FATAL
CROSSING

ABOUT THE AUTHOR

An award-winning author, director of the Michigan Shipwreck Research Association, a partner in the exhibit design firm Lafferty van Heest and Associates, and a recognized and accomplished Great Lakes diver, V. O. van Heest has received the 2017 Joyce C. Hayward Award for Historic Interpretation from the Association for Great Lakes Maritime History and the 2007 State History Award from the Historical Society of Michigan for the collection, preservation, and promotion of submerged maritime resources through interpretation, writing, filmmaking, and exhibit work. Van Heest has written six books and numerous magazine articles, produced a dozen documentary films, been featured in many publications and television news segments, appeared on National Geographic, and the History, Science, and Travel Channels, and is a regular presenter at museums, libraries, and conferences, sharing the dramatic stories of ships and airplanes gone missing on the Great Lakes.

ALSO BY V. O. VAN HEEST

LOST & FOUND: Legendary Lake Michigan Shipwrecks

UNSOLVED MYSTERIES: The Shipwreck *Thomas Hume*
(with William Lafferty)

LOST ON THE LADY ELGIN
Winner - 2011 INDIE Book Award for Nonfiction History
Winner - 2011 Illinois State History Award
Finalist - 2011 Midwest Book Awards

BUCKETS & BELTS: Evolution of the Great Lakes Self-Unloaders
(with William Lafferty)
Winner of a State History Award from the Historical Society of Michigan

ICEBOUND: The Adventures of Young George Sheldon and the S. S. *Michigan*
Winner of a State History Award from the Historical Society of Michigan

FATAL CROSSING

THE MYSTERIOUS DISAPPEARANCE OF NWA FLIGHT 2501 AND THE QUEST FOR ANSWERS

A TRUE STORY

V. O. VAN HEEST

Photographs
As credited and used with permission.
Spread on previous pages: The DC-4 used for Flight 2501,
captured soon before it crashed by aviation photographer Leo Kohn.
The DC-4 in flight on cover is a graphic composite.
Victims on back cover (top to bottom): Captain Robert Lind, Janice Hokanson,
Dorothy Jean Kaufmann, Barbara Freng, and Kenneth Skoug I.
Chapter airplane illustrations: Robert Doornbos.

Published
In the United States of America by In-Depth Editions, 2013
www.in-deptheditions.com
24 23 22 21 20   11 10 9 8 7 6
Sixth Printing, 2020
Publisher Cataloging-in-Publication Data
van Heest, V. O.
Fatal crossing: the mysterious disappearance of nwa flight 2501
and the quest for answers. 352 p. : 98 ill., map
Includes bibliographical references (364-367)
ISBN 978-09889772-1-1 (pbk: alk paper)
1. Aircraft Accidents-Investigation-Great Lakes.
2. United States-History-20th century.
3. Shipwrecks—Michigan. 4. Shipwrecks—Great Lakes—3. Michigan, Lake.
6. Lake Michigan—History.
I. Title II. Author

TL553.52.V364 2013
363.124'65   2013906841

IN MEMORY

THE PASSENGERS

Dr. Leon M. (63) and Siroun (58) Ajemian (m)

Dr. Leslie P. Anderson (50 m)

Merle Leroy Barton (34 m)

Dr. Archibald E. Cardle (51 m)

Anna Nagle Eastman (57 m)

Miriam Frankel (s)

William H. (50) and Rosa Freng (m)

Barbara Freng (17 s)

Mary Frost (29 m)

Alfred W. George (60 m)

Richard P. Goldsbury (21 s)

Rosalie Gorski (27 m)

Evelyn Heenan (54 m)

Benjamin (67 m) and Slava Heuston (60 m)

Thomas Hill (25 s)

Hildegard Hovan (20 s)

John (34) and Catherine (30) Hokanson (m)

Janice Hokanson (7)

Tommy Hokanson (4)

Nora Hughes (50 m)

Arthur E. (25) and Geraldine (23) Jackson (m)

Ruth Johnson (27 s)

Dorothy Jean Parker Kaufmann (42 m)

Mary Keating (24 s)

William Carter Kelty (54 m)

Hilma Larson (62 w)

Leo F. Long (57 m)

Jo E. Longfield (38 s)

Pearl Main (49 m)

Yvette Malby (+/- 30 m)

Dana Richard Malby (3)

Francis McNickle (49 s)

Helen Mary Meyer (23 s)

Karl Neilsen (18 s)

Ralph Olsen (25 s)

William D. K. Reid (43 s)

Marie Rorabaugh (67 w)

Ellen Ross (21 s)

Adelaide Schafer (40 m)

John Schafer (8)

Carl D. (38) and Louise Schlachter (m)

Frank C. Schwartz (58 m)

Joseph Sirbu (55 m)

Kenneth N. Skoug (51 m)

Louise S. Spohn (30 s)

Richard Wyatt Thomson (35 s)

Father Augustine Walsh (45 s)

Eva B. Woolley (64 d)

Leo Wohler (43 m)

THE CREW

Robert C. Lind (34 m)   Verne F. Wolfe (35 m)   Bonnie Ann Feldman (25 s)

Age indicated and (m) = *married,* (s) = *single, (d) = divorced,* (w) = *widowed*

Dedicated to those who have been left behind.
In memory of the victims.

CONTENTS

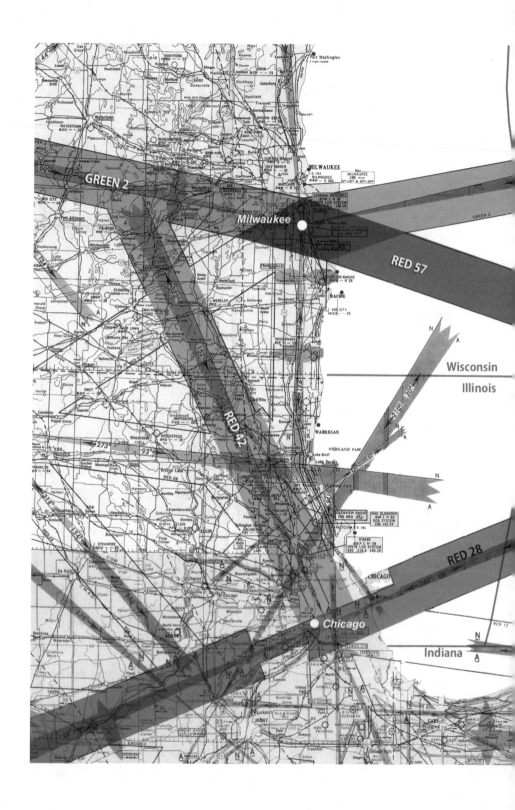

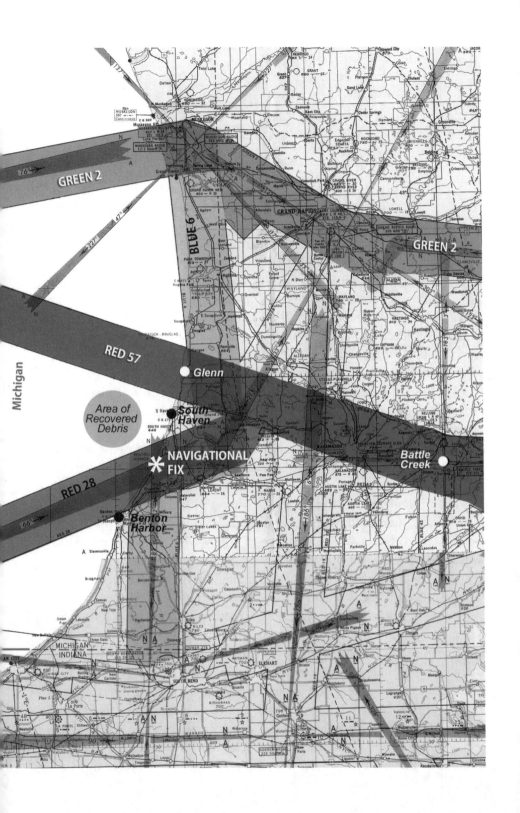

FOREWORD

Just after midnight on June 24, 1950, Northwest Airlines Flight 2501 disappeared into the waters of Lake Michigan, killing everyone aboard, including my mother, in the worst United States' airline disaster at the time. I was only six years old. My brother and sister were just three and two. I had been without my mother's love and guidance for a few weeks while she travelled in Europe and was excitedly looking forward to her return. Instead, I learned her absence would be permanent.

We, and the others left behind, were among the victims of that crash. Before that life had been full of promise; I looked forward to it as a wonderful adventure. After that crash, everything changed. Forever.

I had never experienced losing someone. There was no casket to look into. Worse, I was not even allowed to attend my mother's memorial service. Her loss was an event so jarring that it drove a wedge between reality and my mind. I somehow had to accept what was unbelievable, yet horribly real.

I was too young, too stunned, and too confused to work it out, and there was no one to help me. The friends and family who came around at the beginning offering sympathy and pity were of no help. Being told "your mom is in heaven looking down, watching over you," only made me angry. Those were just words; I needed her here.

In time there was just me, my sister, my brother, and that man who looked like my father. He was never the same after my mother died. He turned increasingly bitter, alienating family and friends, lapsing into depressions that alternated with anxious, paranoiac rants. He was not capable of providing the guidance, security, or love that my mother had given me. He rarely helped me with the problems I brought to him, and there was no one else I could turn to. He kept house poorly; he never remarried; we moved a dozen times or more. Before, when I came home from school, my mother would ask me if I wanted a sandwich or snack. Now my father expected me to make my own.

He was lost in his nightmare world, and for me those first few years after the accident were a big, black emotional void. Strangely, I never cried about it.

Shortly after the crash, someone asked me where my mother was. I couldn't answer with words. Instead, I picked up a pencil and drew a picture of an airplane going down in flames. "She died in a plane crash?" the person asked incredulously.

I guess I must have nodded. Deep down I felt shame in not having a mother and having a father who acted as he did.

As I grew up, I felt different, always left out. The other kids at the dozen schools I attended all had mothers and normalcy. My siblings and I didn't. I always wondered why our life had to be this way. Sometimes friends tried to explain to me that the accident was an act of God. My father would bitterly remark, "What kind of God would take your mother? Don't listen to that religious nonsense."

Up to then, I had received a religious upbringing and was content in my relationship with God and nature as I understood them. Now my father even denied me nightly prayers and never took me to church or Sunday school. I came to feel that I could no longer trust in the God that my mother had taught me about.

Starting far too young, I had to figure out complicated things out for myself; I began thinking about philosophy. I read a lot, but there were no answers to questions like, "Why did this happen to me? What did I do to deserve this fate? Why is my father like he is? Why do we all have to be so unhappy? Is there really a God?"

When I couldn't come up with those answers, I started wondering about the simpler questions like, "What happened to the airplane? Did my mother suffer? Whose fault was it?" Perhaps I just needed someone or something to blame. But, in our household the crash was not discussed, and it disappeared from the news a week after it happened. No one seemed to care anymore. It became a mystery that took its rank among a score of other strange disappearances. The answers would have helped, but there were none.

Eventually I found happiness again; it required time, help, and patient thinking well into adulthood. Today I am a successful professional, a father, and a grandfather. All the same, even though more than sixty-eight years have passed since I lost my mother in that accident, I would still like to know what happened.

-William Kaufmann

PROLOGUE

The brilliant conflagration quickly extinguished minutes after midnight on Saturday, June 24, 1950, as the downpour doused the shattered sections of the aircraft just before the heaving waves swallowed them. Four massive radial engines plunged to the bottom of Lake Michigan many fathoms below the surface, followed by heavy, jagged pieces of the mangled fuselage. The wreckage settled into the soft sand in a twisted heap, barely identifiable as a DC-4 anymore.

Bolts of lightning, just seconds apart, sliced through the pitch blackness of the early morning sky, each flash illuminating the evidence of the devastation still floating on the surface of the lake. Smaller sections of the aircraft's aluminum skin remained buoyed up by the insulation. Shredded plywood paneling from the cabin's interior littered the water. Dozens of ruptured suitcases from the cargo hold spilled out their contents of pants and shirts and ties and dresses. These items began riding the churning swells as the DC-4 had been riding the airstream minutes earlier. Deafening claps of thunder resonated over the debris, and sulfurous smells created a horrid, noxious odor. However, no one was alive to see or hear or smell the aftermath of what would soon be recognized as the worst aviation disaster in the country. Commingled with the floating wreckage were the shredded remains of the 58 passengers and crew, who seconds earlier had been on board the cross-country flight. Their bones had already begun swirling down to the bottom while their blood dissipated into the water, leaving only unidentifiable flesh.

Minutes after the airplane hit the surface, the flotsam began spreading from the site of the impact, carried by currents made crazy by the squall line that had already moved a considerable distance south, leaving a drenching rain behind it. Some debris drifted for a while, then became waterlogged and sank, leaving a trail of destruction on the bottom. The rest rode up the swells and crested down in all directions. Ladies handbags swirled in the water spilling out their contents. A wallet, fat with waterlogged papers, hovered just below the surface. A baby doll with golden hair appeared to have drowned. A checkbook register lay open, ironically revealing the amount the victim had paid for the fatal flight. Floating among these possessions were shreds of foam and fabric that had covered the seats in which their owners had died. As all this, and more gruesome evidence, continued drifting toward the beaches that soon would be filled with tourists, leaving in its wake a mystery that would linger for decades.

PART I
THE SEARCH BEGINS

"A journey of a thousand miles must
begin with a single step."

Lao-tzu

Chapter 1

AN INTRIGUING MYSTERY

O n a spring day in 2002, my husband Jack van Heest, our partner Craig Rich, and I pounded our way out of the channel at Saugatuck, Michigan, over two-foot waves on Lake Michigan, toward the buoy marking the shipwreck *H.C. Akeley*. Over the drone of the boat's motor, Craig yelled, "Northwest Airlines Flight 2501: Now there's a good mystery! We should try to find that wreck next."

That would be a needle in a haystack, I thought. It had taken us four years to find an intact 200-foot-long shipwreck, and in that case we had the benefit of six eyewitness accounts. How could we possibly find a 90-foot-long, broken-up airplane that disappeared *somewhere* over Lake Michigan? But, as I pondered Craig's proposition, I became intrigued. *To find the wreck*, I thought, *would solve a mystery that has lingered for more than a half century.*

Ever since ships have sailed the Great Lakes, they have been sinking. Ever since airplanes have taken to the skies, they have been crashing. A shipwreck usually hides for decades, sometimes centuries, before an explorer comes along and solves the mystery of its disappearance. Most of the time it is no mystery where airplanes crash: The fire and smoke on a patch of scorched ground are dead giveaways. But every so often, an airplane disappears without a trace, on a mountain, in a jungle, or in water. When that happens, the reason for its loss cannot be determined. The most famous case in point: Amelia Earhart. On July 2, 1937, Earhart and navigator Fred Noonan took off from Lae, New Guinea, in a Lockheed Electra, headed for Howland Island, a small speck of land 2,556 miles away. They never arrived. Did the aircraft run out of fuel? Did they encounter bad weather? Did they land on another island or crash into the ocean? The world will never know until the wreck is found.

When Craig Rich proposed a search for Northwest Airlines Flight 2501 in the spring of 2002, we had only just solved our first mystery when a year earlier we discovered the wreck of the *H. C. Akeley* in the southern basin of

Lake Michigan. For me, finding that wreck was the highlight of a quarter-century of adventures that had begun when I first became a scuba diver.

MY FATHER, a navy diver during World War II, and later a swimming pool salesman, introduced me to scuba diving when he strapped a tank on my back and tossed me into the deep end of his good friend Sam Davison's swimming pool. After settling down from the initial rush of realizing I could survive in this foreign environment, I studied the new world around me. The drain, the skimmers, and the textured pool bottom appeared clear, but the world above me was blurred. I could hear nothing but the sound of my regulator as I breathed in and out. At 14 years old, I became hooked on diving.

Two years later, Sam offered me a summer job at Dacor Corporation, the scuba equipment manufacturing company he had founded in Northfield, Illinois. There, I began assembling depth gauges and regulators and was soon promoted to the repair department. Dacor had a policy that all employees learn to scuba dive, and so I earned my open water certification in 1976.

The next summer, I got a job at a dive shop in Skokie, Illinois. I sold gear, learned more about repair work, and swapped stories with the customers. A dive that fall with my old pals from Dacor to the site of the worn and broken timbers of an old shipwreck in shallow water off Greenwood Beach in Evanston, Illinois, would shape my life.

I found it amazing to explore that shipwreck—the *George Morley*—a steam-powered vessel that burned and sank in 1897, even though the sinking event and a century underwater had reduced the ship to rubble. I rooted around piles of twisted metal and charred wood searching for clues to tell me what the passengers and crew might have experienced in the final moments before the ship plunged beneath the surf. I found myself wanting to know more about that shipwreck and how it came to be in 20 feet of water off a popular swimming beach. It would take several years, after graduating from high school and college and obtaining my first job at an architectural firm, before I had a chance to begin satisfying that curiosity.

A serendipitous meeting with scuba divers from the Chicago Maritime Society, when I was 26, reintroduced me to the history-steeped world of shipwrecks. I began working on an archaeological project to document the schooner *David Dows*. After diving the wreck and researching the circumstances of its loss, I felt a connection to the people who sailed on this ill-fated ship. My life since then has been about interpreting the stories of lost ships and their crews. In 1988, I cofounded the Underwater Archaeological Society of Chicago (UASC), a nonprofit organization dedicated to documenting shipwrecks and sharing the results of our work with other divers and the public. I worked full time at an architectural firm and volunteered my nights and weekends running the UASC.

Around that time, Clive Cussler became my author of choice after I read his book *Raise the Titanic*. I soon realized that the book was one of a series of fictional adventures starring the invincible, dreamy, green-eyed diver Dirk Pitt, who while working for the government's National Underwater and Marine Agency (NUMA) saved the world from total destruction on a number of occasions. I read every book Cussler had written and waited with great anticipation for the release of his next one.

In 1994 at a maritime symposium in Dearborn, Michigan, where I presented the UASC's work on the wreck of the *Goshawk*—which was more amusing than insightful due to glitches with the slide projector—another diver approached me to offer his condolences for my botched program. Although he had brown eyes, not the sparkling green of Dirk Pitt, he was as handsome as I had pictured Pitt. I was immediately smitten. He complimented me on my program, despite the foul-ups, and I figured he liked me, too. When he expressed his desire to dive the *Goshawk*, I took my chance. I made an offer to send him the coordinates for the wreck, and he handed me his business card. That night, while gazing at the card, I told a friend that I would marry Jack van Heest, an engineer who worked in Whitehall, Michigan. Indeed, a year later we married. I moved about 140 miles, as the crow flies, northeast across Lake Michigan to settle in Jack's chalet deep in the woods north of Muskegon, Michigan. But it was like a transition to "Green Acres" for me. Living on 11 rural acres—where the closest restaurant was Tim and Tom's, I had to get my hair cut at a barber shop, and buy groceries at Ray's Mini Mart—was a far cry from my high-rise apartment lifestyle in downtown Chicago. Frankly, the house was too far from Lake Michigan. We eventually relocated to Holland, Michigan, when I accepted a position at an architectural firm and settled into a house a mere stone's throw from the lake. The only trouble was there were very few shipwrecks to dive off the shores of our new home.

In the summer of 1995, Jack and I began working with Kenneth Pott, then curator of the Michigan Maritime Museum, and a group of people organized as the committee to establish the Southwest Michigan Underwater Preserve. Michigan's Underwater Preserve system had been created in 1980 to protect clusters of shipwrecks in state waters, and the group hoped to garner state attention for the wrecks off Southwest Michigan out to a depth of 130 feet, the sport diving limit. As archaeologist for the committee to establish the new preserve, Pott had done significant research that indicated dozens of shipwrecks lay in that area, among them the *Chicora*, the most famous of all local wrecks, lost in a January 1895 storm on a run from Milwaukee, Wisconsin, to Benton Harbor, Michigan, carrying a cargo of flour. Its loss, though understandable considering the severe weather, grew into a mystery of legendary proportions when the wreck's whereabouts remained elusive despite multiple searches over the years. The committee organized a side-scan sonar expedition in pursuit of the *Chicora*, but it was not successful.

Around that time, I heard about a new book, *The Sea Hunters,* by Clive Cussler. Figuring the title referred to Dirk Pitt and his sidekick Al Giordino, I bought a copy and settled in for another fun, fictional tale of adventure on the high seas. Instead, I surprised to learn that the book was nonfiction, about Cussler's own adventures on the high seas. Turns out NUMA is a real nonprofit organization, and Cussler uses his book royalties to search the world over for lost ships of historical significance. In the book, he recounts how he has been searching for lost items since he was a kid, tramping through the jungles while serving in Hawaii during the Korean War, seeking burial caves, lost aircraft, or missing people. Back home, he pursues the same kind of adventure, looking for lost gold mines, ghost towns, and prospector artifacts. Cussler did not become a full-fledged shipwreck hunter until 1977 after the success of his book *Raise the Titanic*. For his first expedition he collaborated with an English historian who was researching the story of the *Bonhomme Richard*, the ship that sank from under John Paul Jones as he shouted his famous declaration, "I have not yet begun to fight." Cussler admitted his obsession in that book: "I'm addicted to the challenge of the search whether it's for lost shipwrecks, airplanes, or steam locomotives."

After reading *The Sea Hunters,* I became a fan of nonfiction books. True tales, I started to realize, are way more exciting than made-up ones, even if the main character doesn't save the world. Cussler, 64 years old when he wrote *The Sea Hunters*, had been saving *history* and that was something that I had been trying to do, in my own small way, for many years.

I also learned from *The Sea Hunters* that Cussler doesn't take himself too seriously. Although he studies the ships he searches for—particularly those from the Civil War era—with the passion of a scholar, he really just likes to have a good time and hang around people who know how to have a good time. In recounting a number of his expeditions, he talked more about the antics and the fun he and his friends have while searching, than the methodology of the search.

I came to understand that Cussler has respect for both professionals and amateurs who share his interest in lost vessels, and he often teams up with local divers, historians, and archaeologists in his quests. When he does make a discovery, he leaves the documentation, management, and care of the new-found wreck to the locals with whom he partnered. A line from Cussler's *The Sea Hunters* spoke to me: "To those of you who seek lost objects of history, I wish you the best of luck. They're out there, and they're whispering."

It seemed Cussler was whispering to me. Soon, I set my sights on a new goal for the committee: to find the *Chicora*. Such a discovery, I felt, would offer tremendous potential for another archaeological and outreach project and would continue to generate publicity that might encourage state officials to finally designate Southwest Michigan as the state's tenth underwater preserve. I contacted David Trotter, a diver and side-scan sonar operator whom I had met at the maritime symposium in Detroit, and asked if he might be interested in a joint venture. Intrigued by the mystery of the *Chicora*'s disappearance, always up for a challenge, and eager to expand his work from Lake Huron to Lake Michigan, he agreed to provide his services if we handled local logistics and covered his time and expenses. With little money in the group's coffers, I planned an unprecedented approach in Great Lakes shipwreck hunting: We would attempt to undertake it with the financial support of the public. We announced our project—giving it the catchy title *Quest for the Chicora*—and began planning a fundraising event. If we made a discovery, we would share with the public the location and all that we learned from the wreck. In an arena made up of divers clandestinely searching for shipwrecks to keep the prizes all to themselves, this was revolutionary.

Our April 1998 event raised $5,000. We immediately contacted Trotter to plan the expedition. The water temperature in springtime, he told us, is still cold enough for the sonar to operate most efficiently. During other times of year, there is often a thermocline, a layer in the water where the temperature changes drastically. Like a bank of clouds, the thermocline can limit the ability of the sonar to "see" through it. We scheduled ten days in May, long enough to cover some good territory, but not too long to be away from our day jobs. Jack and I researched the *Chicora* and brainstormed with our teammates a probable search area. Since none of the crew had survived the vessel's sinking, the only information to suggest where the ship went down were newspaper accounts that indicated debris from the ship washed ashore along a 40-mile stretch of beach between Glenn, Michigan, on the north and Benton Harbor to the south. Consequently, our search grid encompassed over 100 square miles off West Michigan within the boundaries of the preserve.

Trotter, who has since been immortalized in the book *Shipwreck Hunter* by Gerry Volgenau, was at the time a 58-year-old diver and newly retired Ford Motor Company executive who had operated side-scan sonar equipment for more than a decade and had found dozens of long-missing Great Lakes shipwrecks. He packed his 100 kHz Klein sonar in his big purple van, hauled it across the state, and installed it on *Rich's Boat*, a 21-foot Cruisers hard top that we had bought from our friend Rich. Jack and I took time off from our jobs for the search.

We learned a tremendous amount about side-scan sonar work from Dave beginning with the proper setup. We secured his sonar, a three-foot long, torpedo-shaped device, referred to as the "fish," on the swim platform at the stern. The fish would be deployed in the water and towed behind the boat. It sends out an acoustical pulse and receives its echo, converts it to an electrical signal, and sends it to a plotter via a long cable. In the boat's covered cabin, we installed the plotter, a box about three feet long and two feet wide. These two units, powered by auxiliary batteries, comprise the side-scan system.

The sonar image, created by a stylus in the plotter, which is somewhat similar to a lie detector unit, is generated continuously on scrolling paper whenever the fish is in the water. By looking at the image from the comfort of the boat's sheltered cabin, the operator can determine the depth of the water, the height the fish "swims" off the bottom, and any potential interference that the water conditions might have on the sonar signal. If the acoustical pulse hits anything of mass sitting on the lake bottom, it will reflect back a signal to the plotter, and the stylus will generate a rough image of the object. Dave explained a sonar image to me. "It's like looking at a Rorschach inkblot, Chief," he said. "It takes a skilled operator to know the difference between just weird bottom and a shipwreck."

Dave called me Chief, I thought, *so he must think I'm in charge.* Then he turned to Jack and winked, "There can be a lot of weird bottom out there, Chief." That's when I realized Dave calls everyone Chief.

We operated out of Saugatuck, Michigan. On the first morning of the expedition, we launched the boat in the Kalamazoo River, hopped aboard, and started the engine. Dave plopped down in the seat next to the captain's chair, and announced, "Let's stick our snoot out and see what the lake is doing."

We motored down the river to the mouth of the channel, where Dave made an assessment. "Just two-footers. We're good to go."

Anything bigger than three-foot waves, he told us, meant it would be too rough to scan efficiently. We throttled forward and shot down the lake several miles until our Loran-C positioning device told us we had reached the northwest corner of a rectangular search grid we had mapped out, where the *Chicora* might be hiding. Before we put the fish in the water, Dave cautioned us not to be too optimistic. "Shipwrecks are hardly ever where you expect them to be."

Deploying the fish was serious business because Dave would be lowering thousands of dollars of equipment into the water. He had a mental checklist of tasks to accomplish and plowed through them one by one. First, he told me to hold the boat steady into the wind. Next, he went into the cabin, turned on the plotter, and directed Jack to rub his hand over the transducers on either side of the fish, while he watched the stylus to verify it was receiving a signal. Then he went out to the back deck and applied dish soap to the transducers to promote good conductivity in the water. After putting on thick rubber gloves, he manhandled the fish out of its box and lowered it into the water. He directed Jack to let out the cable slowly as the fish descended, while he retreated to the cabin to check the plotter to see how deep the fish was. When the image indicated that the fish had reached 30 feet off the bottom, he returned to the stern and clipped a grip on the cable to secure it. Once the fish was set, he asked Jack to motor slowly to the precise starting spot.

We began the first lane's run heading west at about three miles per hour. The sonar sent its signal out on a 20-degree angle toward the bottom on each side of the fish, reaching out about 300 feet on either side of the line we ran. An hour later when we reached the end of that lane, Jack turned the boat around, stepped over 500 feet, and began motoring east on the next parallel lane.

Dave taught us the importance of running methodical, straight lanes back and forth, like mowing a lawn, to avoid veering off course and creating a hole in our search coverage. He also maintained a detailed log of the coordinates of each lane so that the area needs never to be covered again. "Every square mile covered is one mile closer to your goal," he told us, as he jotted down the starting coordinates for the second lane.

The next morning, Dave suggested we stick our snoot out again, and we realized that was another "Dave-ism." That week we heard them all, as well as stories of past discoveries and exciting dives. There's not much to do while searching for shipwrecks except swap stories, swat flies, and nap during the eight or ten hours until it's time to haul in the fish. And Dave had a checklist for doing that, which was even more demanding than deployment because it took some muscle to haul the 60-pound fish up through the water.

The weather cooperated seven out of our 10 days, and we covered about two square miles per day. By the end of our first expedition we had "seen" everything that was on the lake bottom within our 14-square-mile search grid. There was a lot of sand, but no *Chicora*.

"We know where it's *not* located," Dave told us, as he carefully shimmied the sonar box into his big purple van for the ride home. He handed us several rolls of sonar paper that had been used that year. "Here, you hold onto these," he said. "You paid for this knowledge, even if there's nothing there. But, I'd encourage you to scroll through them," he continued. "in case I missed a smudge that might be a shipwreck. We scheduled another expedition for the same time the next year because he said, "Searching is about never giving up."

We unfurled the rolls that night, hoping against hope that the *Chicora* might be hiding on the paper, but no such luck. After our much-hyped *Quest for the Chicora*, it was difficult to report to the local media that we did not find anything. I suddenly knew how journalist Geraldo Rivera must have felt when he opened Al Capone's vault and found nothing inside.

IN EARLY 1999, when we were deep into fundraising for our next expedition, we learned that the Society of American Archaeology would be hosting its annual meeting at the Field Museum in Chicago on March 27. Clive Cussler, who had by then found over 60 lost vessels, would be the keynote speaker delivering a program called "Outrageous Adventures and Grains of Truth." Two other archaeologists would be speaking about their latest projects. Wanting to meet the man who inspired our hunt for the *Chicora*, Jack and I made plans to drive to Chicago and attend the conference with several other dive buddies from Chicago. Knowing two key things about Cussler from his *Sea Hunters* book—that he didn't take himself too seriously and that he liked to have fun— we planned a unique approach to meeting him.

We arrived in Chicago in time to meet our friends before the program. In my purse, I carried a copy of an archaeological report that I had cowritten with a friend, Keith Pearson, a letter to Cussler, a camera, and my copy of *The Sea Hunters*. We jammed into the auditorium with about 200 doting Cussler fans. The first presenter spoke about his work on a shipwreck, which interested us. We couldn't help but yawn during the second presentation about a dig on a prehistoric land-based site. Then, Cussler made his appearance. He didn't lecture. He didn't show slides. He was simply outrageous! He told stories about the fun he and his friends had looking for shipwrecks. He had us all rolling in the aisles, spinning tales as well in person as he does in his books. We were sure he would get a kick out of what we had planned.

At the end of the program, the emcee announced that the three presenters would be in the lobby for a meet and greet. We filed out to see the two archaeologists standing forlornly alone. Everyone else was in a queue to meet Cussler, who sat behind a long draped table, pen in hand, already autographing books his fans had thrust at him. We killed some time chatting with the underwater archaeologist, then an hour later, when Cussler's line was down to just a few stragglers, we meandered over and took our place at the end. When our turn came, Cussler, who looked tired after making small talk with 200 fans, looked up at me, Jack, Keith, and our other friends. None of us held a book. "So, do you folks have any books for me to sign?" he asked.

"Well, no," I replied, starting phase one of our plan. "Since you often search for Civil War-era shipwrecks, we brought you an archaeological report we wrote about a Civil War steamer, the *Lady Elgin*," I explained, pulling the document out of my purse and handing it to him. "Keith and I signed it for *you*."

"Thank you," he said, smiling as he reached for it. He seemed genuinely surprised. "This looks interesting. I will enjoy reading it." Then he deposited it under the table.

I had tucked a letter inside the report, which described our nonprofit organization, our efforts to find the *Chicora,* and an invitation to speak at our upcoming fundraising event. I hoped that he wouldn't just toss the report in the garbage on his way out.

Moving forward with phase two of our plan, I reached into my purse and pulled out a camera, saying, "We were wondering if we might get a group photograph?"

He smiled and said, "Sure."

Using the arms on his chair for leverage, he stood up and started to walk around the table to join us. I quickly interjected, with as straight a face as I could muster, "You can stay there and take the picture of us across the table."

I handed him the camera and backed away to line up with my friends. "You should be able to get all of us in the picture from there," I told him, waving my arms like a director.

Looking confused, he held the camera in his hand, and although I had figured he didn't take himself too seriously, he must have wondered what kind of idiots we were to *not* want his autograph, and *not* want him in our picture. Just as I began to worry that we had gone too far, he raised the camera to his eye and directed a few of us to shift around so that everybody's face showed. He didn't have to tell us to smile, because we could not contain our grins. Then, he snapped. "Do you want me to take another to be sure?"

That's when we all broke down laughing.

"Gotcha!" Keith announced over the guffaws. Cussler immediately realized the joke was on him and shared the laugh with us. We quickly pulled out our copies of his books, and one by one he graciously signed them. Then we arranged to have our photo taken *with him*.

A couple weeks later, I was surprised to receive a phone call from Clive Cussler. "I just wanted to thank you for your *Lady Elgin* report," he said. "I enjoyed it."

We discussed the *Lady Elgin* a bit, then I invited him to speak at our upcoming fundraiser. He declined due to another commitment but asked about the *Chicora*. I launched into a spiel about its mysterious disappearance, hoping, for a moment, that he might want to search for it with us, but he didn't make that offer. One of Cussler's friend's later explained, "When something interests Clive, it interests him. When it doesn't, it doesn't." As much as the *Chicora* interested us, I guess it just didn't interest Clive Cussler.

SOON AFTER MY talk with Clive Cussler, a new guy, Craig Rich, attended one of our preserve committee meetings in South Haven and signed up as a member. He impressed me right away by how confidently he carried himself and how well dressed he seemed even in blue jeans. He could have walked into a business meeting and had people *think* he was in a suit. And he had a deep and resonant voice. "You should be in radio," I commented, immediately thinking that he would make a great narrator if we ever produced another documentary film.

"I was." he said. "My dad and I started a radio station in Zeeland, Michigan, in 1971, and I was the morning deejay and the news and program director."

"So you dive?" I asked, sizing him up to be about 44 or 45 years old.

"Since I was 16," he boasted, probably thinking that would impress me.

"Me, too." I bragged back, thinking that might impress him, but I knew he had at least five years more experience.

"Interested in shipwrecks?" I continued, offering him a chair at the conference table.

"Oh yeah, a little," he said, now sounding humble as he sat down. "I created a web site about local shipwrecks that has been up for a few years."

Great, I thought. *He knows his history and he has computer know-how, too.* So far, he had the makings for a great volunteer.

Craig joined us for pizza after the meeting. I learned he lived in Holland not far from us, he had married his high school sweetheart, they had two young daughters, he was an advertising consultant for the *Grand Rapids Business Journal*, and a member of Holland's City Council since 1982. He told me that he had never missed a council meeting. *Definitely dedicated*, I thought. *He'd make a great volunteer.*

Many people had come and gone since I had taken over the committee, but this guy appeared to have potential for longevity. As it turned out, his commitment, like Jack's and mine, borders on the obsessive.

We hosted our event in the spring of 1999, raised more funds and conducted a second expedition—this time with Craig joining the crew. But, we still didn't find the *Chicora*.

In December 1999, we learned that the State of Michigan had officially approved the Southwest Michigan Underwater Preserve. We hosted a celebration and started soliciting funds for the next year's search. As an official preserve now, the pressure was really on to find something.

We learned persistence from Dave Trotter and Clive Cussler. Dave always reminds us that he spent 15 years searching for the *Minnedosa*, the largest and grandest schooner that Canada had ever built, before finding it in 1993 in Lake Huron. It was farther from shore and twice as deep as the newspaper accounts suggested. Cussler's books recount story after story of how he applied the old adage "if at first you don't succeed...." After three failed expeditions, Cussler kept up his search for the submarine *Horace L. Hunley*. It took 105 days of survey work, 1200 miles of survey lanes, and countless hours doing research before he finally found it. Most importantly, Trotter and Cussler infused us with the thrill of the chase. "If it ain't fun, it ain't worth doing," Cussler wrote. We certainly had been having fun, so we opted to forge on.

In the new century, we picked up where we left off in the old one. However, once again, we failed to find the *Chicora*, which had become the proverbial needle in a haystack. In preparation for the 2001 search, we enlisted the expertise of Arthur Allen, a scientist with the U.S. Coast Guard Research and Development Center in Groton, Connecticut. Allen, who studies drift theory to aid the Coast Guard in its search and rescue operations, is able to forecast where objects will likely drift in the water based on wind and currents.

Although he had never applied drift theory to finding a shipwreck, Allen felt that it would be viable to work backwards in a process called hindcasting. Rather than forecast where debris *would* drift, he would try to determine from what point the debris *had* drifted, in other words, the spot of the sinking. To create a drift model, he needed to first generate a computer animation of the wind, currents, and waves as they existed in 1895. Allen collaborated with David Schwab, a scientist who specifically studies Lake Michigan currents at the Great Lakes Environmental Research Laboratory (GLERL) in Ann Arbor, Michigan. Schwab normally uses digitally archived records of recent weather for his studies, but he would need weather data from more than a century earlier for this exercise. He discovered that the

National Climatic Data Center (NCDC), now a division of NOAA, archives handwritten accounts of wind speed and direction dating back more than a century. He located handwritten records by observers in three different towns near the shore of Lake Michigan for the entire month of January 1895. This gave him enough information to generate the animation. Art Allen then created a series of computer simulations to show potential positions where the *Chicora* could have gone down.

Allen and Schwab's work resulted in an unexpected conclusion: The *Chicora* most likely sank in very deep water, significantly beyond the boundaries of the preserve. We created another search grid, but faced a new challenge. To work in depths beyond 300 feet, we needed to operate with at least 600 feet of cable, which would add considerably to the weight of the sonar. Manpower alone would not be sufficient to haul it in. That's were Jack came in. Using his engineering talents like a contestant on "Junk Yard Wars," he combined a motorcycle wheel rim, a gear reducer, an electric motor, and scrap aluminum, to fabricate a winch and crane to haul in the sonar and cable. It worked like a charm, all for $44 in used parts.

So on May 19, 2001, we took a collective deep breath, dug deep in our pockets for money, and headed out into deep water to resume mowing the lawn, this time going 20 miles offshore. I questioned the wisdom of going that far out in a 21-foot boat looking for a vessel almost 10 times as big that had sunk. It took us over 90 minutes just to get to the starting point of our first lane. Day after long day, we persisted until finally on May 25, 2001, we heard Dave holler from his perch in the cabin, "Bingo!"

There on the sonar printout was a perfect image of a shipwreck that measured about 210 feet long. After having covered 65 square miles of lake bottom, over a total of 28 days in four years, we finally discovered a massive shipwreck in 275 feet of water off Saugatuck, Michigan. Although the wreck was the right size to be the *Chicora*, Dave cautioned, "You won't know it for sure until you see it in person."

That could be a problem. A shipwreck is where it is, not where a diver wants it to be. At the time we found that shipwreck, it ranked among the deepest wrecks discovered in the Great Lakes, making the prospects of getting divers down difficult and dangerous. Although all of us were skilled divers, none of us were certified for tri-mix technical diving, the only safe method to reach depths exceeding 180 feet. Anxious to identify the wreck, we acquired an inexpensive drop camera. Watching through a remote monitor, we saw a wooden-hulled vessel, but after about one minute on the bottom, the camera housing imploded. The brief video was inconclusive, but what we saw was consistent with the *Chicora*.

Because the wreck was outside the boundaries of the Southwest Michigan Underwater Preserve and beyond safe sport diving limits, we formed a new nonprofit organization called the Michigan Shipwreck Research Association (MSRA). Jack, Craig, and I became the board of directors. Our mission: to study the wreck and pursue other deep-water shipwrecks for the purposes of creating educational programming and contributing to the historical record.

IN THE MIDST of much hoopla over our first discovery, my beloved mother died. She was only 74. In a grand scheme I could not begin to comprehend, the void in my heart was filled again when we brought our daughter home from China six months later. Adoption had been our first choice in building a family after learning about all the abandoned girls in China. The paperwork had taken nearly two years, but little Zou Yong Ji—renamed Cella in memory of my mother— was worth the wait. From the first moment I held her, I felt an amazing bond.

I'm pretty good at juggling life's responsibilities, but my new role as a mother was a challenge. However, Cella was already a year old when we got her and didn't require the round-the-clock attention that newborns need from their mothers. By the following spring, I was back in the shipwreck game, with a baby strapped to my back.

In April 2002, we teamed up with a pair of technical divers from West Michigan with the training and equipment to make the deep dive on the shipwreck we had found. Their dives revealed that the shipwreck was not the *Chicora*, but instead the bulk steamer *H. C. Akeley*, lost in an 1883 storm. Although we did not accomplish our goal, we did find a significant ship. There would be much to learn from a study of the *Akeley*. In hindsight, we were lucky to have stumbled on the *Akeley*. Had that been our goal, it would have taken a very long time to find. Surviving crew members reported their ship lost off Holland. We found it off Saugatuck, 20 miles south. We learned firsthand what David Trotter had always told us, "Shipwrecks are rarely where they are supposed to be."

In keeping with our mission, we produced a documentary film and delivered many public presentations about the *Akeley*. I began what would become a professional writing career with my first article called "Searching for a Steamer," published in the magazine *Michigan History*.

It was not too long after this—our first major success—that Craig Rich suggested we go hunting for Northwest Airlines Flight 2501.
"THAT WOULD BE A WASTE of time and money," I replied, leaning in so he could hear me over the noise of the boat motor. "It took us four years to

find the *Akeley*, and it wasn't even the wreck we were looking for," I said. "If it took that long to find a massive steamer, how could we ever find small bits of a busted-up aircraft?"

I am practical—not to mention outspoken—which I realize can be both good and bad. It seems that whenever there is something to be done, whether remodel a house, host an event, or search for a shipwreck, the project manager in me kicks in. I immediately outline the tasks that need to be done, estimate the time, determine the budget, and get the job done. That's the reason I did well in my role as an architectural project manager. However, most people don't like to be managed, or get their ideas shot down.

I knew the instant Craig suggested we mount a search for Flight 2501, it would be an impossible task for our small, low-budget, all-volunteer team. Even though David Trotter had the high-frequency sonar needed to find a debris field scattered on the lake bottom, we could only expect to cover about one square mile per day looking for a small target. Considering that no one survived Flight 2501 to report the position of the crash, and airplanes fly a lot faster than boats sail, the search grid would be immense. We simply could not afford the effort. Plus, if we were to believe the author of the book, *The Great Lakes Triangle*, published in 1976—where I first read about this accident—then the airplane wreckage might not even be on the lake bottom.

In *The Great Lakes Triangle*, author Jay Gourley compares the Great Lakes to the Bermuda Triangle, the region in the southeastern Atlantic Ocean where a number of aircraft and ships have disappeared in supposed mysterious circumstances. The book begins by telling the story of Northwest Airlines Flight 2501 in Lake Michigan. The DC-4, the author wrote, left LaGuardia Airport in New York on June 23, 1950, heading to Seattle, Washington, with three crew and 55 passengers. At 11:51 p.m., when over Battle Creek, Michigan, pilot Robert Lind reported his position and estimated he would be over Milwaukee, Wisconsin, on the other side of the lake at 12:37 a.m. The author noted that Lind's estimate was "exceptionally inaccurate," because at the time the book was published, 26 years after the disappearance, "the plane had not *yet* reached Milwaukee." He insinuated the work of extraterrestrials, by noting the total absence of any aircraft debris on the lake surface, and the spotting by two policemen of a glimmering red light floating high above Lake Michigan at the approximate time of the disappearance.

The balance of the book recounted the loss of dozens of other airplanes and ships, woven together with a common thread of unexplained disappearances, a tactic employed to enthrall readers but one not based on fact. In all likelihood, the author had done enough research to have known

the truth about Flight 2501. Debris from a Northwest DC-4—and a lot of it—
was actually found floating on the surface and later scattered on the beaches
of South Haven in the hours, days, and weeks after the flight's disappearance.
No doubt, Flight 2501 crashed into the lake surface and settled on the bottom,
a mélange of mangled aluminum and tangled wiring, like other airplanes
that have careened into bodies of water throughout the world. The author
was, however, correct when he wrote that the accident was the nation's worst
aviation disaster, the wreck site was never found, and the authorities could
never determine a cause for the accident.

As the years passed and DC-4 propeller airplanes were replaced by jets,
finding the wreckage of Flight 2501 became unnecessary. Investigators seek
cause so that changes can be made to avoid similar accidents in the future, and
no one worried about making DC-4s safer—they had become, for the most
part, obsolete. The accident was largely forgotten except by a few explorers
who thought finding the wreckage would make for a good challenge.

I knew Craig understood how difficult it would be for us to try to
find the shattered carcass of an airplane, and was only half serious when he
suggested we look for it, but he piqued my interest. "It would be a great find,"
I agreed, "Maybe we'll find it accidentally while looking for the *Chicora!*"

We added Flight 2501 to the list of wrecks we hoped one day to find.
That list included the *Chicora, Michigan, Andaste, John V. Moran, Joseph P.
Farnan, William Tell, A.P. Dutton, Hattie Wells, Hamilton*, and a few others.
We hoped that in time new technology might allow us to more easily and
cost effectively mount a search for the airplane. Until then, we turned our
attention back to finding the *Chicora* and decided to also pursue the wreck
of the *Michigan*, a steamer holed and sunk by pack ice in 1885. Because the
entire crew survived and gave a reasonable position where the boat had sunk,
we thought that the *Michigan* would be easier to locate than the *Chicora*.

In May 2003, we set off on our fifth expedition, this time using our
new boat, a 24-foot, hard-top Bayliner. It would be an ideal family cruising,
diving, and searching boat. It has a back deck with a bench seat across the
transom and side-by-side captain's chairs flanking the cabin door with two
steps down into the cabin. The cabin has a small head and kitchenette, a
dinette that converts to a bed, and another bed, called a V-berth in the
bow. For the search, we transformed it into a high-tech research vessel by
adding the electronics, a winch, a crane, and a sturdy sonar platform that
Jack engineered out of aluminum bleacher seats. We named the boat *Cella-
bration* in honor of our daughter. Although we spent ten days with David
Trotter in May 2003 looking for the two lost steamers, one off South Haven

and the other off Holland, we came up empty-handed. Again.

We did not dwell on our failure. Instead, Craig penned an article about Flight 2501. He convinced the *South Haven Tribune*, a small newspaper, to publish it. The editor ran it just after the 53rd anniversary of the accident, and gave it a catchy title: "Area's Worst Airplane Tragedy Relived," with a subtitle designed to make it a current event: "Group Hopes to Find Remnants of Ill-fated Northwest Flight 2501." The editor took some liberties for the sake of exciting copy when—like the reporter had done when he announced we found the *Chicora*—he printed a photo of our team with a caption that read, "MSRA plans to use side-scan to search for the remains of the airplane." In fact, we had no such plans.

Little did we realize that the editor must have had powers of precognition.

IN JUNE 2004 we chose the same approach to searching as we did the prior year: half of our effort looking for the *Chicora* and the other half searching for the *Michigan*. That year we would have the benefit of Dave Trotter's new 50 kHz sonar. This lower-frequency unit meant we could cover much more territory in less time. Rather than "seeing" out 600 feet on either side of the boat, the sonar could reach 1,000 feet on either side. We could now cover almost as much ground in one hour as it had taken us four hours previously. "Don't think there's not a trade-off," Dave warned, petting his prized possession. "This sonar will pick up a large wooden or steel shipwreck," he explained, "but it won't look like much. And you can forget about finding any smaller things out there—they won't even show up with this sonar."

We learned firsthand what Dave meant. On the fourth day of our ten-day expedition in June 2004, as we "mowed the lawn" 12 miles off Holland in deep water looking for the *Michigan*, the stylus plotted out a thin, dark line, little more than an inch long. "Bingo!" Dave declared, pointing.

I thought Dave had drawn a line on the paper with his marker to fool me.

"Shipwreck!" he clarified, with a big grin. Considering how many expeditions had been a bust, this was the happiest I'd seen him since we found the *Akeley*.

"The *Michigan*?" I asked, holding my breath.

"Could be," he replied, leaning in to take a closer look. Although the 50 kHz image did not show detail, the scale on the paper indicated it was about 200 feet long. The line itself was very dark, so much so that the stylus had burned through the paper.

"That's a good sign," Dave said. "A dark image suggests there's metal down there."

Perfect, I thought. *The* Michigan *had been clad in iron.*

"But don't get your hopes up," he cautioned as he rolled up the paper. "It's something man-made for sure, but we'll have to get a closer look to know if it's the *Michigan*."

We returned the next day with the 100 kHz fish. That unit painted a lovely, dark image of a shipwreck, 200 feet long, 35 feet wide, clearly showing two square ends. However, that was a problem. Steamers have one pointy end—the bow.

"If I had to wager, I'd say we've found a barge," Dave noted with a concerned look on his face.

Indeed, when we called upon a trio of technical divers, Robert Underhill, Todd White, and Jeff Vos, who had just begun working with us, they brought back underwater video of a barge. It had been stripped bare, which suggested its owner, probably a local maritime contractor, had scuttled it as the easiest way to get rid of a big hunk of steel, probably long before the prices of scrap metal started climbing.

We had, thus far, conducted six expeditions in seven years and covered 100 square miles looking for the *Michigan* and the *Chicora*. Instead we had found the *Akeley* and a barge. Back to the drawing board. Again.

"Maybe we should take a break from the *Chicora* and the *Michigan* for a year and look for Flight 2501 next time," Craig suggested after we had packed up Dave and his side-scan and sent him home in his purple van.

I just laughed.

Chapter 2

ENTER CLIVE CUSSLER

Craig loves to rub my face in what happened just two months after he again suggested we look for Flight 2501. As he tells it, "It was Sunday, August 8, 2004, at 2:30 in the afternoon. I was out waxing my car when my daughter Catherine slid open the patio door with a smirk on her face and a hand cupped over the telephone receiver, and said, 'Dad, you've got a call.' Then, she rolled her eyes and gave me the phone, announcing, 'He says he's Clive Cussler.'"

Like me, Craig had read every one of Cussler's adventure novels—and they numbered some 25 at the time—and so he recognized his name. So did his 15-year-old daughter, who saw her dad's shelf with Cussler's books every time she went in his office. They both presumed one of Craig's buddies was joking around.

Ready to dish back an appropriate wisecrack response such as "Yeah, Bob Ballard here. How can I help you?" Craig wiped his hands on his jeans, climbed up the porch stairs, and took the phone from his daughter. Then he hesitated, just in case it really was Cussler. "Hello?"

"Is this Craig Rich?" asked a deep resonating voice, that Craig instantly recognized as Cussler from his television series, "The Sea Hunters."

"Yes… hello Clive," Craig replied, glad he had not answered as the famed marine scientist Bob Ballard.

"I hear your group is looking for an airplane," Cussler said, "and I wonder if you want a little help?"

Craig and Clive Cussler talked for about 30 minutes and Craig immediately sent an email entitled "Unbelievable" to Jack and me and our other teammate, Ross Richardson, a researcher and relatively new diver, whom we had recently invited to join our organization. Craig recounted the call and invited us to dinner to discuss Cussler's proposal, letting us know that his wife was planning to serve baby back ribs, corn on the cob, and baked potatoes, as if we needed food as an enticement. We would have come even if we had to bring our own hotdogs.

Dinner at Craig's house was finger-licking good, but Cussler's plan had us drooling. "He's sending Ralph Wilbanks, his sonar expert, to work with us," Craig told us as we gnawed on the ribs. "And, they're going to need to use your boat," he said, looking at Jack and me.

I had read about Wilbanks and his involvement in the search for the *Horace L. Hunley*, the mega-famous Civil War-era submarine that he and Cussler had found off Charleston, South Carolina. I wiped off my hands, stepped into Craig's office, and reached for his copies of *The Sea Hunter*, and Clive's latest nonfiction book, *The Sea Hunters II*, to jog my memory, then also grabbed *Raising the Hunley*, written by two journalists.

Scanning through them, I was reminded that Cussler had met Wilbanks in 1981 on his second expedition to find the *Hunley* when Wilbanks worked as an archaeologist in South Carolina. Whenever they found a wreck—and they found many that were not the *Hunley*—Wilbanks, who Cussler noted was no lightweight, "would start dancing a country jig," making the whole boat shudder when he began stomping. I wondered if our small boat could handle that, but I would be happy to find out if it meant locating Flight 2501.

By the time Cussler returned to search for the *Hunley* in 1995, Wilbanks worked as an independent consultant, and Cussler hired him. Cussler described him as being "as steady and enduring as the faces on Mount Rushmore" and "humorous, with a sly smile fixed beneath a Pancho Villa mustache," noting that "he worked tirelessly day after day, fighting choppy water to keep the search boat on track, with never a discouraging word."

The authors of *Raising the Hunley* offered other insight, noting that his crew "had to occasionally put up with outbursts of Wilbanks' famous temper," and the smell of his favorite snack, pickled okra.

Doesn't matter, I thought. Cussler had written that they "do it big, do it right, give it class, and make 'em laugh," so I knew it was going to be an adventure.

"IT'LL BE A JOINT VENTURE," Craig said, as we carried our dishes to the kitchen, "between Cussler's National Underwater and Marine Agency (NUMA) and MSRA."

"When?" I immediately asked. We were awaiting word from China any day on when we had to travel there to pick up our second daughter.

"Clive didn't say, but definitely this fall. He's waiting on Ralph's schedule."

"Did you tell him fall isn't the best time for survey work?" Jack asked, knowing that the thermocline affects the sonar penetration in the fall.

"Let's not look a gift horse in the mouth," Craig said, depositing his plate in the sink.

Craig explained that the arrangement would be like we had with David Trotter: MSRA would provide boat, crew, and do the research to develop a search grid, and Cussler would provide Ralph Wilbanks, his side-scan, and a boat pilot. However, in this case, Cussler would be footing the bill.

"So, we better figure out where this wreck is," I said, wiping down the dining room table so we could spread out.

Craig retreated into his office, then returned and tossed a document on the table and said, "It's all in here." Big letters across the top said "Civil Aeronautics Board Accident Investigation Report."

Jack reached for it, and I looked over his shoulder and saw that it was only six pages long. The report had been signed by three of the four Civil Aeronautics Board (CAB) members on January 18, 1951, six months after the accident. It was divided into five sections, history of the flight, investigation, analysis, findings, and probable cause. All times were recorded in Central Standard, military time, like 22:37. That confused me because I'm used to a 12-hour clock and because the accident occurred in Michigan, which is in Eastern Standard Time. I reached for a pencil and converted all the times, adding an hour so that I could understand the flight in the time zone where it occurred.

THE OFFICIAL REPORT BEGAN with a statement noting that the DC-4 crashed at approximately 23:25 (12:25 a.m. in Michigan) on June 23, 1950 (Saturday, June 24 in Michigan). The report estimated that the airplane crashed 18 miles north-northwest of the city of Benton Harbor, Michigan. "North-northwest" is one of 16 cardinal points of the compass that specifically represents 331.88 degrees. It is considered a more simplified way to refer to direction.

In reading through the report, I learned a lot more about the accident than I had from reading *The Great Lakes Triangle*. The Northwest Airlines flight began in New York and was scheduled to operate between LaGuardia Airport and Seattle, Washington, via intermediate points of Minneapolis, Minnesota, and Spokane, Washington. It left at 8:31 p.m. with Robert C. Lind as captain, Verne F. Wolfe as first officer, and Bonnie A. Feldman as stewardess, all appropriately certified for the flight and well rested, plus 55 passengers. Prior to the departure, Northwest Airline's meteorologist alerted the pilots to a thunderstorm developing over Lake Michigan near where the flight would cross the lake.

The flight's initial cruising altitude was 6,000 feet, but the pilot was advised to descend to 4,000 when over Cleveland and approaching the vicinity of the storm. After crossing into Michigan airspace, Air Traffic Control (ATC) ordered the flight to descend to 3,500 to increase separation with an eastbound airplane experiencing turbulence at 5,000 feet. At 11:51 p.m., Captain Lind radioed that he was over Battle Creek at 3,500 feet, and estimated the flight would reach Milwaukee at 12:37 a.m. When in the vicinity of Benton Harbor at 12:13 a.m., Lind requested a descent to 2,500 feet, but the report did not state why. ATC was unable to approve the descent because of "other traffic in the area." Lind acknowledged the denial at 12:15 a.m. That was the last communication ever received from the flight.

When Flight 2501 became overdue at Milwaukee, Northwest's radio operator at Milwaukee advised company personnel at LaGuardia and Minneapolis and alerted ATC at Chicago. Radio operators tried to contact the flight on all frequencies, but could not establish communication. At 2:00 a.m., about two hours after the last communication, ATC alerted air and sea rescue facilities. Coast Guard vessels began combing the waters of Lake Michigan, but they did not locate evidence of a crash until early Sunday evening near South Haven, Michigan. The debris included an oil slick, aircraft fragments, personal possessions, and human remains floating on the lake surface. The Coast Guard used grappling devises to try to hook wreckage on the bottom but was unsuccessful. Navy divers went down at one spot where the DC-4 was thought to have crashed, but silt and bad visibility made them abandon the dive.

The CAB members concluded that the aircraft and crew were properly certified for the flight. The crew had been briefed about a forecasted storm, but not given notice that a squall line had developed while they were in transit. They noted that the squall line was located near where the aircraft crashed, and that the DC-4 struck the water with considerable force. Because of severe turbulence associated with a squall line, the board concluded that the accident probably resulted from either a structural failure caused by the turbulence, or because control of the airplane was lost. However, because there was not sufficient evidence to ascertain which of those two possibilities actually caused the accident, the CAB could not determine probable cause.

I wondered how, with so little evidence, the CAB members could so specifically estimate that the crash occurred at 12:25 a.m. 18 miles north-northwest of Benton Harbor.

I pulled from my briefcase a chart of Lake Michigan on which I had recorded all the areas where we had previously searched for shipwrecks. Using a scale ruler, I measured 18 miles, and using a compass, I plotted the spot 332 degrees from Benton Harbor which represents the north-northwest direction.

Although we had searched quite a bit of territory north of there, we had not covered any in that vicinity.

We had learned never to trust just one source of information to prepare a search grid, and we discussed the possibility of applying the hindcasting approach that we had learned from working with Art Allen and David Schwab at NOAA and GLERL while developing the *Chicora* search grid. We knew that we might be able to work backwards to develop a more defined search area if we could determine where airplane debris had been found floating, where any had washed ashore, and where and how fast the wind and currents might have moved it at the time.

Thankfully, our past research had given us some experience in finding that kind of data. I offered to get the weather records for June 1950 from the National Climatic Data Center, Ross would review newspaper accounts to determine where wreckage washed ashore, and Jack would order copies of the Coast Guard log books to hopefully learn where they picked up floating debris. In addition, there were the more mundane issues to take care of, including reserving a boat slip and accommodations for Cussler's team. As it turned out, I would have plenty of time to work on the project. The recent downturn in the economy meant layoffs at the architectural firm where I worked. I suddenly became a full-time mom/researcher/diver/shipwreck hunter.

THE NEXT DAY, before I could order the weather records, I received a telephone call and a photograph from our adoption agency. Han Xin Luan, a 14-month-old adorable baby girl (soon to be renamed Taya) would be ours, and we would need to go to China in late November. Cussler's team would be long gone by then, because the gales of November would blow in. However, we could miss all the post-discovery hoopla if we found the wreck.

Clive didn't waste any time. He called back to let us know that Wilbanks and his boat pilot Steve Howard would arrive in mid-to-late September for at least two or three weeks. Unfortunately for Craig, that was just when he and his family had scheduled a vacation. He would miss out. Jack was planning to winterize the boat before we left for China, but now he had to reinstall the winch, crane, and batteries and get the boat—which by then we had renamed *Chinese Takeout* in honor of our two daughters—ready for an extended time on the water.

The four of us regrouped at our house in late August with our new data in hand. We plotted the wind speed and direction from weather records that gave hour-by-hour readings. We gleaned from newspapers accounts that debris had started coming ashore four days after the crash between Glenn,

Michigan, on the north, and Benton Harbor, 40 miles south.

Unfortunately, we did not yet have the Coast Guard log books. The National Archives operated using snail-mail, and the documents would probably not arrive until after the search ended. We did locate a regional aeronautical chart from 1949 and saw that there were three airways, like highways in the sky, that crossed Lake Michigan, two in the vicinity of this flight. Airway Red 57 ran from Glenn, Michigan, on the east side of the lake, west across to Milwaukee, Wisconsin. Red 28 ran from a point about ten miles north of Benton Harbor southwest to Chicago. We drew a line on the chart showing the airplane's flight path from Battle Creek to Milwaukee, which fell in Airway Red 57. We noted the locations where debris had been found along shore and drew arrows that showed the direction of the wind that night. Several things confused us. The flight's designated route on Red 57 was about 25 miles north of city of Benton Harbor, the reported location of the flight at the time of its last radio call. The debris along shore was found between the two airways. And the estimated position of the crash site, 18 miles north-northwest of Benton Harbor, also fell between the two airways. Why would the Civil Aeronautic Board assume the pilots left a designated airway? Things didn't add up.

"Does anyone know a psychic?" I asked, only half joking, but recalling that Cussler had once called upon the services of a "remote viewer." "Maybe Robert Lind can tell us where he was that night."

Jack, Craig, Ross, and I talked through many different scenarios, hypothesized what Captain Lind might have done that night, estimated the drift of the debris, and put an "X" on the chart where each of us thought the wreckage might be. Our "X"s were in four distinctly different places. After all our efforts, we agreed to begin the search 18 miles north-northwest of Benton Harbor, exactly where the CAB report had estimated the location of the crash.

Chapter 3

LET THE SEARCHING BEGIN

On the afternoon of Wednesday, September 22, 2004, Jack was, in his typical last-minute fashion, bolting the winch to the gunnel of our boat, which sat nudged up behind our garage. "Grab me that wrench," he said, pointing to a pile in the middle of the garage floor.

I stepped gingerly among the ropes and tools and junk heaped in seemingly total disarray and rolled my eyes in frustration at once again being down to the wire for a search.

"It's right there, under that white bucket," he said, pointing.

Somehow what seemed like chaos to me was perfectly acceptable to Jack. He could find a baseball in a blizzard as long as he had thrown it. Each spring before our search, he amazingly managed to finish gearing up the boat just minutes before we had to pull out of the driveway. That is terribly annoying to me, but standard practice for Jack, who faced these same kinds of things working in the ever-challenging world of machine design.

Both of us turned toward the end of the driveway when we heard a loud "kerplunk," which we had come to recognize as the sound of a loaded vehicle hitting the curb at the end of our driveway. A tan extended cab pickup with a topper came to a stop next to our boat. A man about six feet tall, solidly built, with almost all-white hair, stepped out and stretched. I recognized him immediately from his picture in *The Sea Hunters II*. "Hi, y'all," Ralph Wilbanks said with a southern drawl, in what we later came to realize was his signature greeting.

He extended his hand toward Jack and me, as his passenger, obviously Steve Howard, a slightly taller, slightly leaner man, with slightly darker gray hair and a pair of thick-lensed glasses, climbed out and joined us.

The men had left South Carolina two days earlier, stopping overnight halfway during the 1,000-mile journey. We invited them inside, leading them to our kitchen that had become the command post during all our searches.

"Corona?" I offered Ralph nonchalantly, not letting on that I had read about it being his preferred beer.

"Never turn one down," he said, reaching for it.

Steve, too, took the Corona I offered him, and Jack grabbed one as well. After some get-to-know-you pleasantries, we spread out all the data we had collected thus far and got down to theorizing, just as we had done among ourselves a month earlier. Ralph had already read through the Civil Aeronautics Board report and agreed with our conclusion: The search would begin 18 miles north-northwest of Benton Harbor and we would work out of South Haven, the nearest port to the search area.

Planning to load up the boat in the morning, head down to South Haven, and spend a few hours testing everything before beginning the actual sonar work on Friday, Ralph and Steve stayed the night at our house. They would relocate to a hotel in South Haven for the balance of the expedition.

Bright and early the next morning, I awoke to find them already outside pulling a tantalizing assortment of electronics out of Ralph's truck. Their goodies included a Klein Associates 520 side-scan sonar, a 100 kHz and a 500 kHz towfish, a Geometrics cesium magnetometer, two generators, spare cables and circuit boards, tools, buoys, weights, computer cables, and six computers, as well as a jar of pickled okra.

"Breakfast?" Ralph offered up his smelly delectable.

I passed, looking forward to a bowl of cereal.

"Where's Jack?" he asked.

"He's still asleep," I said, glancing up at our boat, which appeared to be all ready. "Looks like he was up pretty late."

Just then, Jack made me a liar. He ambled out of the house with a bad case of bed head and a cup of coffee.

After some more small talk in the driveway, Jack helped orchestrate the loading of the equipment, manhandling the heavy stuff up the ladder that we use to climb into the boat. The components were similar to those we normally worked with so he knew where to put everything.

"Where's the rest of the side-scan?" Jack asked, laughing when he set the 24-inch-long box on the bench.

"That's what it looks like after it has been converted from a paper plotter to a digital receiver," Ralph explained. "I had Garry Kozak convert it for me."

Every serious shipwreck hunter knows side-scan expert and diver Garry Kozak. Not only does he work in the side-scan sonar industry, but he has found a number of wrecks, including the *Dean Richmond*, Lake Erie's treasure ship filed with zinc and lead ingots. Unfortunately for Kozak, because of the depth and position of the wreck, the cargo cost more to recover than it was worth, so he abandoned the salvage effort.

Ralph followed Jack up into the boat. "Can't wait to see this in action," he commented, stroking the winch. "We usually work in shallow water, so we can haul in the cable by hand."

By noon, everything was in place, and Jack headed off to his office for a meeting he could not get out of, while Ralph hitched our boat to his truck. Steve and Ralph would haul it south to South Haven, following me in my car.

South Haven, a more touristy lakefront town than Holland, is about 45 miles south of our house. Although we could follow the Blue Star Highway, the former main north/south thoroughfare that runs parallel to the lakefront, Highway 31 offered a straighter, faster route. It would take us past the twin cities of Saugatuck and Douglas, the only other port towns between Holland and South Haven.

Several miles later, I turned on my directional signal as we approached the main South Haven exit. I led them west a couple miles into the town, which is divided into two distinct areas by the Black River that feeds out into Lake Michigan. The south side boasts most of the shops and restaurants, and the north side is primarily residential, except for the Michigan Maritime Museum and the marina where we would dock the boat. The launch ramp is hidden behind a row of riverfront condos on the river's north side, so I guided them there, and we quickly put the boat in the water.

Steve and I climbed into the boat, planning to motor downriver to the marina. Ralph would drive over and check in at the dock. If all went as planned, we would not pull the boat out again for several weeks. Although *Chinese Takeout* was new to Steve, he had no problems powering it up and backing away from the dock. In fact, I later learned, he often served as captain delivering various boats to sites on the Atlantic Ocean.

"The only trouble with this Bayliner," I said, as I noticed him struggling to keep it headed straight, "is that it handles pretty sloppy."

"Yup, that's the Bayliner's signature," he replied.

His response assured me that he knew what he was doing, and that our boat was in good hands. By the time we arrived at the marina, Ralph was waiting by the slip that would be ours for the duration. Steve did a touch and go at the dock, just close enough for Ralph to jump aboard. They were anxious to test out the equipment in the big lake, so we headed toward the channel, motoring at no-wake speed past the waterfront cottages on the north and the small downtown on the south. Once in the channel, Ralph and Steve got their first sight and smell of Lake Michigan. Although the lake is a deeper blue than the water off Charleston, it must have looked as vast as an ocean but with a crisper smell, different from the fishy, tangy scent of salt water. "So it's true, you can't see Illinois from here," Steve commented.

"Nope," I replied. "It's a good 70 miles straight west at this point. Sometimes when conditions at night are just right, you can see the glow of Chicago's lights reflected off the clouds."

A lot of people who have never been to the Midwest don't realize how large the inland seas are.

"Take her out to at least 150 feet," Ralph told Steve, as he headed below.

"That's a good five to six miles," I hollered to Steve over the engine noise as he throttled forward.

While Ralph adjusted his equipment down in the cabin, I nosed around to get a look at the set-up. Although his sonar is the same Klein brand that David Trotter has, Ralph uses Sonar Wiz software by Chesapeake Technology that records the sonar return digitally in real time on a monitor, rather than a paper plotter. The continuous digital image can later be replayed to review the sonar lanes, much like we can scroll through a roll of plotter paper. If we found the wreckage, Ralph could save the target image as a jpg, complete with exact coordinates. This system is simply a digital version of Dave's sonar.

"So what kind of other work do you do for Clive?" I asked, curious to get to know more about the man with whom we would be working.

"Clive throws a stick, and I fetch," he replied in his slow southern drawl.

Apparently, like Cussler, Ralph doesn't take himself too seriously, I thought, grinning.

I learned that Ralph was raised on the Isle of Palms before it became a swanky gated community. With no way to hide from the water on the seven-mile-long Atlantic barrier island just north of Charleston Harbor, he grew up swimming, water skiing, surfing, and diving. He "blames" Lloyd Bridges and the *Sea Hunt* television series for his career.

"I became interested in underwater archaeology in high school," he told me. At that time underwater archaeology was considered a new branch of archaeology, and few universities taught the discipline. He attended the University of South Carolina and graduated with a bachelor's degree in education in 1970. He joined the University of South Carolina Institute of Archaeology and Anthropology in Columbia, as an assistant underwater archaeologist, which led to his meeting Cussler during his first attempt to find the *Hunley*. Ralph held that position for ten years until he had a revelation in the early 80s: "I took a look at my father and saw how he had grown big. I figured if I got that big, too, I might not be able to dive, so I decided to get into the electronics end of archaeology."

In 1985, Ralph founded his own company, Diversified Wilbanks, Inc., to do exactly as the name implied: diversify. He continued to do archaeology, contracting his services out to a variety of firms, and offering remote sensing, side-scan, and magnetometer surveys. He traveled the world to do the work that he has come to love: Bahamas and Puerto Rico documenting shipwrecks, France doing sonar work at the D-Day beaches, and Alaska, where he located a private airplane in a small mountain lake. He has also worked on the east and west coasts of the United States. Charleston remained his home. At the time we met him, he had just received his master's degree in maritime history.

"I'M IN 150 FEET," Steve hollered down, interrupting our chat as he slowed the boat.

"Time to go to work," Ralph said, sounding much more excited than Jack had that morning when he left for the office.

It takes a minimum of three people to deploy the fish: one to handle it, the other to carefully pay out the tow cable, and the third to keep the boat pointed into the wind. I left the sonar in their capable hands and took the wheel until they got the fish in the water. Then they settled into their positions with Steve piloting the boat and Ralph down below watching the monitor. For the next couple of hours they made adjustments to the depth of the fish and their speed. The biggest challenge was to get the fish far enough below the thermocline to get a good acoustical return. To do this, Steve had to slow to barely one knot so that the fish could settle lower, but at that speed the boat was barely manageable. After several hours testing the equipment, we began the process of retrieving the sonar. Ralph and Steve marveled at the ease of using the winch.

On the ride back in, I joined Ralph in the cabin again. "So, do you think there's anything left out there to find?" I asked about the long-missing aircraft.

"Oh yeah, but it won't look like a plane," he said. "Last year I found a jet that crashed into the Great Salt Lake. All busted up. Only the tail was intact."

Ralph explained that on May 10, 2003, a A-4 Skyhawk owned by a government contractor crashed into the lake after an engine ingested a bird and caused a flame-out. The pilot ejected, but his parachute failed to open and he died on impact with the lake's surface. Ralph was hired to locate the wreckage and found the crash site after only seven hours. However, it took significantly longer to find the ejection seat. "It looked like a grain of pepper on a plate of salt," he said.

We got in by 6:00 p.m. that first day, docked, and buttoned up the boat.

"Jack will meet you here at seven tomorrow," I said, as I got in my black PT Cruiser to head home.

The next morning, in a pattern that would become standard for the expedition, Ralph and Steve got to the marina when it opened and gassed up the boat. Jack arrived as promised. I had prepared a schedule to make sure at least one of us—Jack, Ross, or I—would be on board every day.

BASED ON THE TRIALS performed the day prior, Ralph decided to use the 100 kHz sonar. Overnight, he had mapped out a survey grid seven miles by five miles, with the CAB report's purported wreck location dead center. The water in that area ranged from 180 to 220 feet deep. He plotted the lanes to run north/south, set 300 feet apart to assure ample overlap so that nothing would be missed. He brought the magnetometer on board, although he would only deploy it if a questionable target was found. A magnetometer measures the differences in the Earth's magnetic field, so it could only detect magnetic (ferrous) metals, like iron or steel, which are used in aircraft engines. The majority of the airplane was made of aluminum, which the magnetometer would not register.

Jack immediately noticed an extra piece of "equipment" that Ralph had installed on the dashboard: A six-inch-tall stuffed bear. "That's The Bear God," Ralph explained, sounding quite serious. "He's for good luck."

The Bear God must have been doing his duty, because the lake was flat that day. With Steve at Jack's regular place at the helm, Jack used the time to familiarize himself with Ralph's equipment. He was most interested in the Hypack Max survey software that Ralph used to manage the navigation and track his lanes. This was far more sophisticated than our hand notations.

Soon the story swapping began with Jack filling Ralph in on our past expeditions: "You know, it's possible we could find the *Chicora* out here," he commented, knowing that the steamer's last run on that January day in 1895 followed the course line between Milwaukee and Benton Harbor and ran right through the area where we would be searching for the aircraft wreckage. We had been hoping to find that shipwreck and solve a local mystery since we began wreck hunting in 1998.

"Yeah," he snickered, "wouldn't be the first time something like that happened. We found 18 shipwrecks while looking for LaSalle's flagship *L'Aimable*." That galleon had gone down in 1685 off the Gulf Coast of Texas.

"But sometimes they're easy," Ralph pointed out. "Clive got three for three off Charleston. He found the Civil War battleships *Keokuk, Weehawken*, and *Patapsco* each in less than a day; in fact, he found the *Keokuk* on his second lane, although he bet me he'd find it on the first."

"Then again, we might not find anything," Ralph cautioned. "We went to Maine several times looking in small inland lakes for Nungesser and Coli's *White Bird.*" The French biplane, he explained, disappeared in 1927 during an attempt to make the first non-stop transatlantic flight between Paris and New York. "We came up with zilch."

"What got Clive interested in Flight 2501?" Jack asked.

"Well," Ralph said turning to Jack, "it was a guy who works as a docent at the Air Zoo. He wrote Clive suggesting it would be a good mystery to solve."

The Air Zoo is an air and space museum in Kalamazoo, Michigan, about 40 miles east of South Haven.

"But, I don't think that was enough to really pique his interest," Ralph continued, adjusting a knob on his sonar. "Clive's buddy, Warren Lasch—the guy from Grand Rapids, Michigan, who funded the *Hunley's* conservation—put another bug in his ear."

"How'd he hear about it?" Jack prodded.

"He saw a newspaper article that said you guys wanted to look for it. He suggested that Clive team up with you."

WHEN THEY REACHED the starting point of the search grid, Jack helped deploy the fish and they began the routine of mowing the lawn. Despite the Bayliner's sloppy steering, Steve handled it like a master, not bothering to engage the autopilot as we normally did. He just cranked his hand back and forth on the wheel, maintaining a course line as straight as an arrow. Jack sat below in the cabin with Ralph watching the monitor. The scrolling digital image looked just like the black-on-white image the stylus prints on the paper unit. Any Rorschach ink blots that showed up would still look familiar to us.

About an hour into the first lane, as they neared that specific spot 18 miles north-northwest of Benton Harbor, a small, dark mark about a half inch long appeared on the screen. A white shadow behind the mark indicated it stuck up off the bottom. *Could it be this easy?* Jack wondered, as Ralph zoomed in on the target and captured a screenshot with the coordinates. A minute later, another weird image materialized. "What the hell is that?" Jack asked, pointing, as Steve leaned over to peer down into the cabin.

It looked like a swastika. Ralph estimated the target was about 30 feet square and captured that image, too, declaring in his southern drawl, "I know *where* it is, but I don't know *what* it is!"

In another few minutes, they saw what looked like a field of circles. Then more dark lines and specks. At that point, the boat had already traveled about a half mile from where they saw the first anomaly.

"Gotta be just weird bottom," Ralph said. "Even though that swastika was a great target, now we're seeing all this stuff, which makes me think it's all just geology."

Had it been more concentrated, it might represent the crashed airplane, but a long line of widely scattered debris is not in keeping with an aircraft impacting the surface of the water.

Steve had inadvertently slowed the boat to hear what was being said, and suddenly the image on the screen grew bigger. "Pick it up, Steve," Ralph screamed, when he realized that the slower speed had caused the fish to sink, and it would soon hit bottom. It was his first display of that famous temper we had read about. Ralph and Jack braced as the boat surged forward. As the boat accelerated, the fish rose and luckily didn't hit the bottom.

For the balance of the day, the sonar plotted out smooth sand bottom, with only an unusual speck here and there. They did not experience any insurmountable issues with the thermocline—the invisible layer where the meeting of warm and cold water can distort a sonar image—nor did they find any targets to get excited about.

The weather over the next week was ever-changing. Some days were too rough to survey. Jack and Ross went to their respective jobs, I continued to research the flight, and Ralph and Steve tweaked their equipment, reviewed their search coverage data, and, when they got bored doing that, toured around town. Even good days were not that good, delivering temperature in the 60s, overcast skies, and choppy water. For men used to big, rolling ocean swells, irregular two-footers were annoying. With a potential good day looming at the end of September, I invited David Trotter to join us, figuring there were things that both he and Ralph could learn from each other. However, by the time Dave arrived, the wind had picked up. We holed up at a local diner and swapped the stories that we would otherwise have told on the boat.

Ralph bought along his computer to show Dave the weird targets scanned on the first day and to speculate on what they might be. "The problem with working in deep water is that you can't just jump in and see what those things are," he lamented.

When surveying in shallow water close to shore, Ralph often had a dive team follow in another boat, ready to check out any targets.

Dave understood that well, having worked in water over 200 feet deep for many years. "Yeah, Chief, you just have to suffer through the burning curiosity, until you can get divers down."

We would have to spend a significant amount of time, money, and manpower to check out any deep target. Boat gas to get to and from the site could run as much as $300. The divers would need to fill their tanks with tri-mix, a special blend of gas that reduces nitrogen, which is narcotic at depth, and oxygen, which is toxic at deep depths, and replace those gases with helium. To breathe regular air at extreme depths would be like drinking three martinis, breathing toxic paint fumes, then going out for a drive. A diver would remember little and probably not return safely. The percentages of gases would have to be custom-designed for a specific depth, and each tank—and they would need to carry three or four per dive—would cost about $75 to fill.

Additionally, at least two divers would need to go down for safety, and another two people would need to serve as surface support. A dive to 250 feet, for instance, would require about 45 minutes to suit up, 3 minutes to reach the bottom, 20 minutes on the bottom, and about 60 minutes decompressing, the tedious but critical last step. Decompression is the process of slowly ascending and hovering at specific depths for specific periods of time to rid the bloodstream of accumulated compressed gases. To skimp on that time could result in a case of "the bends," where gas bubbles linger in the joints, causing intense pain and often leaving the victims "bent," unable to straighten their limbs. To skip decompression could result in paralysis or death if the gas bubbles block the flow of vital oxygen to critical organs.

Extended periods of time while decompressing has its own hazards: Hypothermia can set in even when divers wear insulating drysuits. In Lake Michigan, it is not advisable to dive deep until about June when the water warms up enough. In addition, only one deep dive can be made per day because of residual gas buildup in the blood. Therefore, we would only be able to dive on the most promising targets.

"I don't think any of these targets warrants a dive, Chief," Dave assessed, looking at the laptop.

"Yeah, and I think we're done searching," Ralph replied. "The weather that rolled in this morning looks as if it will stick around for another week. We're going to pack it up and head home," he said, leaving enough cash on the table to cover the tab, as we got up to leave.

The gales of November hit early that year. The NUMA team had only been able to survey five out of ten days. On October 1, they rolled out of our driveway. "See y'all next spring," Ralph announced, as he waved goodbye.

Apparently Clive was not going to give up so easily.

Chapter 4

IF AT FIRST YOU DON'T SUCCEED

Although we didn't find Flight 2501 in 2004, that first expedition was important for Ralph and Steve to test the equipment in deep water, become familiar with conditions on Lake Michigan, and get to know us. They had worked with a lot of different people over the years, some professional and dedicated, others amateurs and unreliable. We knew that we fell in the first category, but we would have to continue to prove ourselves the next spring when they would return.

Soon after they left, copies of the Coast Guard and Navy log books arrived in the mail. These official ships' logs documented the search for the aircraft and the recovery of debris from the surface of Lake Michigan. We had difficulty reading the handwriting of different Coastguardsmen. Craig took on the monumental task of transcribing them. Once he was done, we could easily read the recorded activities of the four Coast Guard cutters and a Navy destroyer—all involved in the operation. Crewmen recovered a good deal of debris found floating on the lake's surface. Each log book provided the boat's position in latitude and longitude coordinates and the current activity six times each day. The coordinates were not calculated using satellites like a GPS unit today. Instead, sailors plotted their compass heading, distance, and speed in a method called dead reckoning, and then used a chart to determine their position in latitude and longitude. This method was, of course, subject to inaccuracies depending on wind and currents.

We plotted the coordinates to track the movement and activity of each boat on a lake chart. Once complete, we had a visual image of where the floating debris had been found, most of it northeast of the supposed crash site 18 miles north-northwest of Benton Harbor, and all of it between the northern Airway Red 57 and the southern airway Red 28. Among the flotsam were parts of the shattered fuselage, seat cushions, interior paneling, personal possessions, and human remains.

This information convinced us to continue the search near where we looked in 2004. We made sure the search grid would include an area where the Coast Guard recorded oil and body parts bubbling to the surface—in case the twisted fuselage was directly below and had been slowly releasing its gruesome contents.

In an effort to leave no stone uncovered, we also began a hunt for other government documents that might offer more specifics about the accident than the CAB report did. I queried the National Archives and wrote Freedom of Information Act requests to the Federal Aviation Administration and the National Transportation Safety Bureau, the present-day agency that handles accident investigation. I hoped to find the entire file of data collected by the CAB from which it drafted the final accident investigation report. However, all three organizations responded by sending the same CAB accident investigation report that we already had.

Over the winter, Ralph and Jack each worked on solutions to try to increase daily coverage. Ralph acquired a new Klein System 3000 side-scan that has both 100 and 500 kHz frequencies with 650 feet of cable. The new system would run both frequencies offering the extended coverage of low frequency with the better resolution of the high frequency. The longer cable with the added weight and hydrodynamics of a lead K-Wing would drive the fish lower, allowing them to increase the boat speed. Jack installed a different-pitched propeller that would let the heavily laden boat go faster and reduce travel time to the search area. Together, they estimated that this would double the amount of coverage per day. If we could not pinpoint the site, then at least we could operate as efficiently as possible.

AS WINTER TURNED TO SPRING, we began planning the MSRA annual film festival and our own independent effort to find area shipwrecks. We planned to search for the SS *Michigan,* lost somewhere off Holland, considerably north of the Flight 2501 search area. Considering that debris from the *Chicora* came ashore near South Haven, we figured there was a possibility we would find that wreck while looking for Flight 2501. In fact, our list of wrecks indicated that several other historic ships might be lurking in that area, including the steam barge *Joseph P. Farnan,* the schooner barge *Hattie Wells,* the schooners *William Tell* and *A.P. Dutton,* and the *Sea Mar III,* a 32-foot fiberglass boat that was lost with its crew of four in 1980 while en route from Chicago to Holland. Our research also indicated that a number of small private airplanes had gone down off southwestern Michigan, each with the loss of their pilots, and in some instances a passenger or two.

We scheduled our spring film festival for late April and planned to present a program about the search for Flight 2501. We asked Ralph to be our keynote speaker to share the story of NUMA's successful search for the *H. L. Hunley*. The local newspapers and television stations promoted the event, and the Associated Press picked up the story of our search, which then appeared in a wider array of newspapers throughout the Midwest. In addition to helping fill the auditorium, the media attention had an unexpected consequence. It began to bring people out of the woodwork—mostly senior citizens—who remembered something about Flight 2501.

We received a number of emails and phone calls from individuals who had seen or heard an airplane that night. Each hoped that somehow their recollections might point us to the spot where Flight 2501 had crashed. Retired South Haven resident Jackie Eldred was the first person to contact us. She expressed feeling guilt over not coming forth right after the crash, wondering now if the huge "kaboom" she had heard that night might have helped authorities find the wreck. "I was afraid people would think I was crazy, back then" she told us, "but now I hope I can help you find it."

Several people saw a low-flying airplane near the lakeshore that night; others thought they heard the motors sputtering, still others heard a huge explosion, and several people saw an "orange flash on the horizon." Although everyone seemed very certain they had seen or heard Flight 2501, we reasoned that other airplanes were flying that night and that the sights and sounds of the storm may have mimicked an airplane crashing. We did not hold out much hope that their memories, more than a half century old, would be accurate. However, I felt there were too many similar accounts for everyone to be mistaken.

Ninety-year-old Mary Meier of Big Rapids, Michigan, called to let us know that she had met one of the women victims at LaGuardia. "We chatted for a while," she said, "and laughed when we realized we were both heading to Grand Rapids: she to the city in Minnesota and me to the one in Michigan." Even after more than 50 years, Meier recalled how sad she felt when she learned the woman had died.

One contact would be of particular significance. Chuck Boie, the president of the Mitchell Gallery of Flight, an aviation museum at Milwaukee's General Mitchell International Airport with a membership of historians, pilots, and retired airline employees. Boie had a huge collection of Northwest Airlines' memorabilia and understood flying in the 50s. He offered a great deal of input about what may have happened to Flight 2501 and introduced us to two other people with specific insights. His friend, 92-year-old retired Captain

Frederic Stripe, had been flying in the vicinity of Flight 2501 the night it crashed and had witnessed the violent squall line. And Leo Kohn, an aviation photographer, gave us something we never imagined existed: A photograph of the actual airplane used for Flight 2501. He had taken it when the aircraft was in Milwaukee. Most DC-4s looked identical, but the tail number, N-95425, made it unique. The photograph showed a double-wide aft door, confirming what the CAB report had indicated: that particular DC-4 had been built as a C-54 Skymaster in 1942, then converted to a DC-4 by the Douglas Aircraft Company in 1946. Kohn had found the photo filed among his rejects because it was slightly blurry. Although he was disappointed in the quality, I thought it evoked a great deal of emotion in light of what happened little more than two months after it was taken. The sky was dull and gray and the airplane was taxiing away from Kohn. It seemed to be offering a solemn goodbye.

RALPH WILBANKS AND STEVE HOWARD arrived in May of 2005 as promised and settled into the Comfort Inn once again. Like the previous fall, Jack installed the side-scan gear on our boat, and we divided up the schedule to make sure we supplied a crewmember each day. The new propeller did its job, and the boat operated more efficiently. We deployed the fish and began searching directly adjacent to where we left off the prior fall, working east. With the longer cable and K-wing, Ralph could increase the speed to three or four knots. Mowing the lawn continued day after day. As expected, there was no thermocline in the cold spring water, and the lake proved to be calmer than it had been in the fall.

During the second week of the search while nearing the end of a north run, the boat suddenly lurched and slowed dramatically, though Steve had not touched the throttle. At just that same time, a huge image appeared on the monitor. "Steve! Steve!" Ralph hollered, immediately abandoning his post in the cabin to get to the stern and check on his fish. "What the hell happened?"

Although he asked the question, he was pretty convinced that the fish hit something. While Steve motored slowly backward, Ralph tugged on the sonar cable to see if it was hung up on something, maybe the wreckage of the airplane. Fortunately, it came up and he started the winch to make sure it didn't dig into the bottom. Then he checked the monitor. During all the commotion, the sonar had recorded a massive target. Ralph knew at a glance this was no DC-4. He finished hauling in the fish. Despite the fish having taken an obvious nose dive into muck, evidenced by the coating of ooze, it was undamaged. A burning curiosity prompted Ralph to deploy it again. This time he set it at about 50 feet off the bottom, so that it would not become entangled in whatever was down there. Steve managed to maneuver the boat back into position.

The next few images captured by the sonar revealed what could only be a shipwreck about 100 feet long and almost 60 feet wide in 160 feet of water. It appeared to stand just over 40 feet off the bottom, a massive height considering the length of the vessel. Steve ran back and forth over it several times until Ralph recorded several good images. Then they hauled in the fish.

That night Ralph emailed a jpg of the target. I was stymied. I could not think of any shipwreck lost in that general vicinity that matched the size of the target. The considerable height off the bottom was perplexing. The deck of whatever it was appeared to be wooden because there were lines running down its length. However, the scale of those lines seemed all wrong. We would need to make a dive to understand that particular Rorschach ink blot, but the water was still too cold to risk a 160-foot dive on a target that we knew was not the airplane. We agreed to wait until the warmer summer months.

We would also have to wait to dive on the next target Ralph found. There was no question when we saw the side-scan target what it represented. Clearly, Ralph had found a small pleasure boat, about 30 feet long. The only boat that we knew had gone missing in that general vicinity was the *Sea Mar III*, lost in 1980. Diving this target concerned us since the bodies of the four men lost with the boat had never been found.

The following weekend we hosted our annual film festival, "An Evening Beneath the Inland Seas." Hundreds of people packed into the Knickerbocker Theater on Eighth Street in downtown in Holland. Ralph did a marvelous presentation on the discovery of the *Hunley,* and Craig and I presented a program called "The Disappearance of Flight 2501," about the accident and our initial search effort. Many of the witnesses who had contacted us attended the program, and at the end of the presentation, I introduced them and thanked them for their recollections. Then in the spotlight that nearly blinded me, I found myself ad-libbing something that I had not thought of until that very moment. "Considering all the recent media that brought these people to us," I said, "it may not be long before we hear from a victim's relative."

In those few seconds, I realized that unlike shipwrecks lost more than a century ago, this accident was recent enough that people who knew the victims could still be alive. I wondered if those people would approve of our efforts to find the wreckage or whether it would just open old wounds.

I FELT CLAIRVOYANT, when eight days later, an email popped in from a Ken Skoug. I immediately recognized the name as a passenger on Flight 2501 and for a moment wondered if he had actually survived. Reading the email put that crazy notion to rest. Ken Skoug was the grandson of the victim and lived in the Detroit area. Apparently every so often he searched the internet for anything about Northwest Flight 2501, and this time he happened upon the MSRA web site. He further surprised me with the news that his father, also named Ken Skoug, was alive and well and living in Virginia. They were both very interested in knowing what we had learned about the accident. Hoping against hope that the Skougs had been given some input from Northwest Airlines five decades earlier that might help us in our search effort, Jack and I made plans to visit them in Detroit on the Fourth of July weekend when Skoug's father would be in town. I hoped that by then we would have found the wreck.

Unfortunately, over the next two weeks, we found nothing else on the lake bottom except a lot of what we called "crop circles," which were either landing zones of alien space crafts or, more likely, just hard, clay bottom and rocks. In total, we covered 18 square miles in 2005.

As Ralph and Steve packed up for their return to Charleston, we learned that he would soon be on his way to England to work for Clive on the continued search for the *Bonhomme Richard*. Ralph let us know that Clive wanted him to return to Michigan the following spring. I thought about something Clive had written in *Sea Hunters II*: "There is no monetary profit to this shipwreck hunting madness; I do what I do purely out of a love for our country's history and to preserve it for future generations." I was thankful that Clive felt as we did and had pockets deep enough to make it happen.

JACK AND I and our daughters drove to Detroit to meet the Skougs that July. From the moment we walked into their home, it became clear that the victim Ken Skoug, Sr. was not merely a name on a passenger list. He had lived, been loved, and was never forgotten. A framed photograph of him greeted us as we entered the living room, and we realized that his family had kept his memory alive when we met Ken Skoug Jr, his son, Ken Skoug III, and his grandson, five-year-old Ken Skoug IV. In fact, all three Kens had the same square jaw as Ken Skoug Sr. We spent the afternoon getting to know the man who died in that accident so long ago. It pained me to learn that Ken Jr. never forgot the argument he had with his dad just before his dad boarded the airplane. I considered, too, how sad it was that like my own daughter Cella, Ken III and IV never got to meet the person for whom they were named.

Both Skoug men had a lot of still smoldering questions that the authorities could not answer in 1950.

"Did the plane explode or crash?"

"Did the weather or a mechanical failure cause the accident?"

"Did the pilot make a mistake?"

And, the most difficult of all questions, "Did the passengers suffer before they died?"

As we said our goodbyes and promised to keep them informed of our search efforts, I felt relieved to know they approved of our efforts. I fully realized, in that moment, how our quest to solve an historical mystery would be infinitely more important to this family who, after more than 50 years, were still seeking answers. Finding the wreck suddenly seemed all the more important.

DURING THE SUMMER OF 2005, Jack and I set aside Flight 2501 and returned to the business of shipwrecks. It turned out to be a fruitful summer. Our dives to the shipwreck that Ralph's sonar had slammed into revealed a sizable section of a large steel ship with train tracks on the deck. The ship had plunged into the bottom like a javelin, accounting for the extreme height. However, identifying the wreck did not come easy. We finally uncovered records that an old railroad carferry-turned-barge, the *Ann Arbor No. 5*, had been used nearby in 1968 and 1969 as a breakwall to protect in-water work areas during construction of the Palisades Power Plant. Not until we tracked down the 83-year-old former owner did we learn that after the project was done, the company scrapped two-thirds of the barge. They tried to save money by hauling the intact aft third of the boat to a scrap yard, but the pumps gave out in transit and it sank. We were able to rewrite the history books with that discovery.

Unfortunately, we were not able to write the final chapter of the *Sea Mar III*. The small boat target turned out to be an aged wooden Chris-Craft that had obviously been stripped and scuttled as a way to get rid of a worthless hull. Once again, we were reminded that even when a side-scan image seemed completely obvious, we could not make any assumptions regarding its identity until we had seen it "in the flesh."

When it rains it pours. That summer, while working with David Trotter, we finally discovered the SS *Michigan*. At 275 feet deep, the wreck was too deep for any of us to dive, so we asked for the assistance of technical divers Bob Underhill, Jeff Vos, and Todd White, who were among the most accomplished and experienced divers in Michigan.

Bob Underhill, the senior man of the team, was in his mid-50s. He began diving in 1964 and had logged literally thousands of dives. He could have written the manual for tri-mix diving since he was among the earliest divers to experiment with it. Diving takes precedence over most things in his life, except his wife, Jan, who also dives, although his work as an electrical engineer for a hospital equipment company is important because it pays for his expensive diving habit.

Jeff Vos, the youngest of the group in his late 30s, had logged almost as many dives as Bob because he began diving shipwrecks with his dad not long after he learned to swim. His skills as a machinist and owner of Accutech CNC, a machine tooling shop, gave him an innate understanding of the mechanics of diving and dive gear that allowed him to safely push the limits of diving. His wife, Tamara, also a diver, often joins in on the adventure.

Todd White, the newest diver in the group, was in his early 40s, but he had quickly and methodically advanced through his training, tackling it with the same intensity, organization, and acumen as he does running his restaurant, The Butler, in Saugatuck. Todd's wife, Jody, is also a certified diver.

Thanks to their underwater survey work, we were able to produce a documentary film, and I wrote and illustrated my first publication, a children's book called *Icebound*, about the SS *Michigan*.

AS THE GALES OF NOVEMBER 2005 blew in, we turned our attention back to Flight 2501, trying to strategize where next to look for the wreck. Before I could dig in, I received an email from a Bill Kaufmann, who was just six years old when he lost his mother, Jean, in the crash of Flight 2501. At first I did not want to respond. It had been difficult speaking with the Skoug family and reliving their grief, and I did not relish going through that again. At that point I was more interested in finding witnesses who might have seen or heard something that could help us locate the wreck, however, I felt an obligation to talk with Kaufmann.

Just a couple weeks before Christmas, I called him at his home in California. The conversation was awkward because he seemed distant. He expressed how upset he was over his mother's death and how her loss affected his whole life, relationships, career, and everything; he even wondered if it may have contributed to his divorce. I realized that I was in over my head. While the Skoug men seemed comfortable talking about the loss of their father and grandfather, Kaufmann had difficulty; the accident still seemed very raw to him. I had no idea how to respond, except to tell him about our search effort, hoping that might, in some way, offer him comfort. I spoke carefully because, by that point, I knew a lot about the gruesome details of what had been recovered from the lake. Discussing the accident with unrelated individuals had been perfunctory; to discuss it with Bill would be very personal.

"Have you been in touch with any other families?" Bill asked.

"Just one. The Skoug family. Ken Skoug lost his father." There was silence on the line for several seconds.

"I'd like to talk with him, compare memories, see how he fared after the accident," he said.

I told Kaufmann I would ask Ken Skoug if he would be willing to talk. Then I asked him if he would write down some memories about his mother or how he heard about the accident. I was curious, and I thought maybe the act of writing would be good for him.

"Well, if you need me, why don't I just make plans to come to Holland."

I certainly didn't expect that reaction, but in a flash, I envisioned the perfect get-together—at the MSRA's annual event the next spring when the NUMA team would be in town so that he could meet them too. I wondered if perhaps the Skougs would agree to drive in for the event, giving Bill the opportunity to talk with both son and grandson. *If the planets all aligned*, I thought, *perhaps we will have found the wreckage by then.*

"How about May?" I suggested, then explained my idea.

"I'll be there. And maybe my baby sister, too."

A sister, too, I winced. *Jean Kaufmann left behind two young children.*

As it turned out, the entire Skoug family agreed to come as well as Bill and his sister, Mary Jean, now called Brandi, and her husband, Kurt Holstein. They would be spending considerable time and money to travel here, so I felt obligated to make their trip memorable. We scheduled our event for the first Saturday of May to coincide with the annual Tulip Time Festival in Holland, hoping that would make their visit special. Then, I thought of something that would be even better. "Wouldn't it be great if we could ferry them out to see the search operation in progress?" I said to Jack one day.

"Sure would," he said, "but on what boat?" Ours was not big enough for all four of them plus Jack, me, and our other board members.

"Well, let's see if we have any members who might have a bigger boat," I said, as I started scheming.

Chapter 5

A NEW APPROACH

The NUMA team arrived in late April 2006, earlier than the prior year in order to increase the length of the expedition. That would be just one of several changes Ralph implemented to increase efficiency and cover more territory, because the airplane wreckage was proving to be much more difficult to find than anyone had anticipated. Ralph towed his own vessel, *Diversity*, a 25-foot Parker, from South Carolina to use that year. Although only slightly larger than our boat, it had significantly more deck space to make the setting and retrieving of the fish go smoother, larger fuel tanks so they stay out longer, and better electronics, including a fathometer, radar, and GPS system. In addition, Ralph had come to understand how unpredictable and dangerous the inland seas are, so he obtained a life raft and Mustang flotation jackets and "Gumby" survival suits for each crewman.

All Ralph's boat lacked was a winch, and so Jack built him a custom one like ours. That year, they rented a house in town to make the stay more comfortable, and because each of us with MSRA had day jobs we needed to maintain, Ralph hired a third person, Harry Pecorelli, as crew in addition to Steve Howard. Harry, an archaeologist, whose long, wavy hair I envied, had started working with Ralph on the 1995 *Hunley* search. In fact, he had been the first diver to touch the famed submarine, and later served on the archaeological team to conserve the vessel after it was raised. They quickly got down to the business of mowing the lawn in search of Flight 2501, continuing to build farther north and east from the prior year's search and cover the area where the Coast Guard had recovered the floating debris.

On May 5, 2006, Brandi Kaufmann Holstein and her husband flew into the Gerald R. Ford International Airport in Grand Rapids. Jack and I met them at a local restaurant. Although we were virtual strangers, the circumstance of our meeting was personal. Brandi and I hugged as if we had been friends for years and had a nice evening talking about her mother, Jean.

The next day, MSRA hosted a luncheon for the Skougs and Kaufmanns at a restaurant in town surrounded by gorgeous tulips. We met Bill Kaufmann there for the first time. He had just flown in from California and noted how ironic that his flight had just *successfully* crossed Lake Michigan. He was tall and thin and had bright white hair and full beard. We introduced everyone to each other, and the two families had the chance to talk among themselves. That evening they all attended our annual film festival. I asked Ken Skoug Jr. and Bill Kaufmann to say a few words about the parents they had lost and what the search effort meant to them. After the program, they had a chance to meet Ralph, Steve, and Harry. In preparation for Sunday's activity, I gave them directions to the marina where MSRA members Chuck and Shirley Cooper docked their 53-foot trawler *Seven Cs*. "Let's meet at 9:30," I suggested.

As if the weather on Sunday had been arranged specially for our benefit, the sky was blue, the temperature warm, and the lake was calm. About twenty MSRA members joined Craig, Jack, and me to show their support for the two families. I had asked Pastor Mark Mast from our church to officiate at a small ceremony on the lake. Chuck Cooper skillfully piloted his yacht out of the channel at Holland and south toward the search area. This was the first time that the Skougs and Kaufmanns had been on Lake Michigan. I realized that the journey had the effect that I had hoped it would when, as all of us sat talking in the salon, Bill said to no one in particular, "I always pictured Lake Michigan as a dark, dirty, horrible place, but now I realize my mother died in beautiful surroundings."

It took about 90 minutes to reach the search area. Jack spotted Ralph's boat *Diversity* and pointed it out to those gathered, then we joined the Coopers in the pilothouse. "Can you get us a little closer?" I asked Chuck. I wanted the families to see better how the operation worked.

As we neared *Diversity*, everyone could see the sonar cable angled out behind the boat. Ralph stepped out of the cabin and waved. He had been expecting us. Then he pointed to the black steel dayshape signal with two circles and a triangle mounted at the stern. Shirley, also a licensed captain, recognized its meaning. "That signal means the boat has reduced maneuverability, so we have to stay back at least 100 yards."

Bill Kaufmann joined us in the pilothouse. "So that boat's searching for my mom's airplane now?" he asked, sounding as if he did not quite believe it.

"Sure is," I said. "This is the third season they've been here. They'll be out here every day, weather permitting, through the rest of the month."

After cruising slowly parallel to the search boat for a short time, Chuck headed the boat a bit farther west, then shut down the engine. The quiet on the calm water was deafening. Pastor Mark circulated throughout the salon and on the outer deck asking everyone to join him on the forward deck. He took a position near the bow where we had placed a colorful wreath of flowers and began his service. "We are gathered here on a beautiful day to remember and give thanks for the lives of the 58 people who perished on Flight 2501."

He noted that although more than fifty years had passed between their deaths and our gathering, "it seems but a moment for these families."

Their tears confirmed their still raw emotions.

He continued the service quoting several passages from the Old Testament and spoke words intended for the Skougs and the Kaufmanns, though certainly germane to many. In his sermon he spoke of the questions raised about God in the wake of such a terrible accident, but reminded those gathered that strength can be found in hope, love, grace, and rejoicing that even there in that place, God is present.

The sun twinkling on the surface at that moment seemed heaven sent. Jack, Craig, and I read the names of the 58 victims, then Pastor Mark invited the family members to say a few words about their loved ones. Ken Skoug II spoke from his heart, "Fifty six years is a long time in the history of our country, but just a blink in the eyes of nature. If one has to have a tomb," he said raising his arm and motioning toward the lake, "then my father and the others have a beautiful tomb."

Bill Kaufmann shared memories of his mother and read a passage from the Torah to honor the Jewish victims.

Pastor Mark concluded by asking the families to come forth and place the wreath in the water. When it hit the surface, small ripples radiated out. Then a few flower peddles broke off and began slowly drifting away from the wreath in different directions. I could not help but grasp the irony. Pieces of the DC-4 had done just the same in the minutes after the aircraft hit the surface. As I gazed out over the open water, I wondered how far from our present location the airplane had crashed and hoped we would soon find out. My thoughts were interrupted by the sound of two bells in memory of Jean Kaufmann and Kenneth Skoug, concluding the ceremony.

After the service, it was difficult to launch back into the trivial chit chat that had been so fun on the journey out. For some time, everyone split into small groups, lost in their own thoughts. I could see that even our members were, in their own way, feeling the emotion of the two families.

Bill found me in the salon arranging a platter of meat and cheese. "So is Mark Mast with a church?" he asked.

"Sure is," I replied. "He's with Trinity Reformed in Holland."

"How did this all come together?" he probed.

"I just made some calls and asked our membership for help. That's how we do everything."

"Do you do this every year?"

"No, not a service on the lake," I said smiling, "We did this for you and Brandi and the Skougs because you came all this way to meet with us."

Bill seemed to ponder that, while I opened a bag of bread.

"You know," he said finally, "my family thought I was too young to attend the church service for my mom."

"Really?" I asked, not knowing what to say.

"Today, I finally got to say goodbye to her," he said, with tears brimming. I had no idea the service would mean so much to him.

"No one" he said, wiping his eyes, "has ever done anything this nice for me or my family."

I smiled and offered him a sandwich.

I MET BILL KAUFMANN for lunch the next day before he headed off to the airport. He left his reflective mood on the boat, and got down to the business of the search, turning over his place mat and using a pen to map out the flight path and speculate where the airplane might have gone down. I shared our theories and outlined the area we had already covered.

"I really appreciated talking with Ken Skoug," he said. "I felt so different from all the other kids in my class, growing up without a mother, but now I realize I was not alone in my misery."

It seemed as if the whole experience of the weekend had been therapeutic for him. Then he made a suggestion that in hindsight would be therapeutic for me. "Do you think you can find some more of us—the ones left behind? I think they deserve to know about the search."

That's when it hit me full force. There were literally hundreds of people alive today whose lives, like the Kaufmanns' and the Skougs', had been forever altered by this accident.

"I don't know, Bill," I said, not sure if I wanted to walk down that emotional path.

Bill Kaufmann seemed to be a man on a mission. He did not let me slink away from his challenge. He called me a week after he got home. He explained that he had been looking over the names on the victim list. "I recognized the name Sirbu," he said.

What he said next floored me.

"Just yesterday, I realized why the name was so familiar," he explained.

"I ran into another attorney, Gary Sirbu, who I occasionally see at the courthouse. I took him aside, and asked, 'Are you related to anyone who died in a plane crash in 1950?'"

"How did you know?" Sirbu asked Kaufmann.

"Because my mom died on that plane, too."

Sirbu was shocked that they shared the accident in common, Kaufmann explained. His uncle had died in the crash, and offered to put Kaufmann in touch with his cousins, the grandchildren of Joseph Sirbu.

"I've got their numbers," Kaufmann told me, "I hope you'll call them."

And so it seemed, I would be starting a search quite different from our side-scan operation, one that, ultimately, would be more rewarding and revealing than finding submerged chunks of twisted aluminum.

BEFORE I COULD BEGIN MY SEARCH, Ralph emailed me jpgs of two more targets they had just found. He did not think they represented the wreck of the airplane, but felt they were too unusual to leave unchecked. The first one was 250 feet deep and looked like a giant rib cage—a 30-foot-long single line with a series of perpendicular lines running down its length. Consequently, we called it "Rib Cage." For a moment, I wondered, not too seriously, if an old mastodon walked across the lake one cold winter eons ago and sank through the ice. We called the other "Splat" because it looked like a blob of paint flung at a canvas. Ralph did not think that Splat was the wreckage because the magnetometer did not indicate the presence of any metal.

"Don't rush to dive them," he wrote. "I just need to have you ground-truth these targets to understand what my sonar is picking up in deep water."

For the balance of the month, I kept hoping Ralph would find a more promising target, but after being able to search about 20 of the 30 days they were in town, all we had to show for 23 square miles of coverage was Rib Cage and Splat.

"See y'all next year," Ralph emailed the day they rolled out of town.

BETWEEN THE FLIGHT 2501 search and our shipwreck hunt, which we postponed until July, I had some time to pursue the families. I called Sirbu's grandsons and other members of their family. Like my talks with the Skougs and Kaufmanns, I found it difficult to hear how miserable life had been for them after the crash.

So far, three people had come my way with little effort: Now it was time to turn the tables and do the finding myself.

I pulled out the victim list and began to pore over it. I reasoned that it might be easy to find the families with unusual names like Heuston, Ajemian, and Hokanson. The families of Anderson, Hill, and Ross would be almost impossible to find. I realized I would have a better chance of finding sons or nephews who would have the same last name as the victims, than I would trying to track daughters or nieces whose last names would have changed when they married. There were several victims who died single. Finding their families might be impossible.

I began by Googling the names Benjamin and Slava Heuston and got an immediate bingo. The University of Puget Sound web site listed an auditorium that had been named in honor of the couple. Using whitepages. com, I found two Heustons in Washington, probably sons of the victims, and I jotted down their phone numbers. I realized how strange my call might sound. The person on the other line might assume I was a con artist, so I carefully rehearsed what I would say to attempt to ease the minds of the person who might answer. I dialed Benjamin Franklin Heuston first.

A woman answered. "Hello," I said introducing myself. "I am a researcher from Holland, Michigan. I am studying the crash of an airplane in Lake Michigan in 1950 and I wonder if you might be related to the Heustons who were on board the plane?"

There was silence on the phone as I waited for a response. Then, after a few seconds, the woman whispered. "Yes, they were my husband's parents, but Frank's not going to want to talk about it."

Oh no, I thought, *he is not going to be as receptive as the Skougs and Kaufmanns.*

"But I only wish to let him know that I am part of a team who is searching for the wreck," I continued. As soon as I said that, I wondered if she would think I was phishing for money, so I quickly added. "We don't want anything of you, only to let you know that we are trying to pick up where the authorities left off and determine the reason for the accident," although I wasn't sure exactly how we would figure that out if we found the wreck.

I heard her rustling through papers. "Here, let me give you the number of my husband's brother Paul. He'll probably talk to you."

Indeed, Paul was more receptive, but not much. I told him I had found other families, but clearly he had no interest in connecting with them.

My next attempt was to find the Ajemian family, whose name was even more unusual than Heuston. There was only one Ajemian in the entire country, and thankfully she had chosen her mother's maiden name for her own or I would never have found her. She was about my age and her grandparents had died in the accident before she was born. She arranged for me to speak to her mother.

To find the Eastman family, I searched for Anna Eastman's unusually named son-in-law, Morrow Peyton, whom I had seen listed in a 1950 newspaper story. I found only one person with that name. He lived in Florida, which seemed the perfect place for a man who would be in his 90s. I dialed. When a recorded message said the line had been disconnected, I realized that at 56 years post-accident, I might be too late to reach some of these people.

I had to use detective-like reasoning with some of the more common names. I pursued the family of Dr. Archibald Cardle from Minneapolis by presuming the family still resided in Minnesota. Although there were seven Cardles in the directory, I honed in on the one who was listed as a doctor, presuming a son might have followed in his father's footsteps. Indeed, he had.

I wondered if Rosalie Gorski's husband might still be alive, but there were dozens of Gorskis along the East Coast. Although a newspaper had listed Katherine Kurinka as her mother, too many years had passed to find her still alive. However, I looked up the name because it was so unusual. That strategy worked. A Kurinka cousin led me to Rosalie's husband, as well as her sister.

After a good number of discoveries, I reached a point when I ran out of leads. For the remaining victims, I had only their names, not their next-of-kin. As if in direct response to my quandary, I received a call from a Steve Shei in Chicago, who had seen a story in the *Chicago Tribune* about our search. His uncle, Ralph Olsen, had died in the accident. In addition to telling me about Olsen, he asked if I would like a copy of the victim list his family had received, adding, "It has the names of each passenger's next-of-kin."

Bingo! I thought.

With that list in hand, I was able to track down a number of additional families. Then, in early June, MSRA received an order from a woman named Galloway for a copy of our DVD "The Disappearance of Flight 2501," which we had just begun offering on the MSRA web site. Before I could mail the package, a woman named Larson ordered the same DVD; hours later, so too did a man named Wohler, whose name I recognized from the victim list. I sent out all three DVDs with a note, asking if they had a connection to a victim. Within just a few days, I had personal conversations with three of the seven Wohler kids, all now seniors.

By mid-June 2006, little more than a month after Bill Kaufmann challenged me to find Flight 2501 families, I had found eleven. Because I am a goal-oriented person, I checked off each discovery on the victim list as proof that I was living up to the challenge posed by Bill. However, the discoveries came with a price. Many people poured out their hearts to me—a stranger on the other end of a telephone line—and shared memories of the ones who died. Most of them recounted how they heard about the accident and the effect it had on their lives. Some expressed remorse at something said or not said to the victim. Some cried because of the memories my telephone call dredged up. I found myself empathizing, crying along with them. Sometimes I thought about losing my mother, but that didn't seem as traumatic. I knew she was ill, I had a chance to say goodbye, and I was already grown when she died.

Most of the people I had talked to lost someone close when they were young and the circumstances were horrific. None of them even had a body to bury as a measure of closure. Talking to these people brought the tragedy closer to home. For the first time in my life, I realized that bad things don't just happen to other people. I worried about facing a traumatic loss again myself and worried for my children should something happen to Jack or me. After each call, I would try to pull myself out of the sadness by spending time with my family. I tried reassuring myself that people were resilient. Everyone I talked to had survived and carried on with life.

I felt comfort knowing that none of the people I had spoken with expressed any anger that our search effort was trespassing on their emotions. In fact, each person asked me to keep them apprised of our work and inform them when we found the wreck. However, one theme ran through most of the phone conversations. Many people harbored great bitterness because of the way they received the news of the crash. Rather than a phone call from Northwest Airlines or a visit from the police, many people learned about the accident through the media: either television news, radio or, in some cases, a reporter just showing up at their door.

Although he was just six at the time, Bill Kaufmann recalled his dad's anger when a crass reporter, who had come to his house, positioned him in a chair for a photo and said, "Now let's get your kids in here for a shot."

I realized that if the media was able to jump on the story so quickly 56 years earlier, the story of our finding the wreck would go viral in a matter of minutes with the power of the internet. I vowed to do my best to break the news gently to these families when we discovered the wreck rather than let them find out from the media. But to do that, I would have to find more families.

MY EFFORTS WOULD BE WAYLAID for the start of the diving and shipwreck hunting season that year. The first order of business would be to identify Rib Cage and Splat, no quick effort. Each dive required two divers, a surface support crew, about eight hours, and hundreds of dollars. Our technical dive team, Bob, Jeff, and Todd, offered their services, and Jack and

I ferried them to the site. Rib Cage turned out to be a 30-foot piece of a ship's hull, which piqued our interest: Perhaps the rest of the ship was nearby. Splat was a field of rock and hard clay, just an area of unusual geology. In reviewing our findings with Ralph it became clear that his sonar was capable of picking up very small anomalies in deep water. We felt confident that his equipment would not miss the wreckage even if it was widely scattered in small pieces.

In early July, we began our ten-day shipwreck hunt with three goals in mind. We planned to survey an area where a couple had recorded an unusual lump on their bottom finder while fishing, a small area off Saugatuck that we had not yet covered during prior expeditions, and the area around Rib Cage to see if the ship, from which it had broken off, was nearby. We suspected that we might find the *Hennepin*, a barge that had gone down in 230 feet of water off South Haven in 1927. For all three efforts David Trotter would use his longer range 50 kHz sonar, which can cover a lot of ground but could miss small objects. If by chance we ran over the airplane wreckage while looking for the *Hennepin* with the "50," the image might be too indistinct to recognize it as anything of interest.

Considering that we had been searching for eight years and had found only three wrecks, we figured we had a minuscule chance of finding anything. However, quite unexpectedly, we found three wrecks. The couple's target turned out to be a 200-foot-long steel barge that had been stripped and scuttled. We found a schooner off Saugatuck that we later identified as the *Hamilton*, lost in 1873. And it was a good thing we scrolled through the side-scan paper after the search as Dave always recommended. A smudge on the sonar paper that we had missed seeing during the search turned out to be the *Hennepin*, incidentally missing a piece of its starboard side, just about the size of Rib Cage.

Our work studying the *Hennepin* revealed that it was infinitely more significant than we had originally believed. It began life as an ordinary steamer, but in 1902 had a conveyor system added, making it the world's first self-unloader, a revolutionary development that reduced the time and cost of shipping bulk materials. It became the prototype for all the modern self-unloaders that today account for more than 80 percent of commercial vessel traffic. The *Hennepin*'s significance, as well as the anticipation of one day finding Flight 2501 in deep water, prompted me to pursue technical dive training. By the end of that summer, I had made a dive to the 230-foot-deep *Hennepin*, my deepest dive yet.

AS FALL TURNED TO WINTER, I began working on the Flight 2501 project again, searching for more witnesses, families, and a smoking gun that might point us to the site of the crash.

Over the next several months, I was quite successful in my hunt. I found that one contact would often lead to another source of information. For instance, I talked to Warren Johnson, the son-in-law of passenger Frank Schwartz, who mentioned two things that opened other doors. He indicated that his mother-in-law and several other families sued Northwest Airlines. That immediately illuminated the proverbial light bulb over my head. I wondered if court transcripts might reveal more than the CAB report did about the crash site. I made a note to search for the case files.

Then Johnson threw in a seemingly unimportant fact: "A Northwest radio operator from Cleveland was supposed to testify, but the company transferred him to Shemya."

I jotted down the note, but it seemed insignificant compared to the fact that there had been a lawsuit. Simple curiosity made me Google "Shemya" after our talk, because I had never heard of the place. The first web site that popped up was entitled "Northwest Airlines on Shemya." I couldn't click on the link fast enough and had to pick my jaw up off my keyboard after reading the first few lines. "My name is Rick Cochran. I am now 78. I was on Shemya from July 21, 1950, to April 3, 1951, on temporary duty from my position as a radio operator in Cleveland, Ohio."

I read enough to learn that Shemya was an island in the Alaskan Aleutians before clicking the "contact me" link and sending Cochran an email. I was amazed by his response: "Yes, I was working the night Flight 2501 crashed. I talked to the pilot."

His memories were illuminating.

OF ALL THE PEOPLE I had found thus far, I had not come close to finding the families of any of the crew. The Lind, Wolfe, and Feldman names were far too common to track, and the next-of-kin victim list did not include the crew. I tried a different avenue to find their families. I contacted the Northwest Airlines Retired Pilot's Association, hoping that from among the membership someone might have known the crew and their families. John Olivia, the organization's president, did not think anyone alive today would have known the crew, but, intrigued by our search, he asked me to pen a short article for his newsletter. I obliged him, making sure to note the names of all the Flight 2501 crewmembers and my contact information.

Then about two months after the article appeared in the newsletter, I received a phone call. "Hi, may I please speak to Valerie van Heest?" the man on the other end asked hesitantly.

"Yes, that's me," I replied.

"This is probably going to seem a strange call," he continued.

"Oh, probably not," I replied with a friendly chuckle. I was sure the call was related to the airplane crash so I encouraged him. "I'll bet you're calling about Northwest Flight 2501."

He laughed. "Yes, I am." My name is Brad Frisk. My uncle was Robert Lind, the pilot."

YES!, I screamed in my head, but remained calm enough to say playfully, "I've been looking for you."

He laughed some more, "Well, let me tell you how I found you."

What Frisk described convinced me that coincidences aren't random.

On a recent vacation, while standing outside a bathroom in the Calgary International Airport waiting for his wife, Frisk made small talk with another man also waiting. That man mentioned that he was a retired Northwest pilot.

"Both my uncles were pilots for Northwest," Frisk said. "One of them died when his plane crashed in Lake Michigan."

"Flight 2501?" the retired pilot asked.

"How did you know?" Frisk replied.

"I just read an article about a team searching for the wreck."

The pilot sent him the newsletter. Then Frisk called me.

During our conversation and a later meeting in Minneapolis, I learned all kinds of things about Robert Lind's short life. "Have you talked to the copilot's wife?" Frisk asked.

"No," I said. "I can't imagine she would still be alive."

"I think she is," he said.

She was. Jack and I drove to Wisconsin to meet her and had the surprise and pleasure to also meet Verne Wolfe's sister. She was 100-years-old!

After talking to the families of both pilots, I longed to produce the wreck for them—to somehow give them answers that might be of comfort. So far, our approaches had not worked. We needed something new.

I CALLED DAVID SCHWAB, the scientist at the Great Lakes Environmental Research Lab in Ann Arbor who studies Lake Michigan currents and with whom we had worked with on the *Chicora* project. I hoped he could offer input on the potential speed of lake currents in June so that we could estimate where the flight crashed, based on where the debris was found. Before I could even outline the problem, he asked, "Do you want me to run some simulations?"

As it turned out, I caught him with time between projects. He was able to find the weather records from June 1950 for Milwaukee, Chicago, Benton

Harbor, and Grand Rapids. He used the velocity and direction information, along with what he had learned about the wind's impact on Lake Michigan currents, to create four hindcasting scenarios, one for each city's wind pattern. All four scenarios suggested that the debris would have moved counterclockwise in a northeasterly direction from the impact site. He recommended we search southwest of where we had already looked. He cautioned that his conclusion was far from precise because he only had land-based weather data, not offshore weather, which may have been quite different.

We soon learned from Ralph that while we were attempting to use hindcasting to pinpoint the crash site, Ralph was doing the same thing. He approached Jerry Knisley, an engineer with Hypack, the manufacturers of his sonar software. Knisley had been wanting to develop his own program for hindcasting as a tool that could support Hypack's customers, who, like Ralph, searched for lost objects or survivors adrift after an accident.

Knisley's research led him to Art Allen, the same scientist with the U.S. Coast Guard Office of Search and Rescue (SAR) in Connecticut with whom we had worked on the *Chicora* project. Allen's input helped Knisley to develop his own search and rescue program. At Allen's request, David Schwab provided Knisley with the same 1950 weather data he had used for the simulations he ran for us. I hoped that Knisley's additional studies would help narrow down the search area.

IN NOVEMBER, I RECEIVED A CALL from a Delta Airlines pilot who wished to write an article about Flight 2501 for an aviation magazine. I shared what I knew about the crash and our search effort. Then he asked, "Have you heard about the discovery of another Northwest Airlines DC-4 crash, Flight 4422, in Alaska?"

"No," I replied.

"Well, you ought to look that one up. Two pilots found the wreck a few years ago."

By now, I had learned to pay attention to anything anyone told me related to Northwest Airlines, DC-4s, or Flight 2501, because so many things had led me down important paths I would otherwise not have found. I immediately Googled Northwest Airlines Flight 4422. I found a web site that mentioned the accident. I learned that 24 Merchant Marines and a six-man flight crew died on a return trip from China to the states when the airplane hit the face of Mount Sanford in Alaska in 1948. The Civil Aeronautics Board could not reach the wreckage to analyze it. However, the CAB determined that the probable cause of the accident was the pilot's failure to see Mount

Sanford, which was probably obscured by clouds, or the aurora borealis, or both, while flying a course off the airway.

The inability to reach the wreckage sounded eerily familiar. In reading about the accident, I was struck by the other similarities to Flight 2501. Both airplanes were DC-4s with tail numbers only three digits apart, meaning they were acquired by Northwest at about the same time. Both airplanes crashed in a remote location; one underwater and the other high atop a mountain. Both accidents resulted in total fatalities, each ranking as the country's worst aviation disaster for some time. And, both airplanes were the object of searches more than a half century after they crashed.

The web site indicated that two mountaineers, Marc Millican, a Northwest Airlines pilot from Anchorage, Alaska, and Kevin McGregor, a Delta pilot from Golden, Colorado, found the wreckage in 1997 on their fourth annual expedition. Considering that Millican worked for Northwest, I was curious how the company responded when one of its own employees found the wreckage. By now, I had considerable experience locating the phone numbers of strangers and I found them both quickly. I decided to call McGregor instead of Millican because he lived in a time zone only two hours behind me, rather than four. I dialed.

"Hello?" a friendly voice answered.

"Are you the Kevin McGregor who found Flight 4422?"

"That's me," he replied without hesitation.

I introduced myself and explained that we were searching for a Northwest Airlines DC-4 that crashed in Lake Michigan. He immediately seemed interested, asking a lot of questions. I outlined the circumstances of the accident, the inconclusive CAB report findings, my struggles to find the proverbial smoking gun, our lack of success finding the wreck, and our hope to find records of the lawsuit that might offer additional clues. McGregor said he would help in any way he could. He offered photographs of DC-4s, a DC-4 parts' manual, assistance getting FAA aircraft and airman records, his input as a pilot and researcher, and help with the National Transportation Safety Bureau.

"Do you think the NTSB would get involved? I asked, already having presumed the accident was too old to raise the agency's interest.

"Sure do," McGregor replied. "Even though the NTSB probably won't investigate an accident from that long ago, you are legally bound to notify it when you find the wreck. I have contacts who can help."

That reminded me about the airline. "I see your partner flies for Northwest," I said. "How helpful was the company when you found the wreck?"

"Not at all," he replied sharply. "They wanted nothing to do with the project. Our bigger struggle, though," he said, "was getting a permit from the National Park Service to recover a few pieces of the wreck as evidence. It's on federal land."

That was something else our projects had in common. "Yeah," I said. "We'll have the same problem here because the wreck will be on state bottomlands. We can't raise anything without a permit."

"Good luck getting one," he said sarcastically, sounding like a man who had been given the bureaucratic runaround.

We talked for an hour. Then he asked, "Find any families?"

"Oh, yes, quite a few. You, too?

"Yes, indeed. Not all 30, but I'm getting close," he said.

That generated another hour of conversation about the difficulties of finding people, the various responses, and the emotions in rehashing those terrible memories. As our conversation drew to a close, McGregor was silent for a moment. Then he quietly asked, "Has anything strange happened to you during your search?"

I gripped the phone tighter and drew in a breath because as soon as he posed that question, I knew immediately what he meant. In a flash, I thought of how Clive Cussler had found us, how I had a premonition about hearing from a victim's family, how Bill Kaufmann knew Gary Sirbu, how I was led to Rick Cochran, how Captain Lind's nephew found me, and all the other amazing happenstances.

"Oh, for sure," I said. "There have been a lot of inexplicable coincidences."

"Uh, huh," he said, like he understood. "Let me add one to your list. I don't know where you got this number, but it's the fax line at my parents' house. Even though I don't live here anymore, I just happen to be here visiting. I never pick up their fax line, but when I heard it ring tonight, something told me that I had to answer."

I gasped loud enough for him to hear, as I realized the synchronicity of everything that had been happening.

"When there are unresolved conflicts, especially those that involve death," he said with conviction, "things like that seem to happen."

For a moment I thought he might be a paranormal fanatic, but as we talked about our long lists of amazing coincidences, I realized that he simply accepted that things at play in the universe are bigger than humans can comprehend.

"I never set out to find the families of Flight 4422," he explained, "but it just seemed like something that I was supposed to do."

I realized that I felt the same way. We exchanged phone numbers and emails and agreed to stay in touch. I knew, somehow, that I had just made a friend for life. Then Kevin said something that convinced me that bigger things were, indeed, at play in the universe: "Oh, by the way, I think I know where you can find transcripts of the Flight 2501 lawsuit."

MONTHS LATER, with thousands of pages of those transcripts in hand, FAA airman and aircraft records, and the recollections of many dozens of witnesses and family members, the story of what happened to Flight 2501 and its passengers unfolded in vivid color in much more detail than the six short pages of the CAB report.

Jackie Eldred recalled hearing a low-flying airplane overhead on June 24, 1950, and then an explosion about ten minutes later.

Pilot Kevin McGregor's assistance would be invaluable to understanding what happened to Flight 2501.

William Kaufmann, Brandi Kaufmann Holstein, Kenneth Skoug Jr. (II), and Kenneth Skoug III on board Chuck and Shirley Cooper's yacht for the memorial service. *Photograph by Craig Rich.*

PART II
THE FLIGHT

"Concern for man and his fate must always form
the chief interest of all technical endeavors"

Albert Einstein.

Chapter 6

THE FLIGHT CREW

O n the warm and humid early evening of June 23, 1950, 34-year-old Captain Robert Lind and 35-year-old First Officer Verne Wolfe, checked in at the Northwest Flight Control Office at LaGuardia Airport on Long Island, east of Manhattan. It was just a little before 7:00 p.m., and more than one hour before the departure of Flight 2501.

The airport, renamed just two years earlier for one of New York City's most celebrated figures, Mayor Fiorello LaGuardia, was still relatively new, having opened to commercial traffic on December 2, 1939, as the New York Municipal Airport on land that had once been occupied by the Gala Amusement Park. Seen from the air, the 558-acre complex made a single sweeping gesture following the natural bend of the shoreline. Designed to serve as one of the attractions for the New York World's Fair in 1939, the airport was considered a modern masterpiece. However, as with most new, cutting-edge designs, architectural conservatives found fault with its Art Deco simplicity and symmetry, in this case asserting that the horizontal bands of glass and brick and vertical ribs and grillwork gave it a totalitarian look. After years of flying out of that airport, Lind and Wolfe probably took no notice of the architecture or the signature stainless steel "Spirit of Flight" eagle perched proudly on the roof of the terminal. They would have cared only that the airport functioned for them as pilots. It did indeed serve their needs and as Mayor LaGuardia had intended, was also inviting and efficient for travelers. The airport had already taken its rank as the prototype for all new airports.

Flight dispatcher Richard F. Miller greeted Lind and Wolfe, regulars at LaGuardia, from his chair across the counter at flight control. Miller had agreed to trade shifts with another dispatcher, Bob Gibson, who had been scheduled to work that night. No doubt Lind, Wolfe, and Miller shared some pleasantries before getting down to the business of preparing the flight plan.

That night the two seasoned pilots would be flying the first leg of a three-leg, cross-country flight scheduled to leave at 8:31 p.m. Eastern Standard Time and arrive at Minneapolis, Minnesota, at 1:30 a.m. Central Standard Time. After dropping off several passengers at the Minneapolis airport, Lind, Wolfe, and their stewardess, who Miller informed them would be Bonnie Ann Feldman, would be relieved by a fresh crew. After the aircraft was refueled, the new crew would carry on to Spokane, Washington, then complete the flight upon arriving at Seattle the next morning. Lind and Wolfe had regularly flown this route, often together, especially since Northwest had banned brothers from serving on the same crew and Lind had to give up flying with his younger brother Lloyd. The New York-to-Minneapolis flight worked out well because it got both men back to Minneapolis where they resided with their wives and babies. Lind's and Wolfe's daughters were less than a year apart in age.

Flight 2501 was not a regularly scheduled flight, but an additional flight opened that night in response to the demand for seats on the regularly scheduled Flight 501. As indicated on the June 1950 timetable, a route, time, and cost schedule updated and reprinted in a three-fold leaflet each month, Flight 501 departed New York at 10:00 p.m. every night with stops in Detroit, Milwaukee, Minneapolis, Billings, Spokane, and Seattle. A one-way ticket to Minneapolis cost $41. Spokane ran $88 and Seattle cost $97. Those purchasing round-trip tickets paid double the one-way fare. Reservation agents divided the passengers based on their destinations in such a way that Flight 2501 would leave ninety minutes before Flight 501 and would forego stops in Detroit, Milwaukee, and Billings. The flight, Lind and Wolf learned from the dispatcher, would be filled to capacity that night with 55 passengers.

ON THAT SUMMER EVENING IN 1950, Robert Charles Lind had been a pilot with Northwest Airlines for nine years. Considering that Northwest had not yet celebrated its 25th anniversary, Lind was among the more senior captains. Since 1940 when he first began taking flying lessons, Lind had faced an uphill struggle to ascend to his present position, a struggle that exemplified his tenacity, a character trait that would dominate the last hour of his life.

Robert Lind entered the world on September 25, 1915, and took his place among what would be a brood of seven children born to Charles G. Lind and Rose Sorensen, first-generation Swedish immigrants. On that day, Rose would have paid little attention to the events unfolding in the escalating conflict that would later be called World War I, when British forces launched an attack on German positions at Loos, Belgium. At the time, the Linds lived on Salem Avenue in St. Louis Park, one of many small enclaves developing

around Minneapolis, known soon after its founding in 1872 as "Mill City" for
its flour production. The household must have been lively for young Lind with
sisters Dorothy, Florence, Ruth, and Helen, and his two brothers Donald and
Lloyd. Unbeknownst to young Lind, just days before celebrating his eleventh
birthday, local businessman Colonel Lewis H. Brittin established a company
that would provide him and his brother Lloyd their future careers.

On September 1, 1926, Brittin, an executive with the local business
association, and a group of investors formed Northwest Airways Inc. They
purchased the only hangar at Wold-Chamberlain Field, at the site of the
former Snelling Speedway, an automobile racetrack about 10 miles southeast
of the Linds' home. Brittin had decided that the key to Minneapolis's economic
future would be a direct connection to the rest of country via the air. In 1926,
that meant air mail, the only service that airplanes were used for outside of the
military. In Congress at the time, there was a growing sentiment to take the
government out of business, and the Contract Air Mail Act of 1925 had been
a major step toward that. The Post Office began competitively bidding air mail
contracts, and Brittin resolved for Northwest Airways to become a contractor.
In short order, the company won its first bid. Although the local newspapers
only made brief mention of the new company, the Linds would have become
well aware of Northwest over the next few years because of the regular presence
of the noisy open-cockpit biplanes flying overhead. Washburn High School,
where the Lind kids attended in the late 1920s and early 1930s, was located
directly northwest of the main Wold-Chamberlain Field runway, and the
three Lind boys would have watched the airplanes with great fascination.

Lind graduated from Washburn in June 1931. By then full grown, his
long lean face hid the fact that he stood only 5' 8" tall. At 150 pounds, he
was small, a stature that would later serve him well in cramped cockpits.
His deep-set eyes made him seem distant, but they sparkled. Entering the
work force in the wake of the 1929 stock market crash, Lind could scarcely
afford to plan a future. With a knack for things mechanical, he took the first
job he could get, joining the Serley Electric Company. When that soured,
he went to work for Western Electric. He also signed up for what would be
a three-year stint with the U.S. Naval Reserve, spending many weekends
serving his country while bringing in a little extra money. Although Lind
helped support his family, they had to move to a smaller home at 5737
Garfield Avenue in south Minneapolis, which happened to be even closer
to the Wold-Chamberlain Field and the sputtering noise from the low-flying
airplanes. There in their new home, the family gathered around a small
radio, chuckling along with Amos and Andy, following the drama of Myrt

and Marge, and finding a way to persevere through those tough years.

Northwest Airways certainly felt the squeeze of the Depression as well. Although by 1931 the airline had begun to carry passengers—the very first one on July 5, 1927, in a Stinson Detroiter, the first closed cockpit airplane for passenger service—it operated without profit, still deriving most of its income from carrying the U. S. mail. When the United States postmaster general established lower mail pay rates, Colonel Brittin fought back, plunging boldly ahead with a plan to fight the Depression with expansion, this at a time when there were nearly fifteen million jobless people in the country.

In the early 1930s, Northwest ran primarily between Chicago and Minneapolis and was considered a small, independent airline in comparison to American, United, TWA, and Eastern. The company wished to grow and extend its routes to the West Coast. To do so, it would need to seek approval from the Secretary of Commerce, who since 1926 had been responsible for issuing and enforcing air traffic rules, licensing pilots, certifying aircraft, establishing airways, and operating and maintaining aids to air navigation. And so the "Battle for Seattle" began. Other airlines flew to the West Coast from southern cities, but Northwest executives thought they could do so more economically via a northern east/west route. However, the Secretary of Commerce expressed concern that the northern route would be impossible to fly in winter.

In 1933 an up-and-coming Northwest executive, Croil Hunter, joined Colonel Brittin, who by then was making $1000 per month running the airline. Hunter used his knack for publicity to show Congress, with a "proof in the pudding flight," that Northwest could make it to Spokane even in the snowiest month of the year: January. He invited media-sweetheart Amelia Earhart along for the ride. Captain Hugh Rueschenberg served as pilot, and Joe Kimm—who would later play a key role in analyzing the loss of Flight 2501—served as copilot. Through snowstorms and over mountains, they made a successful round trip. Although Spokane and Seattle remained elusive, by March Northwest received approval to serve Bismark, North Dakota, and Billings, Montana. To gear up, the company purchased a number of Lockheed Electras for the long-haul traffic.

With unemployment still climbing, voters swept Franklin D. Roosevelt into office as U. S. president, with the hope that his campaign song, "Happy Days are Here Again," would become reality. Northwest continued to lobby for an extension of its route to Seattle and encouraged the government to begin the installation of radio range beacons for navigation, a teletype service, and a radio weather service to make western flights safer. By the end of 1933, just as Robert Lind began contemplating taking flying lessons, the Secretary of Commerce granted Northwest its extension to Seattle, a route that would allow the airline to schedule its 501 flights across the country.

Robert and Lloyd Lind followed the news when Wiley Post set a new solo record for a round the world flight in July 1933 in just seven and a half days, and they tuned in to the radio as President Roosevelt launched his fireside chats at about that time. They may have taken notice of fewer aircraft flying out of Minneapolis in February 1934, but not realized that it was because Roosevelt canceled all existing mail contracts with private airlines. The president decided to assign that work to the Army Air Corps, a move that could have put Northwest out of business before the Lind boys could even learn to fly, had it not resulted in a number of delays, inefficiencies, and the death of many an army pilot. Just two months later, on April 16, 1934, Northwest Airways reincorporated as Northwest Airlines, Inc., took back its postal contracts, and increased its passenger service. Economic prospects for the company looked better than ever. This coincided with the start of Lind's aviation career.

Because he lived so close to the Wold-Chamberlain Field, Lind could have ridden his bicycle there for flying lessons. Both he and his brother hoped one day to work for Northwest, the only airline then operating at that field. On August 14, 1937, Lind received a student pilot license allowing him to fly solo, a necessary step to gaining a pilot's license. It would take him over a year of training until he would be ready to sit for the two-part written and flight exam to obtain a private pilot's license. By then, government regulations had changed. President Roosevelt signed the Civil Aeronautics Act in 1938 that established the Civil Aeronautics Authority (CAA) to mandate all certifications, regulations, routes, and establish a three-member Air Safety Board, which soon became the Civil Aeronautics Board (CAB) that would conduct accident investigations and recommend ways of preventing accidents.

Under the new CAA oversight, Lind took his two tests on February 20, 1939, but would face his first of many disappointments. Although he passed the written exam, he failed the flight test. The letter he received a month later indicated that he had to fly at least fifteen additional hours and get a written statement from a flight instructor indicating his belief that Lind had the qualifications to become a pilot. Lind applied himself over the next two months and by April 10 passed the exam and received a private pilot's license. However, he would need a commercial license to fly for Northwest. With more solo flying under his belt, he applied to the CAA for a commercial license on June 26, 1939, but failed the written test. His examiner noted that he would need to pass the theory of flight section before taking his actual flight test. A week later on July 3, 1939, he again took the written test, but, he did not pass again. Clearly, Lind did not intend to give up. After more studying and more flying time under his belt, he passed the written exam on August 28, 1939. Then, right there at the Wold-Chamberlain Field where he had done all his training, he climbed into a Taylorcraft BF and began his flight test. The examiner who rode along with him tested on ten different maneuvers including spins, forced landings, and spirals. Although Lind received passing scores in climb and recovery, he received only average scores in all the other maneuvers. The CAA denied him a license.

When others might have given up, Lind forged on. The additional training he needed would have been costly. Had he passed when he first sat for the exam he might already have been employed in the airline industry. Instead, he took a job at a sash and door company as a machinist to tide him over until he could obtain his commercial license. Seven months later, he tried again. On March 4, 1940, he completed maneuvers in basic flying, airplanes, engines, navigation, meteorology, and civil air regulations. He barely passed three sections with marks of 70; anything lower would have constituted a failing grade. He received his highest score, an 80, in meteorology, yet he failed the section on airplanes and so failed the entire test.

On May 13, 1940, Lind took his third flight exam, checking out again in a Taylorcraft 50, a small single-engine aircraft, and finally passed, receiving his commercial pilot's certificate. However, his flight examiner, J. T. Moynahan, noted about Lind, "although he executed a well-planned flight, his coordination was weak and most of his maneuvers were average." On a scale of 1 to 5, with 1 being the best, Lind received only one 2; his other scores were 3s and 4s. Lind's brother Lloyd, five years his junior, followed in his brother's footsteps and received his private pilot's license just a month after Lind received his commercial license.

In January 1940 Lind received a certification to fly a Stinson aircraft and took a job with a small charter service owned by pilot George Bringhurst. Considering Lind's track record, it is no wonder that in December 1940 when he applied for a flight instructor certificate, he failed the test. However, more than a year later, on March 14, 1941, he passed his instrument test and received an Airline Transport Pilot License. That finally gave him what he needed to join Northwest. He applied and was hired as a copilot on May 8, 1941, and by November obtained his certification to fly DC-3s. His brother Lloyd followed, joining Northwest too, after receiving his commercial license—just before, as it turned out, the outbreak of World War II. The conflict overseas would be good for pilots at Northwest because the company got several lucrative contracts to help support the war effort. Lind began flying troops and supplies to the Aleutian Islands in Alaska as America struggled to fight the Japanese. In the months after the bombing of Pearl Harbor, Japan had deployed a small force to those islands, a vulnerable, little-defended area that poised Japan for an invasion of mainland America. The United States government solicited help from more than 20 commercial airlines. Because Northwest had already been operating a winter route across the northern states, the government decided it was in the best position to handle the transport of military personnel and supplies in Alaska. Northwest became a part of the Army Air Transport Services. The route was soon named the "Flying Boxcar Line." By June 1942, the transport services would be unified and merged into the Air Transport Command (ATC).

Either Robert Lind's new gainful employment, or perhaps the realization of his own mortality brought on by war, may have prompted him finally to settle down. He married his sweetheart, Margaret Wing, in February 1943. She would quickly learn what it was like to be married to a pilot: Lind was assigned cargo transport duty to service Northwest's contract with the Army. He would often fly to Alaska, away from home for weeks on end. Margaret suffered with all the other citizens who had to make sacrifices at that time. Although now making a better salary than he could have imagined, Lind, like so many others living through the war, did not squander his money. He purchased a small piece of farmland (now on the site of the Mall of America) just south of his parents' home and even closer to Wold-Chamberlain Field, by then called the Minneapolis-St. Paul Metropolitan Airport. Rather than hiring contractors to build his home, Lind did a lot of the work himself, even digging his own basement.

With the war in Europe near its end, in April 1945, Northwest assigned Lind commercial service as a pilot to fly DC-3s on the New York to Milwaukee route exclusively. The CAA had just recently granted Northwest that route, which now allowed the airline to offer coast-to-coast service. The company purchased several surplus DC-4s for the route at the encouragement and under the supervision of System Chief Pilot Joe Kimm, who it will be recalled helped establish the western route. On June 26, 1946, Lind passed the exam qualifying him to fly the DC-4. Clearly, his experience had served him well. He scored much higher, receiving marks in the mid-80s and 90s. His brother Lloyd passed the test too, and soon the two brothers were both flying for Northwest, often on the same flight.

ALTHOUGH A FEW MONTHS OLDER than Robert Lind, Verne Frank Wolfe had only begun taking flying lessons around the time that Lind received his commercial pilot's license; as such, he did not have as much seniority as Lind. He would serve as the first officer for Flight 2501 that night as he had for many years. However, he did not intend to remain a copilot his entire career. Just one year earlier, in July 1949, he passed the airline's transport pilot exam, needed to become the pilot in charge, but he had to continue riding the right-hand seat until a pilot's position became available. Remarkably, Wolfe had achieved the same accomplishments much faster than Lind, passing his tests on the first attempt with scores a bit higher than Lind's. He may have been the more skilled of the two pilots assigned to Flight 2501 that night.

Verne Wolfe began his life as the second child of Frank and Lydia Wolfe on June 1, 1915, in a small house at 3323 W. 62nd Street on Chicago's southwest side. Grace, his older sister by eight years, was glad to have a sibling to distract her from her parents' constant talk of war, which had escalated the previous month after a German U-boat sank the British passenger liner RMS *Lusitania*, operating out of Liverpool England, northwest of Lydia's birthplace in London. Wolfe's toddler years spanned America's entrance into the Great War and its end when the Treaty of Versailles was signed just before his fourth birthday.

Life for the Wolfes improved significantly in Chicago in the postwar years when Chicago saw rapid growth as the population rose to over 2.5 million. The family practically watched that growth out their front window as trucks headed west delivering construction materials to build the Chicago Municipal Airport (now Midway Airport) a little more than a mile from their home. It would eventually become the world's busiest airport for a period. As a child during those pre-Lindbergh years, little Verne must have been fascinated by the barnstormers and the early biplanes carrying mail and cargo, taking off and landing at Chicago.

Originally from New York, Wolfe's father, Frank, became an automotive dealer after his move to Chicago. Mechanically inclined, Frank could do most anything with his hands and passed those talents on to his only son.

While Frank worked and Lydia took care of the house, older sister Grace watched over her little brother. "Keep an eye on him," their mother cautioned,"We don't want Gypsies to steal him."

Proud of her little brother, Grace reveled in her new responsibilities and watched with fascination when young Verne pulled the wheels off a toy truck and then started to reassemble it. For Wolfe, it was the beginning of a life of mechanical pursuits. As he got older, his interests turned from toy vehicles to real ones. His first bicycle was probably one introduced by Sears Roebuck or Montgomery Ward just after World War I. Those coveted bicycles came complete with classic features mimicking motorcycles, designed to appeal to boys like Wolfe who aspired to motorized transportation.

One day when Wolfe was in his teens, Lydia looked outside and thought her son had become a thief. Lined up in the back yard was a small fleet of bicycles. She marched out to confront him. "I'm just fixing these bikes for my friends, Mom," he assured her before she could ask.

Before long, Wolfe began working alongside his father at a junk yard in which his father had invested. They bought old cars, tore them apart, and sold them for parts. Wolfe took after his father. He kept the tools spotless, well organized, and properly stowed away. Customers appreciated how quickly they could locate the right parts.

While in high school, Wolfe began helping his paternal grandfather develop the family property in Eagle River, Wisconsin, 350 miles north of Chicago. With the Wisconsin River and hundreds of small lakes nearby, Eagle River was already growing in popularity as a vacation spot, even though it was a full day's train ride from Chicago. During the Depression years of the 1930s, the family remodeled the lakefront cottage on the property and built several more small cottages as rental units. They called it Wolfe's Woodland Resort. Wolfe and his mother would take the train north and work at the resort during the summers. Lydia handled the administrative work and her son took care of all the maintenance and grounds keeping. He would meet the love of his life in Eagle River.

One day in the summer of 1935 while outside gardening, Ruth Zimpelmann, a pretty and vivacious 16-year-old, noticed a young man who sped by her house. Actually, his little convertible, a Ford Model A, first caught her eye. However, the next day she paid more attention to the auburn-haired fellow behind the wheel. At 5' 7" and 140 pounds, he was not a big man, but the sly look in his eyes and a bright smile he flashed her betrayed his adventurous spirit. Ruth thought he was "a cutie."

On the third day the young man passed by her house, Ruth decided to wave. When he waved back, she found herself smitten. The drive-by waving continued for several more days until Ruth began to wonder if she would have to lie down in the road to convince him to stop and talk. Finally, one day he conjured up the nerve. Not only did he stop and introduce himself, but he even invited Ruth to the local fair. By the end of the summer they were an "item," but Ruth was only 16 and Wolfe had already turned 20.

Wolfe could not stop thinking about his dark-haired beauty when he returned to Chicago. He sent her several love letters during the long winter of 1936. The next summer they spent even more time together. He would bring Ruth to his family's resort and they would take the boat out when the guests weren't using it. Ruth found him very romantic.

Wolfe loved adventure almost as much as he enjoyed romance. He zipped around in his Ford at outlandish speeds, getting stopped on several occasions by the local sheriff when his speedometer reached almost sixty miles per hour. It seemed he could never attain enough speed whether on land or on water. He built a surf board-like contraption, connected it to the boat with a towrope, and had a friend pull him around as he held onto the board for dear life. Ruth was an adventurer, too, but after flying off the board on a curve in the river she drew the line, hollering to her boyfriend, "This really isn't so much fun!"

Wolfe never formally proposed: Ruth just knew they would get married once she grew up. On October 4, 1938, a crisp and colorful autumn day, they tied the knot at Christ Lutheran Church in Eagle River, Wisconsin. Wolfe's father traveled north to join the family for the service. Times were tough as the country was still suffering from the Depression. Ruth wore a plain dress. As one of six children, she did not expect her parents to foot the bill. She wrote to her sister Janet, who was married and living in Michigan, "I'm sure Mom and Dad will be glad to have me out of the house—one less mouth to feed."

The Wolfes did not take a honeymoon immediately. In the spring of 1939, Verne came across an article about a man who had driven all the way to Alaska. "Let's try to do this, Ruth," he suggested, showing her the article.

Gasoline and lodging would cost a lot, so they invited Ruth's sister Eleanor along to share expenses. She was a teacher and made about $900 a year, a good wage in 1939. Wolfe brought along an extra set of cotton cord tires for the car, and by the end of the five-week trip, they had replaced them all.

After the honeymoon, the newlyweds took a small apartment in Chicago, not far from Wolfe's parents. Just two months after they set down roots there, Wolfe's mother, Lydia, passed away. She was just 56. Frank Wolfe remarried within a year, and he and his new wife, Belle, relocated to Eagle River to run the resort full time. Verne and Ruth took over his parents' home in Chicago, which was just across the alley from the home where he had been born. There, he found himself back in the shadow of the Chicago Municipal Airport.

Verne had never forgotten watching those airplanes takeoff and land. Perhaps his proximity to the world's busiest airport influenced his decision to become a pilot. Flying lessons were quite expensive, and something the Wolfes could hardly afford, but they found a way.

On July 19, 1940, Verne applied for a student pilot certificate with the Briggs School of Aeronautics. He trained at Harlem Airport, a little field with four sod runways at the southeast corner of South Harlem Avenue and West 87th Street in Oaklawn, Illinois, just a few miles southwest of the Chicago Municipal Airport. Ruth often accompanied him to the field and watched him take off and land with instructor Dewey Briggs.

Just after his 27th birthday on June 29, 1942, Verne passed his first written and flight tests and received his private pilot's license. He continued his training, and by the end of the year had flown 300 hours and attained his commercial pilot's certificate after testing in a Taylorcraft single-engine airplane. By then, the country was already at war with Japan. On May 21, 1943, Northwest Airlines hired Verne Wolfe, who became one of more than 9,000 men and women employed by Northwest for the war effort. Verne began training immediately on the DC-3 and the C-47, its military counterpart. Within five years of his Alaskan honeymoon, Verne found himself back in Alaska. His assignment involved transporting personnel, guns, ammunition, dynamite, and one of the greatest morale boosters—mail—up to Alaska. His own letters would be among the mail cargo; he and Ruth wrote each other letters at least twice per week and talked on the telephone when they could manage.

Verne perfected his flying skills in some of the worst weather conditions over treacherous terrain. By the time he reached Alaska, U.S. troops had annihilated 2,350 Japanese defenders on the Aleutian island of Attu, but it would take several more months before the islands of Kiska and Agattu were secured. During this time, while flying a planeload of troops home, Wolfe's aircraft came under fire from Japanese forces still entrenched on Kiska. Wolfe took evasive measures, but one of his passengers, Flight Surgeon Leonard Clayton Alexander, was hit in the arm with shrapnel. That wound signaled the end of Alexander's military career; he received a Purple Heart and a discharge and would go on to become the dean of the dental school at Marquette University. Years later, he would find himself connected to Ruth Wolfe.

When the war ended in 1945, Northwest laid off many of its pilots, including Verne Wolfe. The company had just lost its lucrative government contracts and needed time to evaluate its work force. Not knowing what the future held in store, the Wolfes moved to Eagle River, Wisconsin, to try to forge a new life, although Wolfe hoped to be called back to Northwest Airlines. In the meantime he partnered with fellow war veteran, Art Sauer, to purchase a pontoon airplane and a small parcel of land that they developed into an airstrip to serve the tourist sightseeing business. The 600 lakes in Wisconsin's Vista County were a major draw for vacationers in the postwar years, and many people wanted to view the area from a vantage point never before available. Verne earned his seaplane rating in June 1946, and he and Sauer began selling their bird's-eye tours. Besides the lone dirt runway, the Eagle River Airport boasted an outhouse and a fuel pump. Ruth pumped fuel for the two or three aircraft that landed there each week.

At the end of summer in 1947, Verne got his wish. Northwest offered him a permanent position. In preparation for their move to Minneapolis, the Wolfes found a nice little fixer-upper at 3012 East 50th Street, but could not take occupancy for six months. Instead, Verne rented a room near the airport, and Ruth moved in with her sister Eleanor in Rice Lake, Wisconsin, halfway between her parents and her husband. Verne and Ruth once again dealt with separation. Nearly fed up with their situation, in January, he wrote Ruth, "Hon, I sure am glad that we are almost done living like this. I like my job, hon, but I don't think anything is worth living like this."

The winters, the war, and now this move, kept the Wolfes apart more than they had been together since they met.

After they settled in their new home, life began to stabilize for the couple. Once a month the pilots and copilots bid for their routes, and Wolfe often found himself paired with pilot Robert C. Lind. The two men frequently flew the Minneapolis to Washington route and the New York to Milwaukee and Minneapolis route, the same one that would eventually bring them together on Flight 2501. The company required a 24-hour rest period between flights so Verne and Bob Lind were able to be home at least every other night. Time together at home did the Wolfes good. On July 3, 1948, a beautiful, nine-pound bundle of joy arrived. Ruth told all her friends that her daughter, Kristy, was a tenth anniversary gift.

Although by 1948 Lind and Wolfe had flown together for a while, Ruth did not meet Bob Lind's wife, Margaret, until her own baby shower, attended by many of the Northwest pilots' wives. Ruth didn't understand why Margaret wept on and off all during the party.

Ruth later learned that the Linds had been trying, unsuccessfully, to conceive a child of their own for several years. Adding to Margaret's misery, was the fact that her husband had to be away for days, and sometimes more than a week, at a time. Her loneliness and neediness stemmed from the fact that she had been raised by an elderly aunt and uncle after the death of her parents when she was very young.

Although Ruth felt compassion for Margaret, she was not especially interested in becoming close with her. "I am maintaining a friendship with her for the good of your relationship with Bob," she told her husband, "but Margaret is an unhappy person, and I don't want her to drag me down."

Ruth noticed that Margaret's spirits soared when the Linds decided to adopt a baby. Margaret told her all about the adoption process. She and Lind had filled out the required papers, had meetings with a social worker, and now waited for a call from Social Services. Once the agency placed a child in their home, the adoption would be finalized six months later, after the social worker evaluated and approved the match.

While Bob and Margaret Lind waited for their baby, Verne Wolfe got used to being a dad. Although he did not take an active role in the diapering or feeding of Kristy, he played with her for hours on end and took her for walks in the park. In the spring of 1950, he purchased a tricycle in New York and flew it home with him.

The Wolfes often socialized with Bob and Margaret Lind, and another pilot, Bob Brennan, and his wife, Lee. While they all enjoyed smoking, none of them drank. Ruth and Lee shared in Margaret's excitement when in early June 1950, she and Bob brought home a beautiful baby girl. Finally, Margaret had the child that she had been longing for.

The new baby must have taken some pressure off Lind, who probably had experienced a difficult time consoling his wife over many years. He had hoped that the baby would provide Margaret with companionship and purpose beyond her lonely life as the wife of an airline pilot. Her neediness and his newly adopted baby may have been on his mind as he prepared for the takeoff of Flight 2501 that would take him home.

Chapter 7

PREFLIGHT PLANNING

The development of the flight plan that night was critical, as it was for every flight. With the input of Captain Robert Lind, Flight Dispatcher Richard F. Miller in New York and Flight Superintendent George Benson at Minneapolis established the route, selected an altitude, and determined the flight times between each checkpoint. Analysis of the existing weather and forecasted weather would be a key ingredient to establishing the plan. To obtain that information, Miller contacted Northwest's meteorologist, Mr. Beresford, at the Minneapolis airport.

Beresford gathered his information from the National Weather Service, which issued general weather forecasts for the Midwest region every six hours and special reports as needed. His job involved interpreting those basic forecasts geared primarily to people on the ground, specifically for use in aviation. His information that night came from Julius Badner, the supervising aviation forecaster in Chicago.

Badner had come on duty at 2:00 p.m. in Chicago for his ten-hour shift. It would be a day like any other for Badner, but one that he would have to live over many times in the coming years. Badner had received his bachelor of science degree in 1937 from the University of Chicago. He joined the Weather Bureau in 1939 as an aviation forecaster, and by 1950 he was the supervising forecaster in Chicago in charge of six meteorologists. His position was still relatively new. It had developed out of a long lineage of trial and error.

A weather observation network began unofficially during the early-1800s and expanded across the United States in the mid-1800s. The development of the telegraph in 1869 meant that weather observations from distant points could be more rapidly collected, plotted, and analyzed at one location. This led to initial efforts toward forecasting. The ability to observe and forecast weather over much of the country would require considerable structure and organization, and so in 1870 President Ulysses S. Grant established the Weather Bureau through a joint resolution of Congress. Its mission was "to provide for taking meteorological observations at the military stations in the interior of the continent and at other points in the States and Territories... and for giving notice on the northern (Great) Lakes and on the seacoast by magnetic telegraph and marine signals, of the approach and force of storms."

Forty-eight years later, on December 1, 1918—15 years after the Wright brothers' historic 1903 flights—the National Weather Service issued the first official aviation forecast using data collected from instrument kites and tethered balloons. Those forecasts would prove to be quite useful for the Aerial Mail Service flyers and other pilots at the time.

In 1950 Badner's role at the Weather Bureau involved developing forecasts specifically for use by airlines in the area between Pittsburgh, Pennsylvania, and Denver, Colorado, and north to the United States border from the Ohio River. These forecasts typically covered the height and thickness of clouds, the visibility, and any precipitation. Typically his forecasts ranged out 12 hours for the entire region: he also prepared forecasts for the major airports in the region and supervised the meteorologists under him.

The first thing Badner did that afternoon was review the weather reports that had been made before his shift and prepare a regional forecast for publication late that afternoon. He transmitted the 12-hour forecast over the teletype circuits at 4:45 p.m. EST. Once he completed that, he began preparing for another forecast to be issued six hours later for the next 12-hour period, as an update to the previous forecast. His 4:45 forecast, written in meteorologist code, covered areas of southern Wisconsin, Michigan, Indiana, Ohio, and Kentucky. Translated, it read in part:

"Cold front near Calumet, Eau Claire, Rochester, Omaha, moving eastward. Clouds and weather: 4,000 to 5,000 broken, variable, overcast, top 13,000 to 25,000...Scattered thunderstorms, visibility 3 miles... Wind, west-northwest, 30 miles per hour with strong gusts, 100 to 150 miles in advance of cold front, spreading eastward and southeastward in advance of front over north and west lower Michigan...Turbulence and scattered thunderstorms in advance of front and in southeast lower Michigan...Brief base 1000 overcast, top 2000, 1 to 2 miles visibility and going over Lake Michigan just north of the cold front."

Beresford analyzed Badner's very lengthy forecast looking for patterns that would affect any Northwest Airline's flights that night. His job would be to condense the forecasts into a shorter, specific versions for use by the airline's pilots flying that evening. Beresford realized that a cold front, high winds, and scattered thunderstorms with brief cloud bases at 1,000 feet indicated the likelihood of a squall, although the forecast did not use that word. He knew that thunderstorms along a cold front had a tendency to form into a semi-continuous line. Each thunderstorm or "cell," usually contained heavy precipitation, frequent lightning, strong winds, and sometimes hail, tornadoes, or waterspouts, all conditions that pilots were trained to avoid. The rain and resulting turbulence in those storms could toss an airplane up and down as much as 1,500 feet. Although it was possible to fly through a squall if the individual cells were spaced far enough apart, it would be difficult for a pilot flying at night to see the squall except during flashes of lightning.

At 4:45 p.m., Beresford issued a Northwest Airlines-specific forecast in which he indicated the development of a dangerous squall and cautioned pilots to proceed with caution:

"Cold front northeast southwest moving slowly eastward along and east of cold front. Expect scattered thunderstorms, line along front broken. Base thunderstorms 3,000 to 4,000 feet. Tops 30,000 to 40,000 feet with some shelf clouds 15,000. Turbulence moderate to severe all levels in thunderstorm and moderate below storms. Advise flights below 10,000 to proceed with caution thru frontal zone. Expect activity to be peak 10:30 p.m. to 4:00 a.m. eastern standard time with possible squall line development in advance of front during the evening. Expect activity to abate rapidly after 4 a.m. Beresford Minneapolis St. Paul 4:45 p.m."

Although Badner's Weather Service forecast had noted the strong winds would spread eastward and southeastward, Beresford interpreted the information and indicated that the cold front and possible squall line would move only east. Flight Dispatcher Miller had access to the full National Weather Service forecast on the teletype, but he was required to utilize the company forecast, considered superior, in planning flights. After laying out the chart and overlaying notes from the forecast, Miller and Lind called Beresford on the telephone and together prepared the flight plan. It would begin at LaGuardia and follow specific airways, like highways in the sky. By that time, the airways crisscrossed the county for a total of over 40,000 miles in length.

The airways were designated by a color and number. The number was assigned according to the geographical location of the airway. Four color designations, Green, Amber, Red, and Blue, denoted their traffic priority. An aircraft flying on a Green airway had traffic priority over an aircraft on an

Amber, Red, or Blue airway. An aircraft flying on an Amber airway only had priority over an aircraft on a Red or Blue airway. Pilots could remember the acronym GARB to designate the traffic priority. The Green and Red airways ran east and west, and the Amber and Blue airways ran north and south. Flight 2501 would follow Northwest's standard route to Minneapolis: Green 3 from New York to Toledo, Red 57 from Toledo to Battle Creek and across Lake Michigan to Milwaukee, Green 2 to Madison, and finally, Red 14 to Minneapolis.

Lind and Wolfe would be "flying the beam" that night. The term referred to the low-frequency radio range (LFR), also known as the four-course radio range, the A-N radio range, Adcock radio range, or commonly "the range," the main navigation system used by aircraft for any higher altitude flight, flight in overcast conditions, or like Flight 2501, a night flight.

WHEN AVIATION BEGAN a little more than four decades before that June evening in 1950, instrumentation for navigation did not exist. Pilots had to follow roads, rail lines, rivers, and mountains to find their way from airport to airport in the daytime. They also had to keep watch on the horizon to make sure they were flying with the aircraft's nose and wings in the proper position relative to the ground, called attitude.

When pilots began flying over large bodies of water, at night, or in low visibility conditions, they learned to use dead reckoning as sailors did, a process of charting their position by calculating the speed, time, and direction from a prior fixed position. Charles Lindbergh used dead reckoning to navigate his way from New York across the Atlantic Ocean to Paris in May 1927, the first nonstop transatlantic flight, one that made him world famous. However, as in marine navigation, dead reckoning in aviation was subject to cumulative errors and exacerbated by natural forces such as wind.

The growth of the airmail service and civilian air transportation after World War I highlighted the need for a technology that would allow airplanes to fly safely at night and in poor visibility. The initial solution again mimicked marine technologies. The government installed lighted beacons, similar to lighthouses, as aids to navigation, but these were only useful for lower-altitude flights in clear weather. Scientists and engineers became convinced that radio-based navigation would provide the all-weather solution.

It took almost a decade to develop a workable solution. In 1926, successful two-way radio air-to-ground communication began, and the first transmitters and receivers were manufactured in 1928. Then, on September 24, 1929, a lieutenant in the U.S. Army demonstrated the first "blind" flight, performed exclusively by reference to instruments and without outside visibility, proving that instrument flying was feasible. This pioneering aviator, James H. "Jimmy" Doolittle, used a radio receiver and newly developed instruments to help him maintain his aircraft's attitude and heading, together with a specially designed directional radio system installed on land. In this way, he safely navigated to and from an airport.

For this system to work nationally, the aeronautical instruments would need to be mass-produced and installed in all aircraft. In addition to radios for receiving the signals, airplanes were soon equipped with a group of instruments known as the basic, or primary six, which included an attitude indicator, a vertical speed indicator showing the rate of climb and descent, an airspeed indicator, turn-and-bank coordinator, a heading indicator showing the magnetic compass course, and an altimeter. The Bureau of Air Commerce began requiring all pilots to get instrument ratings and fly only federally licensed aircraft equipped with two-way radios and approved instruments. The DC-4 used for Flight 2501 had the latest such instruments.

The altimeter that Lind and Wolfe would rely on for their flight was essentially a barometer that measured air pressure: The lower the barometric pressure, the higher the airplane. The device measured the outside air pressure, and, using the barometric formula, calculated the altitude and transferred it to a gauge much like a clock face. Each revolution of a single needle accounted for 1,000 feet, recorded on a numerical odometer-type drum.

To determine altitude, a pilot first had to read the drum to determine the thousands of feet, and then look at the needle for the hundreds of feet. The flight's altitude was planned in relationship to mean sea level, not the height off the ground. At LaGuardia, the elevation is about 17 feet above sea level and the land rises toward Minneapolis to more than 800 feet above sea level, so if the pilots stayed at a constant altitude, the aircraft would get continually closer to the ground as it flew west.

To display altitude above sea level, Lind had to recalibrate the altimeter according to the local air pressure at sea level along his route, to take into account natural variation of pressure over time and in different regions. If he neglected to do this, his altimeter might give a false reading, making him think he was at one altitude when he was really at another. That could be a problem when in the vicinity of other airplanes.

The LFR system that Flight 2501 would be using relied on ground-based radio transmitters that linked all the airways. The U.S. Commerce Department had overseen the development and installation of a countrywide system beginning in the late 1920s. After some trial and error, a "T-L Antenna"

(Transmission Line) was developed; it was later called an Adcock antenna in recognition of Frank Adcock, the British engineer who developed it. By the early 1930s, the government had installed hundreds of radio range stations, each consisting of four Adcock antenna towers strategically located around the country, often near larger airports, approximately 200 miles apart. Some stations had an extra tower in the center for voice transmission so that radio operators and pilots could communicate.

The stations continually emitted low-frequency tones in Morse Code that represented the letters "A" (· —) and "N" (— ·). An Amplitude Modulation (AM) radio receiver in the cockpit would amplify the code into speakers in headsets worn by the pilots. To stay on course, the pilots would tune their radio to the frequency of a particular station that they were headed toward. If they heard an "N" stream (dah-dit, dah-dit, ...) they would need to veer to the left. If they heard an "A" stream (dit-dah, dit-dah, ...) they had to veer to the right. If they heard a steady tone, they would be flying "on the beam," or in other words, on course toward their destination.

The "on course" region, where the A and N audibly merged, was approximately three degrees wide, which translated into width of about 2.6 miles when 100 miles away from a station. The tone would become louder as the aircraft neared the station; when the tone disappeared, referred to as the cone of silence, the pilots would know the flight was directly over a range station. Each station would also transmit its two-letter Morse code identifier once every 30 seconds so that pilots could be assured they were on the correct beam. In some installations, the signal would be stopped briefly to broadcast in voice the current weather conditions. By June 1950, there were some 400 Low frequency Range (LFR) stations throughout the United States. And by then, even children understood the concept thanks to the Parker Brothers' board game *Flying the Beam*, designed by Army pilot Captain William J. Chapman, which they had been playing since it was first manufactured in 1941.

From its beginning in the early 1930s, the LFR was augmented with low frequency non-directional beacons, which were simple, single-antenna transmitters that emitted a uniform tone in all directions. Coupled with a radio direction finder used to detect the incoming waves, these beacons allowed pilots to navigate visually, as well as audibly, using a magnetic compass.

Although the LFR system was groundbreaking for low visibility and night flying, pilots knew its limitations. The course lines would often fluctuate, depending on weather conditions, when the signals from the A quadrant could skip into the N quadrant, or vice-versa, and could fool a pilot into altering his course needlessly. Thunderstorms also often created electromagnetic interference that could disrupt the range signals and produce crackling static in a pilot's headset. Lind knew that to be safe he would have to combine instrument flying with dead reckoning, referencing the charts often and calculating the speed and direction to approximate his location along the way.

In 1926, the Bureau of Air Commerce, a division of the Department of Commerce, began to produce aeronautical charts through the Coast and Geodetic Survey (C&GS), the contractor that had previously produced the government nautical charts. The first series of 31 maps, called Strip Airway Maps, showed topographic and cultural features, airports, beacon lights, and distance and direction lines, the forerunner of the airway system. Radio navigation facilities were added when they became operational.

As the LFR system expanded in 1930, Sectional Charts were born. In time, these charts depicted the entire country and showed the range stations and a series of airways that crisscrossed the county. Using the charts, pilots could navigate from range station to range station to fly anywhere in the country without being able to see the ground. In March 1949, a new layout with enlarged-scale charts was produced, providing even more detail. Lind and Wolfe carried these charts in their briefcases to use on their flight that night.

The LFR system would have been chaotic if not for the network of Air Route Traffic Control Centers (ARTCC, simply referred to as ATC) that managed the flights of all commercial, military, and private aircraft, a system that had been developed alongside the LFR system. The ATC originated when airlines began experiencing an increase in air traffic in the 1920s, which caused growing congestion with associated delays and safety concerns. The airlines concluded that federal action was needed to set and maintain safety standards among all airlines.

Congress responded with the Air Commerce Act of 1926, giving the Secretary of Commerce responsibility for establishing air traffic rules, certifying pilots and aircraft, establishing airways, and developing better, more reliable aids to navigation. The first official air traffic controller began work at Charles Lindbergh's home airfield in St. Louis, Missouri, in 1929. Archie W. League, a pilot and mechanic who had barnstormed around the area for years, set up a "control tower" in a wheelbarrow. He carried a chair, an umbrella for shade, his lunch, water, a notepad, and a pair of signal flags that he used to direct aircraft taking off and landing. League went on to earn a degree in aeronautical engineering, and during a 36-year career, he helped develop the federal Air Traffic Control system. Within a few years, League's signal flags were replaced by "light guns," which focused their beams on single airplanes and communicated with preestablished coded combinations of colors and flashes. However, the emerging technology of radio would allow Air Traffic Control to expand beyond airport boundaries.

The first radio-equipped control room opened in 1930 at Cleveland's airport at a time when nearly all airlines were equipping their aircraft with radio navigation aids. By 1932, the Commerce Department had installed 83 radio beacons across the country and had initiated the construction of two more Air Route Traffic Control centers in Newark and Chicago. In 1936 the government took over all three ATC stations to operate them in coordinated combination.

By 1950 more than 30 centers operated throughout the United States. The route controllers used maps, blackboards, and mental calculations to ensure the safe operation of aircraft. To represent aircraft, they moved boat-shaped weights—called "shrimp boats" because they resembled that vessel in shape—across maps. Personnel at Air Traffic Control had no direct radio communications with pilots in aircraft. Rather, they used telephones to communicate with airline dispatchers, airline radio operators, and controllers in airport towers, who relayed instructions and weather information to pilots via their cockpit radio transceivers.

The teletype also became critical to the Air Traffic Control and the individual airlines. Using teletypewriter technology, first developed in the mid-1800s and made nationally recognized by the likes of Western Union, the ATC controllers could transmit weather and flight information between airlines. Through a land-based wire-system, a key was pressed on a typewriter-like unit at one station, actuating the typewheel at many distant stations to print out the same key.

AFTER GOING OVER THE WEATHER along his route, Robert Lind requested a 4,000-foot altitude to stay under the clouds as much as possible. Before agreeing to the plan, Flight Dispatcher Richard Miller had to have Air Traffic Control review and approve it. He contacted a controller at Cleveland, where the first leg of the flight would be managed. After reviewing the proposed flight plan for Flight 2501, ATC approved the requested route, but could not assign an altitude of 4,000 feet due to other east-moving flights on that route. Instead, it assigned an altitude of 6,000 feet.

Over the phone, Miller and Lind consulted with the flight dispatcher in Minneapolis, and the three men agreed to the plan. Miller wrote it out on the proper form, he and Lind signed it, and then he transmitted a copy via teletype to the dispatcher in Minneapolis for his signature. Although regulations at the time allowed pilots to deviate as much as 25 miles off their planned route, the only way Lind and Wolfe could safely veer farther than that off their route, change airway, or change altitudes would be to request clearance for the change from ATC through a company radio operator.

Lind and Wolfe probably both anticipated a difficult flight during which they would have to keep an eye on the developing weather and make decisions along the way to avoid the thunderstorms. In their years of flying this same route, they had probably encountered similar conditions many times. They picked up their briefcases, donned their sunglasses, and headed out to the tarmac at about 7:40 p.m.

The pilots found their DC-4 gleaming in the rays of the setting sun, nestled up to the long, curved boarding skywalk, a signature feature of LaGuardia. The skywalk extended from either side of the main terminal allowing passengers and the public access to as many as 24 airplanes. The DC-4 with the tail number N-95425 had just come in from a flight from Minneapolis about 15 minutes earlier. Lind and Wolfe met Captain W. F. Dean, the pilot who had flown it in as he wrapped up the flight and climbed down the mobile stairs that ground crew had rolled over to the fuselage.

The mammoth, 94-foot-long DC-4 had been the workhorse of Northwest's fleet after the war. Lind and Wolfe knew the four-engine craft well, both having flown that model and the smaller, two-engine DC-3—the DC to denote their design as the Douglas Commercial—often over the last seven years. Although most of Northwest's DC-4s looked the same, especially painted with the company's signature blue striped body, red tail, and red wingtips—which spanned 118 feet from end to end—the pilots realized that this particular airplane began its career as a C-54A, the military version of the DC-4. The large double cargo door on the port side gave away that fact. This also meant that the aircraft had a more staunchly built floor, and larger wing tanks, which the ground crew had just filled with aviation fuel. At an average burning rate of 216 gallons per hour, the airplane could fly for about 11 hours, significantly more than the scheduled six-hour flight. The DC-4 was considered a very good aircraft for long-range flights.

UNDER THE GATHERING STORM CLOUDS of World War II, Douglas had originally designed the experimental DC-4E to respond to United Airlines' request for a long-range flyer. Ninety-seven-feet-long with a wingspan of 138 feet, a triple tail, four Pratt & Whitney R-2180 Twin Hornet radial engines—among the most powerful engines in the world—and with a pressurized cabin, the benign behemoth was to usher in a new age, but the prototype was too costly for United States airline routes.

A smaller, more pragmatic version, called the DC-4, followed; it gained widespread acceptance and immortality with its single tail and four Pratt & Whitney R-2000 engines. The airplane had not yet entered commercial service when the United States government commandeered its production line just after the bombing of Pearl Harbor in December 1941, skipped the prototype phase, and had the first airplane, labeled as a C-54, the military version of a DC-4, in the air by Valentine's Day 1942. About 1,200 C-54s were manufactured during the war with a wide variety of modifications, and would play a decisive, but unsung, role in winning the war for the Allies. The original model could carry 50 soldiers or 32,500 pounds of cargo. Douglas named the model "Skymaster," which indicates the expectations the company had for the new craft.

The citizens of West Berlin must have thought the DC-4 was certainly a master of the sky between mid-1948 and mid-1949, the bleak years following the war, when that aircraft literally kept them alive by airlifting tons of daily necessities to the city during what became known as the Berlin Airlift.

Franklin D. Roosevelt commissioned a special VC-54C model, nicknamed the "Sacred Cow," which became the first presidential aircraft. It delivered him to the Yalta Conference in 1945 where he, Winston Churchill, and Joseph Stalin discussed Europe's postwar reorganization.

After the war, Douglas built another 74 passenger DC-4s before production ceased in 1947. At the same time, the Air Force began divesting itself of the surplus C-54s. Various airlines scooped them up to fill the demand created during the war. Although Lind and Wolfe would not have given it much thought, they would be flying the airplane with the registration number N-95425 painted in large numbers vertically down the bright red tail. If either of them cared to know, that number could provide insight into the career of that particular craft.

AMONG ALL THE C-54s AND DC-4s built, the airplane used for Flight 2501 could be singled out as special. It was the first C-54—a C-54A with serial number 10270—to roll off Douglas's production line at Orchard Field in the western outskirts of Chicago, a new, two-million-square-foot plant on an expanse of farmland specifically to construct C-54s for the war.

On Friday July 30, 1943, 50,000 people, most of them plant employees and their families, gathered for the dedication of the first Chicago Skymaster, tail number 272165. Illinois Governor Dwight H. Green paid high tribute to the company. Chicago Mayor Edward J. Kelly pointed out the great achievement of turning out the first ship just ten months after the plant's groundbreaking. Plant Manager John D. Weaver praised the employees for their splendid work and cooperation. Major General Harold L. George of Air Transport Command made a prophetic statement. "Chicago may well become the world's air travel hub of the future, considering it sits at the crossroads of many of the great air routes." Indeed after the war, Orchard Field would become the world's busiest airport: O'Hare.

Jennie Giangreco, a 19-year-old riveter elected "Miss C-54" by her fellow employees, christened the aircraft and then gave the signal to start the engines for its maiden flight. Wild cheers and ovations sprang up from the mouths of fascinated spectators as Win Sargent, Douglas' chief test pilot, soared into the setting sun in the Skymaster. He circled over the crowd for 25 minutes.

Just days after the dedication, the airplane was assigned to the Army Air Transport Command for service on segments of the 14,000 mile round-trip between California and Australia across the Pacific. However, the airplane was immediately loaned to the Navy, which was just moving in on the Japanese entrenched at Alaska's Aleutian Islands. For two months it carried supplies to the troops fighting on the islands of Kiska and Attu, and hauled wounded men from that front to hospitals in mainland Alaska. During one takeoff, a piece of the metal mat runway flew loose and tore a two-foot hole in its fuselage. With no time to lose, the Navy kept flying the airplane in that condition, saving the lives of scores of soldiers. After America won the Aleutian campaign, in September 1943, the aircraft was transferred to Hamilton Air Force Base in San Francisco for use by the West Coast Sector of the Pacific Wing for special mission service to and from Hawaii and Australia. Then in late July 1944, United Airlines took control of it for Air Transport Command operations again.

After the war, the government turned it over to a broker, and on February 5, 1946, Venezuelan airline Linea Aeropostal Venezolana purchased the aircraft for $75,000, a deal at the time considering new ones averaged $400,000. Linea sent it back to Douglas for several modifications, including new outer wings of the C-54E type with outer wing fuel tanks and C-54A wing tips, new fuel systems controls, and new Pratt & Whitney 2SD13G engines. Under that ownership, it was registered under tail number NC-91078. The airline did not use it long because the company switched over to the new Lockheed Constellation in early 1947 for international flights. On April 9, 1947, it sold the four-year-old airplane to Northwest Airlines along with another airplane for $1 each plus other "valuable considerations," although what those might have been was not recorded. Northwest re-registered it under the number N-95425 and entered it into its fleet as a cargo airplane on April 11, 1947.

That aircraft and the other 17 DC-4s the airline owned or leased would hold the company over until the arrival of its new fleet. Northwest had ordered ten huge, double-decker Stratocruisers and ten Martin 202s. The Stratocruiser, a luxurious passenger version of the B-29 bomber, could fly

300 miles per hour and carry 83 people. The Martin 202 cruised at 245 miles per hour carrying 40 people. However, huge construction delays on the Stratocruisers left Northwest in a bind when the airline decided to offer an industry first—all-coach service across the country beginning in March 1949. The cost of a one-way ticket would be reduced from $158 to just $97.

To handle the increased demand that the new lower cost tickets created, and still without the much needed Stratocruisers, Northwest was forced in April 1950 to convert N-95425 to a 55-passenger coach aircraft, at a cost of $30,000, installing new seats in a tighter configuration, two on the port side and three across the aisle on the starboard, with a much narrower center aisle. The DC-4 would operate in that new configuration just shy of two months before being assigned to Flight 2501 on June 23, 1950.

AS LIND AND WOLFE examined their aircraft that night, Crew Chief L. G. Goebel, the mechanic who had been going over the DC-4 since it arrived, greeted the two pilots. "Everything looks OK. I didn't run up the engines or listen to them, but I'll do that when you get them running," he told them. "Captain Dean didn't record any issues during his flight, so there are no concerns."

The three men might have quipped about the Stratocruiser delays, hoping they would get a chance to work with those new monsters soon. The DC-4 would have to do, though, for this flight. They would have known it to be safe and reliable, although it had experienced its fair share of accidents.

Lind, Wolfe, and Goebel would have been aware of most of the accidents that had occurred over the last few years, and, like all pilots and mechanics, they would have studied the circumstances of those accidents and discussed the chain of errors to learn from the mistakes of others and take action to avoid similar accidents. Not considering the many fatal accidents that the military had experienced using C54s during the war, since 1943 the civilian C-54s and DC-4s had been involved in 28 fatal accidents that had resulted in the deaths of 649 people. Almost one-third of those accidents—ten total, killing 274 people—had occurred in the United States by U. S. airlines.

Two of those accidents involved Eastern Airlines flights on DC-4s, which combined claimed 108 lives, the highest number of fatalities for any airline at the time. In fact, Eastern's Flight 537 on November 1, 1949, just seven and a half months earlier, had resulted in the largest number of deaths among civilian and military flights, through no fault of the airplane manufacturer, the pilot, or the airline. A Bolivian Air Force Lockheed P-38 trying to land at Washington National Airport crashed into the DC-4 killing all 55 people. There had been talk that Air Traffic Control was to blame.

For Eastern, that tragic accident followed another major disaster two years earlier when 53 people died in a crash near Bainbridge, Maryland. Just after Eastern Flight 605 departed Newark for Miami and reached its assigned cruising altitude of 4000 feet, witnesses watched as the aircraft entered a steep dive, rolled over, and hit the ground. Even after studying the wreckage, the Civil Aeronautics Board, responsible for reviewing all accidents, could not determine what caused the crash.

United Airlines experienced two accidents with DC-4s that resulted in a total of 45 deaths. In each case, the pilots had difficulties in landings and takeoffs. Pennsylvania Central, Pan Am, Alaska Airlines, and Delta each had one accident with DC-4s. Like Eastern and United, Northwest suffered two fatal DC-4 accidents. The first one with more fatalities, occurred on March 12, 1948, when Flight 4422, as previously mentioned, hit the upper face of Mount Sanford in Alaska, instantly bursting into flames and killing all 30 people on board. The CAB blamed the clouds and the aurora borealis phenomenon, also known as the northern lights, for blinding the pilot who was flying off course. Then later that year, Northwest lost two employees on a cargo flight from Minneapolis to Japan. When over Canada, the captain had taken the opportunity on a non-passenger flight to give his first officer some emergency training. He purposely shut down two of the engines and handed the controls to his student, an irresponsible move with so heavy an aircraft. The airplane crashed.

Northwest had also recently experienced two fatal accidents in flights using Martin 202s that Lind and Wolfe would have been very familiar with. On August 29, 1948, Flight 421, traveling from Chicago to Minneapolis, entered the leading edge of a thunderstorm over Winona, Minnesota, and seconds later crashed to the ground killing all 37 people. The accident was blamed on a faulty wing fitting. Then on March 7, 1950, Flight 307, flying from Washington to Winnipeg, Canada, made an intermediate stop at Minneapolis during heavy precipitation, hit a flagpole near the landing runway, and crashed into a house. All 13 occupants and two people in the house were killed.

Lind and Wolfe probably heard the sarcastic slogan bantered around in the wake of those fatal accidents, "For eternal rest, fly Northwest." They would not have been happy to hear that, but even among pilots, those Martin 202 accidents would have been talked about. Lind and Wolfe were probably glad to be flying a DC-4 that, while older, had a more reliable safety record.

In the days preceding this flight, both men probably discussed, with great pity for Air France and its pilots, two back-to-back accidents the company experienced less than two weeks earlier in DC-4s. They each probably had made a mental note never to accept a flight into the Bahrain Airport.

On June 12, 1950, during a flight from Karachi, Pakistan, to the small island kingdom of Bahrain, east of Saudi Arabia, the pilot had trouble with a landing and crashed into the Persian Gulf. Forty-six of the 52 occupants died. Then—unbelievably—just two nights later another Air France pilot flying the same route had difficulty with the same landing at Bahrain and crashed in the water as well, even before the earlier wreck had been salvaged. Forty of the 53 occupants died. Clearly, the substandard airport played a significant role in the deaths of those 86 people. Tragically, all that came out of that accident was a recommendation to equip the Bahrain Airport with radio landing aids and suitable runway approach lights.

Although those numbers seem frightening, Lind and Wolfe were well aware that airplane travel was infinitely safer than automobile travel. In 1949 there had been fewer than 200 fatalities among all the airlines operating in America. The next year, when the government began tracking statistics on automobile fatalities, a staggering 33,000 people would die on the roads.

With the relatively short, 90-mile flight over Lake Michigan later that night, a crossing they had completed without incident many times, Lind and Wolfe would not have given the possibility of a water landing a passing thought. In fact, Northwest had eliminated its prior requirement to have life rafts on board flights that crossed the Great Lakes since its high-speed airplanes could cross the inland seas so quickly.

While Lind and Wolfe were wrapping up their briefing with Crew Chief Goebel just before 8:00 p.m., dispatcher Richard Miller was inside the terminal having a discussion on the telephone with meteorologist Donald Wertz, who had taken over for Beresford in Minneapolis. Wertz had familiarized himself with Julius Badner's 4:45 p.m. forecast and reviewed the hourly sequence reports with actual weather observations that had since arrived from airports around the region. From the information he gathered, he disagreed with Beresford's prediction that a squall line would form and had just issued a revised forecast, considerably less harsh than the earlier one. Miller preferred that the pilots under his control expect the worst and hope for better, so he decided that he would *not* share the new forecast with Flight 2501.

By about 8:00 p.m., the pilots had completed their walk around the aircraft making the customary visual inspections of the engines, propellers, fuselage, and tail, as the ground crew continued loading the baggage. Then, with everything ready to go, and with briefcases in hand, Robert Lind and Verne Wolfe climbed the set of mobile stairs leading into the cockpit.

Chapter 8

BOARDING AND TAKEOFF

Stewardess Bonnie Ann Feldman was working in the cabin when Robert Lind and Verne Wolfe stepped through the small "hamburger" door just behind the cockpit on the starboard side. The door got its name because of the proximity to the propellers. Neither man was very tall, but they both had to duck to get through the arched opening and avoid hitting their heads on the oxygen bottle mounted on a rack behind the copilot's seat. As they took the few steps toward the cockpit, Feldman would have made it a point to greet them. She had worked this flight many times with Lind and Wolfe and knew them well. "We've got a full one tonight—55 passengers," she might have commented.

The flight would be especially hard for Feldman because she had just come down with the flu. She was not due to fly until the next day, but had switched shifts with her friend Louise Johnson to get home early. She hoped to recoup there and be ready for her next scheduled flight. Lind or Wolfe may have noticed that she looked under the weather and asked if she was feeling all right. "No, not too good, but I didn't want to let the company or Louise down," she probably said, just as she had told Louise hours earlier.

Now 25, Bonnie Feldman had been flying for Northwest since 1946. She was born in Red Wing, Minnesota, about an hour's drive southeast of St. Paul, the second child after her sister Beth. She grew up in Bay City, Wisconsin, because her father had been transferred to a bank there. The dark-haired beauty was outgoing and vivacious, perfect qualities for a stewardess. She was the same way in high school, where she had been active in school affairs, junior Red Cross, playing piano in orchestra, and singing in the choir. Plenty of boys chased her, but Feldman had no interest in getting married right away; she had a career in aviation in mind. She had attended Stephens College in Columbia, Missouri, specifically because it set new standards for the roles of women in society; in 1944, it introduced the first aviation program for women. At Stephens, Feldman took flying lessons in addition to normal coursework. Northwest Airlines scooped her up as a stewardess after graduation, and she had been there ever since.

To be close to the airport, she rented a little house just north of the airfield and planned to stay there at least another seven years until she was 32 and would have to resign from Northwest because of age restrictions. If she married before that, she would have to resign early. Consequently, she never dated a particular man for very long. She had gone out with at least 12 men in the time she worked for Northwest. Her parents really didn't approve of her lifestyle, and often encouraged her to marry a rich man, settle down, and have babies. However, Bonnie preferred to fly.

In the hotel earlier that day, Feldman would have prepared for the flight by touching up the polish on her nails and shining her shoes. Then she had dressed, beginning with her regulation girdle, although with her trim figure she hardly needed one: per corporate guidelines, she would not have been working for Northwest if she was any taller than 5'-5" or weighed over 120 pounds. Then she put on her navy blue uniform skirt, white blouse, and matching blue jacket. Northwest demanded a perfect appearance from their stewardesses, so when she arrived at the airport later that day, she would have gone into the ladies' room, tucked back any stray hairs, touched up her makeup, and checked the seams on her stockings to make sure they were straight. This was all recorded on a written checklist, but Feldman had gone through the process so many times that she did not have to refer to it. Lastly, following Northwest's procedures, she had thrown back her shoulders, put a smile on her face to help establish a happy attitude, and headed out to the DC-4.

As Lind and Wolfe took their seats in the cockpit, Lind at the port side seat and Wolfe at the starboard side seat, Feldman carried out her tasks to prepare for the flight. She smoothed down the white cotton headrests, secured the curtains over each round window, made sure there was a pillow and blanket for every passenger neatly folded on the overhead shelves, and checked that the two lavatories near the back of the airplane were stocked and clean.

Since Northwest had begun running coach flights, she had to get used to the cramped conditions of the DC-4 that had been converted for that use. Rather than two seats on either side of the aisle, there were rows of three seats on the starboard side and two seats on the port side for a total of 56 seats. Feldman likely reserved for herself the forwardmost aisle seat on opposite the galley, just behind the cockpit on the port side. Once she completed the cabin preparations, she readied the galley for the snack service. She might have had a few moments to relax before the passengers began arriving.

Meanwhile Lind and Wolfe had been going over their before engine start checklist. Wolfe would have also reviewed the maintenance log, a binder with alternating yellow and white sheets, to see what, if any, issues the previous pilot had noted about the aircraft. "Looks like everything was in working order on the last flight," he would have told Lind.

AS THE PILOTS CONTINUED through their checklist, passengers for several evening flights that night lined up at the counter in the terminal to check their luggage.

Twenty-eight-year-old Mary Meier, a jewelry buyer for Wurzburg Department store in Grand Rapids, Michigan, stood in one of three crowded lines waiting to check in for her North Central Airlines flight home. She, like many others at the airport that night, was returning from a week at the fashion showcase in New York where she had been selecting merchandise for the fall season.

She glanced around and tried to pick out the other fashion merchandisers—she could always spot them because they were usually better dressed than most. In the line next to her she pegged a dark-haired, glamorous-looking woman as another buyer. "Long week at the market?" she asked, initiating a friendly chat.

"Oh, yes, I can't wait to get home," the woman replied in a southern accent. "Where are you headed?"

"Grand Rapids."

"Well, then, shouldn't you be in this line?" the woman asked, motioning her over with her hand. "This plane is going to Minnesota."

"Grand Rapids, *Michigan*," Meier said laughing, "not Grand Rapids, *Minnesota*."

The other woman laughed, too. They chatted for several minutes until Meier reached the head of her line. "Nice talking," she said, before approaching the counter.

"Likewise," the woman replied.

THE WOMAN MARY MEIER had talked to was, in all likelihood, Jo Longfield, the only woman buyer ticketed on Flight 2501. Longfield would have really been looking forward to getting home to Billings, Montana, after a week in New York and two weeks in Chicago before that. As partner and manager of the Mildred-Hazel shop in Billings, she flew frequently. Her buying trips were not without perks. She had purchased several garments for herself, including a fur, all packed in her luggage. Longfield loved her profession, a career she had wanted to pursue since her childhood growing up in Lameda, Texas, where all the other girls thought about was marriage and babies. She studied textile design at the Pratt Institute in New York and first accepted a position in Great Falls, Montana, then made the move to the shop in Billings in 1947.

Even though she was 38, Longfield had only recently started thinking about settling down. There were plenty of movie actors she found attractive, but actually establishing a relationship with an accessible man was a leap she was finding difficult.

Longfield would have recognized two of the other passengers in her line, Leo Wohler and William Kelty, both with Vaughn Ragsdale, a department store in Billings. Wohler, 43 years old, usually did buying trips twice a year and was no stranger to travel either. This was certainly an impressive position considering he began life as one of 16 children and spent the first part of his career as a Lutheran school teacher. An offer from a department store tempted him away from teaching when he was in his early twenties. Then, in 1931, Vaughn Ragsdale offered him a position in its Lewiston, Montana, store. He moved there, met and married Gladys, the woman of his dreams, and was soon promoted to store manager.

Wohler's success had a lot to do with his appearance and attitude. He was tall, maintained a good posture, and wore his clothes well—the epitome of a fashionable man. He demanded respect and offered kindness and positive encouragement. He applied this not only to his employees and customers, but also to his family—which by 1950 had grown to seven children. By then, he had been transferred to the Billings store where he had taken over as general manager.

Wohler traveled with 54-year-old fashion buyer William Carter Kelty. Like Wohler, Kelty had joined Vaughn Ragsdale in 1931, after managing their Bridger, Montana store for seven years before being promoted. He and his wife, Bernice, had no children. Kelty, Wohler, and Longfield would transfer to Flight 501 in Minneapolis to continue on to Billings.

Although none of the Billings-based buyers would have known him, another fashion buyer, Joseph Sirbu, was getting ready to board the flight. Sirbu, with his brother Marvin and his son Jerry, ran their own business as a manufacturer's representative for a line of fine sportswear. Sirbu had just spent a week at the New York market and was on his way to the Seattle market before returning home to his wife, Alma, in Beverly Hills, California. He looked forward to seeing her reaction when the fur stole he had just mailed to her arrived.

AFTER CHECKING IN FOR FLIGHT 2501, New Yorker Frank Schwartz, and his friend John Herbstreit, who had driven him to the airport, stood talking at the terminal window, looking out at the DC-4 that Schwartz would soon board. Schwartz was on his way to St. Paul, Minnesota, to give away his 21-year-old stepdaughter, Joy Bell, at her wedding to Warren Johnson the next evening. Schwartz's wife, Patricia, had flown out to St. Paul two weeks earlier to help her daughter with all the last-minute arrangements. She and Joy were, at that very moment, at the rehearsal dinner at the Northwood Restaurant in St. Paul. His soon-to-be son-in-law would pick him up at the airport when the flight arrived in the wee hours of the morning. Joy had expressed concern that Schwartz would miss the rehearsal, but since the wedding would begin at 8:00 p.m. Saturday, he would have plenty of time the next afternoon to go over the details before the ceremony.

Schwartz had been busy that week at the Fairchild Camera and Instrument Company in New York where he worked as the technical manager. He could not get away any earlier that week, so he had to take the Friday evening flight. He enjoyed the job, which was still somewhat new to him. After college, Schwartz, who was naturally exuberant and friendly, had begun in the hospitality field as a banquet manager in the New Yorker Hotel. At some point, he took an ability assessment test that indicated that he was better suited for a technical position. In short order, he began working for Fairchild doing research and development for flash photography equipment. He did not forget his roots in hospitality, though; he had checked onto the airplane two cases of champagne for the reception the next evening.

Although Schwartz had only known Joy since he began dating her mother about five years earlier, they had become fast friends. He now considered her his daughter. Joy had been born in Hollywood, California, and her father, Morris Bell, died when she was 13. Schwartz was honored that Joy had asked him to give her away at the ceremony and was happy to host the wedding.

"Do you have any trip insurance?" Herbstreit asked as they stood there.

"No."

"Might as well, for a less than a dollar," Herbstreit said, nodding toward the trip insurance vending machine near the Northwest counter. "You can buy a policy there," he said pointing. "It's only twenty-five cents for every $7,500 of insurance."

When the aviation industry was in its infancy, trip insurance was sold by the airlines representatives for a percentage of the airfare. Manpower shortages during World War II had brought about the inauguration of insurance vending machines. The Associated Aviation Underwriters had recently installed the machine at LaGuardia and many other airports.

Schwartz walked up to the stand-alone, counter-height machine and read the three-step process. Reaching into his pants pocket, he pulled out his change and found four quarters. "Guess I'll get a $30,000 policy for Pat," he said to his friend as he inserted the coins.

The machine spit out a policy in duplicate. Below the standard printed disclaimer at the top, he saw boxes that needed to be filled out with his name, the name and address of his beneficiary, the point of departure and destination, the date, the amount of the premium, and his signature. He filled in the information, then folded one copy and tucked it in his wallet and inserted the other copy into the prepaid postal envelope, put his home address on the front, and was about to deposit it in the nearby mailbox when he decided to give it to his friend instead. "Here," he said, extending the envelope to Herbstreit. "Hold on to this for Pat," he chuckled, "just in case."

At that moment, the intercom blared, "Northwest Flight 2501 is boarding now at gate...."

Herbstreit accompanied his friend out to the tarmac, and the two men shook hands as the last of the luggage was loaded into the cargo compartment. "Congratulations on behalf of Joy," Herbstreit said. "Look for me when the plane takes off, I'll be here watching."

Schwartz queued up behind all the other passengers walking toward the stairs that led up into the DC-4.

BONNIE ANN FELDMAN stood at the airplane's port door waiting to greet her passengers enthusiastically despite feeling ill. "Welcome to Northwest Flight 2501 to Minneapolis," she would have said, giving the people one last chance to verify they were on the correct airplane. One by one, she checked their boarding passes, doing her best to remember the passenger's last names and make note of where they decided to sit, so that she could refer to them later by name.

Her list indicated that the passengers included the Hokansons, traveling with two young children; the Frengs, traveling with their teenaged daughter; two mothers, 40-year-old Adelaide Schafer and Yvette Malby, each traveling with their son; and four married couples, the Heustens, Ajemians, Schlachters, and Jacksons. She would have made sure the mothers and couples got a pair of seats together on the port side and would have given special attention to families with children, helping them to seats where they could be together. Perhaps she directed them aft, closest to the lavatories. She knew how best to organize passengers so that the flight was as comfortable as possible for all. The other passengers consisted of 17 men and 19 women traveling alone, although she had probably been given notes that two pairs of passengers, William Kelty and Leo Wohler, and cousins Hilma Larson and Ruth Johnson, wished to sit with each other.

Twenty-one people would leave the flight at Minneapolis and then 10 of them would catch a connecting flight to Billings, Montana. Although Feldman would be replaced in Minneapolis, her list indicated that seven passengers would continue on the flight to Spokane, Washington, and the other 17 would fly all the way to Seattle due to arrive the next morning at about 7:00 a.m., Seattle time.

The final passenger to board was Morry J. Pertofsky, the president of the Columbia Lamp Manufacturing Company, who had been given a seat at the last minute when another passenger did not show up.

A member of the ground crew climbed the mobile stairs and closed the door, then Feldman secured it from the inside while the stairs were rolled away. She quickly walked up the aisle to inform Lind that the cabin and passengers were secure for takeoff.

At that point, Lind would have begun the take off process. "Are the engine areas clear?"

"Affirmative, engine areas clear," Wolfe would have replied.

Then one by one Lind started the engines beginning with number four, then one, then two, and finally three, a burst of smoke coming from each as the propellers began spinning.

FRANK SCHWARTZ'S FRIEND, John Herbstreit, watched with fascination as the propellers became a blur. Just when he thought the airplane was going to begin moving, a man in a long brown gown—a priest of some sort, he presumed—ran past him, waving his arms to the ground crewman handling the portable stairs. Herbstreit watched as the crewman signaled up toward the cockpit, and then one after another the engine propellers stopped spinning. The crewman then rolled the stairs back to the passenger door, climbed the steps with the priest, and opened the door.

Bonnie Ann Feldman stood ready at the door.

"I'm sorry I'm late," Father Augustine Walsh probably announced, panting and holding out his ticket with one hand while clutching his Bible in the other. "I'm supposed to be on this plane."

Despite the inconvenience this late passenger posed, Feldman would have found it hard to get angry at Walsh because of his natural warmth and friendly smile. A monk with the Friars of Atonement at Graymore, New York, Walsh was on his way to the St. Mary's Roman Catholic Church in Deer River, Minnesota, for a temporary assignment.

After checking his ticket, Feldman would have said, "Please wait here," and then headed down the aisle to find Morry Pertofsky, who had been given that seat at the last minute.

At 45 years old, Walsh, who had been born on Christmas morning in Ireland and christened Michael, had already served various positions in Washington D.C., Canada, and in Ireland. He had come to the United States as a small boy and began his studies for the priesthood at St. John's Seminary in 1922, then made his profession of vows in 1927 to Father Paul James Francis, the founder of the society. After completing his studies at the Catholic University of America in Washington, D.C., he was ordained in 1933.

A minute later Feldman returned with Pertofsky, probably offering him some advice as to the next flight he might catch and where to pick up his luggage in Minneapolis since there was no time to off-load it. Then she pointed out the open seat to Father Walsh.

Once the door had been secured again, Feldman quickly reached for her personalized silver container of Wrigley's Doublemint gum, compliments of the gum manufacturer, who had been keeping the airline stocked since the introduction of its "Doublement Twins" advertising campaign in 1939; Philip Wrigley knew how to effectively market his product, as did his father, William, who founded the business. She offered a stick to each passenger to help alleviate pressure in their ears upon takeoff.

As she did that, Lind and Wolfe restarted the engines, carried forth with their final checks, and taxied to the runway. During his career at Northwest, Robert Lind had logged over 900 hours flying on instruments. He had completed a Civil Aeronautics Administration physical that February and during the last 90 days had flown 105 hours in DC-4s, making 15 round trips on the Minneapolis-to-New York and Minneapolis-to-Washington routes. Since his last flight, he had a total rest period of 24 hours. Captain Robert Lind was more than prepared for the flight.

WITH 2,500 GALLONS of fuel pumped into the wing tanks, 80 gallons of oil, and 490 pounds of luggage, the 71,342-pound, fully loaded craft weighed in at just 58 pounds below the maximum permissible takeoff weight. Lind idled the engines on the runway until he heard the voice of the controller say, "Northwest 2501 cleared for takeoff."

Lind released the brakes and pushed the four throttles to the full forward position to provide maximum takeoff power to the whirling blades. "Let's go," he said to Wolfe.

The airplane began to vibrate and the noise inside was jarring, especially in the cockpit. The airplane thundered forward gaining speed until at about 60 miles per hour ground speed, when it reached the 3,500-foot mark on the 5,000-foot-long runway, the wings lifted the airplane. The roar of the engines reverberated from the apartments that lined the south end of the field.

Wolfe activated the switch to tuck the landing gear into the aircraft, and Lind would have made a slight bank over the East River as he climbed 500 feet per minute. "Off at 8:35," Wolfe radioed the control tower.

Twenty-seven-year-old Rosalie Gorski, of Seattle, Washington, a beautiful brunette, probably clutched her stomach as the airplane lifted off, feeling a little more agitation than the other passengers. She was almost three months pregnant and had been having some issues with morning sickness. She and her husband of seven years, Bill, had just spent a month in their home town, Wilkes Barre, Pennsylvania, with her parents, the Kurinkas, between Bill's college graduation and the start of his new insurance job in Seattle. Rosalie had stayed on another three weeks after Bill left and during that time, she had learned of her pregnancy. She planned to surprise her husband with the news when he picked her up at the Seattle airport.

Three weeks away from his wife had been difficult for Bill Gorski. He thought and talked about her often. In fact, he often quoted poet William Wadsworth when describing what he felt when he met her, "She was a phantom of delight when she first gleamed upon my sight."

Soon after having met, he enlisted in the Coast Guard, and she went to work for the American Red Cross in Washington. When his ship was in port one day at Curtis Bay, he found her and proposed. They had married before the end of the war.

Bill Gorski had talked to his wife often from Seattle during those three long weeks. She had called him just the night before expressing her apprehension of flying without him, suggesting she take the train or even buy a car and drive out.

"That would take too long," he had told her. "Don't worry, flying is safe."

TWENTY-THREE-YEAR-OLD Geraldine Reilly Jackson, originally from Connecticut, but now living in Manhattan, probably felt queasy, too. Like Gorski, she was also pregnant, and she and her new husband of two months, Arthur, were taking a belated honeymoon to visit his parents in Sheridan, Montana, to share the good news with them and Arthur's four siblings.

This would make Arthur's father happy, as much as when his son had been accepted at Yale on the GI Bill after serving in the Naval submarine service. Now Arthur worked for Chase National Bank in Manhattan, and his father knew he was destined for an amazingly successful career.

Roaring loudly, the airplane crossed over the Harlem district of Manhattan while passengers on both sides of the aircraft gazed at the beautiful view on the hazy June evening.

FOUR-YEAR-OLD TOMMY HOKANSON, chewing his Wrigley's gum, and his sister, seven-year-old Janice Hokanson, clutching her baby doll, probably had their noses pressed to the windows, pointing and asking questions of their parents. The trip would be a great adventure for the kids because they were going to their grandparents' home on a big dairy farm near Minneapolis. Besides eating lots of ice cream there, they would be meeting their cousins, the children of their father's four siblings. John Hokanson was the only son who had received a college education and left the family dairy business. He had first accepted a position at a milk company in West Bend, Wisconsin, and in 1948 joined the Quaker Maid Company as an executive in the New York office.

Hokanson's wife, the former Catherine Phalen, or Kay as she was known, enjoyed the big family gatherings on the farm. She had grown up as an only child, only acquiring a stepsister—the famous actress Joan Davis—after her mother's divorce and subsequent remarriage in 1941. Kay looked forward to sharing her exciting news with John's parents and his family; she was pregnant with their third child.

DANA MALBY, WHO HAD JUST TURNED three years old, would not have been interested in the view. He was probably crying miserably from the shaking, the noise, and the funny sensation in his ears. His mother would have been rocking and comforting him and maybe suggesting that rather than gum, he chew on some of the popcorn she had stashed in his jacket pocket at the airport. His mother, Yvette Malby, originally from New York, was flying to join her husband, Wesley, after packing up their home to move to Spokane where he had already started a new job at the Washington Power Company.

THE ONLY OTHER CHILD ON BOARD, eight-year-old John Schafer, was traveling with his mother, Adelaide, to Bozeman, Montana, for a visit with her brother. Her husband, a partner in the brokerage firm of Schafer, Miller, and Company in New York, had not been able to take an extended vacation from work, so he and their youngest son stayed home while Adelaide and her son John, from a previous marriage, made the trip without them. It would have taken all her courage to do so. After her first husband, a pilot, had died while flying for the Air Force, she had become petrified of flying.

TWELVE MINUTES AFTER takeoff, Flight 2501 reached its cruising altitude of 6,000 feet and the sky started to deepen in color. Lind would have tuned his receiver into the radio range station at Pittsburgh, the first checkpoint of the flight. "Nothing beats the sound of a four-engine Douglas," he might have commented to Wolfe.

While the engines created a terrific rumble on the takeoff roll, they purred away quietly with the airplane at cruising speed, lulling the passengers with their gentle drone. Millions of lights would have begun to sparkle on the ground below in the gathering twilight. A minute later the flight was over the Hudson River. The ride was smooth and comforting.

Those used to flying might not have bothered to look out the windows. Instead, they could have read copies of the *New York Times* that Feldman had offered before takeoff. Scanning the headlines, readers would have noticed that although printed in black ink, it might as well have been red—almost one third of the major stories dealt with the growing "Red Scare" sweeping the country:

"Chilean Labor Minister Seeks to End Copper Strike that was said to be Communist-Led."

"Trial Begins for Eight New York Teachers Accused of Refusal to Say Whether they were in Communist Party."

"West Coast Scientist Indicted in Red Case."

"Soviets Capable of Atomic Bombing."

The articles illustrated how concerned the United States had become over the spread of communism in the wake of World War II. Tensions had escalated in late 1949 with the establishment of the People's Republic of China following the defeat of Chiang Kai-shek. Then in February, Senator Joe McCarthy riled citizens in a speech in West Virginia when he claimed that, "the State Department is infested with communists."

Although many people felt that McCarthy was just attempting to discredit his opponents, as did *Washington Post* cartoonist Herbert Block, who had recently coined the term "McCarthyism," many others were undoubtedly concerned.

KENNETH NORDLY SKOUG might have tried to focus on something more enjoyable in the news: baseball. He followed the American League with great gusto. He knew that the New York Yankees had played earlier that day against the Detroit Tigers in Detroit, but had not yet heard the score. Instead, all he could do was lament their 2 to 6 loss the prior day despite Joe DiMaggio's great home run. Baseball was a big part of Skoug's life. He had joined the American Legion soon after his discharge from the Navy, and had been managing the Legion's baseball teams as the athletic director in Minnesota. He saw how the game had such a good effect on young boys and was so committed to the program that he had increased the number of teams in the league from just 44 to over 300 in the state.

Skoug's work for the American Legion, as well as his singing in a barber-shop quartet and his playing of the trombone, reflected that he worked to live, not the other way around. Yet, his position had taken him away from his home state, Minnesota, and his daughter, who had already married. His employer of 22 years, Remington Rand, manufacturer of office equipment, had transferred him to New York two years previously as its national director. He and his new wife, Margaret, whom he had married in 1949, about five years after his first wife died of tuberculosis, relocated there, but he kept his house in Minneapolis for his children and for his visits home.

Since the fall, Ken Jr. had been attending Columbia College in New York, and Ken Sr. had been able to see him on weekends. With the school year now over, Ken Jr. was returning home, and his father and Margaret would spend time at home with him, his sister, and her family and attend the American Legion convention in Duluth that month. Margaret and Ken Jr. had driven the car that Skoug had given his son to use while at school. In fact, Ken Jr. had gotten some minor repairs done to it before the trip and the two men had quarreled over who should pay the $7.75 repair bill. Nonetheless, Skoug was looking forward to being together as a family that weekend. He had wanted to arrive for dinner Friday, but office commitments required him to switch to the evening flight instead of the morning one.

IN HIS COPY OF THE *TIMES*, Tommy Hill likely took notice of the article that indicated the Senate had passed a bill extending Selective Service for three years. That might have concerned him because it had a foreboding of potential international conflict. Hill had recently completed four years in the Army during peacetime and would likely be among the first called back should war erupt again. He would not have wanted any part of that. He had just turned 25 the week before, settled into a nice position as an advertising trainee at Benton and Bowles on New York's Madison Avenue and had just gotten engaged to a prominent East Coast girl. He was flying home to Minneapolis to share the good news with his parents.

SIXTY-YEAR-OLD ALFRED GEORGE of Portland, Oregon, a trainmaster for the Portland and Seattle Railroad, would have taken notice of the *Times* article entitled, "Strike Threat For Railroad," about conductors and yardmasters threatening walkouts. He was returning home to his wife, Grace, after having visited his two sisters in his native London. Keeping connected with his two siblings in England, the other two in the states, and his own three married children and grandchildren was especially important to George considering his sorrowful early life. When he was six in 1896, both his parents had died from the influenza epidemic in London that claimed thousands. He and his siblings had been separated and sent to orphanages in London. At 16, he was among thousands of "home children" sent by the British government to Canada as child laborers. He ended up at a lumber camp near Toronto. Four years later, his older sister found him, and eventually he and all his siblings were reunited. They had stayed close ever since.

WILLIAM FRENG PROBABLY READ with great interest the *Times* story entitled, "House Group Votes New Tax Measure." The decisions made that day in Washington would have a definite effect on him, both good and bad. The Ways and Means Committee had called for more than one billion dollars in excise tax deductions on luxury items such as jewelry, furs, and travel. The fur stole his wife, Rosa, wore that day and their planned vacation would have reminded him of all the luxuries she and their daughter Barbara, along with them on the trip, had become accustomed to. However, these tax savings would be offset by an increase in corporate taxes, which would undoubtedly affect his employer, the International Telephone and Telegraph Corporation (ITT).

Freng, vice president and general counsel for ITT, had been at the firm since 1927. Until recently, he had reported directly to its founder, Colonel Sosthenes Behn, and now to the current company president, William Harrison. Although his wife, the former Rosa Funk, enjoyed all that her husband's $35,000 annual salary bought, she was bothered that Behn and then Harrison, thought they had the right to phone her husband day and night to talk business. She was glad her husband had been able to get away to visit relatives in St. Paul, then spend several weeks at the Elkhorn Ranch in Bozeman, Montana She knew this might be the last family vacation with their 17-year-old daughter Barbara. Their other daughter, Mary, had already married, moved away, and started a family of her own, and Barbara was getting serious with her boyfriend.

Although William Freng was undoubtedly the most prominent and well-to-do executive on board the flight, he was a humble, gentle man, active in the Presbyterian Church in Rye, New York, and not frivolous. That is why he chose to fly coach rather than first class.

THE PASSENGERS WERE a diverse group of people: men, women, and children—some single, some married, one divorced, one widowed, one engaged, and one hoping to get engaged soon. Twenty-one married individuals were traveling without their spouses. Their reasons for travel were varied. Twenty-four people were en route to or from family visits, eight were traveling on business, four were relocating, two were attending religious meetings, and one would be standing up in a wedding. The rest were going to or from vacation. Of the 58 people on board, 32 were from the East Coast, 13 from the Midwest, including the crew, and 12 from the West Coast.

Only Karl Neilsen hailed from outside the 48 United States. He had grown up with four siblings on Afognac Island just north of Kodiak Island in Alaska, which had been lobbying for statehood since before he was born. Neilsen was returning home from New York after graduating from high school, where his mother had sent him to get him away from his abusive father. Neilsen would have been glad to know that while he was away, his mother had finally left her husband of 20 years.

Neilsen had been flipping through the pages of the stamp album that he had put together while at school. When he tired of that, he might have glanced through his copy of the *New York Times* to check the weather. Living in Alaska, knowing that the weather could be of life or death importance, Neilsen would have understood the markings on the national weather map several pages into the paper. It showed a big, black, kidney-shaped mass running north and south in the middle of the country with a row of arrows pointing east. This indicated, with graphic clarity, a massive storm front advancing eastward toward Lake Michigan. Undoubtedly Karl Neilsen would have pictured the airplane meeting that front head on and having to penetrate it to reach its first stop at Minneapolis.

Chapter 9

EN ROUTE

As soon as the flight leveled off at 6000 feet, Bonnie Ann Feldman began preparations for the coffee and snack service. She made her way down the aisle, pulling pillows from the overhead shelf and handing them to passengers to place on their laps to hold the small trays she would pass out. On her return up the aisle, she would have begun taking their drink orders for coffee, Coca-Cola, or 7-Up. Most of the passengers probably wanted to get some sleep, though, and did not choose caffeinated drinks. Frankly, Feldman would have preferred them all to have the 7-Up. Although she might not have realized that two year's earlier the manufacturer stopped enhancing the carbonated drink with lithium citrate, a mood-stabilizing drug, she would have known that 7-Up was often chosen for its soothing, medicinal-like qualities, and based on the reported squall, her passengers might need something to calm them.

As the pilots gently turned west over Staten Island on airway Green 3, Carl and Louise Schlachter may have glanced out their window, with some nostalgia, toward their former home in Upper Montclair, New Jersey. They were heading west to a new life in Seattle, where Carl would be taking a position at an architectural firm. A 1933 graduate of Cornell University, he had also studied at the American Academy in Rome and at George Washington University in Washington, D.C. Schlachter, a noted architect and engineer most recently with Walter, Doran & Teague in New York, had worked on modernizing the Panama Canal, the Pentagon, and the Air Force Base at Dayton, Ohio.

Despite these large, important industrial projects, Schlachter really preferred residential design; entering private practice in Seattle would give him that opportunity, particularly because cities on the West Coast were not nearly as developed as those along the East Coast. Seattle would take some getting used to for his wife, who was originally from Washington, D.C. She had met Carl when he was in the Army and they had been inseparable ever since. In fact, whenever they gave a gift, they signed it "Love from Carlou," as if they were one. Louise had been looking forward to joining the board of a branch of the League of Woman Voters, the organization she had served faithfully in New Jersey. The Schlachters had no children, but they did have their beloved cocker spaniel, which flew along with them. To the bemusement of some family members, the couple had expressed their immense love for the dog by putting in writing their wish that in the event of their deaths, the dog was to be put to sleep, not given away.

The other married couples were all heading to or returning from family visits and vacations. Dr. Leon Ajemian, a heart specialist, and his wife, Sirhoun, were on their way from their home in Manhattan to Seattle to visit her sister in British Columbia, Canada. Now 63 and 58, the couple was finally in a position to do some traveling after having worked their entire married lives to provide a good life for themselves and their daughters, Maro and Anahid, both well-known chamber musicians. Born in Armenia, Leon and Sirhoun met in their late 20s and soon married. Then, Leon was captured by the Turkish Nationalists during the 1920 Turkish-Armenian War. He was allowed to live because he had value as a doctor in training, and he eventually became a doctor under Turkish captivity. In time, he escaped and reunited with his wife, who had found safety in Switzerland and was earning a living playing and teaching music. Maro had been born there just before the Ajemians immigrated to America for a life of freedom.

Tacoma residents Benjamin and Slava Heuston, 67 and 60, were returning home after a month-long visit in Queens with their son, Dr. Paul Heuston, to attend his graduation from medical school and visit with Slava's sorority sisters from Mount Holyoke College in Massachusetts. They planned to get off the flight at Minneapolis to spend a few days with Slava's cousin, Ivan Doseff, before continuing on to Tacoma, where their other son, Franklin, an attorney, and daughter, Margaret, lived. All of their children had attended the University of Puget Sound.

Heuston had grown up in Wisconsin and relocated to Tacoma in 1907 after he graduated from Stanford University; there he entered the real estate business and opened his own firm, Heuston and Heuston. He and Slava Balabanoff met in Tacoma and eloped on June 22, 1912. Heuston sent a telegram to Slava's mother, Mrs. C. P. Balabanoff, announcing the news and letting her know "it was unpremeditated." The couple waited more than a year before having the first of their children.

The Heustons were highly educated and used their talents in support of community organizations, including the Boy Scouts, the arts, humanities, education, the local Shakespeare club, and nature conservancies. Whenever he could, Heuston boasted about Tacoma, as he did when he spoke at a 1922 convention, saying, "It is an excellent city, singularly endowed, of unusual loveliness, a youthful city—with the vigor, confidence and enthusiasm of youth—with a praiseworthy past and a brilliant future, a city of destiny."

His eloquent speech gave away the fact that he was also a writer. He kept a daily journal, interspersed with his poetry, written primarily for Slava, especially around Christmas. The previous Christmas he had written a poem entitled simply, *Christmas 1949*. His words captured the spirit of the season, "It seems an urgent human need when months have gone with selfish speed, When days are short and winds are raw, To slow our routine see and saw, And turn to friends and cheer to warm what's left to close the year." His sentiment may also have pertained to the close of life. He had recently been diagnosed with prostate cancer and doctors could do nothing for him. Before the Heustons had left on their trip—the first time that Benjamin would fly on an airplane—a friend joked about the dangers of flying. Although the couple already had a will, the friend's comments, and perhaps concern over his cancer, prompted him to contact his son Franklin to make some revisions to the document.

AS BONNIE ANN FELDMAN delivered the refreshments to her passengers, everyone settled in for the long flight. The few business travelers, including the four fashion buyers, flew often and were used to the routine. Three other business travelers, Dr. Leslie Anderson, Dr. Archibald Cardle, and Merle Barton, would not have been particularly fascinated with the journey. They all looked forward to getting home. All three would have carried leather bags with their instruments inside, but Barton's instruments were not scalpels and stethoscopes; he carried scissors and combs, the implements of a barber.

From Austin, Minnesota, beauty shop owner Merle Leroy Barton had just completed a two-week course at the Robert Fiance School of Beauty Culture in New York City. Barton's wife, Vanessa, and three-year-old daughter, Cathy, anxiously awaited his return. So, too, did his loyal clients at The Beauty Lounge; they looked forward to the new techniques he would be bringing back.

Dr. Archibald Cardle, 51, was returning to Minneapolis via New York from a meeting in Montreal, Canada, for the Northwestern National Life Insurance Company, where he served as assistant to Doctor Karl Anderson, the company's chief medical examiner. He and Anderson had tickets on separate flights, and at the last minute Anderson had offered to trade his ticket on Flight 2501 with Cardle so that Cardle could have a day at home before heading out again. On Sunday, Cardle and his wife, Edith, would be flying to San Francisco where he would attend the annual session of the house of delegates of the American Medical Association as the representative from Hennepin County, Minnesota. Unfortunately, it was too late for the airline to switch their luggage: Anderson's bags ended up on Flight 2501 and Cardle's bags were set aside for the next evening's flight. He had no time to inform his wife of the flight change. Cardle planned to surprise her at home.

All this travel was a far cry from the private practice that Cardle had run out of his home for years. His practice had gotten particularly busy, and he had done quite well financially during the war. Because of his poor eyesight, he could not be sent overseas and was among the few doctors still on the home front. This put pressure on Edith and the children, because one of them always had to be at home to take care of office duties and phone calls. They were able to handle it because they had a full-time maid and the latest in home technology, like an automatic washer and dryer. Working so much, though, left little time for Cardle to be an involved father, although he did set aside one day per month for a date with his daughter, Mary, and played with his son, John, and his train set on occasion. John planned to be a doctor just like his father.

Fifty-year-old Dr. Leslie Anderson, a radiologist who had been schooled at the University of Minneapolis, had been studying at Harvard University in Massachusetts since May. He had not intended to return on that flight, but his wife, also named Edith, heard that the position he had been seeking at the hospital in Yakima had just come available; he had to get home if he wished to be considered for the opening. He thought he had been lucky to get a seat with such short notice. Even though he would be returning home days earlier than planned, he would still not arrive in time to attend his son Robert's graduation from high school that night.

AS FLIGHT 2501 passed Phillipsburgh, Pennsylvania, and Robert Lind radioed his position to the Northwest Airlines' operator, Bonnie Ann Feldman opened the metal chests in the galley and began assembling the small snack trays. In addition to the drinks and snacks, she placed a small red, white, and blue cardboard packet with the Northwest Airlines logo on each tray. It contained three cigarettes that could be enjoyed during or after the refreshments. Then she walked aft and placed the trays on the pillow-covered laps of the two people at the rear and returned for the next two trays.

The Sunbury, Pennsylvania, checkpoint would have been well behind them when Feldman picked up the last of the trays. At that time, about 9:45 p.m.,

Julius Badner at the National Weather Service was busy analyzing the sequence reports from various stations and formulating his predictions for his 10:30 p.m. revised weather report. His forecast would be passed on to Northwest and all the other airlines for analysis. If there was anything new that affected his flight, Robert Lind depended upon his dispatcher to forward that information to him. Although the air was calm and the flight had been smooth thus far, he knew that things would deteriorate when he reached the airspace over Lake Michigan. A squall had been predicted, and he would have to keep his eye on the sky and his ears attuned for any new information about the weather.

After the refreshment service many of the passengers enjoyed their cigarettes, and the cabin filled with smoke. Only the scent of one particular woman's expensive perfume would have competed with the smell of the cigarettes. By then, Feldman had turned down the overhead lights. The married people traveling alone, who were used to having their spouses for companionship and conversation, probably found it rather lonely as the activity quieted down.

Leo Long, 57, of Worchester, Massachusetts, a former pilot during WWII and now a foreman in the drinking cup division of the U.S. Envelope Company, was en route to Seattle to visit his son Donald, his daughter-in-law, and his two grandchildren, whom he had not seen for four years. Then he would go on to Los Angeles to see his other son, Robert.

The rest of the married passengers traveling alone were women, most whose husbands had been unable to get away from work to join them.

Forty-nine-year-old Pearle Main of Spokane was returning home to her husband, Wayne, after a visit with the couple's only child, Kathleen, and her husband, Douglas Carter, in New Jersey.

Anna Nagel Eastman was going home to her husband, Whitney, a vice president at General Mills in Minneapolis, after a visit with her brother, E. H. Nagel, in the Bronx.

Sixty-four-year-old divorcee Eva Woolley of Minneapolis was traveling home after a six-week visit with her daughter, Jane, and her husband, Ralph C. Chase, and her grandsons, John and Steve, of Manhasset, New York.

Mary Miles Frost, 29, a secretary with the Electric Steel Foundry Company, was returning to Portland, Oregon, after a visit with her sister, Alice Bothwell, in Garden City, New Jersey.

Nora Hughes of New York City was on her way to Seattle to visit her daughter, Alice Donovan, and her baby grandson Michael.

Fifty-four-year-old Evelyn Woolpy Heenan, an experienced secretary from New York City, was on her way to Minneapolis, where she had grown up, to spend time with her parents, sisters, and niece. It was just as well that her husband, Bill, whom she had married later in life, did not join her. Her parents were Russian Jews, and even though they were secular, they had never approved of her marriage to a Catholic.

AT ABOUT 10:20 P.M., Flight 2501 crossed over Pennsylvania into Ohio. The pilots checked in with the Northwest Airlines' radio operator at Youngstown, Ohio, at the state's eastern border. All would have been quiet at that point, many of the passengers having already dozed off. Dorothy Jean Kaufmann may have remained awake pondering her life. Over the last two months she had gotten used to being away from her husband, Winfield, and children, but now that she was on her way home, she may have used the dimness and quiet to retreat into thoughts of them. It would have been the first real solitude she had experienced since her trip began in April. She had just returned to the United States on the *Queen Mary* ahead of her two traveling companions after visiting England, Holland, Belgium, Germany, and Switzerland with them. She had been booked on the Thursday evening flight, but when she got to the air terminal at 42nd Street in Manhattan, the agent told her they had pushed up the time of the flight and had not been able to reach her. Instead they had moved her to the Friday evening flight. Kaufmann would now be arriving home on Saturday, and the reality of her life would soon be setting in.

At 42 years old, Kaufmann had three young children waiting at home for her: William, 6, Richard, 3, and her adorable baby girl Mary Jean, 2. Like so many women in the postwar years, she had married and started a family later in life; getting married and having babies right away had not been her priority. Her grandmother and aunts, with whom she had been raised, had been suffragettes, and Kaufmann had been raised to think of herself as an independent, self-sufficient woman. She planned a career and eventually graduated from the University of Washington, then did postgraduate studies at Columbia University to obtain a master's degree. Although her career as a teacher was interrupted by the War when she did office work for the Navy, she taught for many years at Bremerton High School, just west across Puget Sound from Seattle.

Since becoming a mother, Kaufmann had given up teaching, but served as the volunteer vice president of the Seattle Day Nursery Association. Being a stay-at-home wife and mother had been frustrating. She loved her children very much and felt it her duty to care for them at home, but did not feel challenged in her life. Although she did secretarial work for her husband in the wholesale seed and garden supply company that he had recently established, she had not been given a paycheck, and her husband's tight control of the purse strings was difficult for her to get used to. He would often get angry when she bought something that he felt was unnecessary because he had been trying to pay off the house and put money in the bank. She had been considering going back to work once her youngest child was in school but had not yet brought that up with her husband Winfield.

Beside his stranglehold on the money, Winfield's complete aversion to religion disturbed her. She was trying to raise the children as Christians at the First Congregational Church of Seattle, and he continually undermined that with derogatory comments.

Kaufmann was well aware that her husband had suffered a difficult upbringing. Winfield's own father had been abusive, often hitting him without warning or explanation, and his mother was worse than his father. Kaufmann had observed her mother-in-law threaten her oldest son William, when he was a toddler, saying, "If you touch it, I will cut your finger off."

That had sent Winfield into a screaming rage, which Kaufmann considered justified, but his angry outburst surprised her. Lately she had seen him doing that more often over less important issues. Winfield once told her that the only other woman who ever loved him was his aunt, who provided what his own mother did not. Kaufmann felt tremendous compassion for her husband because of this, but the finances and his explosions had to change. The two months away from him in Europe had been her first step in reasserting some independence. Her friends Eve Grant and Adelaide Alexander had suggested the trip, and Kaufmann agreed to go.

From the moment she had told her husband of her plans, he tried to change her mind. She had countered by reminding him that her teaching work had funded his new business, and now she was entitled to a vacation. When his first attempts to derail the trip didn't work, he told her that flying was too dangerous. "Oh, Windy," she replied, putting off his attempt to scare her, "flying is perfectly safe now."

Jean Kaufmann lined up a maid to take care of the house and the children while she was gone, and she made her reservations through the Where-To-Go Travel Bureau. However, Winfield had kept up his protests. On the day of her departure, with no excuses left, he had tried putting his foot down by saying, "I just don't want you to go Jean!"

She had simply replied, "I'm going and that's that."

Once she arrived in Europe, she learned that her husband had dismissed the maid she had hired.

The trip had given her a much needed perspective on her life and her relationship with her husband, and she was ready for the discussion she intended to have with him as soon as she arrived home Saturday morning.

AS FLIGHT 2501 APPROACHED CLEVELAND at about 10:45 p.m. at 6,000 feet, Captain Robert Lind and Verne Wolfe would have been considering the weather, of particular concern since they were getting closer to the forecasted squall line and the much lower cloud cover. Even before takeoff, Lind had requested a cruising altitude of 4,000 feet to keep below the clouds, but his request had been denied due to other traffic at that altitude. Perhaps by the time he reached Cleveland, the other traffic would have passed. At 10:49 p.m. he tuned his radio to the company frequency at Cleveland to initiate his radio check and request, "Cleveland. Two five zero one."

Rick Cochran, the Northwest Airline operator on duty at Cleveland that night, heard the pilot calling on the company frequency. Cochran had been working for Northwest for about nine months. He had already packed a lot into his 23 short years. During summers while attending high school in Harvey, Illinois, he had sailed on Great Lakes ore carriers as an ordinary seaman, while hoping he might one day train to be a pilot. Instead, the war intervened, and Cochran enlisted in the U.S. Army Signal Corp, becoming a radio operator in the South Pacific. After his service, his yearnings for aviation resurfaced, but not as a pilot. He attended Central Radio School in Kansas City and received his second-class radiotelephone and radiotelegraph licenses and a flight radio officer's certificate, desiring to work for an airline. After an unsuccessful trip to New York to find employment, he settled in Cleveland and began his job hunt with the phone book in hand, calling airlines in alphabetical order, American, Braniff, Capitol, and so on. It took until September 1949, when he got to the "N"s, before he found an opening. Northwest Airlines interviewed him the next day and put him to work in the radio room that very same day. Since then, Cochran had been working the swing shift. On June 23, he had come on duty at 4 p.m., taking over for a buddy who had worked the prior eight-hour shift.

Northwest's radio room at the Cleveland Municipal Airport was located through a pair of doors behind the airline's ticket counter. Although much bigger than a cockpit, his work station had some similarities to one. He sat in command on a caster chair at his console station with a transmitter, radio receiver, clock, altimeter, boom microphone, a foot switch to key the remote transmitter, a telephone to the Air Traffic Control Center, and a mill, which is a typewriter-like device, all within easy reach. Nearby two teletype machines were always in use, one to receive the weather and the other to communicate back and forth with other Northwest offices. A speaker on the radio receiver allowed Cochran to move around the room without missing any incoming transmissions. At times of severe static or other reception problems, he had the option of plugging in the headphones, which muted the speaker, making the communications sound a bit sharper.

A few minutes before Lind hailed the Cleveland station, Cochran had heard the bell ring on the National Weather Bureau teletype machine, and the keys began to move as if an invisible typist sat there. The most current terminal forecasts and sequence reports began to print out on the teletype in Cochran's office as well as at dozens of other similar offices throughout the region—all at the same time. The ability to quickly and efficiently send out the same data to so many stations had only been possible for a little over a decade. Not until 1938 did the Department of Commerce establish the teletype network that linked the National Weather Service, airway traffic control centers, radio range stations, and military air bases. Prior to this time, only a party-line telephone circuit connected them.

When the teletype finished printing, Cochran ripped the paper off the feed and carefully went over the weather reports. The information came out looking like hieroglyphics, but Cochran, as well as meteorologists and flight dispatchers, could easily interpret it. As a company radio operator, he had the discretion to contact any flights within his range if he felt the information would be pertinent. That night, he did not have to initiate contact with Flight 2501 because the pilot had already contacted him. Cochran heard some static over the speaker, so he immediately put on his headphones and hit the foot switch to engage him. "Two five zero one. Cleveland. Go ahead."

"Two five zero one over Cleveland at 49 (the minutes after the hour)," the pilot advised. "Request descent from six to four thousand."

Cochran did not need the pilot to tell him the reason for the request. The sequence reports indicated a number of active thunderstorms in the region. Visibility was minimal, and the clouds were low. The pilot obviously wanted to fly under the weather. He acknowledged, "Two five zero one requesting descent from six to four thousand. Stand by."

He disengaged the foot switch, dropped his headset to his shoulders, and while continuing to monitor the radio on speaker, picked up the telephone at his right elbow. This was a hotline connected directly to Air Traffic Control, located elsewhere at the Cleveland airport, which had been tracking the flight and would continue to do so until handing over the responsibility to ATC in Chicago as the flight neared Lake Michigan. An ATC controller picked up the phone in a second or two and said, "ATC Cleveland."

"Northwest two five zero one over Cleveland request descent from six to four thousand," Cochran said.

The controller responded, repeating the request, then said, "Stand by."

As Flight 2501 continued flying west, Cochran typed up notes about the conversation and waited for the response from ATC. It would have taken ATC less than a minute to respond: "Northwest two five oh one cleared to descend to and maintain four thousand." Then the controller signed off with his initials.

Cochran replied, repeating the approval, then closed with "RC." He hit the foot switch which activated the remote transmitter to reconnect with the flight and said, "Two five zero one. Cleveland."

Robert Lind replied, "Two five zero one, go ahead."

"Two five zero one is cleared to descend to and maintain four thousand."

"Understand two five zero one is cleared to descend to and maintain four thousand," Lind acknowledged, "Descending at 52."

Before disengaging the call with the pilot, Cochran quickly tapped the altimeter on his console with his finger to assure a good setting and checked the barometric pressure. Regulations required him to advise any flight changing altitude of the current reading so the pilot could adjust his altimeter to assure consistent height above sea level. "Roger. Cleveland. Kollsman two nine nine one, that's two niner niner one."

Kollsman referred to the "Kollsman Window," the nickname for the manual barometric pressure setting adjustment indicator invented by German immigrant Paul Kollsman, founder of Kollsman Instruments.

Lind acknowledged, "Two five zero one, Roger. Kollsman two niner niner one," as he adjusted the altimeter on his instrument panel, thereby assuring correct altitude above sea level. Cochran ended the call by saying, "Cleveland."

Following protocol, Cochran typed up a summary of the various conversations within one section of the continuous perforated paper on the mill, noting that the entire communication from the flight's initial call to the last transmission took less than four minutes:

CLE   62350
2249   2501 OV CLE 49 REQST DECN TO 4 FROM 6 THSND
CLE   2501 REQST DECN TO 4 FROM 6 THSND STNDBY
2250   NW2501 REQSTG DECN FM 6 TO 4 THSND MAINTN 4
2251   ATC CLRS NW2501 DECND FM 6 TO 4 THSND MAINTN 4

```
        THSND  DW
CLE     R NW 2501 CLRD FM 6 THSND TO 4 THSND MAINTN 4
        THSND RC
2252    CLE 2501 CLRD FM 6 THSND TO 4 THSND MAINTN 4
        THSND
2252    2501 R LVG 6 AT 53.
CLE     R CLE K 2991
2253    2501 R CLE K 2991
        RC 2253
```

When he finished his summary, he reached up and deposited it in a clear plastic slot in a wooden message rack at the upper right side of his console, reserved for any future contacts with that flight. The next operator who came on duty at midnight would file those slips at two or three in the morning, when there was little traffic, as a permanent record of the radio activity that night.

AS LIND BEGAN his descent he adjusted the radio receiver frequency to the Sandusky, Ohio, radio range station, his next checkpoint.

Meanwhile, Donald Wertz, the Northwest meteorologist, was busy analyzing the 10:30 p.m. National Weather Service forecast prepared by Julius Badner that came through on the teletype circuit. The forecast would take effect at 11 p.m. to cover the areas of southern Wisconsin, Michigan, Illinois, Indiana, Ohio, and Kentucky. In part, it read:

"...Clouds and weather: Widespread, base 2500 broken, variable, overcast top 4000 with another layer base 5000 to 7000 overcast, top 15,000 to 30,000 and higher. Visibility 1 mile in heavy thunderstorms with wind northwest, 30 miles per hour with strong gusts along south boundary of thunderstorm area. Developing a squall line moving southward over lower Michigan, north and central portions of Illinois, Indiana and Ohio, into the central portions of Indiana, Illinois and Ohio by 11:00 a.m. (on the 24th) ...Turbulence and thunderstorms south of the front, severe in squall line along the south edge of thunderstorm area, southern Wisconsin, lower Michigan and north and central portions of Illinois, Indiana and Ohio."

Wertz had his hands full trying to keep up with the new information and interpret what it meant to the flights for which he was responsible. Six hours earlier the National Weather Service had predicted thunderstorms for the evening, but did not predict a squall. However, his colleague Beresford had interpreted the information and told all Northwest flights, including 2501, to expect an eastward-moving squall line. Now, the Weather Service acknowledged that, in fact, a squall line had formed but indicated that it was moving south. After analyzing the hourly sequence reports since he came on duty, Wertz was not convinced there really was a squall line—only isolated thunderstorms. He read through all the individual station sequence reports and calculated that the storms had been moving at about 11 miles per hour. Extrapolating that data, he predicted that thunderstorm activity would still be north of Airway Red 57 when Flight 2501 crossed the lake, and so would not cause the flight any problems.

He consulted with George Benson, the flight superintendent now on duty in Minneapolis, who in turn spoke to flight dispatcher Warren Seifert at LaGuardia, who had recently taken over for Richard Miller at the shift change. Both Benson and Seifert thought it prudent not to relay that information to Flight 2501 because it might cause Robert Lind to let down his guard. Instead, they jointly decided to let the 4:45 p.m. forecast stand.

AS THE FLIGHT PASSED CLEVELAND, all four of the children on the flight would have been fast asleep. Little Dana Malby probably cuddled in his mother's arms. Janice Hokanson would have already kicked off her red sandals, clutched her baby doll, and leaned up against her mother's shoulder. Her brother Tommy perhaps slept with his head in his father's lap, a row behind his mother and sister. Likewise, eight-year-old John Schafer probably had fallen asleep resting against his mother.

At 17, Barbara Freng was one year from adulthood and more mature than most girls her age. She had been fending off boys for several years. Her gorgeous good looks and long blond hair attracted the boys, and her intelligence and wit kept them interested. But for the last year, she only had eyes for Howie Bill, whom she had met through her brother-in-law, Dick, Howie's fraternity brother at the Massachusetts Institute of Technology. For the last few months she had been hoping he would propose.

Twenty-one-year-old Ellen Ross, a general duty nurse employed at Passaic Hospital in New Jersey, was also awaiting a proposal from her boyfriend, Allen, back home in Clifton, New Jersey. Maybe her time away that summer would convince him that he could not live without her. Ross was on her way to visit a former classmate in Minneapolis, then to spend the rest of the summer with her aunt and uncle in Livingston, Montana. Her mother had suggested Ellen take a train instead, but when she saw how excited her daughter had been about this, her first airplane trip, she acquiesced. Ross planned to begin classes for her master's degree in the fall.

Another woman on the flight, 24-year-old Mary Keating of Queens, New York, would have been dreaming about her upcoming wedding. She was en route to meet her fiancé, Alan Baron, who would be picking her up at the airport in Minneapolis. From there they would drive to Pine City, where she would meet his parents for the first time. Keating and her fiancé had met at a club in Queens near where she worked as an associate editor of the Ideal Publishing Company. Ever since then, Alan and sometimes a few of his housemates had been joining her and her four siblings at her parents' house for big family dinners.

Looking dashing in his Army uniform, Richard Goldsbury, 21, a private first class, carried a ring in his pocket, intending to ask for his sweetheart's hand in marriage back at home in Milton-Freewater, Oregon. Goldsbury was on a 30-day leave from his unit stationed in New Jersey, and would spend time with his parents as well as his girlfriend and her parents. He was one of those sons that parents dream of having—good grades, never in trouble, and devoted to his mom and dad. Undoubtedly, he had a similar devotion to his soon-to-be fiancée.

While Keating and Goldsbury would have been looking forward to their new lives, 30-year-old Louise Sophia Spohn may have been lamenting hers. She was on her way to the annual meeting with her Christian Scientist teacher in St. Paul. Although she would have looked forward to the session to further her spiritual growth, she had been longing to meet a man to share her life with. A pretty blond with an infectious smile, Spohn did not have difficulty meeting men, but her faith mandated that she find someone who reflected the qualities indicated by the seven synonymous terms for God. So far, no one with those qualities lit her fire, and she had begun to fear she might never meet the right man.

For now, she had her work. An art director at an advertising agency in New York, a position that she had been promoted to several years after her graduation from Cooper Union, Spohn had already broken through the glass ceiling that held some women back. While she made a salary that most women could never dream of, she knew that most men received more for the same position. However, money did not motivate her; family did, and when her parents needed a house, she was glad her financial success allowed her to buy them one. On the outside, it appeared that Louise Spohn had it all—even her watercolors were on exhibit at several galleries—but her work often reflected her longings. In a recent illustration for her client, perfume manufacturer

Prince Matchabelli, she drew a woman in the style of a sensuous Gibson Girl, but placed her in a kitchen wearing an apron. Drawing her own features on the woman was not a coincidence.

Spohn probably took notice of one of the most handsome men on the flight, Ralph Olsen. The strapping man of Norwegian descent lived with his parents in the Westerleigh neighborhood on Staten Island in New York, where he settled temporarily after returning from the war in England. The 25-year-old now worked for the American Steel and Wire Company and had just graduated from Wagner College in New York with a business degree. If either Spohn or Olsen had eyes for each other, they might have managed to sit together. If they conversed, she would have learned that Olsen was also on a pilgrimage to a church conference in Minneapolis, where he would be joined by his sister and brother-in-law, a minister. He, like Spohn, was a devout believer; however, he belonged to the Lutheran Church, which Spohn would have realized was much different from the Church of Christ, Scientist.

Several other single people on board the flight were all traveling to see members of their families.

Former Army Major Richard Wyatt Thomson, 35, of New York City, worked for the New York Life Insurance Company and served as a research director of the Citizens Budget Commission, a nonprofit civic organization. He was on his way to Spokane to visit his father, Francis, who was dying of pancreatic cancer. The apple of his father's eye, Richie had been adopted at the hospital soon after his mother lost her new born baby from spina bifida.

William Reid, 43 years old, had his summer free, having just completed the school year teaching at the Packard Commercial School on Lexington Avenue in New York and taking classes for his doctoral degree at New York University. He would be spending several weeks in Tacoma with his mother and two brothers.

Miriam Frankel, originally of Latrobe, Pennsylvania, was an aspiring interior designer who held a bachelor of science in general studies from the Carnegie Institute of Technology. She was now interning as a secretary for an interior designer in New York, and was traveling to Minneapolis on vacation.

Twenty-year-old Hildegard Hovan of Long Island, New York, the youngest of four children, was on her way to Oregon to visit her family.

Francis McNickle, 49, was returning to Huron, South Dakota, following a visit to Alderkill Camp in Rhinebeck, New York.

Helen Mary Meyer, 23, a receptionist from New Jersey, was on her way to Livingston, Montana to visit relatives.

Sixty-two-year-old widow Hilma Larson, whose husband had died a year earlier fighting a brush fire, was en route to Spokane for a vacation with her 27-year-old cousin, Ruth Johnson, who was returning to Spokane after a vacation in New York.

Sixty-seven-year-old Marie Rorabaugh from Philadelphia was used to traveling alone. Widowed for many years after her second husband's death from a heart attack, Daisy, as she was called, threw all her energies into her family. She was en route to Seattle, where her only daughter, Helen, was due to give birth soon. Helen would pick her up from the airport and take her to her home in Richmond, Washington. Rorabaugh planned to stay for the delivery and through Christmas to help her daughter with her other children, as she had done for the birth of each of her grandchildren, including those of her two sons still living on the East Coast. She had been a doting and helpful grandmother, sewing clothes for the children and helping her children's families in any way that she could.

Creativity ran through Rorabaugh's veins. She had attended the Philadelphia Academy of Fine Arts, but her first marriage had derailed her career in art. Then after her divorce in the 1930s, she remarried. By the time her second husband died, she was too set in her ways to consider a career. She used her artistic abilities only for projects for her children and grandchildren.

On this trip, she carried a considerable amount of cash in her purse to get through the year. Her son, John, and his wife, Gertrude, who had driven her to the airport, were worried about her losing it. She also carried all of her jewelry in a chamois bag, which she planned to give to her daughter. She thought it best for her daughter to enjoy it now rather than wait until her passing. She probably sat clutching her bags, remembering having been admonished by her son for carrying such valuables.

AT 11:02 P.M., ROBERT LIND heard nothing in his headsets, which signaled his passing over Sandusky, Ohio. Visibility was good and he could see the lights from the small city meeting the darkness that represented Lake Erie. He initiated his check call: "Cleveland. Two five zero one."

Once again, radio operator Rick Cochran responded: "Two five zero one. Cleveland."

"Cleveland. Over Sandusky at 02. 4000 feet. Estimate Toledo at 16," Captain Lind said.

"Roger. Over Sandusky at 02. Estimating Toledo at 16. Cleveland."

Fourteen minutes later, Lind again reported in to Cleveland, indicating Flight 2501 was over Toledo at 11:16 p.m. and expected to arrive at Battle Creek, its next checkpoint, at 11:51 p.m.

When his radio receiver went silent again at about 11:40 p.m., Lind realized that the airplane had entered the cone of silence over the Litchfield, Michigan, radio range station that indicated they had just passed from Ohio into the state of Michigan on the way toward Lake Michigan. The pilots might have known that Michigan had been named after the Ojibwa word, *mishigamaa*, meaning "large water." Indeed, Michigan abuts four of the five Great Lakes, contains almost 65,000 inland lakes and ponds, and, claims more shoreline than any other state. However, if Alaska, the key strategic military base during World War II where Lind and Wolfe had both flown during their time in the Army Air Corps, ever became a state, as was currently being considered, it would surpass Michigan in coastline miles.

They knew that Michigan's Lower Peninsula is shaped like a mitten. In fact, Michiganders often hold up a right hand, palm up, to illustrate the state's shape. Lake Erie begins at the juncture of the thumb and the wrist, Lake Huron surrounds the thumb and right side of the index finger, and Lake Michigan runs along the pinky side. The Upper Peninsula, often referred to as "the U.P.," is separated from the Lower Peninsula by the Straits of Mackinac, a five-mile channel that joins Lake Huron and Lake Michigan at the tip of the middle finger. A network of ferry boats ran regularly to transport people across the Straits, although there was talk of building a five-mile-long bridge to connect the two peninsulas. Flight 2501 entered Michigan at the base of the mitten, approximately where the typical life line on the palm meets the wrist.

To the east of the airplane's flight path, Detroit had been a hub of airplane production during World War II, as an outgrowth of the auto industry that began in the 1910s and had grown to define the state. When the demand for airplane production rose because of the war, the government prevailed upon Henry Ford, the founder of the Ford Motor Company, to accept a contract to build B-24 Liberator heavy bombers. Ford built a massive manufacturing complex on a large plot of land he owned in Ypsilanti, about 30 miles west of Detroit, called Willow Run Farm. The new plant, called Willow Run, became the largest factory anywhere in the world. The plant built 8,700 Liberators and employed some 42,000 people, including Rose Will Monroe, who became the personification of the fictional "Rosie the Riveter," made iconic by the 1942 song of the same name. At that time, the U.S. Army took over the Wayne County Airport at Detroit as a staging base for transport of the aircraft to Europe.

After the war, Willow Run had been converted into a luxury passenger terminal called the Willow Run Airport, out of which Northwest Airlines flew regularly, and where the company maintained a radio office to communicate with flights over lower Michigan.

Michigan's terrain and weather became a concern for Lind and Wolfe as they entered that state. The Lower Peninsula is generally level, broken by small hills and moraines usually not more than a few hundred feet tall. The general elevation of the state differs by only a few feet. The lowest point is the surface of Lake Erie at 571 feet, and the terrain rises gradually to Lake Michigan, at 577 feet. Generally, Michigan is considered to be at about 600 feet above sea level. Of significant interest to the pilots of Flight 2501 was that Michigan averages 30 days of thunderstorm activity per year, the most severe in the southern part of the state. True to the statistics, June was dishing up one of its very common storms that night.

WHEN FLIGHT 2501 was between Litchfield and Battle Creek, Captain Norman Mitchell, flying a corporate Lockheed Lodestar east on Red 57 over Lake Michigan, contacted his company's radio operator at Milwaukee behind him to relay his current situation to Air Traffic Control. He was at that time experiencing turbulence causing him to lose as much as 500 feet in altitude. ATC checked the board, and moved the shrimp boat that represented the Lodestar out over the lake. The controller took note of Flight 2501 at 4,000 feet over south central Michigan on Red 57 and quickly saw a potential problem. The two airplanes would meet somewhere near Battle Creek. Because of the reported turbulence, they might not be able to maintain the required 1,000-foot safety separation.

That controller would have been aware of the tragic accident that took place in Kentucky in July 1943. American Airlines Flight 63, using a DC-3, left Louisville, Kentucky, at about 10:00 p.m. for Nashville, Tennessee, and flew through a thunderstorm at 2,000 feet. The terrain in places rises up 700 feet above sea level, and despite the airplane holding at 1,300 feet above the ground, severe turbulence slammed it down into the treetops. Twenty of the 22 people on board perished. The controller knew well that turbulence in a thunderstorm can rise up like a giant and swat down an airplane. He would not take any chances with the Lodestar and Flight 2501 being too near each other.

Through a radio operator, the air traffic controller informed the Lodestar to maintain 5,000, then disengaged and telephoned the Northwest operator at Detroit's Willow Run Airport, the nearest Northwest operator to the current location of Flight 2501.

At 11:27 p.m. Holland Krotz picked up the ringing telephone. "Detroit."

Krotz operated out of Northwest's radio room in Detroit, a set up similar to the one at Cleveland. It, too, was located behind the Northwest ticket counter inside the terminal, and Krotz had an array of equipment nearly identical to Rick Cochran's. He also worked the same swing shift as Cochran and had similar training, although he had been on the job for about 14 years.

"ATC Cleveland. Contact flight two five oh one to descend to 3,500," the controller told him.

Krotz acknowledged the request, put on his headset, and hailed Flight 2501.He heard the familiar voice of Robert Lind answer. "Two five zero one. Detroit, go ahead."

Krotz had spoken to Lind on several dozen occasions, but there could be no pleasantries over the radio. He informed Lind of the need to descend to 3,500 feet. Lind did not question why. He knew that, like a puppeteer, Air Traffic Control could "see" almost everything from above, and he trusted that the controllers pulled the proper "strings." He knew that with Michigan at 600 feet above sea level, the lower altitude would put the flight about 2,900 feet above the ground and the surface of Lake Michigan.

"Detroit two five zero one. Descending to three thousand five hundred at 29," Lind said as he pushed the wheel forward at 11:29 p.m.

Krotz read off the Kollsman reading and Lind adjusted his altimeter. Then Lind tuned back to the frequency at the Battle Creek radio range station and continued flying northwest. Krotz typed up his record of the communication.

Within just a few minutes, Krotz heard the bell from the Weather Service teletype alerting him that the hourly-on-the-half-hour terminal forecasts had arrived along with sequence reports providing the current weather observations. He swiveled around and began reading the text as it printed, then after it stopped he tore off the paper and began digesting the information. The terminal forecasts provided predictions for what would occur at 18 airports in the region. From the hieroglyphics, he would have seen a pattern of thunderstorm activity moving south and southeastward in Illinois and Michigan. The forecasts indicated that at a number of airports in northern Illinois and southern Michigan, the cloud base would drop briefly to 1,000 feet. To the trained radio operator, the low cloud base meant that a squall line would be overhead at that time. Rain would be heavy, winds would be high, and lightning would be frequent. His analysis was interrupted by the sound of Captain Lind's voice hailing him at 11:40 p.m.

This time, Lind requested the current weather at Milwaukee, Madison, and Minneapolis. Krotz realized that the pilot was trying to anticipate conditions at those cities along his flight path after he passed over Lake Michigan. He scrolled down the long teletype sheet and came to the sequence reports for the requested cities and read them off. "Milwaukee ceiling 4,500 scattered 1,000, thunderstorms, lightning in all quadrants. Madison ceiling

14,000 overcast, 6,500 lower scattered, light rain, lightning east occasionally. Minneapolis clear."

These little bits of information gave Lind an immediate visual image of what to expect along his path. The storm, he would have pictured, was still raging at Milwaukee, petering out 75 miles farther west at Madison, and long since passed at Minneapolis. It would have seemed to Lind that the squall line was indeed moving east just as Beresford had predicted four hours earlier when Flight 2501 left New York. In his mind's eye, he might have pictured the squall line running north and south down Lake Michigan like the defensive players of a football team lined up between his current position and the goal line at Milwaukee. Like a quarterback, he would have to plan how to get past the line. However, unlike a quarterback, he was essentially blind; he would not be able to see what the defensive line was doing.

Had Lind requested the weather for cities in Michigan or Illinois, or had Krotz offered up that information, Lind would have realized that the squall line was at that time 400 miles long and running in a northeast to southwest direction. Thunderstorms were currently raging at Bay City, Michigan, and many more thunderstorms formed a semi-continuous line from there southwest through the state to Holland, Michigan, at the lakeshore and across the lake to the border dividing Wisconsin from Illinois. The squall line had been shifting and evolving; the reports now indicated it was moving south, not east as forecasted earlier, and at a much faster speed than either the Weather Service or the Northwest meteorologists had predicted.

AT 11:51 P.M. SILENCE in Lind's and Wolfe's headsets told them they had reached a point over Battle Creek. For the tenth time that evening, Robert Lind initiated contact to report his position, hailing Detroit again, since Northwest did not have a radio operator at the Battle Creek radio range station. "Two five zero one. Detroit. Over Battle Creek at 51 at three thousand five hundred. Estimating Milwaukee at 37."

Holland Krotz at Detroit acknowledged the call, typed up the report, and sent a message on the Northwest teletype system indicating the radio operator at Milwaukee should expect Flight 2501 to check in at 11:37 p.m. CST—a critical time since Flight Superintendent George Benson in Minneapolis would take over management of the flight from Warren Seifert at LaGuardia, and Chicago ATC would take over from Cleveland ATC.

Immediately after the radio call to Detroit, Lind would have tuned his radio receiver to try to pick up the frequency emitted by the radio range station at Milwaukee, 150 miles distant. If he followed his prescribed flight plan, he would be on the ground at Minneapolis in just a little more than two hours. There, a fresh crew would relieve him and continue to Seattle, and he could make it home, looked in on his new baby, and climb into bed with his wife by about 2:30 a.m. Minneapolis time.

At the same time as Flight 2501 passed Battle Creek at 11:52 p.m., a Capital Airlines DC-4, piloted by Captain Charles Renn, was bumping and gyrating its way across Lake Michigan on Red 57. Renn carried only freight. He had taken off from Milwaukee for LaGuardia Airport at 11:35 p.m., about 30 minutes behind the Lodestar on the same flight path, and reached his 5,000-foot cruising altitude as he headed east across the lake at 11:45 p.m. Dispatchers considered Renn a daredevil to take off in the thunderstorm because he had the option to wait out the storm. However, Renn did this kind of thing all the time. He recognized that a squall line is made up of individual cells of thunderstorms that can be spaced several miles apart. He could fly his way carefully through them like a soldier making his way through an enemy minefield. However, once Renn was about 30 miles off shore, he may have thought twice about his decision. Individual storms were hard to recognize when cloud-to-cloud lightning connected them. The moisture droplets in the clouds reflected all of the light, and it often appeared that the entire sky was illuminated, hiding any clear path through the squall. Renn tightened his grip on the wheel, took a deep breath, and continued eastward.

By midnight, the Lockheed Lodestar that had preceded Captain Renn on Red 57 had already made it across the lake and was nearing Battle Creek when it passed 1,500 feet above and south of Flight 2501. If the weather allowed, one or both of the pilots might have seen the lights of the other airplane. In fact, it is quite possible that Captain Mitchell did see Lind's airplane because coincidentally, moments after the two planes passed each other, Mitchell initiated a radio call to the CAA operator at Battle Creek to make a pilot report of the moderate to severe turbulence over Lake Michigan. He instructed the radio operator to relay his report to FAWS, the Flight Advisory Weather Service. FAWS served as an adjunct service to Air Traffic Control to distribute pilot reports via teletype to all the airlines so that they could warn pilots flying in the area. Unfortunately, because of an equipment failure, FAWS never received Mitchell's warning and consequently neither did Northwest Airlines or Flight 2501. However, by midnight Robert Lind and Verne Wolfe were approaching the lakeshore, hearing the static in their headphones that signaled bad weather and feeling the turbulence. So, too, were their passengers.

Chapter 10

TOWARD DESTINY

As Northwest Flight 2501 continued toward its destiny, life along the lakeshore in southwest Michigan carried on as usual for a Friday night in June. The temperature that day had been in the high 80s and the evening brought little respite. Humidity was still extremely high, frizzing the hair of those prone to that. People would have had their windows open, but anyone who had seen the local papers that day knew they would soon be forced to close them when a cold front and rain hit later in the evening. At least there would be some relief from the heat. Like any Friday night, some people had gone to bed early, others were at home relaxing after a long week of work, still others were out enjoying the start of the weekend, and night shift workers were on the job. Many of those people would, in just a few minutes, have an encounter with an airplane that would remain etched in their minds for the rest of their lives.

Men who had gotten together for a game of cards or a drink at a local watering hole probably raved about the game at Briggs Stadium in Detroit earlier that day. The hometown Tigers increased their lead in the American League to two full games with a 10 to 9 win over the Yankees in a ball game that featured a Major League Baseball record of 11 home runs.

More than 3,500 people had attended the first annual Strawberry Festival that had opened the previous day in St. Joseph and would run through the weekend. Located at the Silver Beach Amusement Park, the event featured strawberries grown by area farmers and preserves made by local housewives. The Smoky Mountain Singers had performed that Friday evening.

Many people spent Friday evening reading the St. Joseph *Herald-Press*, the Benton Harbor *News Palladium*, or the *South Haven Tribune*, the biggest publications in southwestern Michigan. Many would have taken an interest in the front-page story in the *News Palladium*. Ninety members of the Benton Harbor and St. Joseph Chamber of Commerce had boarded the huge passenger steamer SS *City of Cleveland III* for its annual meeting cruise to Detroit. The story foreshadowed events to come and a building cold front when it reported fog and heavy lake swells that made the vessel five hours overdue at Mackinac Island.

Sobering news in all the local papers reminded readers that although the war was over, military men were still in harm's way. A United States B-29 bomber stationed on Guam crashed into the sea about 140 miles off the island after a practice bombing run to Okinawa. The Navy was able to locate eight of the 11-man crew, but it could not find the airplane or three crew members who were presumed dead.

Friday night offered a great lineup of prime time shows for anyone who had a console television, a luxury that cost somewhere between $175 and $250—at least as much as a refrigerator, if not more. In those booming postwar years with little unemployment, people were spending on non-necessities, and televisions ranked high on their wish lists. In fact, it seemed that in the not too distant future almost everyone would own one. By June 1950, some six or seven million households, about 14% of the population, had already invested in a television set, about half as many as owned automobiles.

Among the four networks, ABC, CBS, NBC and the Dumont Television Network, viewers in Southwest Michigan had a number of programs to choose from. On Friday, June 23, 1950, most television watchers, whether they had kids or not, tuned in to *Kukla, Fran and Ollie,* a puppet show that aired at 6:00 p.m. starring Burr Tillstrom and Fran Allison. Originally created for children, adults became fans when they realized that the entire show was ad-libbed. Most found it hysterical. Kids may have preferred *Fun House* or the new show featuring a prankish gang, *The Little Rascals.*

Game show fans had to decide between *Quiz Kids* or *20 Questions* at 7:00 p.m. Handymen, or those who wanted to be, could have watched *Walt's Workshop* at 7:30. Though tedious, Walt was funny just because he was so boring, but his tips were generally useful. The frantic theme song of *Man Against Crime,* during which viewers watched the opening sequence of a man running down a deserted street while being chased by a black car, probably stole a lot of viewers away from Walt. Most people knew that show by its more recognizable name: *Follow That Man* starring Ralph Bellamy as private eye Mike Barnett. For simpler entertainment—the kind most people preferred— many tuned into *Ernie Simon,* a variety show hosted by the musician and comedian, at 10:00 p.m.

News at the top of each hour broadcast the most important local and world events. Of particular interest to many was the "cold war" scare escalating overseas. That day in the Senate, members had opened debate on a $1,222,500,000 second-year installment of military aid to free nations fighting communism. The measure was certain to pass according to the reporters covering the story. Of particular concern were the pleas made by South Korea's President Syngman Rhee for support from the United States for his country's American-trained, 100,000-man army daily fighting back communist guerrilla attacks from the north. Rhee made it clear that his army was prepared to fight on the side of the western democracy.

Sports fans undoubtedly watched *The Gillette Cavalcade of Sports* at 9:00 p.m., followed by *The Greatest Fights*, a boxing show, at 10:00. By the time Flight 2501 had reached a point halfway between Battle Creek, Michigan, and the lakeshore, the 10:30 p.m. movie and the local weather were just ending, and all the networks would sign off at midnight. That evening, no one needed a reporter to tell them that a storm was on the way—the rumbling of distant thunder had already been delivering that news.

For those without television sets in southwest Michigan—and there were many—the radio would have provided their source for entertainment that Friday night. The news and weather had aired early and again later in the evening. Many people listened to *Ozzy and Harriet, MGM Theater, Jimmy Durante, Doris Day, The Lone Ranger*, or *The Cisco Kid* in the early evening. *The Life of Riley*, starring William Bendix, was a favorite at 9:00 p.m. on WMAQ. Word had recently leaked that a comedian who played Riley for a short time before Bendix, would be taking over as host of the television variety show *Cavalcade of Stars*. Jackie Gleason was among the many radio personalities who were making the transition to television.

Music stations, including WHFB-FM in Benton Harbor, WELL-FM in Battle Creek, and WJEF-FM in Grand Rapids, broadcast the current hit tunes late into the night, although the approaching thunderstorms may have created static that would have been annoying. No doubt, in the late evening hours almost every radio station played the romantic tune *Sentimental Me* by the Ames Brothers, which had just taken rank as the number one billboard song. Other new favorites from the top of the charts included Eileen Barton's fun, fast tune, *If I Knew You Were Comin' I'd've Baked a Cake*; the big band-style song, *Hoop-Dee-Doo*, by Perry Como with the Fontaine Sisters; and Teresa Brewer's *Music! Music! Music!*, otherwise known as *Put another Nickel In*, a corny, novelty song with infectious vitality, Brewer's first big hit.

FOUR OR FIVE MINUTES after the television stations went dark at midnight, Northwest Flight 2501 was approaching the shore of Lake Michigan over the small town of Glenn, located directly beneath the center line of Airway Red 57. At the same time, the Capital Airlines cargo flight under the command of Captain Charles Arnold Renn was approaching the lakeshore near the same area and in the same airway, but flying from the opposite direction and trying to hold at 5,000 feet, 1,500 feet higher than Flight 2501. It had been a difficult trip thus far for Renn, but he felt that he had never put his airplane or himself in jeopardy: He knew how to fly in those conditions even when the turbulence pushed the airplane up and down several hundred feet and cloud-to-ground lightning was frequent. Within just a couple miles of the lakeshore, the turbulence increased from just moderate to severe, but he made it through little worse for wear. Despite the rough air, it did not occur to him to radio a pilot weather report for FAWS, as Captain Mitchell in the Lodestar had done about 15 minutes earlier. However, even if he had done so, the system was down and, like Mitchell's report, it would not have reached Flight 2501. By that point, nothing could have provided Captain Lind any better warning than the turbulence he was already experiencing and the storm activity he was seeing and hearing. In fact, the circumstances would have constituted an emergency.

Some pilots might have considered penetrating the storm. Flying between cells of thunderstorms was possible, but not acceptable with passengers. Northwest's policy dictated that pilots avoid areas of severe turbulence for the purposes of passenger safety and comfort, even if the pilots felt the airplane could withstand the weather.

On any one of the dozens of times that Lind had approached this very spot near Glenn, Michigan, in clear weather at 3,500 feet above mean sea level, he would have seen pinpoints of light on the ground representing the homes, street lights, and cars in that rural area. The lights would have appeared progressively closer spaced and brighter as the airplane neared the towns of South Haven and Benton Harbor to the left and Saugatuck and Holland to the right. On a very clear night, he might have even seen the glows coming from Chicago to the southwest, and Milwaukee to the northwest, framing the vast black canvas that represented the 300-mile-long by 100-mile-wide Lake Michigan.

Flight 2501 would be crossing the big body of water about two-thirds of the way south from its northernmost point at the shores of the Upper Peninsula. However, flying at 3,500 feet in the conditions that night, Lind would not have been able to see much through the clouds.

Although Lind had known to expect thunderstorms and an east-moving squall line over the Lake, until that point he really had no idea what he would actually encounter: Each storm, like a fingerprint, is different. They follow certain patterns, but no two are identical. Now before him, flashes of lightning inside a massive cloud bank appeared like a defensive lineup of football players trying to block his forward movement. Static electricity in the air may have interfered with the radio reception from the Milwaukee range station. The jerks and bumps and ups and downs meant that Lind, the pilot and "quarterback" of the airplane, would have to rethink his game plan: It was his discretion as the captain to "call an audible."

Lind had to determine what action to take based on what he could see for himself out the small windows that framed his view. Considering that the aircraft was flying at about three miles per minute, he had precious little time to decide. He may have consulted Wolfe, but ultimately the choice would be his and his alone as the captain and supreme commander of the airplane. He had only three options: turn around, turn north, or turn south. Continuing forward, west toward Milwaukee, would have been a deadly mistake.

Lind could have retreated from the storm and flown to another airport to land and wait for the squall to pass. Although he knew that he had the right to do whatever he felt was necessary for the safety of the airplane and his passengers, he also knew that Northwest, like all the other airlines, preferred its pilots to avoid the significant extra costs involved in intermediate stops for any reason. He could see that turning north would be no better than going forward, since lightning flashed in that direction as well. Instead, he made the decision to turn south in an attempt, like a quarterback, to make an end run around the defensive lineup of the storm, as pilots often did in that region when encountering storms.

There was no pilot requirement to request a change in his flight plan when an emergency presented itself. He knew a pilot's responsibility was to aviate, navigate, then communicate, in that order. And he knew, based on the chart Verne Wolfe would have had open on his lap, that Airway Red 28, 22 miles south of Airway 57, offered him another route across Lake Michigan away from the path of what he thought was the east-moving squall.

At about 12:09 p.m., with hands gripping the wheel, Robert Lind turned it to the left and began an arc south. Once out of Airway Red 57, he knew it was reasonably safe to descend without clearance to fly with visual navigation south along the lakeshore until he reached the other airway, a short diversion that would take him seven or eight minutes. In such an emergency a pilot had to do what he must to avoid an even worse situation. Where the dotted lights along shore at South Haven met the pitch-black body of water provided a nice, straight line to follow south.

Once out of the immediate danger of the squall, Lind could now navigate. He probably tuned his radio receiver to the frequency of the radio range station at South Bend, Indiana, which shot its signal straight north along Blue 6, the airway that ran north/south several miles inshore of the lake. While flying within view of the ground at that point, he knew he would have to begin ascending back to his prescribed altitude so that he would be higher when he reached the other airway. The chart indicated that the signal from the Chicago radio range station intersected the signal from South Bend at the Benton Harbor navigational fix, located in the center of Airway Red 28. The unique audible tone would tell him when he had reached that point, which is actually about ten miles north of the city of Benton Harbor. As he kept his eyes on the ground, his ears to his receiver, and his hands firmly on the wheel, he would have carefully reviewed his new plan and prepared to communicate his intentions to Air Traffic Control. What he could not know from the view south out his windows was that the storm was right on his heels.

AS ROBERT LIND AND VERNE WOLFE were beginning their emergency detour south, retired airplane mechanic 54-year-old William Bowie, his wife, Lillian, and their son Billy sat outside of the gas station they owned in Glenn, three-quarters of mile east of the lake. The power had just gone out in their small town, so with nothing else to do, they and their neighbors, some seven other people including June Marring, Ivan Orr, Danny Thompson, and truck driver Arnold Rapp, shared a few beers and watched the approaching storm with the same fascination as they had watched television earlier.

From their perch at the northwest corner of the intersection of Blue Star Highway and 114th Street that marked the heart of the little village, the group could see the sky light up when flickers of lightning raced between the clouds. Seconds later, their conversations were drowned out by the deep claps of thunder, the sonic boom of the lightning that took longer to reach their ears. Anyone who regularly watched storms would have known that as the interval between lightning and thunder decreased, the storm was getting closer. At that time around midnight, the line of the storm was still a couple miles away. There would be just enough time for the storm-watchers to finish their beers—if they drank quickly—and shoot a little more bull before the rain hit.

A few minutes after midnight, to the best of Bowie's calculation, the sound of droning motors captured his attention. Looking around to the north, he spotted the source. Flashing lights in the sky revealed an airplane heading south, almost straight toward them, right above the Blue Star Highway. The conversations all halted when the others took notice, following Bowie's gaze north. Even over the noise of the storm and the wildly moving trees, Bowie detected something about the sound of the engines that did not seem right. "Bring that plane down here, buddy, and we'll fix it up for you," he hollered, lifting his beer toward the sky.

Looking up, Thompson probably took a swig of his beer, then announced, "That thing sounds like a stock car with a blown head gasket."

Bowie, whose gas station was directly under the intersection of Red 57 and Blue 6, saw a lot of airplanes flying overhead, but at much higher altitudes. This one stood out because it was so low. He thought it seemed out of control. As it flew south past his gas station, he noticed an odd yellow light trailing the aircraft. "I wonder if that's a wing on fire or if it's just the exhaust," he commented to no one in particular, as he watched the airplane head south then disappear behind the treetops.

Edwin and Marion Kuban, asleep in their lakefront home in Glenn, both woke up to the sound of a low-flying airplane. They only heard it for a few seconds before a flash of lightning and the immediate boom of thunder signaled the arrival of rain and drowned out the motors. The clouds opened up and poured down their contents. The Kubans tried to fall back asleep and those gathered at the gas station hightailed it home. The low-flying airplane would be a source of conversation early the next morning when the townspeople would awaken and begin cleaning up the downed tree branches that would litter all of Glenn.

SEVEN MILES SOUTH OF GLENN, sometime after midnight, 20-year-old Donald Bassi stood on the bluff just outside his parents' lakefront cottage along Northshore Drive, one block west of the Blue Star Highway. If it had been daytime, he would have been able to see the channel markers at South Haven about two miles south of the cottage, but in the pitch black of night, all he could see was the dim glow of the lights in town. He had been concerned that the high winds might knock out the power, but South Haven still had light.

Bassi had gone outside at about 11:45 p.m. when he began seeing distant flashes of lightning and hearing the approaching rumble of thunder, a sound that, as an amateur meteorologist, he always found thrilling. He and his parents had been at the cottage for a few weeks already, having arrived in early June to stay for the summer as they had every year for as long as Bassi could recall. That summer was bittersweet because instead of returning home with his parents to Chicago in the fall, Donald would be heading off to college. His life was changing, and he wondered if this might be his last summer in South Haven.

Although a warm breeze from the southwest had accompanied him when he walked over the lawn to the edge of the bluff about 20 minutes earlier, it died down almost completely now. Then, as he stood there, a sudden breeze hit him in the face. The trees seemed to come alive as their leaves rustled, adding to the symphony of the storm. The winds increased dramatically: Bassi estimated they grew to at least 50 miles per hour. He had to be careful not to get too near the edge of the bluff. One big gust of wind and he could find himself tumbling nearly 50 feet down the incline to the beach.

As Bassi directed his gaze northwest over the Lake, the lights from South Haven at his back cast a glow out over the Lake and revealed a massive wall of clouds heading toward him. Then a brilliant flash of light and another immediately thereafter silhouetted the clouds. Within seconds the incredible sound and light show intensified. Bassi watched, enthralled, as each flash of lightning illuminated the entire stage. As plain as day, he saw a long, moving cloud bank stretching as far as his eye could see from the southwest to the northeast. It seemed to be tumbling right toward him. As he watched it progressing, the bursts of light revealed more lines of clouds behind the first, like ranks of advancing soldiers. He counted at least five lines of storm clouds running parallel to and behind the first.

Bassi had been sailing on Lake Michigan since he was a child, and he had learned to pay attention to the weather. He knew a squall line when he saw one, and this one was a multi-layered monster. *What a weird storm*, he thought. It was perhaps because the storm was so unusual that he made a mental note of the scene. The clouds, he figured, looked to be about 800 feet above the water, and the tops extended up to about 1,200 feet. He was surprised to see that despite all the wind, the surface of the Lake had not yet whipped up to a frenzy.

In the next flash of lightning, he saw his neighbor, Jim Roberts, several dozen yards away standing near the bluff. "Looks like we're in for a big one," he hollered to Roberts, over the noise of the wind.

"Sure does, kid," Roberts shouted back, glancing in Bassi's direction.

A wall of cold air suddenly hit Bassi, and the temperature dropped several degrees in an instant, as if the door of a giant refrigerator had opened. That must have been too much for Roberts. "I'm heading inside," he said, turning. "You best do the same."

No way, Bassi thought. *The show is just beginning*. He hugged his arms around himself for warmth, leaned into the wind to maintain his footing, and watched. On the immense stage before him, something small caught his eye. A cluster of tiny lights flashed in the sky, moving toward him from the north. As the lights became slightly bigger, he heard the drone of engines and realized it was an airplane. He gauged it to be about two or three miles from him. Although he was not very familiar with airplanes, he could see that this one had multiple engines on its wings. *Strange,* he thought, *as long as I've been coming to the cottage, I've never seen a plane here.* It seemed to be flying in front of and parallel to the squall line but on a slightly divergent path south away from it. In the next series of lightning flashes, the sky reversed, and the airplane became a silhouette. He seemed certain the time was shortly after midnight. Within 30 or 40 seconds the airplane disappeared from his view.

Soon thereafter, the first squall line passed over Bassi, and he looked straight up into its underbelly. In the deafening roar of the wind and the thunder, he could feel the moisture in the air and hear the rainfall approaching. It took about five minutes for the next line of clouds to pass over and another five for the third. Then the rain hit, coming down strong, and Bassi hustled into the house.

THREE MILES SOUTHEAST of Donald Bassi's cottage and two miles directly east of downtown South Haven, 11-year-old Evelyn Kulczy could not sleep. Although her dad, Paul, a justice of the peace, had tucked her and her sister in over an hour ago, the approaching storm and the excitement for the coming weekend kept them up. They huddled around their open bedroom window which looked northwest toward the Lake. From there they could see Phoenix Road, which ran straight west toward South Haven, and the lights from Sherman's Dairy just across from the farm. With each flash of lightning the sky lit up. Suddenly Evelyn spotted an outline of a dark object low in the sky during a particularly bright flash of lightning. "Look, an airplane!" she said excitedly pointing west.

The sky went dark again before her sister could see it, but as her eyes adjusted, Kulczy saw little flecks of light where the airplane had been. "See that?" she coaxed her sister again, pointing. "That must be the lights of the plane."

"I'll bet those people are scared," her sister said, spotting the airplane.

"Keep an eye on it," Kulczy directed her, turning quickly from the window. "I'm going to get Dad."

AROUND THE TIME that Evelyn Kulczy spotted the airplane, a South Haven teenager, Oscar Bergstrom, and a pal who had been out carousing that night, were driving south on Dunkley Street in South Haven, heading almost straight west toward the bridge over the Black River. Suddenly, Bergstrom heard a deep rumble directly overhead that sounded nothing like the storm. His car began to shake. Looking out through the windshield, he saw the lights of a very low flying airplane heading southwest out over the pier head. "Holy cow!" he exclaimed to his friend. "That was close."

INSIDE HIS HOUSE ON INDIANA AVENUE, half a mile south of the bridge at South Haven and three blocks inland, 15-year-old David Allers, the son of fishing boat Captain Julius Allers, was up late reading. He had turned off the radio because the reception was so bad. He didn't bother going to bed, knowing he would not be able to sleep during the storm. The wind was so strong it blew the curtains almost straight into the house. Suddenly, at what he figured was a little after midnight, the family's two dogs started howling. He put down his book and listened. Over the howling of the wind and between the claps of thunder, he heard the unmistakable sound of a large aircraft flying overhead. He had never heard an airplane over his house before and wondered what it was doing there in the midst of a storm.

SOMETIME AFTER MIDNIGHT inside a little house on 13th Street, about two and a half miles south of downtown South Haven and just a few blocks from the lakeshore, newlywed Jackie Eldred woke up with a start and sat straight up in bed. She and her husband, Meryl, had turned in early that night and had been asleep for a couple hours. She could hear the distinct sound of an airplane flying overhead, and the engines seemed to be sputtering.

Her thoughts turned to a frightening night years earlier when she was a kid living on her parents' farm. A small airplane had crash-landed close to their house, and her dad had always said, "Just a few yards farther and we would have all been killed." Now it seemed another airplane was going to crash. Very frightened, but not wanting to disturb Meryl, who had to work the next day, Jackie laid back down, pulled the sheet up over her head, and continued to listen, fearful of what she might hear.

TWO BLOCKS WEST of the Eldreds' home where 13th Street dead-ended at the lakeshore and where Deerlick Creek trickled out into the Lake, a young couple were locked in a passionate embrace in a Chrysler parked at that local make-out spot. George Bartholomew thought the night all the more romantic because of the storm brewing outside. Then all of a sudden, in mid-lip-lock, his date pulled back. "Do you hear that?" she asked, cocking her ear toward the window.

My God, Bartholomew thought, listening, *that's a plane*. "Duck," he yelled over a clap of thunder, wrapping his arm around her to shield her from what he expected would be the concussion of an airplane crashing.

When nothing happened, the two sat up and looked around outside, surprised that they didn't see a flaming mass of burning wreckage. "Let's get out of here, George," his date pleaded, sliding back to her side of the seat. "Whatever that was, I'm scared."

Bartholomew turned the key, started the engine, quickly backed up, and jockeyed the car around on the narrow road. Then, he hit the gas. Embarrassed that he was as frightened as his date, he steered the accelerating car down the road as the tires dug into the dirt. He must have passed right by the Eldreds' home as he gunned the engine, heading east on 13th and then making a right on River Road, south to 14th, which would lead him to the Blue Star Highway and home.

ALTHOUGH GEORGE BARTHOLOMEW likely sped right past the home of 16-year-old Norma Quinn, who lived on 14th Street not too far from the Lake, she took no particular notice of any cars out late that night. Instead, she sat trembling by her bedroom window, shaken by the very loud, strange noise she had just heard while watching the storm overhead. She had no idea what it was, but she remained focused on the sky out over the Lake and the massive, rolling wall of thunder clouds.

IN THE LAKEFRONT RESORT NEIGHBORHOOD of Crystal Beach, about three-quarters of a mile south of Norma Quinn's home, Stella Nowlan sat frightened by the howling wind outside. Her 17-year-old daughter Punky was on a dinner cruise out of Benton Harbor with her friends Betty Sue and Carol and their boyfriends. The closeness between the flashes of lightning and the claps of thunder told her that the storm would soon be upon them, and she worried that her daughter's boat would be in danger. Her husband was still out, and her 11-year-old daughter, Marilyn, was reading. "Grab your raincoat, honey," Stella suggested, trying not to sound panicked as she put on her own coat and reached for the umbrella. "Let's go out and see if we can see Punky's boat."

The wind fought mother and daughter as they wrestled their way to the bench atop their bluff. Stella wrapped her jacket tightly around her and sat down, pulling Marilyn into her lap. She began to scan the Lake during every flash of lightning, looking for the boat.

It would be a hopeless mission. Benton Harbor was about 15 miles south, and, even in the daytime, she could never have seen a boat at that distance. Moreover, any captain worth his salt would never have ventured out into the big lake with a storm approaching. The boat had probably just cruised up and down the St. Joseph River. However, Stella didn't know that, and, like any mother, she was concerned. She and Marilynn sat there keeping watch.

ABOUT THREE AND A HALF MILES south of Crystal Beach in the wooded lakefront community of Palisades Park Country Club, ten-year-old Doug McCain was shocked awake by a big clap of thunder that seemed to vibrate the back seat of the car where he was lying. He sat up and looked around to get his bearings. McCain could not believe he hadn't awakened sooner because the noise was so loud. "We're almost to the cottage, Doug," he heard his mom say.

She reached over the seat back to pat his head. Just then several flashes of lightning illuminated the inside of the car, and Doug saw his mother's reassuring look.

Because he was groggy, it took him a few seconds to recall that he and his folks had left their home in Homewood Park, Illinois, earlier that evening after his dad had gotten home from work. They would be staying at the cottage for several weeks. Now that they were almost there, McCain became excited. He knew that in the morning he would be meeting up with several pals whose families also spent their summers at Palisades Park. As his dad negotiated his way down the dirt road through the woods, he made a sweeping turn to the right past the Country Club; McCain knew that if he looked left he would see the Lake through a clearing. As the line of violently swaying trees came to an abrupt end, he quickly stuck his nose against the left side window. He had expected to see a dark void that would be the Lake, but instead saw a series of bright lights that he immediately recognized as the windows of an airplane. He even thought he could see heads in the windows. "Mom, Dad, there's a plane out there," he said banging on the window. "It's really low." As soon as he uttered those words, the car re-entered the woods.

"You just woke up, son," his dad said focusing on the road. "You were probably dreaming."

Maybe I was, McCain thought, craning around to look back, *but it sure looked like a plane to me.*

McCain, of course, didn't know that his neighborhood was located almost directly under the intersection of Red 28, which led from Battle Creek southwest to Chicago, and Blue 6, which ran parallel to the lakeshore. The intersection of those airways marked the aeronautical navigation point, or in other words, "a fix," at Benton Harbor, even though the actual city was ten miles south. Of course, since Palisades Park was under a heavily trafficked airway, McCain, and anyone in that vicinity, might have noticed any number of aircraft flying that night. However, most airplanes did not fly as low as the one he had seen.

ALTHOUGH IT CAN NEVER BE KNOWN exactly what took place in the cockpit of the DC-4 at 12:13 a.m. when the airplane was, according to CAB report, "in the vicinity of Benton Harbor," the flight initiated a radio call. Verne Wolfe probably consulted his chart for the frequency of the closest Northwest radio station, which would have been Chicago's Midway Airport, and tuned the radio to that frequency. Then Lind would have spoken into his microphone: "Two five zero one."

Flight 2501 was probably just approaching the Benton Harbor navigation fix, along the shore of Lake Michigan, that spot about ten miles north of the city of Benton Harbor, where the east/west airway, Red 28, intersected the north/south airway, Blue 6.

The operator would have replied through the microphone on his desk "Two five zero one. Go ahead."

Although there is no transcript of the exact words spoken by the pilot, and the CAB report provides only paraphrased commentary, protocol required that a pilot request clearance to change routes. Lind would have had to provide his current location, his direction of travel, and his next intended checkpoint. All that is specifically known, however, is that Flight 2501 requested descent from 3,500 feet to 2,500 feet.

At that moment, according to the weather sequence report that Julius Badner was just posting on the teletype, the squall line ran directly east/west from Flint, Michigan, to a point at the lakeshore about 15 miles north of Benton Harbor and west across the Lake to Rockford, Illinois. By then, the squall line was plowing straight south at a rapid rate. Robert Lind had been, unknowingly, flying just ahead of the leading edge of the squall.

"Two five zero one requesting descent from three thousand five hundred to two thousand five hundred," the radio operator would have repeated, as he jotted the request in a form of shorthand. "Stand by."

The operator might have been curious why the pilot requested the descent, but radio protocol warranted keeping transmissions as short as possible. He would have left the radio line open, then telephoned the Air Route Traffic Control center at Chicago's Midway Airport, the world's busiest at the time. There a controller, who had just come on duty at the midnight shift change, picked up the telephone, saying, "ATC Chicago."

On behalf of Flight 2501, the operator made the request. Then the controller repeated the request and said, "Stand by."

At that point, about 30 to 45 seconds had elapsed since Flight 2501 had initiated the radio call, and the DC-4 may have reached the Benton Harbor navigational fix. The controller in Chicago was taking over management of the flight from the Cleveland ATC center, and he would have placed a "shrimp boat" that represented Flight 2501 at that position The controller would have analyzed the current positions of aircraft in the region and their flight paths and to determine if any were flying or were scheduled to fly at 2,500 feet. The controller took note of another airplane, still on the ground at Milwaukee, that was scheduled to depart soon and fly toward Chicago. He must have determined that if he allowed Flight 2501 to descend to 2,500 feet, it would encroach upon the 1,000-foot separation required between the two airplanes.

That analysis would have taken anywhere from 45 to 60 seconds. Then the controller responded to the Northwest radio operator: "Northwest two five zero one is not, repeat NOT, cleared for descent to two thousand five hundred due to other traffic in the area."

The operator acknowledged by repeating the response. "Roger. Flight two five zero one not cleared to descend. Maintain three thousand five hundred."

Then the radio operator hung up and re-engaged radio communication with Flight 2501, informing the pilot that his request had been denied due to other traffic in the area.

At 12:15 a.m., Captain Lind would have replied, "Roger. Two five zero one maintaining three thousand five hundred feet."

After the Northwest operator ended the transmission, he would have typed a transcription of the conversation on his mill, torn the sheet off the roll, and deposited it in the bin at his console as a record of the conversation.

Exactly what happened after that last radio call would be a source of official and unofficial debate for many decades to come.

SOON AFTER MIDNIGHT, in the town of Coloma near Paw Paw Lake, 10 miles northeast of the city of Benton Harbor, several people took notice of a very low-flying propeller aircraft over the small inland lake. Two police officers and a woman, Mrs. Marty Jones, saw it flying almost right above the treetops.

About two miles closer to Lake Michigan, in the tiny town of Riverside, a foundry worker, Doyle Cleveland, leaned against a wall under an overhang of the foundry sometime after midnight, smoking a cigarette and watching the storm, unhappy that he had to work second shift. Suddenly, he saw a low-flying airplane heading west toward the Lake. He could not believe anyone would be flying through a storm and so low.

About a quarter past midnight in a torrential downpour, newlywed Web Geezer pulled his black, 1948 Pontiac to the side of the Blue Star Highway near Hager Shores, about eight miles north of Benton Harbor. "It's not safe to drive in this," he said to his new bride, sitting next to him, and their friends in the back seat. They were returning home to Bangor from the Strawberry Festival in St. Joseph, and the windshield wipers could not keep up with the flow of water. Geezer turned off the engine. Thunder and lightning enveloped them. As the couples were wondering when the worst of the rain would pass, they heard a low droning noise far different than anything a storm could dish up. "That sounds like an airplane," Geezer said, leaning forward to try to see out the rain-streaked window.

The noise grew louder, and he reached for his wife's hand. They instinctively ducked their heads as if trying to avoid getting hit from above. As the sound petered out, Geezer ventured another peek outside and saw the lights from an airplane flying very low—almost at the tree-top level—heading out toward the Lake. "My God, that was close," Geezer said with a gulp. They continued to sit in the car, chattering about the airplane, waiting for the rain to let up.

Sometime after midnight, 62-year-old retired Navy Commander R.P. Helm aimed his high-powered telescope north out over the Lake and toward the approaching squall line. Though he normally gazed at the stars, his equipment would have offered him an up-close view of the raging storm. The large bay window of his lakefront home on Rocky Gap Road, about three miles north of Benton Harbor, afforded him a panoramic vision south, west, and north. Each flash of lightning gave him an amazing view of the rolling thunder clouds.

Suddenly, with his naked eye, he saw the lights of an airplane heading southwest out over the Lake. He took note that its lights were flashing and he thought, for some reason, that it was in trouble. He estimated the time as 12:20 a.m. As he continued to watch the lights, he saw a brilliant flash of lightning and then a red-and-white flash where the airplane had been. Keeping his eye trained on the flash, he saw what he thought was smoke. *My God*, he thought, *that plane just disintegrated*. He had no way of calculating the distance, but from his years in the Navy, he made an educated guess. Whatever happened to that airplane, he figured, occurred about 15 to 20 miles out. He presumed that if he had seen it, so too had the local Coast Guard, so he didn't bother to call them. He tossed and turned all night, worried about what he had witnessed, hoping against hope that the airplane had not crashed.

At what might have been the same time as R. P. Helm saw the flash,

George Cole, who lived four miles north of Helm, saw an airplane flying very low over his lakefront farm, out toward the Lake where it disappeared in a brilliant flash. Sixty-year-old Bertha Busse of Bridgman reported seeing a flash in the sky off St. Joseph. Web and Ramona Geezer and their friends, who were parked along Blue Star Highway near Hager Park, heard a tremendous boom that felt like it rocked the car. Although neither Cole, Busse, or Geezer could calculate how far away the flash or the noise was, experts indicate that an explosion can be seen for about 25 miles, and heard even farther over water because there is no ground or vegetation to absorb the sound.

Several other people within a few miles south of South Haven saw or heard something that seemed so significant they would never forget it, though they would not mention it to anyone for decades.

As Stella Nowlan held vigil at the bluff in Crystal Park with her daughter Marilyn scanning the Lake for any sign of her other daughter's boat, she recoiled when she saw an orange ball of light somewhere on the Lake. It seemed so bright that it lit up their beach. Whatever it was, Stella felt sure it had nothing to do with her daughter's boat, but she and Marilyn would never forget what they saw.

Norma Quinn, the teenager who had been gazing west out her window saw an orange flash over Lake Michigan. It rattled her to the core, but she vowed then and there she would never say anything to anyone because she did not want to sound crazy. Later, she would feel guilty for not coming forward.

Jackie Eldred, who had for the last several minutes been trying to calm herself after awakening to that low-flying airplane overhead, heard a tremendous "Kaboom!" She presumed in an instant that the airplane she had heard crashed. "Meryl," she cried, shaking her husband, "Wake up! Wake up!"

He just groaned and rolled away from her, clutching his pillow.

"Meryl, wake up," she pleaded, almost yelling and pushing against him with both hands.

Finally he rolled onto his back and opened his eyes, blinking to try to make sense of what his wife was shouting. "What's wrong woman?"

"I heard a plane fly over our house real low about ten minutes ago. It was sputtering," she cried, clutching Meryl, "and, just now, I heard it crash."

Certain that she was just dreaming about that incident with the airplane at her parents' farm, her husband grumbled, "You're imagining things, Jackie. It's just the storm. Go back to sleep." He rolled away to the far side of the bed.

By the end of the weekend, Meryl Eldred would feel guilty about how he had disregarded his wife.

AT ABOUT 12:20 A.M., Capital Airlines pilot Captain Frederic Stripe saw before him the telltale signs of a squall line over Lake Michigan. The wild electrical storm stretched as far as he could see. Lightning broke out of the clouds and struck the ground as if Zeus himself were hurling thunderbolts in anger. Stripe was flying a cargo aircraft from Detroit to Milwaukee on Red 57, about 15 minutes behind Northwest Flight 2501. Although he had been warned of thunderstorm activity over Lake Michigan, until he saw the intensity he had not thought it would pose any problem. He knew in an instant that there would be no safe way to pass through the storm to Milwaukee.

Freddie Stripe had seen plenty of storms in his 20-year flying career. He became fascinated with flying in 1918 when he was five years old and watched airplanes taking off and landing at the old Curtiss Field in Waukegan, Illinois, where he had grown up. In his early teens, he hung out at the airport, helping with chores, and had the thrill of his life when the pilot of a Curtiss Jenny biplane took him up for a spin. On that day, he became hooked on flying.

When he was old enough and had saved enough money, he began taking flying lessons. In 1931 he received his private pilot's license. Back then, pilots could fly only in the daytime, using landmarks like railroad tracks or rivers, to navigate. For the next six years, during the Great Depression, Stripe gave flying lessons and barnstorming demonstrations to keep his skills up to date and make enough money to keep training. By 1936, he had earned his commercial license. About that time, the implementation of the radio range system gave him and other pilots the tools to navigate at night and in poor visibility. Now, instead of flying around weather where there was no visibility, he could use the range system to navigate in or around storms. Stripe flew through a lot of bad weather after Capital Airlines hired him in 1940, first as a copilot, then as a captain two years later.

Like most captains back then, Stripe had little time to mature before being called into the U.S. Army Air Corps in 1942. He became an Air Transport Command captain in the Military Transport Division and began flying C-47s, C-54s, and several other types of aircraft overseas. He returned to Capital Airlines in 1945 after the war.

In recent years, Capital had gotten approval to fly some of the same routes as Northwest Airlines, and the company poised itself to compete for its share of that market. Over the last two months, Stripe had been crossing the Lake as many as eight times per day, flying between Detroit and Milwaukee. He had encountered many thunderstorms along that route.

Stripe knew that lightning like he saw that night had been responsible for blinding many pilots. Consequently, he always carried welder's goggles for just such an emergency. However, he was not about to get close enough to the storm to need them. On previous occasions, he had been caught unaware in a storm at night because the lightning remained embedded, or in other words, hidden within the clouds. On one occasion, high winds buffeted his airplane, and he realized the winds would flip him over if he made too sharp a turn. Instead, he carefully navigated his way out of the weather flying at 30-degree increments until he reached clear air. However, a couple years earlier he had to work much harder to save his and his passengers' lives.

While flying a DC-4 between Washington and Chicago, Stripe found himself enveloped in a severe squall over Pittsburgh at about 8,000 feet. The winds were so strong they tossed the airplane up and down as much as 2,000 feet. At some point the airplane began vibrating so badly the stewardess came into the cockpit to express her concern on behalf of the frightened passengers.

Stripe tried to stabilize the airplane with the help of his copilot, but no matter what they did it continued to shudder. Then it began a sudden and dangerous downward descent. He tried to adjust the orientation of the elevators, the fabric-covered surfaces on the tail that he could move up and down to change pitch, but they did not respond to level out the airplane. Stripe realized that something had gone very wrong with them. He knew what he had to do. "Button everyone down," he told the stewardess, who quickly hurried back to do as she was told.

By then they were at 3,000 feet. "We're still going down, aren't we?" the copilot asked incredulously, while pulling back the wheel.

"Yeah, we are," Stripe said, with a hint of fear in his voice, "unless…." Then he hit full throttle and pushed the wheel forward, pointing the aircraft even further toward the ground.

"What the hell are you doing?" the copilot screamed.

There was no time for Stripe to explain. Suddenly, the airplane caught air and started heading up at a severe angle. Stripe blacked out for a few seconds, and when he came to, he realized the airplane was still on an upward path. "I've got it," he hollered to his copilot, who was just becoming alert, as he quickly adjusted the trim tabs.

The airplane began to level out, and Stripe reduced the power. Although the vibrations continued, Stripe was able to successfully land at Cleveland. There, a mechanic set up a stepladder so that Stripe could inspect the elevators at the tail. What he saw confirmed his suspicions: The fabric covering of one of the elevators was missing. The high winds partially tore it off, and it flapped violently, causing the terrible vibrations and disabling the lift of the elevator. Stripe's maneuver of going full speed toward the ground created enough lift to propel the aircraft upward at an even greater speed, which ripped the fabric off. Then, the elevator became operable again. That experience served as a big warning for Stripe in the Michigan storm that night.

"We're getting away from this mess," he told his copilot as he turned the wheel to the left.

Then he tuned into the familiar frequency of the Capital Airlines radio operator at Detroit to inform the company he planned to return to Detroit to wait it out. His chief pilot, he knew, would not be happy about the extra expense of grounding a flight, but that would cost less than losing the airplane and the pilots. "Detroit," he hailed the Capital Airline operator, providing his flight number. "Returning to Detroit at five thousand."

After the radio operator coordinated the change of flight plan with Air Traffic Control, Stripe tuned the LFR receiver to the frequency of the Detroit radio range station. His decision to turn back that night just might have saved his life, and a long one it would be.

IN ADDITION TO Capital Airlines pilot Freddie Stripe, at least four other pilots elected to turn back that night. Three had taken off from Detroit shortly after midnight, heading west in various directions, and all three decided to return to the safety of Detroit.

Mary Meier, the professional jewelry buyer and frequent flyer who had boarded a flight at LaGuardia earlier that night, was on board an airplane that turned around. During the approach to the Kent County Airport in Grand Rapids, Michigan, at about 12:30 a.m., she sat clutching the arms of her seat, more frightened than she had ever been. The airplane was swaying back and forth and bumping up and down like a car hitting deep ruts in a road, and she felt terribly nauseated. Outside, lightning lit up the sky and thunder boomed all around her. Just as she was reaching for the airsickness bag, she felt the airplane bank to the left at the same time she heard the crackle from the intercom. "Ladies and gentlemen, due to the thunderstorm, we will be diverting to the Lansing Capital City Airport to wait for the weather to clear."

Meier breathed an audible sigh of relief. Lansing, she knew, was about 70 miles southeast of Grand Rapids. *So near and yet so far*, she lamented, *but I'm glad that the pilot didn't risk everyone's lives trying to land.*

Once the airplane reached the ground in Lansing, Meier and the other passengers were guided inside the terminal to wait. She had no one to report her delay to, but other passengers were using the telephones at the counter to contact their families. Over all the hubbub that accompanied the airplane delay, she overheard a conversation between two frustrated passengers that caught her attention. "Well, apparently not all the flights have been grounded," one passenger bemoaned. "Several planes have been rerouted south around the storm over Lake Michigan."

That comment reminded Meier about the fashion buyer with whom she had chatted while waiting at LaGuardia—the woman traveling alone who had confused Grand Rapids, Michigan, with Grand Rapids, Minnesota. *She'll probably reach Minnesota long before I'll get to Grand Rapids*, she thought, looking up at the clock that showed it was nearly 2:00 a.m. *In fact*, Meier, thought, *She's lucky. She's probably asleep by now.*

Much later that day, when Meier stepped out of a cab amid debris from the storm in front of her apartment on Fountain Street in Grand Rapids, she saw the headline of the *Grand Rapids Press* glaring at her from inside a newspaper box: "DC-4 FALLS IN BIG LAKE: 58 LOST."

After reading the article, she realized that the woman she had talked to was, in fact, not lucky at all. That thought would haunt her for the next half century.

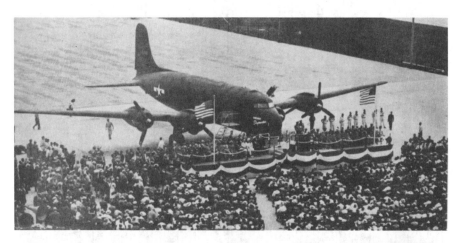

Fifty thousand people gather for the dedication of the first C-54 to roll off the production line at Orchard Field in Chicago, Illinois, on July 30, 1943. That aircraft that would eventually be used for Flight 2501. *Chicago Airview News, courtesy of Martin Hendren.*

Captain Frederic Stripe, Capital Airlines pilot, in the 1950s (left) and in 2007.

Rick Cochran, Northwest Airlines radio operator, in the 1950s (left) and in 2007.

Robert Charles Lind, pilot   Verne Frank Wolfe, copilot   Bonnie Ann Feldman, stewardess

Siroun Ajemian

Dr. Leon M. Ajemian

Dr. Leslie P. Anderson

Merle Leroy Barton

Dr. Archibald E. Cardle

Anna Nagle Eastman

William H. Freng

Rosa Freng

Barbara Freng (17)

Miriam Frankel

Mary Frost

Alfred W. George

Richard Goldsbury   Rosalie Gorski   Benjamin Heuston

Slava Heuston   Thomas Hill   John Hokanson

Catherine Hokanson   Janice Hokanson (7)   Tommy Hokanson (4)

Nora Hughes   Geraldine Jackson   Arthur E. Jackson

Dorothy Jean Kaufmann

Mary Keating

William Carter Kelty

Ruth Johnson

Leo F. Long

Jo E. Longfield

Dana Richard Malby (3)

Pearle Main

Francis McNickle

Helen Mary Meyer

Ralph Olsen

William D. K. Reid

Marie Rorabaugh   Ellen Ross   Frank C. Schwartz

Carl D. Schlachter   Louise Schlachter   Joseph Sirbu

Kenneth Skoug, Sr.   Louise S. Spohn   Richard W. Thomson

Fr. Augustine Walsh   Eva Woolley   Leo Wohler

A navigator is pictured here in the cockpit of a typical DC-4 behind the pilot, but Flight 2501 did not have a navigator. Note the oxygen bottle rack on the right, as it will be referenced later. *Courtesy of the Northwest History Center.*

Flight 2501, a coach flight, had three seats on the starboard side and two seats on the port side, accommodating more passengers than the typical DC-4, pictured here. Note the open shelves above the seats. *Courtesy of Northwest History Center.*

PART III
THE SEARCH CONTINUES

"What we anticipate seldom occurs:
but what we least expect generally happens."

Benjamin Disraeli (1804 - 1881)

Chapter 11

TRY TRY AGAIN

As I wiped off my kitchen island, I saw the familiar tan, extended-cab pickup truck pulling into our driveway. "They're here," I hollered to Jack, Craig, Bob, Todd and Jeff, all gathered in the living room.

If anyone had suggested that we might be working with Clive Cussler's team for this long, I would never have believed it. Here it was, April 25, 2007, and we were kicking off our fourth expedition with dinner at our house. I had a casserole in the oven, and Ralph and crew arrived right on schedule, at 6:30 p.m. With no need for the formality of doorbell ringing anymore, they pushed open our side door, and I heard Ralph's familiar greeting, "Hi y'all," as he, Steve Howard, and Harry Pecorelli filed down our hallway toward the kitchen.

Ralph plopped a case of Bud Light on the counter, and I wondered if he had changed his beer of choice. Jack had a case of Coronas cooling in the refrigerator.

We exchanged greetings and handshakes. Harry gave me a big bear hug, like we were long-lost friends, even though we had only met a few times the year before. Shipwreck hunting has a way of bonding people, plus Harry is the kind of person who ignites a friendship quickly. His warmth and friendliness endear him to most people instantly.

I liked these first gatherings of our expeditions best, when hope was in the air. Everyone was in a jovial mood; we caught up like the old friends that we had become, reminisced about past failures that the passage of time had made humorous, and thought only of the positive: Because of the many square miles we had already covered, we knew exactly where Flight 2501 was NOT located. As long as we kept meticulous records of where we had searched, then every additional square mile covered would bring us closer to the goal.

Since our search began, we had covered over fifty square miles, and I felt confident we would find Flight 2501 because, in addition to the witness reports along the lakeshore and the DC-4's last reported position in the vicinity of Benton Harbor, David Schwab's scientific drift models had considerably narrowed down the search area to a position off Benton Harbor southwest of where we had already searched. Although I had located only half of the victims' families, I looked forward to being able to inform them of our discovery, when the time came, in a much more gentle way than they had been told of the accident decades earlier.

We crowded chairs around our kitchen table. As we dug into the casserole, our conversations filled the gaps that a year leaves in its wake. After putting our plates in the sink, we gathered around the kitchen island, ready to get down to business. Ralph opened his computer case and pulled out his laptop and a bunch of papers. I grabbed my materials and added them to the pile.

Ralph took the lead, sharing his thoughts on the new search area. He showed us the hindcasting charts that Jerry Knisley, the Hypack software engineer, had created using his search and rescue program. He explained that Knisley had placed digital markers into a program that approximated the movement of the waves and currents on June 23, 1950. After running the program numerous times with different "drop zones," representing potential places where Flight 2501 might have crashed, Knisley saw a pattern. "He is calling it the goal post theory," Ralph explained, pointing to two dots on the map representing the posts. "He believes the debris drifted through these posts clockwise and swirled southeast. Therefore, the plane probably went down out here," Ralph said, pointing to an area northwest of the goal posts, much farther northwest of where we had previously searched.

Debris drifting clockwise from the northwest? I mused, with a confused look on my face. I reached for Schwab's hindcasting charts, realizing Knisley's conclusion was the complete opposite of Schwab's. Schwab surmised the debris would have drifted counterclockwise from the southwest.

"We've blocked out an area two miles wide and fifteen miles long to try to cover this year," Ralph continued. "We'll approach this in one-square-mile areas beginning with the most probable square mile and working from there until we find it."

It seemed as if Ralph had made up his mind about where to search, but I held more faith in the theories of a scientist who had spent his career studying Lake Michigan currents. I decided to pursue a discussion. "Funny," I commented, gently pushing David Schwab's chart closer to Ralph. "Jerry used the same weather records as David Schwab, but their conclusions are totally different."

"Yeah, this isn't an exact science," Ralph shot back.

I knew then that nothing any of us could say would change his mind.

Although Schwab and Knisley's differed on what direction they thought the debris had drifted after the crash, they both agreed that the debris could only have drifted so far given the wind and current conditions on the lake in the days following the accident. With their combined input, we were able to define the overall boundaries of the search by drawing a circle 25 miles in diameter around the epicenter of where the debris was first found 45 hours after the crash. This was based on the presumption that the debris did not travel more than one quarter of a mile per hour in any direction after the crash. The 500-square-mile circle encompassed a vast area between the two airways and included small segments in Airway Red 57 to the north and Red 28 to the south. We had already covered a good deal of territory in the center of the circle where we had initially theorized the airplane crashed, so it was time to give our partners a chance to test their theories.

Five weeks later, after more than twenty days on the lake and over thirty square miles of additional coverage, Ralph was not nearly as jovial as the night he arrived. The wreck was not behind the goal posts, and Ralph and crew had to return to Charleston without making a touchdown. Ralph would soon be moving on to England to keep up with the *Bonhomme Richard* search, as he had been doing every summer after he left Michigan. He was having similar luck in the North Atlantic finding everything but the famed warship. He even located a German U-boat and a Russian spy trawler.

I had a difficult time calling and emailing all the families to report our lack of success, but most of them expressed gratitude. Arthur Jackson's sister-in-law, Marge, wrote, "I appreciate all your effort and energy. May God bless you."

Rosalie Gorski's husband, Bill, wrote, "Over the years I have carried the memory of my precious Rosalie in my mind, heart, and soul. She is remembered daily in my prayers. Your interest in and concern for Rosalie and the other victims of this terrible tragedy is deeply appreciated."

"I'm really very interested in what your group is doing," Marie Rorabaugh's daughter, Helen Seymour, wrote. "I hope you keep me up to date on the findings and conclusions reached by MSRA and NUMA."

A Freng granddaughter, Barbara White Morse wrote, "My sister Mary and I appreciate, more than words can ever express, all you and Mr. Cussler have done to help us know more about the loss of our grandparents and aunt."

CLIVE CUSSLER CALLED me soon after the 2007 expedition ended. "You know, Valerie," he began, "a wreck will only be found when it wants to be found."

I laughed, although I realized the wisdom of his statement. Despite the best efforts, fate played a hand in this. "If nothing else," I replied, "your efforts have been of comfort to the families. And, you've already spent more than 60 days longer on the search than the government did in 1950."

"This reminds me of an airplane that went down in Kentucky Lake in Tennessee," he replied. "The sheriff couldn't find it and gave up. The family turned to me for help. It's not the kind of thing I do, you know," he continued, "but I thought, why not? I'll try to help."

He told me that he had sent Ralph in search of it. "Sure enough," Clive said, "after two days Ralph found it, and he gave the coordinates to the sheriff. You know what the sheriff asked Ralph?" Clive asked me.

"No, what?" I bantered back to this consummate storyteller.

"He asked him, 'How do you know you actually found the plane?' You know what Ralph answered?"

"No, what?"

"Because I tied a God-damned buoy to it for you!"

We shared a good laugh. That was the kind of story Clive told with great flair in his *Sea Hunters* books, but it was even more enjoyable hearing it in his own voice.

Clive and I spent the rest of the conversation talking about Flight 2501: the facts and the suppositions. We discussed the various witness accounts and how some were believable and others were not. We discussed the two opposing scientific hindcasting theories and scratched our heads over which one to believe."Let's try southwest next year," Clive announced at the end of our conversation.

"Southwest it is," I replied.

I FACED 11 MORE MONTHS before we had another shot at finding the wreck, but looked forward to our annual MSRA expedition and the possibility of finding the *Andaste*, a massive, steel self-unloading freighter that we had set our sights on that year. However, our expedition that June was a bust. On the bright side, I hoped that all the disappointments were serving to build my character.

As had become a habit, I turned to other projects. I continued to research local ships gone missing and write about them. I tracked down more Flight 2501 families, built up the new museum exhibit design business that Bill Lafferty and I had launched after the success of the *Hennepin* project, and continued on the lecture circuit, sharing stories of West Michigan's submerged maritime history with audiences in the Lake Michigan region. At one of those lectures, I had a chance encounter that would add a key member to the MSRA team and lead to a very important discovery related to Flight 2501.

After my lecture at the annual meeting of the Berrien County Historical Society, a friendly woman who appeared a few years younger than me introduced herself as Chriss Lyon and commented, "I've been following you and your organization since your discovery of the *Akeley*."

I felt flattered.

"Are you still looking for Flight 2501?" she asked.

"We sure are," I answered, "but we won't get back out until next spring."

"Have you found any of the victims' next-of-kin?" she inquired.

That question caught me off guard. I wondered why she would be interested. "Yes, some," I said, hesitating to say much more.

"Oh, good," she kept going. "I was going to start looking for them."

Oh no, I thought. *The last thing these poor people need is to have yet another researcher picking their brains.* I felt I had been imposing too much already. "What's your interest?" I asked, probably sounding defensive.

"I'm a genealogist," she said. "I'd like to offer my help."

That piqued my interest. In the space of a few minutes, I learned that her interest in genealogy began with research into her own family and had grown from there. Her primary job was as a supervisor for a 911 station in the Berrien County Sheriff's Department, where she dispatches the police, fire department, and Coast Guard to handle emergencies. Ironically, had Chriss been alive in 1950, she might have been coordinating aspects of the Flight 2501 search and rescue operation. In time, her interest in history prompted her to offer her services as the Sheriff Department's historian.

I took Chriss up on her offer of help. The next day she called me. "Got a pencil?" she asked. "I found Ellen Ross' sister."

Chriss' skills went way beyond finding people. She had a knack for tracking down historic archives as well. When I realized her full capabilities, I challenged her, "What do you suppose was done with all the human remains found in the lake?"

"Let me look into that," she offered.

We set off on different paths. I pursued coroner records, eventually connecting with Jeff Filbrandt of the Filbrandt Funeral Home in South Haven, who used to work for Van Buren County Coroner Fern Calvin's funeral home. Filbrandt hit a dead end. "Records were not kept until 1953," he told me a couple days later.

Chriss had better luck. She called me about a week later sounding very excited, "Can you meet me in St. Joseph? I found the grave where all the remains were buried."

She explained that she had elicited the help of Robert Cooley, a member of the Berrien County Genealogical Society, who transcribed the records of local cemeteries. It had taken him only two days to locate a notation in the sexton register of Riverview Cemetery in St. Joseph, Michigan, indicating that on July 3, 1950, unknown parts of bodies from an airplane wreck in Lake Michigan had been buried in lot 535, section 3, space 4.

Later that week, I met Chriss at the cemetery. We parked our cars along the southernmost road on the grounds and made our way to the last row in the cemetery. Numerical markers led us to the specific plot, a patch of unmarked grass. On either side of the plot, granite headstones, level with the ground, marked the graves of other individuals. We both kneeled down on the grass. "I can't believe that the remains of the victims were buried here," I said, touching the grass, "and there is nothing to acknowledge them."

"It's disrespectful," Chriss agreed.

"Wouldn't it be nice if we could change that?" I commented, the cogs in my head starting to click into gear.

THE TELEPHONE AND MY COMPUTER became my two most prized research tools. I never strayed too far from my desk, and I slept with my phone close by, not knowing who would call next. It turned out to be retired Coast Guard officer Larry Otto, who at the time of the accident was a junior officer on board the *Woodbine*, one of the Coast Guard cutters sent to the scene. In fact, we had seen his signature on many of the logbook pages. His recollections brought alive those pages with sights, sounds, and smells of what he had experienced. "This was my first search and rescue mission, and I was so excited," he told me as he described the radio call he received ordering his vessel to duty. He also underscored the terrible tragedy. "When we got to the site, I realized there was no one left to rescue—the scene was so horrible."

I asked him about the location of the wreck, wondering if, perhaps, there had been some kind of gag order, and the Coast Guard really had found the crash site.

"No, we never found the wreck," he told me, dashing my hopes.

Otto suggested I call two other Coast Guardsmen who served under him on the *Woodbine* during the search. Wayne Tovey and Carl Gilbow had vivid memories of the four days they had spent hauling up gruesome debris from the aircraft. By that point, I had talked to many individuals who knew the victims, witnesses who said they had seen the airplane that night, and now Coast Guardsmen involved in the search and recovery. However, I had not talked to anyone from management at Northwest Airlines. That was about to change.

I had subscribed to the Northwest retired pilots newsletter; one day I pulled the latest copy out of my mailbox and quickly scanned it while I was standing at the end of my driveway. On the back cover was a picture of an elderly man with the caption, "98-year-old Joseph Kimm pictured at the Northwest retirees picnic." I had seen Joe Kimm's name in the CAB report and in newspaper accounts about the accident investigation. My screams echoed through our neighborhood: "He's aliiiiiiiiive!"

Joe Kimm, who sounded as sharp as a man half his age, had been very involved in the accident investigation. He offered several details but, unfortunately, could not recall anything that would help us in our quest. "We tried, but could never find the plane."

Next, I received a call from a woman I knew, but was unaware that she had any connection to Flight 2501. Judy Schlaak, the registrar at the Maritime Museum in South Haven, who had previously assisted me with ship research, had heard about our search and wanted to help. Her father, a commercial fisherman, had set his gill nets just before Flight 2501 crashed. "My dad brought up some interesting things in his nets a couple days after the accident," Judy told me. "They might point you to the wreck."

We agreed to meet for lunch. She brought me a package. Carefully folded up in a plastic pouch was a peach-colored, short-sleeved men's shirt. "This was in a suitcase that my dad recovered—I want you to have it."

Wow, I thought, holding the shirt reverently in my arms. *This belonged to one of the passengers, perhaps even someone whose family I had spoken to.* I had never imagined that anything recovered from the accident still existed.

Chapter 12

QUITING IS NOT AN OPTION

April 2008 was soon upon us. That month, Northwest Airlines ceased to exist; it merged with Delta Airlines. We no longer had to be concerned with the airline's reaction if we found the wreck.

Ralph reserved the same house and boat slip in South Haven, but brought along a different third crewmember, Cameron Fletcher, who took Harry Pecorelli's place, since Harry and his wife had just had their first baby. A student of archaeology, "Junior," as Ralph called him, would be getting an extra education from his six weeks of work on Lake Michigan.

Mowing the lawn would begin in earnest the next day. The team would be searching in the southwest sector of the circle, as Clive had promised.

About two weeks into the expedition, I received an email from Ralph. "Clive will be here late this week to work with us."

Not only would this be the first time that he personally joined in the hunt for Flight 2501, but also his first time working on the Great Lakes. I wrote back, "Great. How about we all get together for dinner at our house one night?"

Ralph suggested the next Friday night after Clive's first full day on Lake Michigan.

Right on schedule that Friday, I saw Ralph's truck pull into our driveway. We had a bigger than normal gathering for the dinner, because everyone wanted to meet the Grand Master of Adventure. Our teammates brought their spouses, and David Trotter, Kevin McGregor, and Chriss Lyon joined us. Ralph led the team in the side door, as usual. I lay in wait, ready to tease Ralph, "So…Clive's first day on Lake Michigan," I said smiling at Clive, while shaking Ralph's hand. "You probably found Flight 2501?"

Without missing a beat, Ralph replied, "No, but we did find what appears to be a small airplane and two shipwrecks."

"Really?" I asked, not knowing if he was kidding.

Ralph didn't answer; he headed into the kitchen, toting his computer bag. I shook Clive's hand and welcomed him. Although this was the second time I had met him, I treated it as my first, since I was sure he didn't recognize me from that archaeological conference in Chicago almost a decade earlier.

Jack and I played hosts, introducing Clive to everyone and pointing out their roles on the MSRA team. Once our guests seemed comfortably settled with drinks in hand, I found Ralph. "Did you say something about shipwrecks?" I coyly asked.

"I was wondering when you were going to start pestering me," he joked, reaching for his computer bag. "Where can I set this up?"

"How about right over here in the sun room," I motioned, leading him from the kitchen to the adjacent room and pointing to the desk on which our computer sat. "You can plug in here."

I collected Jack, Craig, Bob, Todd and Jeff, the people for whom this would mean the most, and hustled them into the sun room. By then, Ralph had his computer running with the familiar Lake Michigan chart on the screen. I saw three dots, all pretty close to each other. *Ralph wasn't kidding*, I thought, *three new wrecks*.

He clicked on a file and called up an image of the first wreck. "We picked this up while running north on our second lane of the day," Ralph announced.

I knew immediately it was a good-sized shipwreck. The detail was so extraordinary that I could practically see wood grain. "That looks like an engine," Jack said, pointing to a distinct shape near the stern."

"Sure does," Ralph replied.

"How big?" Craig asked.

"About 150 feet long."

"How deep?" Bob asked.

"160."

Great, I thought. *Jack, Craig, and I will be able to do the 160-foot dive.*

"So a 150-foot-long wooden steamer?" I proposed, not being very clever with the naming.

No one commented because Ralph was clicking away with his mouse. "Then on the very next lane going south, we found this," he said, opening up another file. "It's only about a mile away from the steamer."

Another shipwreck materialized. "This one is about sixty feet long and at the same depth," Ralph noted.

The side-scan image appeared to be boat-shaped, pointy on one end and square on the other, but it had little shadow. Shadow on a target would appear light, not dark, and would indicate approximately how high the vessel sits off the lake floor. "Not much to it," I commented, referring to the lack of shadow. "Did you take another pass at this one?" I asked, knowing that depending on how the sonar signal hits an object, it can look completely different.

"No. It's not what we're after. We didn't waste time scanning it again," he replied. "I'm calling it the 'Flat Wreck.' You can dive this one easily enough."

"What about the small airplane you mentioned?" Craig asked, reading my mind.

"Wait till you see this," Ralph said, calling up the third target.

I gazed at the most perfect side-scan image I had ever seen. It looked as if an airplane had gently landed on the lake bottom. I could see the nose cone, two wings, and the standing tail. "Wow, come here, Kevin," I hollered into the living room, knowing that as a pilot and diver, who had found a small airplane submerged in an Alaska lake, he would be interested in seeing this.

He joined us in the tightly-packed room and looked over my shoulder. "Shit, that looks just like my Cessna. I'd hate to have been that pilot."

"This one's in about 180 feet." Ralph said

Another wreck I could dive, I thought. "I hope the pilot isn't still in his seat," I commented, wondering how I would react if I saw a body underwater.

"Did you get another view of this target, Ralph?" I asked.

"Nope. It's clearly not a DC-4, so I didn't bother."

While we were scrutinizing the airplane target, Craig opened the MSRA website on our computer and called up the page where we maintain a list of the all the missing ships and airplanes off West Michigan.

"Well, it looks like we have two good possibilities," Craig said.

All eyes turned to the other screen, where there was a photograph of a Piper Apache PA-24, lost in October 1979. Craig read the text out loud. "A pilot, Stewart Dreger, was en route from Palmira, Wisconsin, to Detroit, Michigan. Air Traffic Control lost radar contact with the airplane about twenty-five miles west of South Haven."

"This target is about twenty miles offshore," Ralph pointed out.

"Close enough, considering an aircraft like that flies at about 185 miles per hour," Kevin pointed out.

Craig called up the other small airplane on our web site. "This one's been down there a lot longer," he noted.

A Boeing Stearman PT-17 went missing on August 5, 1946. Craig read the text. "Benton Harbor pilot, William L. Hood, was lost while flying from Naval Air Station Glenview in Illinois to Benton Harbor. Dozens of planes searched for Hood and his plane, but no trace of either was found."

"William Hood...," I said, remembering an email from a couple years earlier. "His nephew contacted us wanting to know if we ever found his uncle's plane."

"Looks like you might have a phone call to make," Kevin said, "depending on which plane wreck this is."

I made a mental note to look up the Dreger family. After tracking down Flight 2501 families from 1950, I knew I would have little trouble with 1979.

"I'd suggest," Ralph said, "that you dive that target while we're still here. If it is a private plane, we're going to have to inform the State Police."

The new finds infused the balance of the evening with excitement. We ate, we talked, and my daughters asked Clive for his autograph in their copy of *The Adventures of Vin Fiz*. Our evening would have been great if they had found nothing, but three wrecks served as icing on the cake.

"Never mind The Bear God," I said to Clive while escorting him to the door at the end of the evening, "you're the good luck charm!

"What can I say?" he replied, laughing, as he headed out the door.

"HAND ME MY MASK, please," I said to Jack, from my perch sitting on the transom of our boat a week after the airplane target was found.

If I had tried to bend over, the weight of the double tanks on my back would have pitched me head first onto the deck of the boat. Donning my mask was the last thing I had to do before joining Bob Underhill and Jeff Vos, who were already in the water, hanging onto the buoy line that Ralph had dropped near the small airplane target earlier that morning.

May was very early in the season to be doing a deep dive like this. The water was still cold and so was the air. There was no sun that day to warm us up before we entered the water or, more importantly, when we returned. Hypothermia was a real risk. However, if this was one of the missing private aircraft, it was too important to delay. We planned to limit our bottom time at 180 feet to just fifteen minutes, which would require another fifteen minutes of decompression.

I spit into the lens of my mask and rubbed my saliva around, preferring natural anti-fog juice to the stuff that comes in a bottle. Jack climbed onto the swim platform and made sure both my tanks were turned on and the valve that connected them was also in the on position so that the tri-mix breathing gas could flow freely between the two. He would serve as surface support, but was ready to make the next dive depending on what we found.

I swung my finned feet over the transom and stood up on the swim platform with Jack's help, since the tanks weighed me down. Fortunately, in the water, they would not feel that heavy. Then, I took a giant stride into the lake, holding my mask in position so that when I hit the water, it would not be ripped off. The extra weight of the tanks forced me under, but the buoyancy of my drysuit and my "wings," the flotation device around my tanks, helped propel me right back up to the surface.

The water was little more than 40 degrees, but all of my skin was covered with a layer of thermal protection, except around my mouth. I would be chilly, but it would be bearable. I touched my right hand to my head to signal I was OK, then kicked my way to the down-line where Bob and Jeff waited with video cameras in hand. As soon as I got there, I purged the air from my suit with the valve on my left arm and did the same to my wings. Then I began sinking, following Bob. Jeff followed me. We had agreed on that order because I had no intention of going near the cockpit windows where I might come face to face with the pilot.

The water was amazingly clear because it was so cold. In a few months, after it warmed, the visibility would decrease a little but would still allow us to see some sixty feet distant. The clarity of the water still astounded me some sixteen years after it made its remarkable transformation. When I began diving in Lake Michigan in 1976, five foot visibility was the average, and the water became pitch black at about 100 feet deep. Now the blue-green shade of the water darkened as we got deeper, but the daylight followed us down, never fading from view. Our deep-diving team had even encountered ambient light on wrecks as deep as 275 feet.

We owed the extraordinary visibility to the zebra and quagga muscles, invasive species indigenous to Russia and the Ukraine that entered the Great Lakes in the early 1990s through the discharge of ballast water from foreign freighters. They have been a double-edged sword; the filter-feeding mollusks help clean the water, but they attach themselves in clusters to any hard surface, like wood of a shipwreck or aluminum of an airplane, making it hard for divers to see the details of the wreck.

At ninety feet deep, I could begin to make out the sandy bottom below. I rotated around as I continued to descend, but I could not see the wreck. About two minutes after we left the surface, we reached the bottom and saw the weight to which Ralph had secured the down line: a concrete block. He wanted us to recover it after our dive so he could use it again in the future. I hovered about six feet off the bottom, careful not to dangle my fins in the sand, which would undoubtedly raise a cloud of silt that would obstruct our view. I saw Bob head off in one direction from the buoy and knew he must have spotted the plane. I followed far enough behind him so that his fins did not hit me in the face. Then I spotted the wreck about 40 feet away. It looked small, but I figured that was because I was still quite far from it. As we closed the gap, I got a better view. *Geez*, I thought, *the plane has sunk into the muck so far, I can only see the very top of the fuselage and the wings.*

I felt a little relief, knowing that the cockpit windows would be buried. When Bob reached a point about fifteen feet from the wreck, I caught a view of him against the airplane and thought that, even buried, it seemed too small. Then Bob swam to the right, and I got an unobstructed view of the target.

"It's two pieces of wood!" I screamed into my regulator, knowing in that instant that we had wasted an entire day and hundreds of dollars on boat, truck, and breathing gas. We had been fooled by side-scan targets before, but no target had ever been so convincing.

All I wanted to do was turn around and go up, but I had to wait for my buddies. It is always so frustrating in a situation like this because we can't communicate well underwater. Bob swam the length of the wood from right to left, and Jeff swam the opposite direction. I hung back, ascended a few feet, and started scanning out over the lake bottom, wondering for a moment if this wood was just random garbage and the airplane was lurking nearby. However, from that higher vantage point, I realized that the wood was, in fact, the airplane target. It appeared to be two long and large timbers joined perpendicularly in the proportions of a Christian cross. At the base of the cross, I noticed the sand had scoured away, creating a triangular-shaped trench. I realized that the trench had created the illusion of an airplane tail on the side-scan image. At that moment, although I cursed the side-scan, I realized that if it could detect pieces of wood no longer than twenty feet, it would never miss a pile of mangled DC-4.

Three minutes into our bottom time, Bob and Jeff circled back, and we all headed to the up-line. We did not need to decompress because of the short dive, but, as with any deep dive, we "hung" on the line for three minutes at 10 feet as a safety measure. As I held onto the up-line, looking up through the crystal-clear water, I could see the bottom and side of our boat and the outline of Jack looking down at us. He must have been wondering why we had come back so early. Until one of us surfaced, he would still be presuming we had dived on an airplane. He would be awaiting our identification of it as an Apache, a Stearman, or some other type of aircraft and the news about whether there were any bodies inside. When our three minutes were up, I kicked my way up to the surface to break the bad news to Jack as quickly as possible. I spit out my regulator and hollered the 10 feet across the water. "It's not a plane, it's two pieces of wood in the shape of a cross."

"What?" he asked, cupping his hand over his ear.

I swam closer. "It's not an airplane."

Once we had all climbed out of the water, recapped the dive for Jack, taken off our gear, and numbed our disappointment with beer—even me having one too—the guys began the process of hauling up the concrete block. They took turns, huffing and puffing. It must have been like pulling up a boulder with a string. Finally the block reached the surface, and Jack and Jeff hauled it over the side and dropped it onto the deck with a thud. "Holy crap," Jack exclaimed. "Ralph used the biggest, baddest block he could find."

That's when I got an idea how we could break the news to Ralph about the "plane."

I checked my cell phone and saw, surprisingly, that I had reception even that far out on the lake. Hoping Ralph did, too, I called his number.

"So what do we have?" he asked, skipping a greeting.

"Did you have to use *such* a big concrete block, Ralph?" I asked doing my best to sound seriously upset. "You dropped it right through the cockpit window and into the pilot's lap!"

There was silence on the line for a couple seconds, and I figured that Ralph was squirming. Then Jeff and Jack started laughing, and Ralph must have heard them. "No, really, what is it?"

I told him.

He didn't say much.

On the way in, I pulled out my copy of the side-scan image of the "Small Plane." Even though I had seen the target in person, it was impossible not to "see" an airplane in that Rorschach ink blot. I realized that the angle of the sonar beam hit the target in just such a way as to be deceptive. Had the sonar hit it from any other angle, it would have looked completely different, probably not warranting a dive.

CLIVE RETURNED TO ARIZONA, but with our good luck charm gone, we didn't find anything else. Ralph wrapped up the expedition at the end of May. "Let me know what those other two targets turn out to be," he said as we bid our goodbyes at the South Haven house.

We waited until June to dive on those targets. After being duped by the "Small Plane" target, we were afraid to presume that a target that looked like a 150-foot wooden steamer was really a 150-foot wooden steamer. However, in that case, it turned out to be a 150-foot wooden steamer. Clearly the ship had burned to the waterline before it sank, which confirmed that it was the *Joseph P. Farnan*, a steamer that caught fire and sank in 1898 while en route from Benton Harbor to Escanaba after delivering a load of lumber. It had settled deeply and solidly into the loose, silty lake bottom.

The Flat Wreck turned out to be very flat indeed. All that remained of the sixty-foot schooner was the lowest portion of the hull, and it was almost completely buried in bottom muck. Were it not for a small section of the forward rail, we never would have found it. Hazarding a guess as to its identity was impossible at that time because there was so little left of the vessel. Those two wrecks gave us something to work on that summer, a good thing because we came up empty-handed again after a second attempt that June to find the *Andaste*.

REAL LIFE, as Jack and I refer to everything besides shipwrecks, kept going, but like a throbbing toothache, Flight 2501 was always present. When we would get together with our non-diving friends, I'd often recount my conversations with Flight 2501 families or solicit input on where the wreckage might be, and I'd see their eyes glaze over. When my cousin shared the joyous news of her daughter's pregnancy, telling me how she planned to surprise her husband that weekend, I reminded her that Rosalie Gorski waited to tell her husband that she was pregnant and died before she did. My cousin did not appreciate my input. The phrase, "get a life," was thrown in our direction often.

Soon, Jack and I came to realize that we would lose our "normal" friends if we didn't find other things to talk about. We began to keep our Flight 2501 discussions private, but our kids often heard us talking. We could not even take our daughters to the beach without pointing out at the horizon line and theorizing where Flight 2501 crashed. Whenever we were outside doing yard work and heard an airplane taking off from the private airstrip nearby, we would stop, look up, speculate about its altitude, and time how long we could hear it, analyzing the many Flight 2501 witness accounts.

Even unrelated things could lead to thoughts of Flight 2501, like when my daughter Cella was reading and asked me the definition of "barrier." I told her that "a barrier is an obstacle that prevents movement or access, like a barrier in a road." Then I told her the word could also be used metaphorically; for instance, "Many pilots that night saw the storm as a barrier, but Captain Lind didn't. He continued across Lake Michigan."

I was finding it hard to get a life.

ON SEPTEMBER 20, 2008, fifty-eight years after the accident that ended the lives of fifty-eight people and changed the lives of the hundreds of others, a procession of cars turned east off Niles Avenue in the city of St. Joseph, in southwest Michigan. They passed a low stone wall, atop which stood a plaque with an etching of a setting sun over Lake Michigan welcoming them to Riverview Cemetery, where the remains of flight 2501 victims had been interred.

The drivers circled around to the south end of the ninety-acre, lushly landscaped property, along the banks of the St. Joseph River. Towering oaks and plump evergreens sheltered more than 10,000 monuments dotting the memorial park, all but one commemorating a single person, a couple, or a family. One by one, the cars came to a stop along the one-way, narrow roadway at the southeastern corner of the cemetery; doors opened and out came the occupants, securing their sunglasses to protect their eyes from the brilliant rays. They walked slowly toward a grouping of chairs carefully arranged between the flat stone markers that adorned that portion of the cemetery.

Talking in whispers, they slowly and reverently approached a new headstone—the only upright headstone in the area—toward which all the chairs faced. Flower arrangements in autumn hues of russet, gold, and crimson surrounded it, reflecting in the shiny, black granite surface of the impressive monument. Under the spreading branches of a gnarled elm that reached toward the stone as if to protect it, those gathered drew out tissues and wiped their eyes. They all wore pictures of their departed loved ones near their hearts, where they stored their memories. Almost six decades after the tragic loss that ended so many lives too soon, the mourners' emotions appeared to surface again, though tempered by the passing of years.

One by one, the Wohler children, Roberta, Leona, Dorothy, Leo, David, Darlene, and the toddler John, now sixty-one-years old, each walked up to the monument, bent down, and placed a single rose at its base. Those seven precious flowers represented the siblings' collective love for their father, still so strong after all those years.

The weather could not have been more different from that night fifty-eight years earlier, but it reminded those gathered that there is always light after dark and good after bad. At eighty degrees, the day was warm, but a gentle breeze rendered the temperature quite comfortable. For Michiganders who knew the gales of November were just around the corner, the beautiful day carried melancholy, an appropriate mood for the ceremony that was about to begin.

A four-member color guard began the service, parading in with gently wafting flags, circling behind the monument, and proceeding off toward the river.

"Good afternoon. Please be seated," Pastor Robert Linstrom, of Peace Lutheran Church in South Haven, said to begin the service. Then he described the reason for the gathering:

"On June 23, 1950, Northwest Airlines departed New York's LaGuardia Airport on a balmy night for a flight to Minneapolis. We are gathered today in memory of the fifty-eight people who died that night fifty-eight years ago. As we gather at the site where the remains of those people have been buried, a site long-lost to the memory of those of us who came after that terrible loss of life that fateful night, we come with the amazing gift and witness of family who lost loved ones. We gather here with all of you as witnesses and keepers of the legacy of those who died. We gather to give thanks this day. We give thanks for the proper accommodation for those we loved. We give thanks for the privilege of marking this place as hallowed ground. We give thanks for this moment in time made sacred by our gathering. In this hallowed place and in the grandeur of Lake Michigan's depths, the fifty-eight who died are entombed and we pause this day in reverent remembrance to commend them to God. Please join me in a word of prayer."

With my own children and Jack at my side, I listened, grateful for the beautiful day and all of the people who joined together to make the ceremony possible. Chriss Lyon, without whom I could not have found this grave site or many of the families present, sat solemnly near the back. Kevin McGregor, the pilot who initially helped me understand that this had all been divinely orchestrated and who helped me seek the answers, stood at the side near a towering pine.

I retreated, for a few moments, into the dark corners of my mind where I knew that bad things don't just happen to other people and could, in fact, happen to me. My biggest fear surfaced—that one day I might have to again attend a memorial service for someone close to me, someone whose life was cut significantly short—something that I had never worried about until my mother and my nieces died prematurely and until I came to know, almost personally, the fifty-eight people we were honoring and remembering that day. I also feared losing my own life prematurely, not for my sake, but for the suffering it would cause those who love me, just as the people gathered that day had been affected by their loved ones' deaths in the crash of Flight 2501.

When I first read about Flight 2501 so many years earlier, I could never have imagined how fifty-eight people from twelve different states—who were complete strangers to me—could come to feel like friends. However, in a grand plan I could not comprehend, they had. Because of that and because I was largely responsible for the day's gathering that brought together so many of their families who shared a common grief, I felt the need to say a few words. Working through my own emotions, I mustered the following:

"Before us today sit the sons, daughters, a grandson, nieces, and a cousin of several of the individuals lost in this accident so long ago. Despite the passage of over a half century, these families have never forgotten their loved ones lost in this tragic, life-ending and life-changing day. In addition many more family members who could not be here are with us in spirit. William and Daisy Hahnebach from New Jersey, whose brother and uncle, Carl Schlachter, and his wife, Louise, perished, have sent this beautiful flower arrangement with one flower representing each victim.

We are also honored to have with us today retired Coast Guard Officer Larry Otto, who on the day after the crash was among those who set out on a search and rescue mission. However, were it not for Larry and the other Coastguardsman, we could not be here today in this cemetery honoring those buried here.

As you know, we haves been searching Lake Michigan for the wreck of Flight 2501. In the process, we found something much more important: the place where your loved ones have rested for all these years. When I first encountered the barren plot of grass more than a year ago, I realized a great injustice had been done in never marking it and in never telling any of you that it even existed. Jeff Filbrandt of the Filbrandt Family Funeral Home in South Haven, Michigan, whom I had met in the course of the search for this grave, felt the same way and endeavored to do something about that. Today, through Jeff's generosity, we have this extraordinary monument that now honors those lost so long ago in this tragic accident."

All eyes gazed at the granite memorial that stood above all the others in that section of the cemetery. Across the top is the inscription: "In Memory of Northwest Flight 2501, June 23,1950. Gone but Never Forgotten." The names of all the victims are engraved in two columns, joined forever in the hereafter.

Pastor Linstrom continued with a scripture reading from the Old Testament; even those not familiar with the Bible would recognize the words from the tune made famous by the Byrds:

"There is a time for everything, and a season for every activity under the heavens: a time to be born and a time to die, a time to plant and a time to uproot, a time to kill and a time to heal, a time to tear down and a time to build, a time to weep and a time to laugh, a time to mourn and a time to dance, a time to scatter stones and a time to gather them, a time to embrace and a time to refrain from embracing, a time to search and a time to give up, a time to keep and a time to throw away, a time to tear and a time to mend, a time to be silent and a time to speak, a time to love and a time to hate, a time for war and a time for peace."

Ken Skoug and Bill Kaufmann, the first two individuals I met who had been scarred by this accident and who encouraged me to search for the other families of Flight 2501 victims, took turns reading the victims' names. A bell tolled after each one, giving those present a moment to remember. In those moments, I remembered my mother and the slowly tolling bell I was sure I had heard when she died.

Elizabeth Schulze, a graceful, soft-spoken woman of seventy-two, traveled from California to participate in the ceremony. "It was really hard to make this trip," she later said, "but I thought, it's just one day in my life that I really don't want to miss." Her uncle William Reid died in the crash. "I was 16 when it happened and I can remember when my mother told us about the crash. I thought maybe he didn't get on the plane, maybe he's safe somewhere, but of course that wasn't true," she said. "I never quite closed the door on this because there wasn't any closure."

The ceremony provided her that closure.

"We don't know what remains are buried here, but I assume my mother's are," noted Bill Kaufmann, with his snow-white head of hair and beard hiding his 64 years, who also traveled from California to attend the service for his mother, Jean. "For the first time it seems she's not lost. Of course she's dead, but I no longer have to wonder what happened to her."

"There's not so much sadness, because after all it's been fifty-eight years," Robert K. Williams told me that day. His cousin Thomas Hill was among the victims. "But this is a completeness, like tying up loose ends." He traveled from Minnesota to participate.

Mar Rouston, the niece of Mary Keating, came from New York to honor her aunt. "In a way, this helped to connect me to her because I was born after she passed."

The Color Guard retired the flags, marching back as a bagpiper came forward to play *Amazing Grace*. That song drew tears from those who had, until then, held in their emotions. As the last notes of the bagpiper faded as she walked slowly toward the river, I read a letter written by Mary Fenimore, the daughter of Mary Ann Freng, the sole remaining member of the Freng family:

> "We all share one sad, common thread: that in a blink of an eye, we lost someone who meant a great deal to us. For me it was three people, my grandmother, grandfather, and aunt: William, Rosa, and Barbara Freng. While I never had the opportunity to know these caring and thoughtful people, I am nonetheless profoundly affected by their loss. Never did I get to know the feeling of sitting on my grandfather's lap while he told me a brilliant story about his amazing travels abroad. Never did I get to play in my grandmother's beautiful garden learning the names of her prized roses, and never did I get to share secrets with my aunt. My mother lost her entire family. She no longer could share the events of her day with her mother, attend parties with his sister, or show off her first baby girl, born just three months after the crash. Although she tried to spare me her pain by never discussing the accident, there is no doubt the events of June 24, 1950, affected her deeply."

The accident had effected me deeply as well. I longed to find the wreck and solve the mystery of its loss even more after meeting so many more individuals who had lost a loved one.

Chapter 13

DISAPPOINTMENT & DEVASTATION

In late April 2009, NUMA arrived for our sixth expedition. Jim Lesto, a quiet, mild-mannered man, served as the third crewman. He retired early, lives in Charleston, like Ralph and Steve, and works for Ralph on a per-job basis. In his free time, he dives the many cave systems in Florida and snow skis, when weather permits, in West Virginia.

Clive, who must have taken seriously his power as a good luck charm, joined them a few days later. He found three shipwrecks. After the prior year's "Small Plane" misjudgment, I didn't know where we got the audacity to specifically name the three targets, but we did. Rather than call the first one "The Big Canoe," we dubbed it the *Hattie Wells*. Rather than name the second one a "sixty-foot Mystery Schooner," we called it the *William Tell*. Instead of calling the third one simply "The Box," we called it a forty-foot barge.

As it turned out, we were right about all three shipwrecks. Bob, Todd, and Jeff dived on the *Hattie Wells,* a schooner barge lost in 1889 in 250 feet. All of us dived the *William Tell*, a schooner lost in 1869 in 180 feet, and the barge in 125 feet.

We were familiar with the history of the *Hattie Wells* and *William Tell* from our research, but how and when the barge sank was a mystery. The two bigger barges that we had found previously had been stripped and scuttled, an illegal act that could have resulted in a stiff fine if the owner had been caught, but this barge still had equipment on it, which suggested it had been lost accidently. As we later learned, someone was fined over this barge, but not the owner. I discovered an article in the August 21, 1968, *South Haven Tribune* entitled, "Teens Fined for Vandalism." The article described how two Oak Park, Illinois, youths were apprehended after they set loose two vessels from the construction site of the Consumers Power Plant at Palisades. The article indicated that one vessel was a forty-foot barge with about $1,800 worth of equipment aboard. Bultema Dock and Dredge owned both vessels.

This discovery would mark the second Bultema vessel we had found.

Although these were significant shipwreck finds, our main goal still eluded us. Disappointment was becoming a very common emotion that I had been experiencing each spring for the last six years.

As usual, I reported our lack of success to the Flight 2501 families, then threw myself back into my regular work, as well as my pursuit of the remaining Flight 2501 family members. By that point, I had found relatives of forty-seven victims. I had no idea that I was about to experience, one after another, the shock and emotion of what those individuals went through in the days after Flight 2501 went missing.

ON JUNE 1, 2009, the nightly television news, internet news, and newspapers throughout the world announced a tragedy that captured my attention in the same way that the disappearance of Flight 2501 had captured the public's attention in 1950. I followed the story along with millions of other people:

"JET HIT STORMS OVER ATLANTIC. Plane carrying 228 people from Rio to Paris falls off radar. SAO PAULO (AP)—A missing Air France jet carrying 228 people from Rio de Janeiro to Paris ran into lightning and strong thunderstorms over the Atlantic Ocean, officials said today. Brazil began a search mission off its northeastern coast. Chief Air France spokesman Francois Brousse said 'it is possible' that the plane was hit by lightning.

Air France Flight 447, an Airbus A330, left Rio yesterday at 7 p.m. local time (6 p.m. EDT) with 216 passengers and 12 crew on board, said company spokeswoman Brigitte Barrand. About four hours later, the plane sent an automatic signal indicating electrical problems while going through strong turbulence. The plane crossed through a thunderous zone with strong turbulence at 0200 GMT today. Brazil's Air Force said the last contact it had with the Air France jet was at 0136 GMT, but did not say where the plane was at that time.

The head of investigation and accident prevention for Brazil's Civil Aeronautics Agency, Douglas Ferreira Machado, told Brazil's Globo TV that he believes the plane must have left Brazilian waters and could have been near the coast of Africa by the time contact was lost, based on the speed it was traveling. 'It's going to take a long time to carry out this search,' he said. 'It could be a long, sad story. The black box will be at the bottom of the sea.'"

Wil S. Hylton of *The New York Times* reported that the crash "was easy to bend into myth" because "no other passenger jet in modern history had disappeared so completely—without a Mayday call or a witness or even a trace on radar."

London's *Daily Telegraph* quoted Dr. Guy Gratton, an aviation expert from the Flight Safety Laboratory at Brunel University, about Flight 447: "This is an air accident the likes of which we haven't seen before. Put bluntly, big passenger planes do not just fall out of the sky."

These experts were obviously not familiar with American aviation history. Fifty-nine years earlier, Flight 2501 had done exactly that.

As the Air France tragedy unfolded in the days that followed, I continued to see uncanny similarities to Flight 2501. More than twenty-four hours after the disappearance, searchers found evidence of the crash including an oil slick, pieces of aluminum, and portions of the seats, but no signs of life. Newspapers began profiling many of the victims. The Brazilian Navy brought in divers, but authorities expressed concern that they would never be able to find the wreckage in waters as deep as the *Titanic* sank. By June 7 authorities announced they had found two bodies and a briefcase with a Flight 447 ticket inside.

JUST EIGHT DAYS after that international aviation tragedy, I received a text message that would put me in the same shoes of all the relatives of victims of Flight 447 and Flight 2501. While at a book signing on June 9, 2009, I heard the familiar tone of my phone signaling a text had arrived. I glanced down at the screen and saw a message from my cousin, Jacqueline, who was more like my sister to me. The words were distressing. "Morgan and the girls were in a car accident. We're at Butterworth Hospital. Come now."

Morgan, my ninetween-year-old "niece"—the daughter of Jacqueline and her husband, Steve, and the older sister of our "nephew," Collin—was the mother of two infants, two-year-old Jordyn and four-month-old Hannah.

I forwarded the message to Jack, telling him that I would pick him up in ten minutes, expressed my apologies to event organizers, and dashed to my car. Once on the road, I dialed Jacqueline's number, hoping for a good report on their condition. "Hello," she said quietly.

"How are they doing?" I asked immediately.

Jacqueline's response felt like a stabbing pain coursing through my body: "Morgan's gone."

"Nooooooo!" I screamed in a voice that still reverberates through my head. I pulled over, just a mile short of Jack's office, afraid I would crash my car otherwise.

When I found my voice again, bubbling up through uncontrollable sobs, I managed to ask, "Jordyn? Hannah?

I heard her take a deep breath. "Jordyn survived, but Hannah is not expected to live through the night."

I had never—not even when my mother died—sobbed so much. *Children, and especially babies, are not supposed to die*, I raged in my head.

I managed to make it to Jack's office, where he was pacing outside. I struggled out of the car, unsure if I could stand, then fell into his arms. "Morgan's dead!" I screamed at the top of my lungs, in anger, I think, while spit and drool gushed from the corners of my mouth. I repeated what Jacqueline had told me about the girls, breaking down again. His eyes became red and tears welled in them, but he remained solid, managing the calm he must have realized he would need to drive us to the hospital.

After being silent for a half of the 45-minute drive, I said with a clairvoyance that would unfortunately be spot on, "Nothing will ever be the same again. Jacqueline and Steve will divorce, Collin will turn to drinking and drugs, and we'll never see Jordyn."

"Don't say that," Jack implored, sounding angry that I had even voiced such things out loud.

"I'm sorry, but I don't see how they will survive this intact," I said, knowing Jacqueline better than he did, imagining how a young teen might cope, and assuming Morgan's young husband would not stay in touch. I worried about how my own kids would deal with this. Just two weeks earlier they had snuggled with their adoring cousin Morgan and her two daughters—babies they thought of as little sisters. It seemed too much to handle.

Many hours later as we drove home on the deserted highway after baby Hannah had joined her mother, we talked about the accident and how we would explain it to Cella and Taya. We had learned that Morgan had been in a hurry to get to her parents' house for dinner. She missed a stop sign, and a big truck plowed into her car, killing her instantly and throwing the babies out of the vehicle.

In the wee hours of that morning, I thought about how the families of Flight 2501 victims had gotten the news of the accident and the difficulties they had all faced trying to pick up their lives and move on. I could not help but to mourn alongside Wesley Malby and Oscar Schafer, who each lost a wife and son; the three Kaufmann children, who lost their mother; the seven Wohler children, who lost their dad; and Mary Ann Freng, who lost her entire family. Then I had an outlandish thought about the Hokanson family, the mother, father, and two young children who had died on the flight: *They were lucky because they died together. At least none of them had to suffer losing their closest loved ones.* The tragedy that I was now facing brought me closer to understanding the aftermath of Flight 2501.

Ralph Wilbanks on his boat *Diversity* pointing out the sonar gear during the expedition. *Photograph by the author.*

Harry Pecorelli monitoring the side-scan feed in the cabin of *Diversity* during the 2007 expedition. *Photograph by the author.*

The NUMA/MSRA team gathered in 2010 at the author's home. Pictured from left to right are Cameron Fletcher, Chriss Lyon, Jeff Vos, Todd White, Jack van Heest, Clive Cussler, Ralph Wilbanks, Craig Rich, the author, Ross Richardson, David Trotter, and Kevin McGregor. Steve Howard was present but not in the room. *Photograph by Mickey Trotter*

Although this side-scan sonar image looks like a small airplane, it is actually two pieces of wood, illustrating how important it is to dive a target to confirm its identity. *Side-scan by Ralph Wilbanks.*

From left to right, Todd White, Jeff Vos, and Bob Underhill, who made the deep dives to rule out certain targets as Flight 2501. *Photograph by Rene Mireles.*

From left to right, the NUMA crew: Jim Lesto, Steve Howard, Clive Cussler, and Ralph Wilbanks during search operations in 2010. *Photograph by the author.*

After the memorial service of September 20, 2008, the Flight 2501 families gathered for a group photograph near the memorial stone. Organizers are pictured at the right: the author, Chriss Lyon, and Jeff Filbrandt. *Photograph by Kevin McGregor.*

In Memory of
NORTHWEST FLIGHT 2501
June 23, 1950

Gone But Never Forgotten

LESLIE P. ANDERSON MD	WILLIAM C. KELTY
DR. LEON & SIROUN AJEMIAN	HILMA LARSON
MERLE LEROY BARTON	LEO F. LONG
DR. ARCHIBALD E. CARDLE	JO E. LONGFIELD
ANNA NAGLE EASTMAN	PEARLE MAIN
MIRIAM FRANKEL	YVETTE MALBY
WILLIAM & ROSA FRENG	DANA RICHARD MALBY (3)
BARBARA FRENG (17)	FRANCIS MCNICKLE
MARY FROST	HELEN MARY MEYER
ALFRED W. GEORGE	KARL NIELSON
PFC. RICHARD GOLDSBURY	RALPH NORMAN OLSEN
ROSALIE GORSKI	WILLIAM D. K. REID
EVELYN HEENAN	MARIE RORABAUGH
BENJAMIN & SLAVA HEUSTON	ELLEN ROSS
THOMAS HILL	ADELAIDE SCHAFER
HILDEGARD HOVAN	JOHN SCHAFER (8)
JOHN & CATHERINE HOKANSON	CARL D. & LOUISE SCHLACHTER
TOMMY HOKANSON (5)	FRANK C. SCHWARTZ
JANICE HOKANSON (7)	JOSEPH SIRBU
NORA HUGHES	KENNETH N. SKOUG
ARTHUR E. & GERALDINE JACKSON	LOUISE SPOHN
RUTH JOHNSON	RICHARD W. THOMPSON
DOROTHY JEAN KAUFMANN	REV. AUGUSTUS WALSH
MARY KEATING	EVA B. WOOLEY

LEO WOHLER

THE CREW

R. C. LIND   VERNE F. WOLFE   BONNIE ANN FELDMAN

The Flight 2501 granite monument sits impressively high along the south edge of the Riverview Cemetery in St. Joseph, Michigan. The inscriptions were designed by the author and the monument was donated by Jeff Filbrandt of the Filbrandt Family Funeral Home in South Haven, Michigan. The cemetery later placed directional markers to the monument after seeing the number of individuals visiting specifically to pay their respects to the victims of Flight 2501. *Photograph by the author.*

PART IV
THE AFTERMATH

"Oh! I have slipped the surly bonds of Earth...
Put out my hand, and touched the face of God."

Excerpt from High Flight *by*
John Gillespie Magee, Jr.

Chapter 14

FLIGHT 2501 IS MISSING

At 1:00 a.m. on June 24, 1950, 45 minutes after the last transmission from Flight 2501, and 80 minutes before the flight was due to land at the Minneapolis-St. Paul Airport, Northwest Airlines contacted the Michigan State Police and asked Air Traffic Control (ATC) to alert air and sea rescue facilities in the region to a possible crash. Technically, the aircraft could not be presumed down until dawn when its fuel supply would be exhausted, but the storm, combined with the lack of communication with the flight indicated that a tragedy of horrendous proportions had occurred.

Officer Lyle Hall of the Michigan State Police took the radio call from the Northwest operator at the Willow Run Airport at 2:32 a.m. The airline reported the flight overdue at Minneapolis and asked the police to report any aircraft accidents to Northwest. Hall typed up the complaint and assigned it case number 6581. He forwarded that information to other posts throughout lower Michigan. At the same time, ATC contacted the Ninth Naval District at Lake Bluff, Illinois; the Ninth Coast Guard District at Cleveland, Ohio; and the State Police in Illinois, Indiana, and Wisconsin, setting in motion what would become over the next few days the largest search and rescue operation in the history of the Great Lakes. It would be focused on the southern portion of the 22,000-square-mile Lake Michigan plus areas on land surrounding the lake in four states.

Admiral James A. Hirshfield, commander of the Coast Guard's Ninth District who was responsible for the entire Great Lakes region, was awakened and briefed. He was no stranger to pressure. While in a convoy on the North Atlantic during World War II, he had commanded the cutter *Campbell*, which engaged six U-boats, and sank a seventh all in the period of two days, earning the Navy Cross for his actions.

He ordered a search and rescue operation to commence and summoned Captain Nathanial S. Fulford, one of his chief officers, who was based in

Chicago, to carry out his orders. Fulford had been with the Coast Guard for 30 years and had been awarded a Bronze Star for his leadership during amphibious invasions of both the Gilbert and Marshall Islands during the war.

Hirshfield's counterpart in the Ninth Naval District, Rear Admiral James C. Jones, was also awakened and briefed. He issued orders for the involvement of personnel, vessels, and aircraft from the Naval Training Station Great Lakes and the Naval Air Reserve Glenview, both in northern Illinois.

While the cogs of all the big wheels were clicking into gear, an armada of small boats, airplanes, and individuals were already on the job throughout the lower Lake Michigan region. Because witness reports were widely scattered on each side of the lake, and since Flight 2501's scheduled route had crossed the lake, no area could be ruled out on land or in the water. The State Police alerted Civil Air Patrols. Many volunteers began trekking through remote wooded areas looking for a downed aircraft. The Air National Guard in Grayling, Michigan; Mitchell Field in Milwaukee; Selfridge Air Force Base north of Detroit; and even Lowry Field in Denver readied, collectively, several dozen airplanes for the search. Local Coast Guard stations began preparing to deploy their small, motorized life-saving boats.

As word traveled, private airplane and boat owners also offered to lend a hand. Although the thunderstorms of the previous evening had already passed south of Lake Michigan and would not hamper search operations, searchers would have to wait for the light of the dawn to be effective.

AS THE VARIOUS search and rescue participants swung into action, word of the potential disaster was just beginning to reach those who would be most affected: the families of the people on board. Verne Wolfe's wife, Ruth, may have been the first family member to learn about the missing airplane. She always waited up for her husband, and that night would be no different, even though she did not expect him home until around 2:30 a.m. Soon after midnight in Minneapolis, she phoned the Northwest desk at the Minneapolis-St. Paul International Airport to check whether the flight was on schedule. After identifying herself to the agent, she heard some whispering in the background: "Tell her we'll call her back in a little while."

Ruth was not prone to worry, but she knew at that moment that something was wrong.

An agonizing hour later, she saw the headlights of a car pulling up outside her house at 3012 E. 50th Street about two miles north of the airport. She hurried to the front window, hoping to see Verne. Instead, she saw Northwest pilot Keith James, his wife, Mary, and another pilot's wife, Lee

Brennan, coming up the walk. *Verne's dead*, she knew in that instant, tears welling up in her eyes.

She opened the door and stood on the porch trembling, clasping her arms to her body.

"Ruth," Keith James said, before he even entered the house. "I'm so sorry to have to tell you this, but Verne's airplane is missing."

Ruth broke down sobbing when she heard those words out loud.

Mary James put her arms around Ruth and guided her toward the sofa in the living room as her husband paced. "Listen, Ruth," James said, "They have enough fuel to fly until dawn. It's possible they tried to fly around the storm."

Ruth had been a pilot's wife long enough to know that when communication is lost, so is hope. "Where do they think it went down?" she asked, looking at him through reddening eyes.

James hesitated for a few seconds, knowing the answer would be even more disturbing. "Lake Michigan," he said quietly.

The trio of messengers settled in for a long wait until Northwest could provide more information. Ruth managed to call her sister Eleanor in Rice Lake, Wisconsin, who indicated she would leave immediately and be there in a few hours.

Lee Brennan phoned the Wolfes' pastor and made arrangements for a neighbor to care for Ruth's baby, Kristy.

"What about Margaret?" Ruth asked, referring to Robert Lind's wife.

"She knows by now," Mary said gently.

Through her own pain, Ruth could not help but have sympathy for Margaret even though she did not much care for her. She knew that Margaret and Bob Lind had just recently adopted a baby daughter, and Margaret had already suffered the loss of her parents.

AS WITH RUTH WOLFE, the airline probably sent representatives to Margaret Lind's home, less than a mile south of the airport. It is likely that one person stayed with the baby, while another drove her to the airport so that she would be there when news of the flight arrived. Although she frequently badgered her husband about being late, she would have been more worried than angry this time, especially now that she had a baby to think about.

AT ABOUT 1:00 A.M., Warren Johnson, the soon-to-be son-in-law of Flight 2501 passenger Frank Schwartz, entered the terminal of the Minneapolis-St. Paul Airport to pick up Schwartz, due in at 1:30 a.m. A couple hours earlier, after his wedding rehearsal dinner, he had dropped his fiancée, Joy Bell, and her mother, Patricia, at his grandmother's house where they would stay the night. He had said a long, romantic goodbye to Joy. The next time he would see her, she would be walking down the aisle at 8:00 p.m. Saturday at the Arlington Hills Lutheran Church. He could not wait to see her in her wedding dress. He knew she would be even more beautiful than when she was a princess at the 1949 St. Paul Winter Carnival.

The two lovebirds had met while attending college, he at the University of Minnesota and she at the nearby Macalester College in St. Paul. Johnson knew little about Joy's childhood; she had always been reticent about that. All she had told him was that her father, Morris Bell, had died and her mother later married Frank Schwartz.

Johnson approached the Northwest passenger counter to inquire about the flight. In front of him, another man, Ken Skoug Jr., beat him to the question, "I'm here for Flight 2501. Is it on schedule?"

The agent raised his eyebrows and said, "Please wait here," then he disappeared through the doors behind the counter.

Johnson knew the radio operators worked in offices through those doors and would know the status of the flight. He had graduated college with an engineering degree the year before and for the last several months had been working for Northwest Airlines in its routing department. He already knew a lot about how the airline functioned.

Before the agent came back, several other people began filtering up to the counter. James Woolley was there to pick up his mother, Eva Woolley. Alan Baron anxiously waited for his fiancée, Mary Keating. Margaret Skoug joined her stepson, Ken, to await news about the arrival of her husband, also named Ken Skoug. Warren Johnson noticed a woman behind the counter, who was smoking a cigarette and pacing. She didn't look like an employee and she looked angry.

A few minutes later, the agent returned to face the small group of people. He made an announcement to everyone. "The flight has been delayed in Detroit," he said, sounding stiff. "We are not sure when it will arrive, so you should all return home and call us in the morning."

The agent may have made an honest mistake or been told to stall for time, because, in fact, it was Flight 501, the regularly scheduled evening flight to Minneapolis that had been grounded at Detroit. Dispatchers probably did not want to risk that airplane crossing the lake in the storm after not yet being able to locate Flight 2501.

The idea of going home and waiting did not sit well with Ken Skoug, who was visibly agitated. He had argued with his dad, Ken Skoug Sr., just before his trip and was feeling quite guilty over it now and wanted to apologize. The wait would be agonizing, but he and his stepmother decided to do as the agent suggested. The others grumbled a bit, asking more questions, but the agent just repeated his suggestion to go home. Some took his advice. Others, including Woolley and Baron, settled into seats to wait. Johnson did not say anything; he just watched how each person reacted.

When he was alone at the counter, Johnson spoke up to the agent. "My name is Warren Johnson, and I work for Northwest in routing," he said, clearly seeking special attention. "I'm waiting for Flight 2501. When did it land in Detroit?"

The agent cast his eyes downward at the desk without saying anything, turned, and retreated through the door. He returned after a few minutes. "Look, Mr. Johnson," he said quietly, not making eye contact with him. "We are actually not sure where Flight 2501 is right now."

Johnson remained calm, but had a gut feeling that the airplane and his future father-in-law were gone. "Not sure? What do you mean?"

"Well, sir," he said keeping his voice low so as not to alert the others. "Our radio operators have not heard from the flight since a little after midnight in Michigan. There's a thunderstorm in the area and the radio reception is spotty. We're hopeful though," he said, glancing toward the woman pacing behind the counter, "The pilot's wife is here waiting."

The agent did not need to say anything more. Johnson knew that no communication for the last two hours meant that the woman's husband was probably dead, and with him, Frank Schwartz and all the other passengers. He remained calm, but he was starting to break down inside thinking of Joy and her mother asleep, dreaming about what was supposed to be such an exciting day tomorrow. Instead, it would be the most terrible day that either would have to face—the loss of a husband and the father. Johnson wrote down the phone number at that desk and indicated he would call within the hour.

When he got back to his parents' house and made the call, the agent had nothing new to offer. Johnson mournfully awakened his parents and told them what happened. After some discussion, his father phoned and woke their minister, the man who would be performing the service the next day, and asked him to meet them at the house first thing in the morning when Joy and her mother awakened. Then they made coffee and began gathering the telephone numbers of the 300 guests who were to attend the reception the next day. Of course, they would have to cancel the celebration. Johnson was not even sure Joy would want to go through with their vows, but he hoped that she would. *She'll need me now more than ever*, he thought.

AS THE JOHNSONS WERE GRIEVING, 500 miles away on the southeast side of Lake Michigan Chief Oscar Halsted and two crewmen left the St. Joseph, Michigan, Coast Guard station in their motor lifeboat. It was still pitch black, but they knew that the dawn would begin breaking in about two hours. By then they would be considerably offshore in the right place to begin their search.

Meanwhile, at 3:00 a.m., the radio operator on duty aboard the Coast Guard patrol boat *Frederick Lee*, moored at its home port in Chicago, knocked on the cabin door of Captain John Dalin, a 44-year-old lieutenant. Used to being awakened at all hours while serving in the Pacific during World War II, Dalin quickly hopped from his bed, already alert, and opened the door, smoothing back his hair, which made his long, narrow face resemble movie actor Clifton Webb. The operator handed him a typed message from Captain Fulford, reporting that a DC-4 with 55 passengers was presumed missing in Lake Michigan. A civilian had reported that he thought he had seen an airplane go down off Port Washington, Wisconsin, so Dalin was ordered to proceed north and begin a search there.

Dalin immediately called his crew to order and recalled those on shore leave. By 4:30 a.m., the *Frederick Lee* left its regular berth and headed toward the Chicago locks and out into Lake Michigan. Already twenty-three-years old, the 125-foot-long *Frederick Lee* was among only a handful of currently operating Coast Guard vessels that had been built long before World War II. It had been designed for trailing "mother ships" along the outer line of patrol during Prohibition and was named for a well-respected Revenue Service captain who commanded the cutter *Eagle* in the War of 1812. After duty overseas during World War II, the *Frederick Lee* had been sent to Chicago.

As soon as the *Frederick Lee* passed the outer breakwater at Chicago at 4:40 a.m., Dalin stationed a number of seamen as lookouts, but at a maximum cruising speed of thirteen knots, it would take the cutter over six hours to reach the primary search area.

"EXCUSE ME, CAPTAIN," a seamen said as he knocked on the cabin door of Lieutenant Frederick Goettel, commanding officer of the Coast Guard buoy tender *Woodbine*. It was 6:11 a.m. and the sun was just rising in Michigan that Saturday morning. "You're wanted on the telephone. It's Captain Fulford."

Goettel, who was already awake, opened the door while buttoning his khaki shirt across his broad chest. *This must be important for Nathaniel*

Fulford to want to speak to me directly, he thought, as he followed the radioman up the ladder stairs to the radio room above his cabin.

He knew that the forty-nine-year-old Fulford reported directly to Admiral Hirshfield, who had control over all the vessels throughout the Great Lakes.

Goettel pushed open the door of the small room and picked up the telephone. "Lieutenant Goettel here for Captain Fulford," he said.

"Hold, please," an operator replied.

"Fred," the Asheville, North Carolina, native said in his thick southern accent, "we've got a Northwest Airlines DC-4 that crashed in the lake somewhere between Benton Harbor and Milwaukee last night. I need you on search and rescue duty now."

"I can have the ship ready in twenty minutes," Goettel replied promptly.

The *Woodbine* had just moored the morning before in the harbor at Frankfort, Michigan, after sailing overnight Thursday from its home port in Grand Haven, Michigan, to show its colors for the Frankfort Centennial Celebration taking place over the weekend. However, search and rescue, known as SAR duty, would take precedence. Although SAR operations had been few and far between for the *Woodbine* since Goettel had assumed command in September 1949, he understood the work well, having attended the Coast Guard Academy in 1939 and served as an officer in the Coast Guard since 1942. In addition to regular duties tending aids to navigation, the *Woodbine*—as well as any of the other thirty-eight United States Coast Guard buoy tenders—could be called up for SAR operations or law enforcement missions at any time.

The eight-year-old *Woodbine*, a class-A steel cutter, was among 13 identical vessels specially designed in 1939 for setting and retrieving navigational buoys. It got its name from a North American woody vine, also known as Virginia Creeper, and carried the number W289 on its black hull, which offset its bright white superstructure. In 1944, the *Woodbine* was deployed to the Pacific and took part in an amphibious assault on the Mariana Islands and the Okinawa Campaign. After the war, the *Woodbine* was transferred back to the United States and resumed the primary work for which it had been commissioned, arriving in its new home port of Grand Haven in September 1947. With its two Cooper Bessemer diesel engines and 30,000-gallon fuel capacity, it was capable of long journeys. To hoist buoys and cargo, it had an A-frame structure that straddled the superstructure and supported the lifting boom. It carried two twenty-foot motor launches and a crew of fifty.

Fulford informed Goettel that he had already sent the *Frederick Lee* to begin the search and would be contacting several other Coast Guard cutters and local stations to aid in the operation. "As the highest ranking captain, you'll be in command when you arrive on site," Fulford told Goettel.

Fulford quickly wrapped up the conversation after Goettel let him know he would stay in touch via radio. Goettel exited the radio room and took the ladder a half flight up to the bridge deck to relay the orders to the on-duty crew. There he found twenty-three-year-old Ensign Lawrence J. Otto, one of his three deck officers. Otto had come on duty at 4:00 a.m. for an eight-hour shift. "Mr. Otto, prepare to get underway," Goettel ordered. "We will be conducting a search and rescue mission in southern Lake Michigan for a Northwest Airlines DC-4 lost sometime after midnight this morning. Better schedule the seamen six on and six off."

Otto knew that the normal eight-hour shift meant that only one-third of the crew would be on duty during each period. The new schedule would put half the crew on duty each shift. "Yes, sir," Otto responded calmly and professionally, just as he had been trained. However, inside he was excited. *Just two days on the job and I'm an officer on a search and rescue mission,* he mused.

Otto knew from his years in training that some men waited years to be involved in such work. He imagined how thrilling it would be to actually pull survivors out of the water.

BEING ABLE TO HELP SAVE LIVES had been one of the big draws that influenced Larry Otto's decision to enlist in the Coast Guard. That, and the fact that his father, a civil servant mechanic who worked for the Coast Guard, encouraged him to do so when his draft notice arrived in April 1945, a month before his 18th birthday. His dad told him that the Coast Guard would afford him better opportunities to move up in rank than the Army. On May 1, three weeks before his high school graduation, Otto went to the local recruiting office in Milwaukee and signed up. However, at five-foot, six-inches tall and only 129 pounds, he did not meet the minimum weight requirement of 135 pounds. "Go home and eat and drink a lot," the recruiter him, "then come back tomorrow."

Otto did as he was told, but he was still three pounds shy the next day. "A pint's a pound the world around, kid," the recruiter hinted, "Go drink a lot of water, then come back in here right away."

Again, Otto followed orders, practically drowning himself, and an hour later he weighed in at just the minimum. He passed his on-the-spot physical, then hurried to the bathroom. He was sworn in and immediately boarded a train for boot camp at Manhattan Beach in Brooklyn, New York. Adolph Hitler's suicide and the approaching end of the war in Europe, which had just hit the front page of newspapers that day, were all the talk on the train trip east.

Otto felt quite relieved when the Japanese finally surrendered during the last quarter of boot camp, after the second atomic bomb was dropped on Japan. He graduated on August 20, with little concern that he would be sent overseas. In fact, he qualified for the Coast Guard Academy Prep School in Groton, Connecticut, and if he made it into the Academy he could look forward to four years of college before active duty.

Otto was given a month off to return home, before beginning classes in late September, to review his high school courses and earn chemistry credits necessary to meet the Academy entrance requirements. In May 1946, just one year after joining the reserves, he and about one thousand other cadets sat for the nationwide entrance exam. Otto was among the top 250 men who passed and were offered appointments to the Academy. Only 160 men accepted. They received orders to report to the New London, Connecticut, Academy across the river from Groton. Otto spent the next four years as a cadet in the engineering program. The classes were difficult and there was a lot of attrition: Some quit and others failed. Otto was among only 68 cadets who graduated. He was never too proud to admit to any one who asked, "I was 67th in my class."

Upon graduation on June 2, 1950, the new officers, all with the rank of ensign, were offered their choice among sixty-eight billets aboard various ships. Otto picked the *Woodbine*, home ported in Grand Haven, because it was the closest position to Milwaukee and his family. He was given fifteen days of leave to return home, then reported aboard the *Woodbine* on June 21. He was surprised to learn that Frederick Goettel would be his commanding officer: He had trained under Goettel at the New London Academy. The very next day, the cutter set sail to show its colors for the celebration in Frankfort. Now it was on SAR duty.

QUARTERMASTER WAYNE TOVEY, who was in the chartroom behind the bridge, overheard Goettel talking to Otto. At twenty-four, Tovey had been in the Coast Guard for almost six years and was older and had more seniority than most of the crew. Once Goettel left, Tovey approached Otto. "So, I heard 'The Beef' say we're heading out for SAR?"

That was the first time that Otto heard his commander's nickname. *"The Beef," certainly fit his stature*, he thought. "That's right," he replied, not commenting on the nickname, "chart a course to intersect a line between Benton Harbor and Milwaukee."

Otto immediately began issuing more orders. Using the communication system, he alerted the ship's engineer to start the engine, blew the whistle to recall the sea detail, then made a general announcement to call the crew to order and prepare to get underway.

By 6:30 a.m., the *Woodbine* began moving toward the channel that led to Lake Michigan, where it would head on a course 208 degrees southwest. Twenty-year-old Yeoman Carl Gilbow was in his office when he heard the announcement. He went on deck and learned through scuttlebutt that they were off to rescue passengers from a downed airplane. He pictured people floating in life jackets and looked forward to being a part of the rescue. Gilbow had only been in the Coast Guard for one year.

As the *Woodbine* left the Frankfort channel, action was intense on board the ship. Some crewmen began removing the covers from the launches. Others started clearing the deck for the inflatable airplane life rafts they expected they would be bringing aboard, and still others began gathering clothing and blankets. There was an air of excitement among everyone because no big airliner had ever crashed in the lake. *This will certainly be more exciting than sitting at the festival*, Gilbow thought.

The lake was still dishing up swells from the storm the night before, the temperature was in the high sixties, and fog blanketed the lake. One of the crew noted that the boat seemed to be floating on fog and that in spots he could not tell where the lake left off and the fog began. It would take until late afternoon before the *Woodbine* could slice its way through the fog and reach the area off Milwaukee to rendezvous with the *Frederick Lee*.

AT 5:18 A.M. ACROSS THE LAKE, minutes after sunrise and about ten minutes after Commander Fulford ordered the *Woodbine* to SAR duty, Rear Admiral James C. Jones ordered the Naval Reserve training vessel *Daniel A. Joy* to begin SAR operations. If the wreck was found, Navy divers would be needed to go down and identify it because the Coast Guard had let its frogman program lapse after the war. Lieutenant L. G. Edgerton, standing in for Commanding Officer Joseph R. Antink, who had taken emergency leave the prior day, received the radio message and alerted his crew that early morning.

The *Daniel A. Joy* had been built as a destroyer escort, commissioned in April 1944, and used for escort, patrol, and antisubmarine duty just before the end of the war. After the allied victory, the *Joy* was sent to San Francisco to be used as a Naval Reserve training vessel, then decommissioned in February 1949. Just ten months later, it was recommissioned, refurbished, and sent to the Ninth Naval District for use in training reservists on the Great Lakes.

At the time the radio call came in, the *Joy* was engaged in an anchoring exercise off Whitefish Bay, Wisconsin. Edgerton ordered the anchors hauled in and a course set south toward the site of an oil slick near Milwaukee, Wisconsin, spotted by a Northwest pilot.

By 7:00 a.m., it reached the spot and found the slick and a few pieces of floating paper, but no bodies or any survivors. Edgerton figured the slick emanated from the wreckage of the aircraft, and he would need divers to go down and confirm it. The crew marked the head of the slick with two life rings attached to a grapple line in sixty-six feet of water. Following orders, Edgerton then set a course for the Milwaukee Harbor. While underway at 7:45 a.m., a small craft delivered Captain George A. Parkinson, head of the Naval Reserve, to the *Joy*. By 8:12 a.m., the *Joy* docked at the south side of the Sanitation Pier at Milwaukee where all fourteen-day reserve trainees disembarked along with Captain Parkinson. Commander Joseph Antink boarded the vessel and relieved Edgerton of command. Antink had been ordered to confirm whether the remains of Flight 2501 lay beneath the oil slick.

Chapter 15

THE UNIMAGINABLE

M ore than ten hours after the disappearance of Flight 2501, news of the probable tragedy had not yet reached the public. The only citizens who knew anything was wrong were the pilots' wives and the friends and families of the Minneapolis-bound passengers who had been at the Minneapolis-St. Paul Airport to meet the flight—and all they had been told was that the airplane was late. The families of Spokane- and Seattle-bound passengers remained unaware of any problem because the flight was not yet due in those cities.

That would all change within a few hours after Captain George Parkinson stepped off the *Daniel A. Joy*. Parkinson had been sent out in the vessel to acquire first-hand information about the oil slick.

A fifty-year-old former teacher, four-year veteran of World War II, Bronze Star recipient, Naval Reserve captain, and director of the University of Wisconsin-Extension at Milwaukee, Parkinson broke the story when he spoke with a reporter from the *Milwaukee Journal*. Whether he had specifically approached the *Milwaukee Journal* or whether a reporter intercepted radio transmissions and met the cutter at the dock is unknown, but Captain Parkinson would have had the authority to speak to the media. Although the reporter focused on the accident, not the person providing the information, Parkinson could not have been a more appropriate man to talk to about a wreck on water. In 1944, as commander of the Destroyer USS *Thomas,* he delivered the final death blow to the *U-233*, a German submarine found prowling in the North Atlantic. After it sank, he retrieved the survivors. In this case, however, the Navy had not found any survivors, only an oil slick.

The *Journal* broke the news on the front page of its second edition on Saturday June 24, with the headline, "Report Finding Air Liner Trace in Lake." The story continued, "Coach carrying 58 vanishes in storm. Bubbles sighted on the water's surface about seven miles off South Milwaukee. Capt.

George A Parkinson, head of the local Naval Reserve, said that the Destroyer Escort *Daniel A. Joy* had discovered what may be the sunken wreckage."

Parkinson would probably not have been so bold as to conclude that an oil slick signified the finding of wreckage. It is more likely that the reporter took that leap. Suddenly Milwaukee became the center of attention.

Northwest Airlines reacted like a deer caught in the headlights. Clearly the company was not yet ready to announce the loss of the airplane in Lake Michigan. In fact, a Northwest official told reporters that, "the plane might have been blown off course with its radio out of commission and gone down in the northern woods of Wisconsin."

The *Journal* even began prematurely profiling the victims, providing brief outlines of the three crew members, as well as Mrs. Whitney (Anna) Eastman, who had lived in Milwaukee, and Kenneth Skoug, who often did business in the city.

Even before the *Journal* hit newsstands, the *Milwaukee Journal*'s own radio station reporter, George Compte, broadcast news about the search effort live from aboard a private Coast Guard Auxiliary boat just after 10:00 a.m. After that, newspapers from around the country began picking up on the story, most referencing Milwaukee as the original source, and most suggesting that wreckage had been found.

Behind the scenes, Northwest officials were likely scrambling to reach the passengers' next-of-kin. They had a list of passenger names, addresses, and phone numbers, but if no one answered at the number, they had no way to track down relatives. In many cases, the media would be responsible for drawing out the families of the victims, and some editions of various newspapers around the country printed the entire passenger list, giving journalists what they needed to pursue personal interviews. Many were not compassionate in their quest for a scoop.

AT ABOUT 10:00 A.M., the doorbell rang at the house where Patricia Schwartz and Joy Bell, wife and stepdaughter of passenger Frank Schwartz, were staying in St. Paul, Minnesota, before the wedding. "I'll get it," Bob Rigg said to the group of mourners.

Rigg, the best man, had come over as soon as Johnson had called that morning. Pastor Melvin E. Hammerberg from their church had helped Johnson break the grim news to Joy and Patricia. Soon thereafter, a representative from Northwest Airlines had called to confirm the airplane and all the passengers were presumed gone. Patricia and Joy had been sobbing ever since.

Rigg opened the door to find a man with a pad of paper and pencil standing there. "I'm sorry for your family's loss," he said, sounding not all that sincere. "I'm with the *St. Paul Pioneer*. May I speak with the bride?"

"No, you may not," Rigg said angrily. "Have a little respect."

Johnson overheard the conversation and was amazed that a reporter had gotten to them so quickly. He had just mentioned the wedding in passing when the Northwest employee had offered condolences.

"I'd just like to know if the wedding is still on for the evening?"

"That's none of your business," Rigg replied, knowing that the couple had not yet made that decision.

"The public has the right to know!" the reporter countered.

"The public has no rights, mister," Rigg said with authority, closing the door behind him and stepping out on the porch with the reporter. He grabbed his arm and pulled him down the front steps, then escorted him briskly to the street. "We're done here," he said, giving the reporter a shove.

Inside, the pastor was trying to convince Joy to go ahead with the wedding. "You're going to need Warren to go back to New York with you and your mother tomorrow to deal with things," he counseled, "and it would not be proper if you two weren't married."

Joy wanted to marry Warren, but thought that would be disrespectful to her mother. She looked at her mother, asking approval with her eyes.

"Go ahead, Joy. You've got to live your life," Patricia said, with tears running down her face.

Joy looked up at her fiancé and smiled through her own tears, then turned to the pastor, "All right, but only family. We'll have to cancel the reception." As she said that, she began crying again, mourning the loss of her beautiful reception at the Riverwood Inn along the bluffs of the Mississippi River and their honeymoon at the historic hotel in Stillwater, Minnesota.

Rigg, who had rejoined the group, offered his help, "If you have your guest list," he said to Joy, "I'll start making calls."

By 8:00 p.m. that evening, Rigg and the other members of the wedding party had been able to reach all but eight guests. Joy and Patricia did not have the heart to turn them away when they arrived at the church. The annoying reporter from that morning actually had the audacity to show up at the wedding, although he was not let in. He wrote the story anyway, and it appeared the next morning in the *St. Paul Sunday Pioneer* alongside other stories about the tragedy: "Kin of Plane Victim Wed—Joy Bell of St. Paul went ahead with her wedding Saturday night, although she and most of the party were on the verge of tears. In the quiet of the Arlington Hills Lutheran Church, thoughts were far away on Lake Michigan's waters where the search for the missing Northwest Airlines DC-4 was still going on."

Throughout the ceremony, and for the next many days, weeks, and years, Warren Johnson would agonize about the accident, wondering why the pilot flew into a storm and deprived them of a father and future grandfather.

SIX-YEAR-OLD BILL KAUFMANN awoke Saturday morning in Seattle to the sound of the telephone. He lay in bed rubbing the sleep from his eyes and listened as he heard the muffled voice of his father, Winfield. Just then he remembered that his mother was supposed to be arriving home that morning. She had been away for almost two months and he could not wait to see her.

He had last heard her voice just two nights earlier when she called from New York. His father had held the phone away from his ear so that Bill could listen in. "I'll be home Saturday morning instead of Friday," she had said. "I'll explain later, but I've got some nice gifts for the children, including a doll for Mary, and a cowbell for Bill."

"Hi, Mom," Bill had interrupted her.

"Hi, Sweetie," she had said. "Mommy doesn't have time to talk now. I'll see you Saturday. I love you!"

Bill had kept listening as his mother wrapped up the call. "Winny, we've got some things to talk about when I get home," she said.

"All right, Jean," his dad had replied.

Bill imagined she would have a lot to talk about after such a long trip in Europe, but he didn't care about that, he just wanted to see his mom. He threw back the covers and ran out to the living room, but his mother was not there. Instead, he saw his father sitting in a chair bending forward with his hands over his face. "Oh, my God, oh, my God, oh, my God," his father kept saying.

Bill had no idea what was wrong. He heard his little sister crying from her crib, but his father seemed deaf.

"Your mother is not coming home," he said when he saw Bill.

Just then the doorbell rang. His father just sat there looking sicker than Bill had ever seen him. Then he got up to answer the door. Bill saw two people he did not recognize come straight into the living room. One was carrying a camera with a big flash bulb. They talked to his father, but Bill didn't really understand what was being said. Then, one of the men walked right past Bill up to the mantle where a framed photograph of his mother sat. "I'll need this," he said, pulling it down.

"Do I hear another child?" the other man asked, nodding toward the crying coming from the other room.

That's when Bill's dad seemed finally to hear his daughter. He left the room and came back a few minutes later carrying the baby with Bill's little brother Richard in tow.

"All right, that's good, sir," the man said. "Could you please sit here," he said, pointing to the living room chair. "Son, can you go sit on your dad's lap, please?" the man asked Richard. "And how about you stand behind your dad," he said to Bill.

Then the man with the camera took a book off the shelf and handed it to Bill's dad. "Here, why don't you read to the children?"

His dad just stared at the book and then Bill saw a big flash.

The next day the picture accompanied an article about the airplane crash in the Sunday *Seattle Times*. The caption read, "Winfield Kaufmann at Seattle yesterday reading to his three children as he waited anxiously to hear positive information about his wife, who was returning home on the plane after a trip to Europe."

ON THE EAST COAST, reporters were practically trying to beat in the doors of other people who had lost someone on Flight 2501. Alan Baron had called his apartment to break the news of the death of his fiancée, Mary Keating, to his five housemates. He sent them over to Keating's home to fend off the reporters pestering her distraught mother. Likewise, Richard Spohn, Louise Spohn's younger brother, who had heard the news on the radio, had to force gathering reporters away so that he could speak to his parents in private.

ALTHOUGH REPORTERS DIDN'T reach all of the victims' families, news reached them nonetheless. In the outskirts of Billings, Montana, sixteen-year-old Roberta, called Bobbie, and fourteen-year-old Leona Wohler were up that Saturday morning at their grandmother's house doing chores while their grandmother was at the market. They had arrived from their home in Billings earlier in the week to attend a church camp and spend some time with their beloved granny. Their mother, Gladys, was home with the other children, twelve-year-old Dorothy, ten-year-old Leo, five-year-old twins David and Darlene, and toddler John. Leona was upstairs making the beds while listening to the radio. At the top of the hour the announcer began reading the news: "Fifty-eight people are presumed missing on a Northwest Airlines DC-4. Flight 2501 was heading from New York to St. Paul-Minneapolis when the plane disappeared over Lake Michigan."

Leona dropped what she was doing and ran to the top of the stairs, "Bobbie," she screamed, "What airline did Dad fly?"

"Why?" Bobbie asked, walking upstairs, not understanding why her sister was screaming.

"There's a Northwest plane missing—Flight 2501."

God forbid, Bobbie thought, so many things now swirling in her head. "I think it was Northwest—Oh, my God—what else did the radio say?"

"Everyone is gone," Leona whimpered.

Bobbie sat down on the bed, grabbed a pillow and squeezed it as hard as she could. She could think only of the premonition she had earlier that week when she said goodbye to her dad in their kitchen as he was leaving for the airport. Ever since he had been involved in a bad car accident when returning from the Vaughn Ragsdale store in Columbus, Montana, she had worried about her father, but that goodbye felt different. She sensed she would never see him again. She recalled studying every inch of his face and body so that she would never forget him. Even now, she could picture his soft, smooth face, his dark, slicked-back hair, his thin mustache that sometimes tickled her when he kissed her, and his penetrating eyes that always let her know she was the center of his universe. In her mind's eye she could feel the texture of his dark brown, tweed sports jacket and see the leather patches on the elbows. He always dressed so well, whether in a suit or in his more casual clothes. *He had never looked more handsome than he had that morning*, she thought.

Leona pulled her sister out of her thoughts. "Even if the plane crashed, Bobbie," she said, still shaking, "I'm sure he survived."

"You're probably right," Bobbie said, trying to be strong. She pictured her dad struggling to shore after the crash, perhaps with a case of amnesia, which is why he hadn't called home.

As they talked through the situation, they decided to call Mr. Johnson, the manager of Vaughn Ragsdale, the clothing store where their father worked, hoping that he would know something about their father's flight plans. His response was unnerving. "I'm going to send Mr. Wittier from the Lewistown store to meet you."

The girls quickly arranged for their uncle to drive them home to be with their mother and siblings. Wittier arrived at the house shortly thereafter. He approached their mother directly, but could not have chosen worse words to break the news: "Well, Gladys, it seems Leo is at the bottom of Lake Michigan."

ON SATURDAY MORNING at about 9:30 a.m., Mr. Ross and his fourteen-year-old daughter Alice, the father and sister of passenger Ellen Ross, were golfing at a course in New Jersey near their home. On the radio, they heard that a Northwest Airlines airplane was missing.

"Didn't Ellen fly on Northwest?" Alice asked.

"Oh my God!" her father replied. "I think so."

They left the golf course immediately, hurrying home to be with Ellen's mother, stopping only briefly to purchase a newspaper. They had a momentary respite from their fears when they saw that Ellen was not listed among the lost passengers. However, soon after they arrived home, the phone rang. A representative from Northwest Airlines delivered the terrible truth. In fact, Ellen had been on board the flight. For the rest of the day, the Ross family prayed that the airplane had crashed on land and that Ellen had survived.

IN ONE CASE, great lengths were taken to keep a pregnant woman from hearing about the accident on the radio. As Mary Ann Freng White and her husband, Dick, were driving their blue Chevy sedan south on US Route 1 near the outskirts of Richmond, Virginia, on that warm, dismal morning, they had no idea that a Virginia State trooper was in hot pursuit of them. The trooper carefully maneuvered between the cars that sporadically dotted the rural route, attempting to catch sight of the car that his sergeant had told him to find. He had a message to deliver that would turn the occupants' world upside down, especially the woman's. His orders were to get her back to Chevy Chase, Maryland, to the home of her husband's employer.

Traffic was light that Saturday morning and the Whites had been on the road for a couple of hours. They had left Maryland early that morning heading to North Carolina, where their new home awaited. Wearing a sleeveless maternity dress and her signature pearl choker, Mary looked as glamorous as she always did. She had a heart-shaped face accentuated by an intriguing widow's peak. Petite, she managed to keep a good figure during the first six months of her pregnancy. Only her swollen belly gave away her condition. Although Mary was a bit of a rebel, not always playing by the rules of her conservative family, Dick hoped that her impending parenthood would ignite her own maternal instincts and soften her attitude toward her parents.

Dick felt well rested after a vacation over the previous two weeks, a break between assignments. On Monday he would begin a new position as a consulting mechanical engineer at a plant run by his employer Kurt Simonds. At only twenty-five-years old, he had already worked for Simonds for over two years, ever since graduating from the Massachusetts Institute of Technology. His first assignment had been in Lawrenceville, Georgia, where the couple lived after the elaborate wedding Mary's father had thrown for them in Rye, New York, at the Rye Presbyterian Church. Between the two assignments, the Whites stayed first with his parents in Bronxville, New York, and then with hers in Rye, just before her parents and sister, Barbara, left for a vacation in Billings, Montana.

As the Whites drove on, the state trooper began to catch up to them.

White had spent the last two days at company headquarters in Chevy Chase, Maryland. He knew that if he kept performing well at work, he would be promoted. Although even as a teen, he had set a goal to succeed in business, he felt some additional pressure from his father-in-law, the formidable William Freng, a vice president for ITT Corporation, to provide for Mary in the same way that her father had. His fraternity brother at MIT, Howie Bill, who had been dating Mary's sister and planned to propose that summer, felt similar intimidation from the elder Freng, and the two men discussed the issue often. White's concerns had started to lessen after the previous week when he and Freng played golf together for the first time. Although White clearly could not keep up with Freng in the game, his father-in-law took him under his wing, treated him with kindness and respect, and introduced him proudly as his son-in-law to a number of people at the Rye Country Club.

Hanging over his head was a concern that Freng's respect would end immediately if he ever found out that the young couple had actually married during White's last year of college. He had met Mary while she attended Wellesley College. One of the "majors" of all MIT men was to spend time at the all-girl college just a few miles southwest of Cambridge. After a year of dating, the couple decided to marry. An elopement fit Mary's rebellious personality, but she was not brave enough to admit it to her parents. A year later, White went through the motions of asking Freng for his daughter's hand in marriage, months after they had already married. The couple could not say no to the extravagant wedding her parents had offered to host.

The trooper soon spotted the blue Chevy and accelerated until he was cruising right behind the car. He gave a quick, short blast of the siren, not the multiple signals he would have given for a traffic offense, but enough to catch the attention of the driver.

In the rearview mirror, White saw the officer flash his headlights and point toward the side of the road. He had no idea what he had done wrong, but he pulled over immediately. He watched as the trooper stopped his vehicle a car's length behind his, opened the door, stepped out, took off his hat, and hesitated for hesitated, staring at the ground. *He looks more nervous than me*, White thought.

The officer finally approached White. "Good morning," the trooper said, swallowing, "Are you Richard White?"

Surprised that the trooper knew his name, White responded, "Yes, what's this all about?"

"I have a message from your employer," he said, bending down and glancing into the car, making eye contact with the woman and smiling, "and I need you to come back to my vehicle."

White looked at his wife, shrugged his shoulders, and said, "Sit tight, honey, I'll be right back." Then he opened his door, got out, shut it behind him, and followed the trooper back to his car. The officer reached in through his open window, grabbed his notepad, referenced it, then said, "A Kurt Simonds contacted us this morning after receiving a phone call from your parents. It seems that a Northwest Airline's plane has gone missing."

White slumped back against the car and covered his eyes with his hand, immediately realizing that his wife's parents had flown on Northwest Airlines to Minneapolis. "Your wife's family is presumed dead," the trooper said.

White doubled over as though someone had kicked him in the stomach. The officer kept talking, but he didn't hear what the man was saying. "Sir, sir," he finally heard, as the officer touched his shoulder. "Kurt Simonds suggested you return to Chevy Chase and meet him at his house, then break the news to your wife there."

That statement drew White out of his own shock and to thoughts of his wife and their unborn child. She had just lost her entire family, and the shock might cause her to lose the baby, too. He realized, as Simonds must have, that it would be best to tell Mary in a private place, where she could lie down or get medical attention quickly. Then he thought of his friend, Howie Bill, who had intended to propose to Mary's sister. White would have to notify him. Through the clouds swirling in his head, he heard the trooper say, "You better get going. Keep your radio off, because the story is already being broadcast."

Ten minutes later, the couple was in transit back north to Maryland. White had composed himself and simply told his wife, "There's been some complication and Kurt wants us to meet him back at his house."

Mary had protested, asking why they couldn't just discuss it on the phone. All White could do was stay level-headed, drive safely, try to keep his wife calm, yet not lie to her. "If Kurt asked us back, it must be important," he said.

After a tense car ride in which they did not talk much, White angled his car into the driveway of his boss's home. Simonds and his wife must have seen them coming because they left the house and stepped out onto the porch. White took a deep breath, got out of the car, walked around to the passenger side, and opened the door for Mary. He held out his hand to help her up, and escorted her up the front stoop. White and Simonds exchanged hesitant glances before Mrs. Simonds invited them inside to sit down in the living room. There, White reached for his wife's hand and eased into matters as gently as he could, "Mary, there's been an accident."

"They're gone aren't they?" Mary asked, tears welling in her eyes as she realized why her husband had turned the car around. Kurt Simonds intervened, picking up a copy of the *Washington Democrat* and handing it to her. "We don't know much more than this," he said, pointing to the headline, 58 PRESUMED MISSING. "Your in-laws called me because they were concerned about you."

Mary sank back into the sofa and began weeping.

FOR SOME PEOPLE, news of the accident brought great relief. After awakening at her mother's home at Manzanita Beach on Vashon Island, Washington, Rosamond Schlosser retrieved her mother's copy of Saturday's *Seattle Daily Times* from the front porch. The headline caught her eye: "Last Minute Change in Plans Put Seattle Woman on Lost Plane." Her hands began to shake as she read the article about a Jean Kaufmann who had lost her life on Flight 2501 and realized her own last-minute change had, in fact, *saved* her life and that of her three-year-old son, John. She had exchanged her June 23 ticket on Flight 2501 for one a day earlier in order to extend the visit with her family.

Arlene Savitt, another woman spared by chance, was awakened that Saturday morning in Long Island, New York, by a pressure on her body. As she blinked sleep from her eyes, she realized her sister was hugging her tightly and sobbing, "Something happened to the plane you were supposed to be on."

Arlene had been living in New York since December 1949 when, after a visit to her sister's home, she decided to stay on the East Coast. She had been working in the accounting department of the American Society of Composers, Authors, and Publishers, a perfect job for her as an aspiring singer and songwriter. In May 1950, she was asked to join the Rockefeller Center Choir and sang regularly in the plaza. She had purchased a ticket for a visit home to Minneapolis on Flight 2501, but returned it when her sister urged her to drive there with her instead. "I feel like a walking ghost," Arlene told her sister that morning. She began wondering why she had been spared.

BY EARLY AFTERNOON, the Navy Destroyer *Daniel A. Joy* was back on Lake Michigan searching for any kind of floating debris to indicate that the oil slick off Milwaukee really did come from the DC-4. By 4:00 p.m., they had found nothing and returned to the place where they had dropped a marker at the head of the oil slick. They set a buoy and requested the assistance of a well-known local diver, Jack Browne, who came to the site in his converted PT boat *Morning Star II*, but he was unable to locate any wreckage. Using long lines and grapnel hooks, the crew then dragged through the area hoping to hook any wreckage on the bottom, but they found nothing. The commander at the Ninth Naval District ordered Captain Antink to proceed to Chicago and await new orders.

WHILE THE NAVY was engaged in the dragging operation, the United Press and the Associated Press picked up the story, and within a few hours, newspapers throughout the country were printing afternoon editions of their Saturday papers. Most of the articles repeated the accounts of wreckage found off Milwaukee, which had already been disproved by the Navy. By that time, 18 hours after the last communication with the flight, most reporters assumed that everyone on board had perished although they still had no idea how, where, or why. Many Saturday headlines, like the *Herald-Press* in St. Joseph, Michigan, declared the sad reality, "58 ON PLANE DIE IN LAKE." However, in that same edition, a Northwest Airline official was quoted as saying, "The company still hopes the plane might turn up unharmed." He indicated that it held enough fuel to fly to Montana.

The *Herald-Press* and the Benton Harbor, Michigan, *News Palladium*, were the first papers to shift the center of attention away from Milwaukee to the east side of the lake. They both reported that an oil slick had been found twelve miles northwest of the St. Joseph Harbor. As it turned out, Chief Oscar Halsted of the St. Joseph Coast Guard, who had departed his station at 3:00 that morning, found the slick. Both papers also printed accounts from several locals who had seen a low-flying airplane along the lakeshore. The articles quoted a Commander Helm and Bertha Busse who each reported seeing an explosion far offshore, presumed to be Flight 2501. That new discovery and new witness accounts, plus the understanding that the Navy had not found any wreckage off Milwaukee, alerted the search and rescue teams that the effort needed to be relocated and expanded.

The Coast Guard decided to bring in more resources. Although the cutter *Mackinaw* was in Lake Huron, at 11:15 a.m., Captain Fulford contacted its commander, Captain Carl G. Bowman, and ordered him to proceed and assist in the search for the missing airliner. The *Mackinaw* was one of the largest and most recognized Coast Guard ships on the lakes. The 290-foot vessel had been authorized by Congress in December 1941, just ten days after the attack on Pearl Harbor, as an icebreaker to keep the upper Great Lakes open for shipments of iron ore, limestone, and coal necessary for the production of steel. Three years passed before it went into service out of its home port in Cheboygan, Michigan. During the ice-free months, the cutter was used for law enforcement, patrolling regattas, resupplying Coast Guard land stations, and search and rescue, like the current mission.

The *Mackinaw* had been in Lake Erie and was on its way back to Cheboygan when the new orders arrived. It entered Lake Michigan by 4:00 p.m., but fog slowed its progress. At 7:45 p.m., it had reached a spot near North Manitou Island, and the crew prepared the deck for the landing of a Bell-47 helicopter from the Coast Guard Air Station at Traverse City. By 8:00 p.m., the helicopter had been secured and the pilots had been assigned cabins. It would take another twelve hours before the *Mackinaw* would reach the search area.

By 8:00 p.m., the buoy tender *Hollyhock* was also underway to the new search area. Captain Fulford had ordered its commander, Captain B. K. Cook, to proceed and assist that day at noon when it was off Charlevoix refloating a buoy. Although much closer to the search area than the *Mackinaw,* the maximum speed attainable with its triple-expansion steam engine was just twelve knots, so it would not rendezvous with the other vessels until Sunday afternoon. The *Hollyhock* had been commissioned in 1937 as one of three 175-foot tenders for the U.S. Lighthouse Service. When that agency became part of the Coast Guard in 1939, the ships became the property of the Coast Guard and had been faithful servants ever since.

WHILE THE SEARCH CONTINUED on Lake Michigan, hundreds of people on the East Coast, Midwest, and West Coast—friends and family of the passengers and crew—were struggling to get through the day, a day that most would never forget, a day they wished had never happened, a day that would forever change their lives.

The tragedy also touched many people who did not even know any of the victims, including the President of the United States. Late that evening at his home in Independence, Missouri, Harry Truman was briefed about the crash of Northwest Flight 2501 in Lake Michigan. He had read about the missing aircraft that morning in the *Washington Democrat*, while scanning newspapers in his limousine on his way to the airport. There had been a lot, in addition to the disaster, to absorb that day. The *Washington Post* ran a story about David Greenglass, the former army sergeant charged with espionage for his part in the Fuchs spy ring. The *New York Times* reported that the Hollywood Ten refused to cooperate with the House Un-American Activities Committee. The *Washington Democrat* reported that FBI agents in Indianapolis had nabbed Henry Harland Shelton, one of the nation's most desperate criminals. Other articles told of Communist regimes springing up around the globe and anti-Communist propaganda in the United States. "Better Dead than Red" was the slogan of the times. The airliner story was just one of many events the President had to keep track of.

Truman undoubtedly thought of the missing DC-4 and its occupants when his DC-6, *The Independence*, took off that morning for Baltimore, Maryland, where he would speak at the dedication of the new Friendship Airport at 11 a.m. Dark clouds on the western horizon, his aides told him, were the aftermath of the violent thunderstorm that had probably caused the airplane to go down.

The Independence had landed while the Marine Corps Band played "Hail to the Chief;" the mayor of Baltimore and the governor of Maryland greeted the President and escorted him to the bandstand. The mayor began the dedication explaining how the new airport was a miracle of engineering, planning, and cooperation between federal, state, and municipal governments. The archbishop of Baltimore blessed the new facility and offered a prayer for peace. Then President Truman took the stand. He also spoke of peace. "We would not build so elaborate a facility for our air commerce," Truman said, "if we did not have faith in a peaceful future."

Truman pointed out that the airport's name had been chosen with that sentiment in mind.

After the dedication, the President had flown to Missouri to spend the weekend at home with his wife. He had been reminded again of the airline accident when his pilot had to fly an alternative route to avoid the squall line that was still moving south. That evening, his aides confirmed that the Northwest Airlines airplane was not just missing, but in fact had crashed in Lake Michigan killing all fifty-eight people, taking rank as the country's worst aviation accident. Truman knew that in the coming weeks and months he would have to meet with Delos Rentzel, the head of the Civil Aeronautics Board. An accident of that magnitude, Truman must have worried, could certainly frighten people away from flying, and how ironic, he must have thought, on the very day of a new airport dedication. Later that night, he went to bed haunted by the image of charred bodies from the airplane washing ashore. He was just starting to fall asleep when the phone rang with more bad news. Secretary of State Dean Acheson informed him that the North Korean army had just crossed the 38th parallel and invaded South Korea.

Chapter 16

SEARCH AND RECOVERY

Sunday morning dawned foggy at 5:15 a.m. along the Wisconsin shore. The *Woodbine* had arrived at Milwaukee the prior day, done some searching, and anchored near the *Frederick Lee* in the Milwaukee River for the night. At 5:30 a.m. both cutters prepared to get underway. Captain Frederick Goettel ordered each vessel to run a ladder pattern back and forth across the area underneath Airway Red 57 and look for floating wreckage.

At that time, the *Hollyhock* and the *Mackinaw* were in mid-Lake Michigan and would soon intersect the search corridor. The *Mackinaw* began sending out its helicopter to do more distant reconnaissance, but the fog hampered visibility of the lake surface. The boats blew their fog signals continually as they cut through large swells left over from the storm. Between patches of fog, the crewmen on all four vessels could see airplanes crisscrossing the lake. There were also a number of airplanes flying out of Illinois that passed near the *Daniel A. Joy* moored in the river awaiting orders for sonar work or diving.

THE PEA SOUP fog and scorching hot, humid weather was not about to stop the tens of thousands of fishermen on Lake Michigan, who had been looking forward to Sunday, June 25, all winter and spring. The day marked the start of sport fishing season, and reporters estimated that some 400,000 Michigan-based fishermen with permits in hand would be out on the Lakes that day. Many fishermen from the Milwaukee area would have gotten an especially early start, hoping to do double duty—catch some fish and maybe even help solve the mystery of the big airliner disappearance.

In South Haven, Michigan, Julius Allers, the captain of the *Elsie J*, piloted the 48-foot, steel fish tug down the Black River toward Lake Michigan. He, Alex Washegesic, and Walt McCash, who all worked for the boat's owner, Chris Jensen of Jensen Fishery, had other concerns that morning besides the airliner lost off Milwaukee that they had read about in the newspaper. They had set a gill net on Friday, and because of the bad weather could not recover it on Saturday. Although they typically did not work on Sunday, they needed to recover their catch.

Allers negotiated his way past a pack of rowboats and small motor boats all filled with fishermen champing at the bit to get out to the big lake. Up ahead, he saw the fish tug belonging to the Chambers Brothers, their main competition, as well as the Coast Guard motor lifeboat from South Haven. He waved to Joseph Bartunek, the boatswain's mate, and seamen Kenneth Richie and James Bryson, figuring they were heading out to oversee the start of fishing season. In fact, they were going out to search for any sign of the aircraft.

Likewise, Kyle Sinclair, manager of South Haven's small airport, had just taken off in his private airplane to aid in the search effort.

Once the *Elsie J.* passed the piers that were lined with fishermen, it quickly left the pack of sport fishing boats behind: Allers' crew would be heading farther out to water about 100-feet deep where they had set the gill net for whitefish. They hoped for a good catch that day, particularly since it had not been a very profitable season thus far.

Allers had been fishing most of his life. Born in 1903 at the Sleeping Bear Point Life-Saving Station in northwestern Michigan, where his father worked, he had spent his youth on Beaver Island after his father's transfer there. Fishing was a way of life on the island. For the last ten years, he had been working for Chris Jensen, but by that summer he was beginning to wonder if he had to find another occupation. The trout population was diminishing. Ever since the record trout catch in 1940, the tonnage had been declining and rapidly. Sea lampreys were to blame. The eel-like creatures, native to the Atlantic, began slowly invading Lake Ontario after the Erie Canal opened in 1825. By 1945 Jensen and Allers were finding lampreys—some as long as three feet—attached to almost one-third of their catch. A lamprey would use its round, suction-like mouth to attach to the underside of a fish, dig into the fish's flesh with its sharp teeth and tongue, and then begin sucking blood, killing the host fish slowly. By 1950, Jensen fished primarily for whitefish, but the lampreys had taken a toll on their population, and smelt and chub populations were growing, causing the whitefish population to decline.

The 75-horsepower Kahlenberg engine thumped rhythmically and spewed black smoke from its stack as Allers passed the end of the breakwall. The fog had dissipated a bit, but it still hung in the air. He had to go slow, sound his horn frequently, and keep an eye out so that he did not ram any other boats. He took a bearing with his compass and headed the *Elsie J.* southwest from the channel.

The boat had been built in 1945 by the Burger Boat Company in Manitowoc specifically for Chris Jensen and was a solid and reliable craft. That was important to Allers, especially after the loss of two South Haven-based wooden fishing tugs, the *Richard H.* and *Indian*, both lost during the Armistice Day storm of 1940. As the *Elsie J.* passed several small boats already trolling, Allers wondered what he would find in the net that morning. Sea lampreys, as it turned out, would be the least of his problems.

About an hour later, Allers spotted the wooden buoy that marked one end of the several-hundred-foot-long net that, underwater, would have looked something like a massive tennis net stretched across the lake floor. Lead weights along the net's bottom edge weighed it down and cork floats across the top kept it upright. When a curious fish swam near, its gills would get caught in the netting.

Allers throttled down and glided to a stop near one end of the net. As Washegesic opened the port side hatch, Allers donned his oilers and pulled on plastic sleeves to keep his arms dry. At five feet, nine inches tall and rather hefty, Allers looked like most of the fishermen, but smelled a lot better. His Old Spice aftershave always masked the smell of fish. The threesome began the process of hauling in the net. First, Allers grabbed the end of the net with the gaff and fastened it to the power lifter. Washegesic powered up the lifter and the net began coiling around the reel. Allers stayed nearest the door to make sure the net came in untangled. He and the other two men pulled the fish off the net one by one and tossed them into boxes of ice. The first few whitefish were fine specimens.

The net kept coming and the men kept grabbing fish.

"What the hell is this?" Washegesic asked a few minutes later, pulling a clump of flesh from the net and opening his palm to show the others. "It looks like someone has already skinned and filleted the fish for us."

"I don't know what that is, but get rid of it," Allers said.

As the reel made another revolution, Allers saw a huge hole in the net. "Stop the motor," he hollered to Washegesic, carefully examining the tear. "Damn it. How the hell did this happen?"

Allers had personally crafted the net with his wife over the winter and it had been in perfect shape when they set it. The net would require a time-consuming repair before being used again.

"Keep hauling," he grumbled to the others.

As the net continued coming in, Allers saw something familiar, yet completely out of place, tangled in it: a suitcase. It was mangled and partially open. He grabbed the gaff, kneeled down, and wrestled the suitcase carefully from the net so as not to tear it any more. "Son of a bitch!" he screamed suddenly, recoiling backward and falling on his rear end. The suitcase landed at Washegesic's feet.

"What's the matter? McCash asked. "It's only a suitcase."

It wasn't the suitcase that had shocked Allers; it was the basketball-sized object that rolled out of the net near the suitcase. "I think I saw a human head," Allers groaned.

"What the hell are you talking about, Julius?"

Allers was quiet for several seconds and got to his feet. "The airplane!" he declared, realizing that was where the suitcase came from. "It must have crashed right here."

The three men all threw out theories for the suitcase and torn net, hoping Allers was wrong about the crash. "Open it up," McCash encouraged, pointing to the crumpled suitcase.

The hinges were twisted, but Allers forced it open. Not much was left inside, except for a couple of neck ties and a man's shirt still folded and pinned up as though it had come from the cleaners. He picked it up and saw that it was ripped in a few places, but realized it had been a fine shirt, made of a peach-colored, lightweight rayon material, with long sleeves that buttoned at the wrists, a flap on each of the two breast pockets, and an open collar, the kind that would be worn without a tie. He noticed that it was hand-stitched, denoting an expensive shirt. The label indicated it was size medium, made by the McGregor Company.

Although Allers would not have known, the McGregor-Doniger Company was a maker of men's and boys' sportswear. By 1950, it was one of the leading men's sportswear companies in the country, profiting greatly from the recent trend toward more casual clothing.

"We're going to have to report this," McCash said.

"Yeah, but we gotta get the net in first," Allers replied, "then we'll set a marker here."

They started the retrieval process again, fearful of what else might show up. There were fewer fish than the prior week's haul, and the men hoped it was because of whatever had happened to the net, not a declining fish population. Then Allers found another clump of what looked like a filleted fish. This time he had a better idea what it really was. "Hand me a bucket, Alex," he said, trying, as he reached for the flesh, to imagine it was just another fish. He tossed it in the bucket that Washegesic extended, shivering as he did despite the heat.

By the time they had retrieved the net, they had collected, besides whitefish, some strips of fabric, several pieces of foam rubber, and a bucket half filled with chunks of flesh.

As they entered the harbor later that afternoon, Allers blew the whistle as he usually did when they passed the Coast Guard Station, knowing it would signal his wife, Paula, that they were in. As always, she and the kids, David, Mary Jean, and Judy, were waiting at the Dykman Avenue dock to check on the amount of fish and find out how long it would take him to clean them and get home. This catch was different from all the others. After explaining what they had found and what he suspected had happened, Allers gave his wife the shirt and ties and told her to take them home. The shirt wouldn't fit him, but he could put the ties to use on Sundays. "I'll get there a little later than usual," he told Paula, knowing he had to report his find to the local Coast Guard station.

Allers arrived home a couple hours later, but instead of going inside, he grabbed a shovel from the garage, dug a hole as far away from the house as he could, dumped the contents of the bucket into it, and filled the hole with dirt, saying a little prayer as he did. Frank Rydlewics, the Coast Guard chief petty officer he had talked to, had not been very concerned. "Just get rid of that stuff," he had told Allers about the flesh. However, Rydlewics did keep the suitcase and noted the location of the discovery.

It is likely that Rydlewics clearly understood the truth of what Allers reported. He probably radioed the reported location to his crew in the lifeboat, because, coincidentally, just a couple hours later at 6:00 p.m., Chief Petty Officer Bartunek, who had left the harbor that morning with seamen Richie and Bryson, radioed that they had found debris from the airplane. Bartunek noted that they had recovered the partial skull and hair of a woman, the raw flesh of a man's back down to his legs, human intestines, clothing, a gray blanket with the letters NORTHWEST stenciled on it, and the maintenance log book of the aircraft filled with alternating yellow and white sheets of paper. Officer Rydlewics ordered them to head directly to the St. Joseph station twenty miles south to deliver the recovered items. Then, he telephoned Captain Fulford with news of the discovery, probably proud that his station had cracked the case.

AS RYDLEWICS WAS MAKING THAT CALL, Captain Goettel on the *Woodbine* was plotting his next move and that of the other cutters. He had spoken with a Civil Aeronautics Agency official and learned that the airplane had been in the vicinity of Benton Harbor when the pilot last radioed. He plotted the possible flight path between Benton Harbor and Milwaukee and decided to move the *Woodbine* south about twenty miles and continue his ladder pattern across the lake down there.

Captain Goettel and Ensign Otto were in the wheelhouse about 30 minutes later when the radioman approached them. "Sirs, we received a call from Captain Fulford. He said that debris from the downed airliner was found twelve miles off South Haven. He ordered us there."

Here we go, Otto thought, hoping that even after forty-two hours in the water, people might still be alive.

"Mr. Otto," Goettel said. "You heard the man. Proceed and assist."

The *Woodbine* was already underway and heading in that direction, so Otto ordered the wheelsman to increase speed. At 7:00 p.m., the lookout leaned inside the wheelhouse. "Ensign, I see debris dead ahead."

Otto stepped outside. The sky was dull and overcast, but there was still plenty of light; the sun would not set until about 9:30 p.m. The seas had calmed. He raised his binoculars. As far as he could see ahead of the *Woodbine,* specks dotted the lake surface, some in clusters, others by themselves. Some things were dark, others were light. A few pieces had some mass, floating up and above the surface, but most lay flat on the water. He steadied his elbows on the rail and scanned the surface for any movement. He noticed a dark and slightly iridescent strip of water in the area, about 100 feet wide and at least a half mile long, that he figured was an oil slick. Everything was still and nothing looked big enough to be a person. He was sickened to realize this would be a recovery mission, not a rescue mission.

Just then, Goettel appeared on the wheelhouse. "Ensign, prepare to stop the engine and launch the boats."

"Yes, sir."

Otto grabbed the microphone, "Boat crews, report to your stations."

The chief boatswain's mate assigned seamen to the two boats, while the vessel slowed to a stop. Wayne Tovey and Carl Gilbow both pulled duty in the starboard boat. They stood by as several crewmen began operating the falls to lower the boat from the davits. From their vantage point on the deck some 12 feet above the lake's surface, they could see the scattering of debris, but had no idea what it consisted of. Tovey, the older and more experienced of the four men, had the sense that this was not going to be pleasant. Everything from parts of the fuselage to people's possessions would be out there: anything that could float, maybe even bodies. Gilbow, on the other hand, was excited. This was his first SAR duty, and he had not given the accident much thought—the search would be more like a treasure hunt. The words "ready, boys," spoken by one of the seamen, pulled each of them from their thoughts.

One by one, Tovy, Gilbow, and the two other seamen stepped over the low side rail, climbed down the wooden-tread, rope ladder that had been thrown over the side, and jumped into the boat.

"Thirty-two degrees off the starboard bow, one-eighth mile," Otto blared through the megaphone from his position atop the bridge wing twenty feet above the main deck. From there he could see a large cluster of debris. Then he strode through the wheelhouse to the other bridge wing to give direction to the boat crew on the port side.

Tovey started the motor and let it warm up a bit. A seaman cast off the lines securing it to the ship, and they pulled away heading in the direction Otto had commanded, motoring very slowly. Within a few minutes, the boat approached something in the water that looked like a heap of fabric, and Tovey put the engine in idle. Using a gaff hook, Gilbow leaned over the starboard side, stabbed at the object, lifted it, dripping, and swung the saturated material into the boat, where it fell with a slap onto the deck. Water rushed off, finding its way out the scuppers near the stern. One of the seamen picked up the material, wrung it out over the side, and unfurled a pair of brown tweed men's pants, with a belt still through the loops, slashed as if the man inside them had been attacked with knives.

That's when the tragedy hit Gilbow. *There's nobody left—no one bobbing in life jackets,* he thought. The pants made it real for him.

Tovey continued, seeing a cluster of flotsam and a small flock of gulls hovering overhead that must have been what Otto had directed them toward. He idled the boat as the debris became more concentrated. A seaman hoisted a small section of silver aluminum, backed with some kind of yellow puffy material, into the boat. One of the men tossed in what was clearly foam from a seat cushion with blue patterned fabric still adhered to one side. "What the hell is this?" he hollered, looking with horror at his forearm and shaking it over the deck. A lump of stringy tubing fell from his arm.

"That, my friend, is probably what's left of the guy who was sitting in that seat," another seaman joked, recognizing it as human intestines.

"Jesus Christ," he cried, stumbling backwards, away from the gory mess. He quickly turned around and began retching over the side of the boat.

"Get it together, boys," Tovey said. "There's a lot more of that here."

The boat had just glided into a huge field of debris, the bow pushing it to either side of the tender. "Go ahead, start grabbing," Tovey said.

"But we got nothing to scoop it up with," Gilbow protested.

"You got hands, don't ya?" someone said.

Tovey joined in, too, bending over next to the helm and heaving things into the boat. They picked up all kinds of debris, including aluminum, foam, thin pieces of wood, a purse, loose papers, a small suitcase, a blanket, more clothing, and a baseball-sized object that could only be a child's heart. More lumps of flesh appeared, none bigger than a basketball.

As fast as they could pick up debris, more appeared. In fact, it seemed to be bubbling up from below. Fortunately for the men, little of the human remains, so far, were identifiable. It might as well have been meat from the butcher shop: there were no bones, no heads, no limbs. Then one of the seamen near the stern hollered, "Hey, Johnny, you're a ladies' man. Why don't you help this lovely woman into the boat?"

Startled momentarily, thinking someone was alive, Tovey rushed aft, looked over the side, and saw what could only be a human breast floating upright. "Have some respect," he shouted, then bent over and scooped it up.

He knew that sailors often used dark humor like that to alleviate stress, but he didn't like it.

Then one of the other men vomited.

Tovey knew he had to cut this short. His crew could not take much more, plus the boat deck was nearly full with debris. He decided to go back and suggest only twenty-minute shifts on the water. He pushed the throttle forward, turned around, and headed back to the *Woodbine*.

Despite the hum of the boat's motor, he heard running through his head the Northwest advertising jingle that ran regularly on the radio:

"Give wings to your heart,
Your spirit soars,
Manhattan to the Orient,
Miami to Hawaii's shores.
Fly the best when you fly Northwest!
Northwest Orient (Gong) Airlines."

Yeah, Tovey thought sarcastically, *your spirit certainly does soar on Northwest Airlines—right on up to heaven!*

He made a vow never to fly on an airplane.

OTTO SAW THE SMALL BOAT heading back and climbed down to the ladder to the main deck. One of the deckhands was preparing the lines to secure the boat. As it approached, Otto saw a heap of debris lying on the deck. He began looking around for something to put it in. He spotted a garbage receptacle. *The thirty-gallon metal canister would do just fine,* he thought. *It has two handles that we can tie lines to for lifting.*

"Seaman," he said to a man nearby. "Put together a detail and collect all the garbage cans. Distribute them to the two boat launches."

By the time Tovey's boat had been secured to the starboard side under the davits, Otto got a firsthand look at the types of things they had been recovering. *The plane must have completely disintegrated when it hit the water,* he thought. *Nothing is bigger than a breadbox.*

"Got something we can put all this stuff in?" Tovey shouted up to Otto.

"Yeah, I'm sending it down now."

Using the boom normally used to lift buoys, a deckhand lowered a trash can and Tovey grabbed it, pulling it down to the deck. The four men started placing the debris inside, not bothering to sort through things. One of them tossed a few of the larger, heavier pieces up onto the deck of the *Woodbine*. "Haul her up," Tovey yelled, once the canister was full.

One by one the men climbed the ladder, looking like they had just come back from battle.

Tovey and Otto discussed the conditions out there, the amount of human remains they had found, and the need to limit the crews' time in the boats. Tovey described the "hot spot," as he called it, where debris seemed to be bubbling up and expressed his opinion that the wreckage was located just below. He suggested that they drag the area and try to hook it. "Oh, and we're gonna have to have something to scoop the stuff up with, instead of our hands," he commented. "It's pretty gruesome."

"How about some pots from the mess?" Otto offered.

"That'll do."

Otto sent a deckhand off to collect the pots. By 8:30 p.m., two fresh crews had been deployed to the small boats and were heading out to collect more debris. By then, Goettel had decided they would work continuously throughout the night. The sky was already getting darker. They would need all the spotlights to illuminate the water.

Ensign Otto's duty shift ended at 10:00 p.m., just after the two boats had returned for a third time, delivered their canisters of gruesome debris, and gone out again. He briefed the next officer in charge, then stepped out to the bridge wing. The sun had just set and it was now dark. The humidity was almost gone, and the air was warm but not oppressive. The night seemed calm and deathly still. The only sounds were from the distant voices of the crew in the boats, although he could not make out their words. Every so often, he heard a retching sound that he knew was another crewman losing the contents of his stomach. Then a rumble from one of the small boats firing up its motor, probably to chase a piece of debris, drowned out the voices.

From his vantage point, Otto could see the beams of the spotlights illuminating the surface and the glow of lights off in the distance marking the other Coast Guard cutters, some as far away as a couple miles, and each a hub of activity just like on the *Woodbine*. Between the *Woodbine* and the other cutters, he counted ten small boats, two deployed from his tender, and two each from the *Hollyhock* and the *Frederick Lee*. Only the mighty *Mac* had four boats. Their individual spotlights made the boats look like fireflies dancing around the night sky. *It looks so beautiful*, he mused, but then cursed himself for having such a thought considering the reason they were there.

A flash of light caught his eye and he realized that a spotlight had hit a piece of aluminum in the water at just the right angle. Just then "The Beef" joined him on the bridge wing. Otto had not been able to get that nickname out of his head ever since he heard it the day before. Making conversation, Otto commented. "The debris seems to be moving pretty steady, even though the water has calmed."

"It's the current," Goettel replied. "It's pushing everything northeast toward shore."

Otto thought about how hard it had been for the men in the boats to handle the human remains. He could not imagine how a child playing on the beach would react if debris drifted ashore. That thought fueled his commitment to the work, but he would not come back on duty until 4:00 a.m.

After a restless few hours of sleep, Otto took over at the morning shift change. During the briefing he learned that a boat from the St. Joseph Coast Guard Station was en route to the scene to transport the recovered debris. CAA, CAB, and Northwest officials had gathered there and wanted to look everything over. Thirty minutes later, motor boat CG83428 arrived and edged up to the *Woodbine*. The deck crew began the process of lowering the containers, ten or fifteen by some counts, to the small boat, while gulls squawked madly overhead. Then the boat motored off to repeat the procedure with the debris collected overnight by the *Frederick Lee* and *Mackinaw*.

Only the *Hollyhock* was gone, sent in by Goettel to deliver its load, then ferry a contingent of officials out to the *Mackinaw* for a big on-site meeting. In the *Woodbine*'s spotlight, Otto saw much less debris on the lake. The small boats were running farther from their mother ships to pick up stray flotsam. The helicopter on the *Mackinaw* was being readied to take off to scout for more debris at daybreak. Looking over the chart, Otto saw that the four boats had recovered debris scattered over about seventy-five square miles. Wherever the airplane had hit the water, the debris probably spread out in all directions, moving with the currents like a jar of marbles dropped on a hard surface.

MOTOR BOAT CG83428 arrived at St. Joseph Coast Guard Station at dawn on Monday morning, carrying the grisly evidence, followed shortly thereafter by the *Hollyhock*. The crew of both boats off-loaded the containers of debris and eight Northwest blankets in which they had wrapped the clothing, and carried them into the boathouse. Berrien County Coroner Louis Kerlikowske, and owner of the Kerlikowske Funeral Home, took charge of all the human remains.

As he began to examine the flesh and organs, some of it riddled with metal fragments, he noted the lack of bone. He concluded immediately that the force of the crash had been so extreme that it stripped the flesh off the bodies. He indicated that unless more intact bodies were found, he would have to recommend a mass burial.

Captain Fulford had driven in from Chicago and took great interest in seeing the debris. Officials, including Third Region CAB Acting Chief W. G. Golkowake, CAB member George R. Clark, CAA Supervising Agent R. Halsimon, and Northwest officials Ralph E. Geror, Paul Benscotter, and Felix Perry, Flight Operations Technical Advisor H. E. Morphew, and System Chief Pilot Joseph Kimm, all had arrived from Minneapolis or Chicago.

This would not be the first accident investigation for Kimm. He had started flying in 1929. At seventeen, he joined Northwest as a steward and by eighteen was a copilot, making $150 per month. Just two years later, he and Captain Mal Freeburg survived a terrible mishap when one engine broke loose and lodged in the landing gear. They managed to shake it loose over the Mississippi River, then land safely. That daring maneuver netted him and Freeburg an audience with President Roosevelt a year later. And that same year, he had a chance to serve as copilot on a "proof of the pudding flight" with Amelia Earhart to prove Northwest could fly from Minneapolis to Spokane. Although his career had many high points, especially after he had been promoted to captain, he had suffered through having to investigate four fatal crashes and the death of pilots and crew he knew and respected. This was his fifth accident investigation.

Kimm and the other men focused on analyzing the airplane debris. There was quite a bit of foam and fabric from the seats and armrests, torn white fabric from headrest covers, plywood from the inside of the fuselage, and shattered sections of the fuselage that had floated because of the still-attached insulation. Kimm took particular interest in a rack from the cockpit that had been mounted behind the pilot's seat and once held an oxygen bottle. He deduced from its damage that the airplane had hit the water on its side and angled down.

Several dresses were found with price tags still attached, some perhaps belonging to Jo Longfield, who had made several purchases in New York.

Other items of clothing, torn from the passengers' bodies or lost from their luggage, included trousers, jackets, dresses, sweaters, undergarments, a fur jacket, and a cloth jacket that still carried the scent of expensive perfume.

Because of markings or sizes on some items, they could be associated with individuals. A suit coat with a label from a Worchester, Massachusetts, store would have belonged to Leo Long, who was from that city. A Bible likely belonged to Father Augustine Walsh. A tiny blue coat with a kernel of popcorn inside, rubber pants, and baby shoes, were the perfect size for little Dana Malby. A girl's red sandal and a boy's black oxford probably belonged to Janice and Tommy Hokanson. A baby doll, had probably also belonged to Janice, the only little girl on the airplane.

Identifiable personal items included a handkerchief monogrammed with the name Evelyn Heenan, a Salvation Army card belonging to William Freng, a stamp album inscribed with the name Karl Neilsen, a wallet containing a trip insurance policy for Frank Schwartz, a briefcase containing papers belonging to Ken Skoug, a medical case belonging to Dr. Archibald Cardle, and a torn coat with papers in the pocket belonging to Dr. Leslie Anderson. A pair of boy's corduroy slacks had a laundry mark with the name Schafer, indicating they had belonged to seven-year-old John Schafer. Only a few Northwest airlines flight kits, including brochures and schedules, like all the passengers received, survived its long immersion.

As the officials pored over the evidence in the closed boathouse, more than forty newspaper reporters, photographers, radio commentators, newsreel cameramen, and television news reporters descended upon the station from metropolitan centers in four states. St. Joseph, Michigan became the news capital of the nation that morning with representatives of every major news agency present, including the Associated Press, the United Press, and the International News Service, plus the major papers from Chicago, Milwaukee, and Detroit. Some of the television networks were satisfied to shoot film of operations at the Coast Guard Station to broadcast later that day, but most wanted to be ferried out to the site of the operations on the lake. Captain Nathaniel Fulford of the Coast Guard agreed to take forty members of the press to the site on the *Hollyhock* along with high ranking officials of CAA, and Northwest who had to rendezvous with the *Mackinaw* for an on-board meeting. The reporters were told to choose one representative who would be allowed to board the *Mackinaw* to report on the meeting—all the others would remain on the *Hollyhock*. They all boarded the cutter at about 8:30 a.m.

Several victims' next-of-kin also appeared at the station, but they were not invited out to the site, perhaps out of compassion. Northwest Airlines had offered them accommodations at the Whitcomb Hotel in St. Joseph, which had become the hub for out-of-town CAB and Northwest officials. James Woolley, Eva Woolley's son; Alan Baron, Mary Keating's fiancé; Howard Hill, Tommy Hill's brother; Sylvia Frankel, Miriam Frankel's sister; and a few others gathered, still hoping against hope their loved ones had survived or that their bodies had been recovered for a proper burial.

Meanwhile Michigan State Police Lieutenant Dale Shoemaker arrived at the Coast Guard station to oversee the disposition of the debris recovered from the lake. Coroner Kerlikowske turned over all human remains to Doctor H. J. Frost, the St. Joseph pathologist, and noted that Joseph Kimm of Northwest Airlines kept possession of all the personal affects so that they could be returned to the families. Floyd Barton, the brother of Merle Barton, the barber, was allowed to look through the debris for items that might have belonged to his brother. He found Barton's checkbook, sales receipts, a suit jacket in tatters, and a coat in almost perfect shape. Three families left as soon as they realized that there was no chance of finding anyone alive.

The *Hollyhock* arrived on site at 11:30 a.m. Monday and transferred the small contingent of meeting participants to the *Mackinaw*, as well as Patricia Bronte, a reporter with the *Chicago Herald American,* who had been selected as the media representative, and a Fox studio cameraman. The cameraman would not film the meeting, but instead be taken up in the *Mackinaw's* helicopter to film the ongoing recovery operation from the air.

They joined Captain Frederick Goettel of the *Woodbine* and Captain Dalin of the *Frederick Lee*, who had arrived minutes earlier, in the meeting room. Pots of coffee awaited them and nearly everyone lit cigarettes: The air was smoky and solemn.

Captain Fulford took command of the meeting as the highest ranking Coast Guard officer in attendance. By that point he and the cutter captains had collectively seen all the recovered debris and agreed that it painted a vivid picture of what had occurred somewhere in the vicinity soon after midnight two days earlier. Patricia Bronte hurriedly scrawled notes as each captain presented his report, conclusion, and recommendation for further action. She must have been thrilled to be the one chosen for this assignment, especially over her male peers, but all eyes would be upon her and she knew she had to deliver something good. She began drafting her article during lulls in the conversation: "Four Coast Guard officers at the shipboard conference develop a composite theory of what happened to Flight 2501, supported by the evidence of floating debris, indicating the complete breakdown of the craft."

In conclusion, Commander Goettel indicated that, based on all the debris he had seen floating on the lake surface, he believed the only whole parts of the airplane on the bottom would be the engines.

After every participant had spoken, the group made a decision about how to proceed, then Captain Fulford adjourned the meeting. One of the *Mackinaw's* small boats took the participants back to their respective ships, and the *Hollyhock* set a course back to St. Joseph. After briefing the 39 other reporters on the *Hollyhock*, Patricia Bronte retired to a private cabin to write her firsthand account of the meeting. Considering the raw and frank statements made at the meeting, and the fact that little salient information about the accident had been given to the victims' next-of-kin, it seems inexcusable that the authorities had allowed her to attend, let alone print her dramatized version of the theories expressed. Bronte's article, later repeated in a number of newspapers, must have torn through the hearts of the victims' loved ones with as much intensity as the airplane had torn through the victims. It certainly provided fuel for lawsuits that were already being drafted:

> "The 58 persons were buffeted about in the heavens in abject terror before their bodies were chewed to bits as the four-engine craft smacked into bits in a stone-skipping crash 10 miles west of South Haven. The ill-fated craft flew into a line squall which battered the helpless, out-of-control craft around the skies, blew it miles off course, and undoubtedly jarred its passengers viciously about the inside. For at least two minutes the passengers suffered a horrible awareness that disaster was near as the roughness would leave no doubt that the craft was in uncorrectable trouble. With terror at its height, the big craft slammed into the lake waters which were calm from heavy rain despite the squalling winds. The plane tumbled over and over and skipped and tumbled more over a four or five mile area. As the plane ripped itself apart, the bodies of its passengers were twisted and torn too."

Even if Bronte's story represented the theory of the Coast Guard, it is understandable that Northwest Airlines and the CAA disagreed with the description of the final moments of Flight 2501. Joseph Kimm, Northwest's chief pilot, refused to publicly theorize why the airplane crashed because he felt it was too early to draw a conclusion.

An investigator for the Douglas Aircraft Company, which manufactured the aircraft, offered a statement damning the DC-4, but, of course, he asked that his name be withheld. He said that the airplane probably plunged into the lake on its back at a speed of 400 miles per hour, noting, "there have been eight cases in which planes of the same type were flipped onto their backs by high winds, but righted themselves after falling about 6,000 feet."

Of course, at an altitude of only 3,500 feet or less, Flight 2501 would not have had enough time to correct the problem before hitting the surface.

EVEN BEFORE BRONTE'S ARTICLE hit the papers, decisions made at the meeting had been carried out. The *Mackinaw* and *Hollyhock* were dismissed immediately from search and rescue detail that Monday afternoon, and the *Woodbine* and *Frederick Lee* were sent to St. Joseph to deliver the other debris they had recovered while the meeting was taking place. The decision about whether to continue recovery operations or whether to send the Navy's *Daniel A. Joy* out for sonar and diving work would be made by Northwest Airlines and the Civil Aeronautics Board.

When the *Woodbine* docked later that afternoon in St. Joseph, Quartermaster Wayne Tovey lowered the gangway to accommodate the unloading of the debris. By then, the press and officials had departed. Only a few remaining next-of-kin waited at the Coast Guard station for answers. One of them approached Tovey as he was overseeing the unloading, and asked, "What about survivors?"

Tovey pointed to the containers being carried off the cutter. "I'm sorry, sir; everything we recovered is in those barrels."

JUST AS CITIZENS from the twin cities of Benton Harbor and St. Joseph began to learn about the gruesome evidence of the crash being delivered to their Coast Guard Station, the late editions of Monday's papers also reported news of another tragedy that would directly affect their community and compete for front page news over the next few days. The cruise ship SS *City of Cleveland III*, which left the twin cities the prior Thursday evening with 90 members of the local Chambers of Commerce, had been involved in a fatal accident. The previous day, the Norwegian freighter *Ravnefjeel* collided with the *Cleveland* in heavy fog on Lake Huron and tore a massive hole in the superstructure. Four men perished, including former Benton Harbor Mayor Mervyn Stouck, Police Chief Alvin Boyd, and local businessmen Fred Skelley and Louis Patitucci. Three other men were seriously wounded. That tragedy and the crash of Flight 2501 would leave a lasting impression on many people.

WHEN ENSIGN LARRY OTTO came on duty at 4:00 a.m. Tuesday, June 27, the *Woodbine* was docked in St. Joseph. During his shift briefing, he was told that his boat would conduct dragging operations in the vicinity of the "hot spot," where Tovey had reported bubbling debris. The *Frederick Lee* would attempt to recover any still-floating debris, and the *Daniel A. Joy* would conduct sonar operations and send a diver down if any targets were found.

Once the *Woodbine* arrived on site, the crew deployed two heavy weights spaced fifty feet apart, connected by a chain, and began motoring slowly, hoping to hook the chain on the wreckage. The dragging operation netted nothing, but the *Frederick Lee* had recovered some additional debris including sections of a wing and a bulkhead. By mid-afternoon, both vessels were dismissed and sent back to their home ports.

Larry Otto would never forget his first five days as an officer on the *Woodbine* and his deep sadness that he was unable to help save lives.

AND THEN THERE WAS ONE: Only the *Daniel Joy* remained on site, with its crew, five divers, and Roy J. Clark of the Civil Aeronautics Board. As they began conducting sounding operations that Tuesday, a solemn requiem mass was taking place at St. John's Catholic Church in St. Joseph for the fifty-eight victims of the crash. A few Flight 2501 families probably attended, but most of the 100 people present were locals thoughtfully showing their respect for the many victims.

At noon Tuesday on the *Daniel A. Joy*, the crew recorded a couple unusual targets about ten miles off South Haven. Diver Edward Doherty climbed down onto the barge that had been set in place and sat while a fellow diver fastened his hard helmet to his suit. He was lowered to the lake bottom at 1:00 p.m. and returned an hour later, reporting visibility only eight inches, and a mucky, quicksand-like bottom three- or four-feet thick. The bottom condition that Doherty described was incorrectly reported by some newspapers as being thirty- to forty-feet thick and led to a theory that the wreckage must have been sucked into the soupy bottom and now lay deeply buried. At 3:00 p.m., another diver went down on a different target. He, too, reported finding nothing.

The next morning, as a result of a joint decision by officials at the CAB and Northwest Airlines, the *Daniel A. Joy* was ordered to cease and desist sounding and diving operations. All parties felt it would be fruitless to continue searching for the wreck. Five days after the country's worst aviation accident— and the only commercial airline crash in the Great Lakes—the largest search and rescue operation in the history of Lake Michigan ended.

Newspapers around the country reported the failed results of the search on inside pages. Front page headlines shifted to other, even more disturbing news: TRUMAN ORDERS PLANES AND SHIPS TO AID SOUTH KOREA.

Chapter 17

GRUESOME EVIDENCE

"**H**i Jack, it's Max Norris," the South Haven city engineer said, gripping his telephone receiver on Tuesday morning June 26, 1950.

"Hi Max," answered John Fleming, the Van Buren county health inspector. Everyone called him Jack because his grandfather and three uncles were all named John.

"You know about the plane crash…right?"

"Sure do, Max. I've been worrying about…uh…the possibility of bodies showing up on the beach."

"Well, looks like that's happened—not bodies, though—just parts."

Norris had gotten a call from Officer Otto Buelow of the South Haven Police. A Jessie McCormick of Casco Township reported seeing debris from the airplane just north of South Haven. When an officer checked it out, he found pieces of foam rubber, several items of clothing, a woman's white sock, a boy's undershirt, and human flesh. In addition, Coast Guardsmen at South Haven and St. Joseph had inaugurated a beach patrol and found several coats, pieces of the airplane's deck, and more human flesh—much of it swirling just outside the south pier at the mouth of the channel.

"I'm going to need your help, Jack."

The thirty-one-year-old Fleming was not unaccustomed to helping in any way he could. As a teen growing up in Marquette, Michigan, during the Depression, he actually walked to Sault St. Marie, a trek of 160 miles, to live with his aunt and help the family by working in a grocery store for three dollars a week. When the economy began to improve in 1939, he was able to pursue his interest in biology at Western Michigan University. There, he met Rita Minar, whom he would eventually marry after his service in the U. S. Army Medical Corps in Europe during World War II. In 1947, the couple relocated to Paw Paw, Michigan, where Jack had accepted a position with

Van Buren County as the health inspector. Fleming had earned his master's degree in public health from the University of Michigan just a few weeks before the call from the city engineer came in.

The two officials began to assemble information about the lost flight, the passengers, and what was known of the recovered human remains. They decided on three courses of action: to ask Mayor Charles Tait to close the beaches, to assign patrols to scour the beaches both north and south of town for more body parts, and to watch closely the city water intake, located west of the south pier. If human remains got sucked into the system, the water would be unfit for drinking.

Norris and Fleming did not take the beach closures lightly. Masses of tourists—some 10,000 if the predictions were correct—would be arriving in South Haven that Friday at the start of the long Fourth of July holiday weekend. Ever since the big passenger steamers had begun running to South Haven regularly in the late 1880s from ports in Illinois and Wisconsin and even farther away in Lakes Huron and Erie, the small city had become a destination, largely for its beautiful beaches.

With the advent of vehicles and a network of paved roads, South Haven started bustling every summer. Billboards advertised the city as the "Center of Vacationland," with the "World's Finest Beaches." Resident business owners counted on tourism for the bulk of their summer income, and the Fourth of July weekend usually brought in the most people.

Now those vacationers would not have access to what drew them to South Haven. The airplane crash could become a significant financial disaster for South Haven, but the officials had no choice—a grisly encounter with human remains on the beach just might send vacationers running, never to return. "Let's get the beach cleaned up as quickly as we can," Norris concluded, "in time for the weekend."

"Will do," Fleming replied, then hung up.

He quickly straightened up his desk, knowing he would be away for a while, and set off on what would be a week-long effort. He collected a number of containers and loaded them into the back of the county's red jeep for whatever he might encounter on the beach. Tuesday, the first day of his assignment, would be a busy day.

THAT MORNING, TEN-YEAR-OLD DOUG MCCAIN was down at the beach with his neighborhood pals as he had been every day since his family had arrived the previous Friday night at their summer cottage at Palisades Park several miles south of South Haven. By then, McCain had all but forgotten the low-flying airplane he had seen in the wee hours of Saturday morning. The surf was still running high, like the day before, and his mother had forbidden him to go swimming. However, the water tempted him. Just walking in the water, he reasoned, wasn't the same as swimming, so he and the other boys waded in up to their knees. Looking out to where the waves crested, McCain spotted something that reminded him of what he saw Friday. "Look!" he hollered to his friends over the pounding surf, pointing to a suitcase. "I'll bet that came from the plane I saw."

They all stood in knee-deep water waiting as the suitcase surged closer to shore. It seemed to take forever. One wave brought it almost within reach, then an undercurrent sucked it back out. Finally McCain was able to grab it. As soon as he lifted it out of the water, it fell open. Nothing was inside. *Darn*, he thought.

McCain dragged it up the beach away from the water's edge and returned to the group to see what else he could find. The boys split up and went in different directions, like a scavenger hunt. McCain could hear each boy yell as he found something new—a piece of foam, an item of clothing, or some plywood. They delivered their finds to the suitcase, dropping them inside. The fun came to a screeching halt when McCain saw something he never expected. It was clearly a piece of human flesh; he could see a distinct belly button.

He hollered to get the attention of the other boys. They formed a circle around it, just staring; no one was going to touch it. "What'll we do now?" someone asked.

Just then, McCain spotted a red Jeep driving toward them. Feeling like he was about to get caught doing something wrong, he stepped in front of the flesh and the other boys followed suit. Sure enough, the vehicle came to a stop a few feet from them, and a man climbed out. "Boys, you'll have to go back home," Jack Fleming said with authority. "This stretch of beach is closed."

No one said anything for a few seconds. Then McCain spoke up. "Is it because of this?" he asked, stepping aside and pointing at the remains.

Fleming did not want to upset the boys any more than they probably already were, so he replied calmly, "Yes, son. Because of things like that. Now go on home. I'll take care of this—and that too," he said, pointing to the suitcase.

As McCain retreated to the woods, he looked back and saw the man putting on gloves and picking up the hand.

YOUNG MCCAIN AND HIS FRIENDS were not the only ones scavenging debris from the beach that morning. There were so many people that Fleming could not talk with each one. He contacted Van Buren County Sheriff Fred Roper to request assistance. Roper, in turn, contacted Berrien County Sheriff Edwin H. Kubath, who called in his mounted posse and the Coast Guard. Soon, these officials began patrolling the beaches for souvenir hunters. The sight of so many officials probably prompted some people to come forth with their discoveries. Floyd Frazee, who ran the store at Covert Park, turned in a green cloth purse, indicating he had gotten it from the Hale boy. Inside, the police found a pair of lady's' size seven black gloves and a man's Westclox wrist watch.

A few miles south of Palisades Park, eleven-year-old Dianne Savage, her siblings, and her dad were walking along the shore at the Hager Township Beach, the closest beach to their home in Paw Paw, Michigan. Her dad told them that an airplane had crashed last Friday night, and he wanted their help looking for anything of value that might have washed ashore. Dianne thought the beach looked quite littered, but it all seemed like junk. Then she saw something that looked like the mess on the barn floor after her dad had gutted and hung a deer to bleed out. Her dad quickly hustled the children back to the car. Diane knew that what she had seen was not from a deer, and it frightened her.

Little more than an hour later, ten-year-old Jeannine Kucera gripped her mother's hand as they walked the two blocks from their summer home to the beach. Just as they neared the stairs that led down to the water, her mother stopped. "Honey, we can't go down there. It's blocked off."

Jeannine saw a big rope and a sign that said, "Beach closed." "It must have something to do with the storm," her mother said, probably not wanting to upset her by mentioning the airplane crash.

The little girl remembered the storm well. She and her parents had been huddled in one big bed with a candle lit, which her mother said would keep them safe. At some point, when Jeannine had almost fallen asleep, a big boom awakened her. Her mother said it was just thunder. However, the adults had been talking about an airplane that crashed nearby.

Jeannine didn't know what was going on down at the beach, but as they started walking back home, she saw men on horseback riding along the shore. She had never seen that before.

WITH HELP FROM the mounted officers now patrolling the beach, Jack Fleming drove his Jeep from person to person to collect any human remains; he did not worry about airplane parts or personal possessions. He knew other officials would tend to that. About a mile south of the South Haven channel along Evergreen Bluff Drive, a woman flagged him down. "Are you in charge here?" she asked.

"Well, ma'am," he said introducing himself, "I'm one of the people in charge. I'm collecting...ah... ...human remains."

"Oh, what a tragedy," she responded, shaking her head and closing her eyes for a moment. "My son found something and I didn't know what to do with it so I put it in my refrigerator."

"I'd be happy to take it off your hands, ma'am."

"Give me a couple minutes," she said, retreating back up the incline toward a sizable home.

She returned shortly with a brown paper bag. "I don't know what this is," she said, handing it to him.

Fleming opened the top of the bag and peered inside.

"Ma'am, this is a human lung."

BY THE END OF TUESDAY, Fleming had filled several of the containers in his Jeep. Although he had dealt with corpses before, he had never seen anything like this. It looked like the passengers had been cut up with knives. He didn't even see any arms or legs or heads. Instead, he just found just mutilated flesh and organs. He could not even begin to guess how many people were represented by the remains in his vehicle.

Evidence of the disaster continued to wash ashore on Wednesday. In Grand Haven, more than forty miles north of South Haven, two little girls, Marilyn Regelin and Jean Engel, found a two-foot-by-two-foot-square structure and called it to the attention of their dad. One side was made of a composition material and the other plywood. There was a continuous aluminum flange riveted to one edge and the other edge was jagged, as if torn from its original mount. He thought it might have been from the airplane and turned it in to the police.

Ten-year-old Danny Goodwilly and his pal Bob Hamilton turned in a brown-and-gray striped lady's' coat with a pearl button and part of an arm rest that they found near the Chesebro Resort at Evergreen Bluffs.

Near Deerlick Creek south of South Haven, a Coast Guard searcher found what he believed to be a surgical kit with the name Merle Barton on it. In fact, it was a barber's kit.

Just north of the channel at South Haven, Jim Mitchell and his brother, owners of Mitchell Brothers' Block, pitched in to help Coast Guardsmen and Jack Fleming comb their lakefront property from which they normally mined gravel. Fleming encouraged the brothers to collect anything that looked human. To Jim, it was all so gruesome. Two things haunted him—a heart and a hand that he saw Fleming place in bottles.

Fleming had received an alert from the Van Buren county coroner to be on the lookout for hands so that the police could provide next of kin with any positive identification. As soon as he picked up that hand, he knew that it was too badly damaged to retrieve fingerprints. Another day would pass before usable evidence would wash ashore.

ON THURSDAY AFTERNOON, nineteen-year-old Verley Bunyea, her boyfriend Allen Russell, Bunyea's brother George, and a few other teenagers climbed down the small dune to the beach at Glenn about a mile west of Bunyea's house. She loved going down to the water ever since her dad, a tool-and-die maker, had relocated the family there three years earlier from Mt. Greenwood, Illinois, where trips to Lake Michigan had been rare. Six nights earlier, she had huddled with her siblings and parents in their basement, worried that a tree would fall on the house during the big lightning storm; now she was walking along the water's edge looking for souvenirs from the airliner that had crashed that night.

As the sand shifted through her toes, and the breeze blew through her hair, Bunyea clutched a cigar box she had brought along to store any treasures. Just then something dark blue in the sand caught her eye. She bent to pick it up and realized that it was a portion of a hat with a broken brim. She turned it over in her hands and saw a band of white material inside. Large block letters spelled LIND. She wondered what that stood for and passed it around for her friends to see. "Looks like a pilot's hat," someone commented.

"Oh, yeah, I guess it does," she said, having no idea what the pilots' names were, but tucking it inside her box.

She and the others picked up some fragments of foam, a few pieces from what must have been a suitcase, and something that appeared to be made of straw. Nothing had any burn marks. As she continued walking south, flipping sand with her feet in the hopes of uncovering something, a bright white object bobbing in the water caught her eye. It rose and fell on the crests of the small waves between the first and second sand bar about 30 feet offshore. "What's that?" she asked pointing.

"Looks kind of big," Russell said. "I'll go see."

He had short pants on, so he just waded out. Anxious to learn what it was, Bunyea hiked up her dress and followed him into the water, still holding her cigar box, but she stopped when she saw Russell's shorts get wet as the water got deeper beyond the first sand bar. She watched as her boyfriend took three more strides, then stopped at the object. She saw him lean over to examine it, then reach down and flip it over. Then she heard him scream, "Holy Christ!"

Frightened, Bunyea began backing away as Russell stumbled and fell up to his neck in the water. He kicked and struggled and finally managed to get to his feet, and ran toward her screaming "It's a body! It's a body!"

"Ahhhh," Bunyea screamed, running through the water to the shore and back up the beach. Everyone else ran too until they all reached the grassy area at the top of the rise. Bunyea looked out at the water and could still see the speck of white. Some of the others collapsed on the grass, huffing and puffing. "What the hell, Allen?" one of the guys asked, sounding mad, but probably just embarrassed that he had run along with the girls.

Allen Russell bent over, bracing his hands on his knees as if to catch his breath. "It was a woman," he managed to say between gasps of air, "wearing a girdle…it was horrible…no head…only one arm…shredded flesh."

The teenagers were quiet, probably pondering the horror of what they had just seen. Then Bunyea broke the silence: "We've got to tell someone."

"There's a phone at the store," her brother said, referring to the small market kitty-corner from William Bowie's gas station at the intersection, three-quarters of a mile from the beach. "Come on."

They all started jogging east along 114th Street. "Wait," Russell hollered, stopping in his tracks. "One of us has to keep an eye on it. You all go on."

About forty minutes later, Bunyea and the others watched from outside the market as a South Haven police car and a hearse from the Calvin Funeral Home headed past them toward the lake. "Let's go home, George," she encouraged her brother, picking up the cigar box.

"You shouldn't be taking that stuff," he said, glaring at the box, "especially after what we saw."

"They don't want this stuff, George," she said, trudging off with her souvenirs.

When South Haven Police Sergeant Purlette Hinckley and Van Buren County Coroner Fern Calvin reached the beach, the body had already washed ashore. Hinckley noticed a ring on the ring finger, suggesting the woman had been either married or engaged. They loaded it on a stretcher, got it into the hearse, and took it to the funeral home. There, Sergeant Hinkley learned that another woman's left shoulder, arm, and hand, found on South Haven's north beach, had been brought in. That hand bore an engagement and wedding ring set. He attempted to take fingerprints from both left hands, but did not have the appropriate equipment. Instead, he asked Coroner Calvin to remove the tips of each finger at the first joint. He carefully put them in separate bottles, marking each one with the correct digit. Then he made arrangements for the fingertips to be driven to the State Police Identification Bureau at East Lansing the next day. Fingerprint expert Sergeant Leroy F. Smith was later able to pull acceptable prints although they were somewhat blurred due to the long immersion in water.

MEANWHILE, DEBRIS KEPT COMING ASHORE. Many things were undoubtedly carted home by the finders, but others were turned in. A Mr. McVey, who operated a store near Lake Michigan west of Douglas, Michigan, twenty miles north of South Haven, had collected a number of things. On Friday, June 30, he turned everything over to the South Haven police. Among the items were a red leather bag, a torn lady's' dress with a label from Nelson-Caine in New York, a man's double-breasted suit coat from the Vaughn Ragsdale Company, and a pair of men's brown wool trousers.

Everything was sent down to the St. Joseph Coast Guard Station boathouse and kept under lock and key. On July 1, the debris was removed and trucked off to a warehouse near Northwest Airlines' headquarters in Minneapolis.

Two days later, recent high school graduate Robert Ketelhut, who worked part time for his father, the sexton at St. Joseph's Riverview Cemetery, watched as Berrien County Coroner Louis Kerlikowske brought in a container that his father later told him held human remains from the airplane crash. The remains were buried that afternoon in an unmarked plot provided free of charge by the city.

Mayor Tait was able to open the beaches of South Haven on July 3 with a level of confidence that nothing more would show up on the beach. Reports from the local water plant indicated that nothing had been found in the intake pipes. The holiday would proceed, just a little later than planned.

OFFSHORE, THE HORROR WAS NOT OVER. As tourists sunned on the beach and played in the water, South Haven fisherman Al Schieie hauled in his gill net and found flesh and other debris, presumably from the airplane. When he arrived back in South Haven, he called the police. Officer Otto Buelow met him at the fishing shanty on the northwest side of the Black River, near Jensens' Fishery, to look over the debris. There he learned that another fisherman, Wallace Chambers, believed that he had snagged his nets on the wreckage the day before. Chambers provided a compass heading and distance from the channel at South Haven and showed the officer his damaged net. He explained that when he activated his lifting machine, the net didn't budge, and he knew it had hooked something on the bottom. After some effort by hand, the crew managed to detangle it, but the net came up torn and with a streak of rust.

THE TRAGEDY DID NOT END upon the death of fifty-eight people. Representatives at the adoption agency that had placed the baby girl with Robert and Margaret Lind visited the new mother and widow. In short order, the agency determined that she would not have the financial capability to raise the child alone, and the baby would be better off if placed in a two-parent home. In the wake of the tragic loss of her husband, Margaret Lind also lost the long-awaited and beloved daughter she had already bonded with in the short time she had been the child's mother.

ON JULY 13, 1950, the Civil Aeronautics Board convened an inquest at Chicago in a conference room in the Stevens Hotel on Michigan Avenue. Delos Rentzel, chairman of the board; Oswald Ryan, vice chairman; and members Josh Lee and Harold A. Jones were in attendance to hear the testimony. Francis H. McAdams, an attorney and former naval aviator in World War II, presided over the hearing.

Over two days, the CAB heard the testimony of thirty-two witnesses in an effort to determine an official cause for the accident. One after another, the witnesses, participants, and experts offered up their accounts and theories about the incident. Julius Badner of the National Weather Service reported on the weather predictions and actual weather that night.

Richard Miller, the Northwest airlines flight dispatcher on duty when the flight left New York, outlined the scheduled air routes, which included flying over Lake Michigan on Airway Red 57. He said there was no indication of a thunderstorm over the lake when the pilot was briefed at 7:30 p.m. While technically true, apparently Miller avoided discussing the weather forecasts that indicated the storm would move over Lake Michigan and did not address weather updates that Northwest received while Flight 2501 was in the air.

Captain W. F. Dean, who flew that particular DC-4 to New York just before Flight 2501, testified that the aircraft was in fine working order. Northwest radio operator Donald Wertz recounted conversations he had with Flight 2501. Captain Norman Mitchell testified about the heavy turbulence he experienced flying on Red 57 that night.

William Bowie, the owner of the gas station in Glenn, Michigan, told investigators that he had seen a four-engine airplane flying very low, apparently in trouble. Arnold Repp, a truck driver who was with Bowie that night, confirmed the sighting. Donald Bassi recounted his sighting of an airplane heading into the severe electrical storm. Retired naval commander R. P. Helm from Benton Harbor, Michigan, described seeing a low-flying airplane disappear in a flash about twenty miles offshore at about 12:20 a.m. Lieutenant Frederick Goettle described the search operation and the debris recovered from the lake. John Pahl, a structures specialist with the CAB, rendered his opinion that the airplane impacted water and fractured into small pieces. A Navy captain, Kenneth Earl, testified about the diving operation and how time consuming and hopeless it would be to try to find the wreck.

Lastly, Joseph Kimm, chief pilot for Northwest Airlines, testified. Along with his comments about how he believed the DC-4 impacted the water, based on his study of the recovered debris, a newspaper quoted him as saying, "Three planes over the same airway followed by Flight 2501 turned back and landed at Detroit that night. Their captains reported severe turbulence over Airway Red 28. We believe that whatever happened came shortly after his 12:13 a.m. request to change altitude. We have no doubt whatsoever that he was right on course—despite the wild rumors that put him elsewhere."

Kimm's comment contradicted Flight Dispatcher Richard Miller and other witnesses who testified that the flight plan called for the airplane to cross the lake on Airway Red 57. It seemed likely that either Joseph Kimm made a mistake or the reporter who quoted him did. Kimm also made a statement that could render Northwest Airlines liable for the accident through the actions of its pilot, *if* any lawyers pursued it: "Robert Lind could have turned back, but he didn't."

With over 400 pages of transcribed testimony recorded in those two days, Francis H. McAdams adjourned the hearing. The four members of the board would spend the next many months analyzing and discussing the testimony in preparation for writing the final report.

AFTER THE HEARING, Commissioner Donald Leonard, head of the Michigan State Police at East Lansing, began attempting to match the fingerprints taken from the hands of the two partial female bodies that had been recovered. The task would be problematic because fingerprints would only be available for those female passengers who had at one time worked for the government or an employer that required fingerprinting. At his request, the United Press drafted a request for fingerprints that was published in papers throughout the country. Sam Frankel, the father of victim Miriam Frankel, was the first to respond.

He had a set of fingerprints he had personally recorded of his daughter's right hand. Leonard wrote him back, indicating that unless he could provide prints of the left hand, they would be unable to make a comparison.

In the days that followed, Mary Keating's mother, Dorothy Jean Kaufmann's father, and Nora Hughes' husband, each contacted the Michigan State Police to let them know that their loved one had been fingerprinted at one time. Leonard suggested they appeal to the Federal Bureau of Investigation to search through its records and forward copies of the prints to the Michigan State Police. He provided the address of J. Edgar Hoover at the FBI.

Hoover had been appointed director of the Bureau of Investigation—predecessor to the FBI—in 1924 and was instrumental in founding the FBI in 1935. However, by 1950, concern had arisen that Hoover was exceeding the jurisdiction of his position, using it to amass secret files on political leaders and collect evidence using illegal methods. President Truman had recently started speaking out about him, accusing him of transforming the FBI into his private, secret police force.

Regarding the investigation of Flight 2501, Hoover was initially quite obliging. In response to the requests from the families and the Michigan Police Commissioner, Hoover's staff located Nora Hughes' prints from her alien registration card and forwarded them to the Michigan police. They were not a match. Hoover probably regretted giving up control, because on July 24 he wrote Commissioner Leonard asking him to instead forward the fingerprint cards from the victims' hands to the FBI, advising that, "The Bureau will be glad to compare any fingerprints with the fingerprints we have on file of all the persons having the same names as those listed as missing passengers."

Leonard could not argue with Hoover, so he forwarded the print cards and waited.

By this time, more than a month after the accident, lakefront city managers had little concern of more debris surfacing, however, they were in for an unpleasant surprise. A young Grand Haven, Michigan, bait catcher, Jack Robinson, hauled in his eighty-foot-long net and found a number of pieces of flesh that he knew were not minnows. He collected the flesh in a five-gallon bucket and gave it to his father, who contacted the police. The local sheriff came out and retrieved the bucket. Then, Robinson began talking about his discovery around town. Soon thereafter, the sheriff caught up with him to announce that the flesh he had found was just fish. "You need to stop talking about body parts, Jack," the sheriff said, looking him straight in the eye, "or there will be consequences."

Jack took that comment as a threat and stopped talking about his find.

However, he felt sure that the flesh he had found was not fish. The police were obviously ready for all this to be put behind them.

Finally, on August 15, Hoover replied to Commissioner Leonard's request for fingerprint analysis and indicated that the prints taken from the two hands did not match the prints they had on file for Bonnie Ann Feldman, Barbara Jane Freng, Rosa Freng, Louise Spohn, or Dorothy Jean Parker. Leonard sent him another letter specifically asking about prints for both Mary Keating and Miriam Frankel, whose next-of-kin indicated had worn rings on their left hand. On September 1, 1950, Hoover responded, "My dear Commissioner: You are advised that on the basis of the information furnished, a search was conducted, but no fingerprint records could be located. Assuring you of my desire to be of assistance in these matters, I am Sincerely yours, John Edgar Hoover."

Upon receipt of that letter, all hope of ever identifying the two partial bodies ended. Northwest Airlines President Croil Hunter sent condolence letters to each family on corporate stationary, offering the brief sentiment, "I am sure you know how deeply I sympathize with you in the great loss you have suffered. I realize no words of mine can soften your sorrow but I want to express to you, both personally and on behalf of the company, our deepest and heartfelt sympathy. I only wish it was within our power to alleviate the sadness that has come to you."

FOUR AND A HALF MONTHS LATER, the Civil Aeronautics Board completed its report. Delos W. Rentzel, chairman of the board, met with President Harry Truman on the afternoon of January 17, 1951, perhaps to discuss the findings of the board. The next day the report was made public. The 6,209-word document provided an approximate location of the accident, eighteen miles north-northwest of Benton Harbor, although it indicated the wreck had not been found. The CAB surmised that turbulence likely caused the crash, but concluded that, "The Board determines that there is not sufficient evidence upon which to make a determination of probable cause." Rentzel, along with board members Josh Lee and Harold A. Jones, signed the report. Vice Chairman Oswald Ryan did not participate in its adoption.

Now it would be up to the lawyers representing the families to try to prove blame in a civil court of law, a difficult task in the face of the CAB's inability to do so. They would focus on Northwest Airlines, in an attempt to extract from the company's deep pockets some restitution for this tragic accident.

Chapter 18

PLACING BLAME

"All rise! The United States District Court in the southern district of New York is in session," the clerk of the court announced on October 11, 1957. "The honorable Edward J. Dimock presiding."

The flag of the United States fluttered as the judge passed by it and took the bench. Twelve jurors and three alternates stood to his left in the jurors' box.

"Please be seated," the clerk announced after the judge sat down.

The court had consolidated the cases of four plaintiffs into one trial proceeding for efficiency. John Rorabaugh, the son of Marie Rorabaugh; Freda "Patricia" Schwartz, the wife of Frank Schwartz; William Ramsey, the executor of the estate of the Frengs; and Oscar Schafer, the husband and stepfather of Adelaide and John Schafer, had initiated their individual suits against Northwest Airlines immediately upon the release of the Civil Aeronautics Board report in January 1951. Northwest had entered into settlements with most of the families, but, at various points in the process, the negotiations had broken down with these parties. This trial would be their last resort. Most of them sat in the courtroom waiting to testify.

By this time, seven and a half years after the accident, the other families who had initiated suits had already settled with the airline. Alma Sirbu, wife of San Francisco clothing merchandiser Joseph Sirbu, had been among the first, filing a $395,000 suit against the airline. She settled for an undisclosed amount. Likewise, Winfield Kaufmann, husband of former teacher Dorothy Jean Kaufmann, settled for $25,000 with another $25,000 in a trust fund for his children, with twenty-five percent of those amounts going to his attorney. Of course, no amount of money could begin to compensate for the loss of his wife and his children's mother, and Kaufmann wished to avoid a costly and risky trial and the pain of reliving the tragedy, so he accepted the settlement.

Patricia Schwartz had been well on her way to settling; however, the airline, through its attorney, suddenly recanted on its offer, giving her little option but to pursue a lawsuit. By that time, seven years after the accident, the trip insurance money that she had received would have been nearly gone.

Sixty-seven-year-old Judge Dimock adjusted his spectacles on his nose as the clerk swore in the jury. Dimock, who graduated from Yale in 1911 and obtained his law degree from Harvard University three years later, had served as a federal judge since his nomination by President Harry Truman in June 1951, after years of private practice and teaching. Dimock had received some embarrassing media attention a few years earlier when he offered thirteen convicted communist leaders a choice: either go to Russia or go to an American prison. However, American law did not allow banishment, and Dimock had to recant when the defense attorney pointed that out. "All right, we'll have no more of it," he had replied, rather sheepishly.

Judge Dimock went over ordinary housekeeping items pertaining to the trial, which was slated to last two weeks or more. He pointed out that although the case was being tried in a federal district court, the law and statutes of the state in which the accident occurred would prevail regarding any damages that might be awarded to the plaintiffs. The jury would need to first determine in which state the airplane crashed.

After his initial comments, Dimock invited the plaintiffs to make an opening statement. The four plaintiffs were represented by three attorneys: Edmund H. H. Caddy and R. N. McCann, of Patterson, Belknap & Webb in New York City, had been retained by the Freng and Rorabaugh families. Martin N. Kolbrener of Guggenheim & Untermyer, also in New York City, represented the Schwartz and Schafer families. Kolbrener would be the lead attorney over the consolidated case. Forty-seven years old, a New York native, and the son of Jewish immigrants from the Galicia crown land of Austria prior to the outbreak of World War I, Kolbrener took a special interest in the Schwartz case. The victim, Frank Schwartz, was a distant cousin.

Kolbrener alone handled the opening remarks, outlining what he and his co-counsel intended to prove: that the airplane fell into the lake when it met the squall line entirely due to Northwest Airlines' failure to fully inform the pilots of the weather. Kolbrener took this case quite seriously, not only because he represented a relative, but because success would bring him closer to his next career goal. Trials were becoming too stressful for him, especially after his coronary several years earlier. He planned one day to become a judge. However, he was at a disadvantage. His firm, which had been in business since the 1850s, did not normally try aviation cases, nor did the four-decades-old general practice of Patterson, Belknap & Webb. Kolbrener and his co-counsel would be up against John G. Reilly, an experienced and crafty aviation law specialist of the firm Bigham, Englar, Jones and Houston.

In his late sixties, defense attorney Reilly must have impressed the jury with his confidence and seniority over the plaintiffs' attorneys. His firm had been engaged in the practice of aviation, maritime, and insurance law since 1909, and he had defended Northwest and several other airlines in a number of similar cases. In fact, his firm had recently been responsible for obtaining a defense verdict of not-liable in the case over Northwest Flight 4422, the DC-4 that crashed on Mount Sanford in Alaska in 1948. Like Flight 2501, its wreckage had not been found.

Reilly knew that the burden of proving negligence rested on the plaintiffs, and without the wreck they would have a difficult time convincing the jury the accident was the airline's fault. However, he would have been aware that juries tend to side with individuals over a corporation. After the plaintiff concluded opening remarks, it was Reilly's turn. He started by appearing sympathetic, "However tragic, however regrettable this incident was—and it surely was a most tragic one—my client is in no way responsible for it."

Reilly explained that the four suits would not be an action for grief, sorrow, anguish, or the deprivation of companionship, acknowledging, "I concede to you right away that all the money that has been minted could not compensate for any of those things. Only pecuniary, or rather monetary, damage," he explained, "suffered by the next-of-kin can be considered."

Reilly's strategy was to eradicate the impression of blame on the airline. However, in the event of his failure to do so, he would try to prove that none of the plaintiffs had suffered any monetary damage. He eased into the topic: "I take it I need not say anything which must be in disparagement or derogation of these people because I say right now that they were all very lovable people."

That elicited tears from the family members in the courtroom.

Then Reilly got down to business, laying out the reasons why he felt that three of the four plaintiffs were not due any damages according to the law. In the Rorabaugh case, he noted that the victim, Marie Rorabaugh, was sixty-seven years old, widowed, with three grown and married children; one had recently died. "They sustained no pecuniary injury by reason of that lovely lady's death," he noted.

In the Freng case, he acknowledged that while the loss of Mary Ann Freng's entire family "beggars description," as a married twenty-one-year-old, she was adequately provided for by her husband.

In the Schafer case, he pointed out that Oscar Schafer, a forty-one-year-old stockbroker at the time, sustained no financial damages through the loss of his stay-at-home wife, and even if the jury found that he did, it could only be based on a limited period because he married again soon after the accident.

Only in the case of Frieda Schwartz, widow of Frank Schwartz, did Reilly acknowledge pecuniary damages as a result of his death. He even emphasized that saying, "there is no question about that whatsoever."

This admission must have taken the jury by surprise considering how forcefully and succinctly he had derided the claims of the other three plaintiffs, but the jurors would not have known about the settlement negotiations with Schwartz, which had begun with a suit for $250,000 and broken down after Northwest reneged on a $25,000 offer and reduced it back to the company's preliminary and paltry offer of only $7,500, representing little more than the victim's annual salary. Reilly had something up his sleeve, which may have been the reason Northwest retracted the larger offer. After cleverly acknowledging damages, he said, "Frank Schwartz left behind no children," leading carefully into his next, seemingly casual, comment, "but in the interest of accuracy there was a child of his widow, but not his child."

Reilly planned to bring out facts about the child later in a way to benefit his client.

Over the next hour, John Reilly outlined the details of the flight, Northwest Airlines' operations, the aircraft, radio conversations, and weather that were not contested. Then he launched into the key to his defense: "Where the plane disappeared, when it disappeared, how it disappeared, or why it disappeared, no one has ever been able to find out."

In saying this, he suggested that if the cause of the accident could not be determined, that Northwest could not be found negligent. For the benefit of the airline, he would need to prove the accident was an act of God.

The next two seemingly subtle and offhanded comments were clearly designed to shift blame. He explained that during the last communication with the flight, Air Traffic Control denied the pilot's request for clearance to descend to 2,500 feet. "I will show you," he promised, "that traffic was still on the ground when they refused it to him and this is one of the tragic incidents in this case."

In pointing out that ATC had based their denial on the flight path of an airplane not yet even in the air, he insinuated that had clearance been given, Flight 2501 might not have crashed. Reilly clearly was attempting to shift blame to others rather than Northwest Airlines. He went on to discuss a turbulence report made by a pilot flying a Lockheed Lodestar, saying "but Air Traffic Control never gave this information to FAWS (the Flight Advisory Weather Service), despite the recommendation of the pilot. This is another of the tragedies of this case."

Although the plaintiffs may have considered suing the United States for the errors of Air Traffic Control, the legal right to do so had only existed for a short time. Prior to that, the government could claim sovereign immunity from most non-criminal claims. It had taken an aviation accident, ironically, to generate support for the bill that would allow citizens to sue the government. On a foggy morning in 1945, Lt. Colonel William Smith, piloting a U.S. Army B-25 bomber to Newark Airport, asked for a weather report. Because of low cloud cover, the controller suggested that he land, but Smith requested and received permission from the military to continue on to Newark. He descended below the clouds only to find himself in the middle of Manhattan. He managed to miss several tall buildings, but smashed into the Empire State Building, killing himself, two people in his aircraft, and 11 office workers. The military, which had allowed the flight to continue, was blamed.

As a result, in 1948 Congress passed the Federal Tort Claims Act. Since then only one suit against Air Traffic Control had been won. In 1955 the United States was found liable for the negligent actions of an air traffic controller for a 1949 collision between Eastern Airlines Flight 537 and a Bolivian military aircraft while attempting to land at the Washington National Airport. However, the precedent-setting ruling occurred years after the plaintiffs began preparing their cases over Flight 2501, and by then it may have been too late to consider suing the government.

By late afternoon, Reilly concluded his opening statement, "Before I leave you, there is one thing I wish to impress upon you. See if the evidence does not establish that those two *competent* pilots were the sole judges of the weather they were observing, and it was within the ability of that pilot, if he saw fit, to put down at Chicago, turn back, or declare an emergency and proceed at any level."

There would be no argument regarding the pilots' skills, likely because a pre-trial motion in favor of the defendant precluded it. There probably had been no evidence to suggest incompetent behavior.

Finally Reilly implored, "However tragic these losses may have been, I ask you, on evidence as you find it, to return a verdict on behalf of my client."

Judge Dimock concluded the first full day of the trial by sending the jurors home with a warning not to discuss the details of the case with anyone and ordered them to return on Monday, October 14, at 10:00 a.m. The jurors had the entire weekend to ponder Reilly's defense.

REFRESHED FROM THE WEEKEND, the jury first heard the evidence of Northwest meteorologist Donald Wertz, who was on duty when the airplane crashed. Because by the time of the trial Northwest had reassigned him to duty in Tokyo, Japan, the company claimed hardship in having to bring him back for the trial. Instead, his deposition would have to be read out loud.

It was Reilly's intent to show that Wertz acted with the utmost safety of the flight in mind when he decided *not* to transmit the 10:30 p.m. National Weather Service forecast to Flight 2501 because he felt that forecast was less severe than the forecast his counterpart, Beresford, had given the pilot before the flight. Wertz remained resolute in his contention that the earlier forecast provided ample warning of a squall.

On Wednesday, the fourth day of the trial, Martin Kolbrener called National Weather Bureau meteorologist Julius Badner to the stand in direct rebuttal to Wertz's testimony. He intended to have Badner outline the various forecasts he had developed that night and the actual weather observations in the region where the airplane went missing. Kolbrener hoped to establish how significantly the weather changed in those few hours and how negligent Northwest had been in not providing the update to Flight 2501. First he began by asking Badner to define a squall line.

"A squall line is a line along which there are almost continuous thunderstorms," Badner testified. He went on to say that turbulence in a squall can be severe, causing updrafts and downdrafts that can force an airplane up or down as much as 1,500 feet.

Through questioning over that afternoon and all the next day, Kolbrener was able to paint a vivid picture for the jury of the significant weather developments as they occurred from 4:45 p.m. to 12:30 a.m.

Badner explained how from 4:45 p.m., when he issued his regional forecast, until 10:30 p.m., when he would issue his next one, he used actual weather observations, called sequence reports, from 18 airports in the region to predict the future weather. After he issued a new and updated regional forecast at 10:30 p.m., he prepared a forecast for each airport, called a terminal forecast, specifically for use in aviation. Although regional and terminal forecasts predicted the weather for a twelve-hour period, each was updated every six hours, providing the most up-to-date weather information. The National Weather Service transmitted every forecast through the teletype circuit, which was available to all airlines for use in planning and managing flights.

To highlight the changing weather, Kolbrener asked Badner to read all 18 terminal forecasts within the region of Michigan, Indiana, Illinois, and Wisconsin that he issued at 11:22 p.m. that night. The reading sounded like droning repetition, almost hypnotizing to the jurors. Translated from meteorological jargon into words a layperson could understand, it was still confusing. The last report from Saginaw, Michigan, read much like the other seventeen forecasts: "Base 3,000, overcast; top 5,000 with another layer above; base 6,000, overcast; tops above 30,000, visibility four miles in thundershowers; wind south southwest fifteen, with fresh gusts, briefly base 1,000, sky obscured; tops above 30,000, visibility one mile in heavy thundershowers; northwest thirty-five with strong gusts."

Even Judge Dimock seemed overwhelmed. "What does 'briefly' mean?" he asked Badner.

Kolbrener must have smiled, realizing this would bring out the testimony key to his case.

"For brief times during the forecast period," Badner began answering, "clouds will move down to the lower limit, and incidentally those are the times that the squall line is expected to pass the airport."

"Objected to!" Reilly shouted.

Realizing that he had been responsible for eliciting the testimony that Reilly objected to, Dimock turned to the jury, "This would be a good time to recess for a short period."

Once the jury left the room, Dimock and the attorneys could argue about the objection. Clearly, Reilly did not want specifics of the squall line to come out, but he tried to diffuse the matter by objecting to the reading of weather at Saginaw and other places he claimed were too far from Lake Michigan.

"The only reason I think these places are important is this," Kolbrener said, getting to the heart of his case, although unfortunately out of earshot of the jury. "They show that at a given time, a pattern was developing that if a meteorologist was watching—say Northwest—he would see a pattern developing that this squall line was moving south and southeast."

Dimock attempted to clarify, "Do you suggest that if this man Badner could have forecast the squall, then the meteorologist for Northwest could have forecast it?"

"That's right, "Kolbrener replied forcefully. "And if this forecast went out at 11:22 p.m., then, with the half-hour lag, Northwest got it no later than 11:52, when the plane was still heard from."

Dimock turned and looked directly at Reilly "I don't think he has gone too far," he said, indicating he would allow the questioning to continue.

ONCE THE JURY RETURNED, Kolbrener began a line of questioning that would help the jurors better understand the implications of all those repetitive sequence reports. He set up a map of Michigan, which showed all of Lake Michigan, and marked the scheduled route of Flight 2501 from

Sandusky, Ohio, to Battle Creek, Michigan, and across the lake to Milwaukee, Wisconsin. Then he continued his questioning: "At 10:49 p.m., when the plane is reported at Cleveland, where was the squall line?"

Badner got up from the witness chair with his sequence reports in hand, walked to the map and, referencing the reports, used a red marker to place a dot at all the airports that reported low clouds, high winds, and heavy rain at that time. Then he connected the dots, revealing a red line running from Madison, Wisconsin, east across the lake to Gladwin, Michigan.

"Was that information available to any meteorologist that night?" Kolbrener asked.

"Yes, it was."

Kolbrener repeated the same questions for 11:02 p.m., when Flight 2501 was at Sandusky, Ohio; 11:51 p.m., when at Battle Creek, Michigan; and 12:15 a.m., when the pilots were last heard from.

After Badner finished, the map offered an easily understandable image of how the 400-mile-long squall line, which ran east and west, had swept down from northern Lake Michigan to the southern end of the lake in little more than an hour. A quick calculation by an astute juror would have shown that the squall was moving almost directly south at about 100 miles per hour.

Most significant on the map was the red line representing the squall at 12:15 a.m. It ran from Rockford, Illinois, east across the lake through Battle Creek, Lansing, and Flint, Michigan. It crossed the lake's eastern shore south of South Haven. It was clear that at that very rapid rate of travel, the squall would have reached Benton Harbor by about 12:25 and Chicago by about 12:45 a.m.

Kolbrener must have felt confident in what he had been able to bring forth through Badner. After having established that the weather data was available to Northwest's meteorologist, he hoped that the jury would find that Northwest had been negligent in not providing that information to Flight 2501.

On re-cross examination, Reilly tried to redirect the jury's attention to his contention that no matter what information the company gave or didn't give the pilots, they were the best judge of the weather. "So at 12:15, you say the squall line was 50 miles above Chicago, right?"

"Yes," answered Badner.

"So, there was nothing that would preclude the passage of a plane there? At Chicago?"

"No, there was nothing to prevent a plane from passing over Chicago."

Then, Reilly shifted topics and attempted to undermine all the information that Kolbrener had just so smoothly revealed. "Did the terminal stations speak of a squall line?" he asked.

"No observations spoke of squall lines," Badner answered. "The observations," he continued, "are to be interpreted…"

"I move that go out!" Reilly shouted, drowning out Badner's last statement.

Judge Dimock cleared his throat to get attention. "Can you only answer yes or no?" he asked Badner directly.

"No, it needs clarification," Badner replied. He wished to explain that a squall line cannot be seen as a visible line at any place—it simply looks like a thunder and lightning storm from any one vantage point. Only when a meteorologist recognizes that a series of thunderstorms line up, can he determine that a squall line exists.

Judge Dimock pressed to get the answer. "So none of those reports used the word squall line?"

"That's true," Badner said confidently, but then he became quiet. He probably realized that the judge had just outsmarted him.

Dimock turned to Reilly with a smug look on his face, "Is that what you wanted to bring out?"

"Thank you," Reilly said, smiling.

Not wishing to leave the jurors with a question in their minds, on redirect Kolbrener attacked the issue a different way.

"Can you tell us whether or not the plane, which reported over Battle Creek at 11:51 p.m. and was heading to Milwaukee, intersected the squall?"

"It is objected to," Reilly said.

Kolbrener rephrased, but Reilly objected again. He rephrased a second time and Reilly objected once more. Finally Dimock helped Kolbrener with an acceptable question. "Suppose you just ask him if the squall line intersects a direct line from Battle Creek to Milwaukee?"

Kolbrener rephrased as suggested.

Then Badner stated the obvious: "Yes."

The jurors probably wondered why Reilly fought so hard to keep that out. It was clear to anyone who saw the map that the flight path intersected the squall line at the Michigan shoreline.

Then Kolbrener asked his most critical question. "Was this information known to any meteorologist who paid attention?"

"Object," Reilly said loudly, "on the grounds that he can't know who paid attention."

Kolbrener rephrased four more times and Reilly objected four times, until finally Judge Dimock chimed in. "He told us previously that the forecasts were sent to all meteorological stations."

ON THURSDAY, OCTOBER 17, the fifth day of the trial, Martin Kolbrener called Coast Guard Commander Frederick Goettel to the stand. In the space of the seven years since the loss of Flight 2501, Goettel had been promoted from the rank of lieutenant to commander. After establishing that he had served as the captain of the *Woodbine* in June 1950, Kolbrener began his questioning, taking Goettel through from the point his vessel was assigned search and rescue duty to the moment he first encountered floating debris. "Where were you at that time?" Kolbrener asked.

"Within an area eight to twelve miles from the Michigan shore...halfway between South Haven and St. Joseph."

Then he questioned Goettel about the debris his crew recovered. Goettel described the flotsam and human remains in detail. The jury members must have cringed, and the families present would have been horrified. Kolbrener was interested in bringing this out for two reasons: to establish that the airplane and its passengers had been torn apart and to try to show that the accident had occurred in Michigan. Michigan law had no compensation limits in a wrongful death suit, and, more importantly, all the evidence pointed there. To drive home the point he asked Goettel, "Did you observe from where the debris came?"

"Yes, we recovered it from the surface of the water, but I saw it floating from below the surface of the water right under my searchlights."

Kolbrener didn't press the issue further. He felt that the testimony suggested the wreckage was directly below the floating debris eight to twelve miles off shore and therefore established the crash occurred in Michigan. Satisfied with Goettel's testimony, he turned the witness over to Reilly for cross-examination.

Reilly began by establishing Goettel's credentials, which seemed counterproductive if he intended to discredit his testimony, however, his true objective soon came out. He hoped to establish that although the aircraft debris was first found in Michigan waters forty-two hours after the last communication, the airplane crashed somewhere farther west and the debris merely drifted eastward. If the accident occurred in Illinois or Wisconsin, that would benefit Northwest because wrongful death statutes in those two states had financial limitations. "As a skipper of a boat on the Great Lakes," he asked, "are you familiar with the currents and winds and the prevailing direction of the wind?"

Kolbrener understood immediately what he was trying to do and objected on the grounds that Reilly was attempting to elicit expert testimony from a witness.

Dimock allowed Reilly to proceed.

"Isn't it true that some of the debris you observed floating eventually washed up on shore," he asked, "and so the movement of the debris was in what direction?"

"Northeasterly."

Kolbrener asked that the answer be stricken out. Dimock overruled the objection and encouraged Reilly to continue.

"Isn't it a fact that you began your search at Milwaukee?"

"Certainly, yes, sir," Goettel replied.

Kolbrener objected again and the attorneys argued. Again Dimock allowed Reilly to proceed.

"You had information that brought you to Milwaukee, did you not?"

"Oh, yes, a number of reports."

"Tell the jury, was there a large object, such as…"

"Just a minute!" Kolbrener shouted, stopping Reilly in mid-sentence. "I object to that as hearsay."

This time Dimock sustained the objection. Reilly asked a similar version of the question five times, Kolbrener objected five times, and Judge Dimock sustained the objection five times. The jury listened as the two attorneys argued. They must have been curious about whatever had been seen at Milwaukee. Frustrated that he had come all this way and had information to share, Goettel asked the judge, "Can't I just tell you?"

Judge Dimock probably mused at the commander's naiveté, but replied quite professionally, "That's not the way the law works, Commander. Please just answer the questions directed to you."

Kolbrener realized that after all the discussion and argument, the jurors might think he was trying to hide something important. He spoke up angrily to get the judge's attention, "Mr. Reilly has already poisoned the jury's mind with something on the surface. Let Goettel tell everything because this is an insidious way of creating a suspicion in the mind of the jury. I withdraw my objection."

"It is highly objectionable that he did not follow my instructions," the judge said, glaring angrily at Reilly. However, since the objection had been withdrawn; he consented to let Reilly pursue his question.

Without further interruption, Goettel described five civilian reports of floating debris, presumed to be from the aircraft, in various places west and south of Milwaukee. Then, as Goettel began to say that upon investigation he had found nothing, Reilly interrupted him with another question.

"Your honor," Kolbrener pleaded, "he interrupted the witness."

Dimock could stand it no longer. "There was nothing there?" he asked directly of Goettel.

"No, nothing," he replied.

Now it was Reilly's turn to be angry. He had an agenda and intended to pursue it. "Those winds were blowing toward Michigan, rather than away from it?"

"Yes," Goettel answered.

"Is it not your experience that with human or other objects lost off the bathing beaches of Chicago, searches are inevitably conducted in the region of Benton Harbor?"

"I am going to object," Kolbrener piped up again.

"Sustained," Dimock agreed.

Reilly pursued the matter of drifting debris in a different manner. "Tell me, sir, in the southern waters of Lake Michigan, is there is not another component entering into drift besides wind?"

Reilly was undoubtedly referring to currents, but Kolbrener objected again on the grounds of that being expert testimony. Dimock again sustained the objection. Although not satisfied he had proven the crash occurred outside Michigan boundaries, Reilly knew that Michigan's unlimited damage statute would only come into question if Northwest Airlines was were found negligent, and he did not intend to let that happen. "I am finished," he consented.

OVER THE NEXT SEVERAL DAYS, Kolbrener, Caddy, and McCann brought in a series of witnesses for the plaintiffs.

"I call Donald Bassi to the stand," Kolbrener announced on Friday.

Bassi had witnessed the squall line roll south over Lake Michigan that night and had testified at the Civil Aeronautics Board hearing in Chicago held a month after the accident about his sighting of a "four-engine plane." Bassi described how he watched it fly south, almost into the storm, shortly after midnight. On cross-examination, Reilly tried to discredit Bassi's testimony by pointing out that at the 1950 hearing, he had reported seeing the airplane just after 11:00 p.m.. Unfortunately, Kolbrener did not bring out the fact that the CAB report noted all time in Central Standard Time, and 11:00 p.m. Central is the same as midnight in Eastern Standard Time.

The plaintiffs' next witness, Oscar Lappe, an aeronautical engineering scientist at New York University, was hired as an expert witness to address the hazards of flight in areas of turbulence. His testimony showed how turbulence could have contributed to the loss of Flight 2501 if it encountered the squall line.

Kolbrener also hired Marcus Plante, a professor of law at the University of Michigan, to testify about Michigan's wrongful death statutes in the event that the jury would determine that the accident had occurred in Michigan. While the jury was out of the room, Plante outlined a number of precedent-setting Michigan cases in which grown and independent children, like those suing in the Rorabaugh and Freng cases, had collected pecuniary damages from parents who had been killed, even though those parents no longer had legal responsibility for their children.

After that Dimock recalled the jury, and Kolbrener called the plaintiffs to the stand one by one to present their cases for financial damages.

Helen Rorabaugh Seymour, her brother Charles Rorabaugh, and his wife, Gertrude, testified about the financial loss they experienced after their mother, Marie Rorabaugh, died. It was difficult for all three to establish a financial value for a woman they loved so much. Helen was reduced to tears on a number of occasions. Through the testimony of all three, they established a pattern of gifts and household assistance that Marie had provided and would have continued to provide had she lived.

Reilly countered this by pointing out that those gifts were not of great value and that each child was financially self-sufficient. Reilly also made it known that the children had collected life insurance and stocks from their mother's estate, but the judge told the jury to disregard that.

Reilly did the same in the Freng case, although the value of the gifts and inheritance given by the very successful William Freng to his married daughter was much higher than it had been for the Rorabaugh children.

Mary Ann Freng White could not testify for herself. She had recently been hospitalized for pneumonia, and, even after seven years, she could not discuss the accident without breaking down. May Ramsey, a close family friend and executrix of the estate, testified on her behalf. So too did Charles Hiles, a superior of William Freng's at ITT. Hiles explained that had Freng lived, he would have eventually been promoted to vice president or even president of the company. "At his past history of pay increases," Hiles explained, "he would have made well over $100,000 annually."

Reilly countered by eliciting testimony that ITT often hires its top executives from outside the company, instilling doubt that Freng would have been promoted from the inside.

Oscar Schafer, the husband of Adelaide Schafer and stepfather of John, spoke for himself, outlining a solid case that his wife had not only taken care of their ten-room home on six acres, but also assisted him as a part-time secretary in his stockbroker business. He provided documentation of the money he had spent for household help and secretarial services since his wife's death.

Reilly countered by drawing out testimony that Schafer had seen an increase in his annual salary from $15,000 to $20,000 in the years since his wife died and had inherited valuable property from her estate. And he reminded the jury that Schafer had remarried 11 months after the accident and, in effect, had replaced his household help with his new wife.

Freda Schwartz had, unquestionably, the most solid case for monetary damage. Married five years to Frank Schwartz, who had adopted her daughter, she had been solely dependent on her husband, who had made about $6,000 annually.

On cross-examination of Schwartz, Reilly began heading down a path that seemed to meander far from her financial struggles in the wake of Frank Schwartz's death: "I take it from your earlier comments, you have been previously married?"

"That is right."

"Would you tell us when you contracted that marriage?"

"Objection, immaterial," Kolbrener interjected.

"Overruled," Dimock replied.

"Well, I was twenty years old," she answered, hesitatingly.

"So, if you were born in 1908, then you were married in 1929?"

"Well, that must be it," she said, almost in a whisper.

"Can you tell me the place you were married?"

"Uh…I don't recall."

"You mean you really can't remember where you were married?"

"Well…in Chicago."

"Where in Chicago?"

"In a judge's chamber."

"When did your first husband die?" Reilly asked, trying to move forward.

"I don't remember," she said beginning to shake.

"Are you serious that you don't remember?"

"Well, I was not very fond of him," she said, starting to whimper.

"How many months was he dead before you married Mr. Schwartz?"

"Well, I have a rough idea."

Realizing he was beginning to wear her down, Reilly tried something different. "What was your first husband's name?"

"Morris Bell."

"Did you have a daughter by that marriage?"

"Yes."

"How long after the marriage?"

"About a year."

"I assume you know your daughter's birthday?"

"April 20, I think, 1929."

"Did you meet Frank Schwartz before Bell died?"

"Yes, I think I met him the year of the World's Fair."

"1939?"

"That sounds right."

With 5:00 p.m. drawing near, Judge Dimock adjourned for the day. Kolbrener signaled Schwartz to follow him out of the courtroom, so they could talk privately.

The next morning Reilly began questioning Freda Schwartz again.

"Your maiden name is Freda Larson?"

"That is right," she said quietly.

"Were you known as Laverna Bell at any time?"

"Yes," she said, realizing that Reilly was not going to let up.

"Were you employed in cabarets?"

"Yes, I worked in the Lexington Hotel."

"Did you assume the name of Pat?"

"I think so, since I was sixteen or seventeen."

"Were you christened as Laverna?

"Yes."

"Was your husband's last name actually Belosky?"

"He used that at times," she said, beginning to break down. She knew Reilly had somehow discovered all her secrets. With tears starting down her cheeks, she whimpered, "I have a confession to make, Mr. Reilly. I have told the truth, but not wholly. I have to tell the whole truth, even though it is an awful thing to tell." She was quiet for several seconds before finding the resolve to continue. "I was never married to Mr. Bell," she said, starting to cry. "and I have kept that a secret from everyone, including my daughter, for all these years. My attorney didn't know this until just last night."

"But you have under oath indicated that you were married, have you not?" Reilly pressed unsympathetically, having achieved his goal of catching her in not one, but several lies.

Over the next hour, on redirect, Kolbrener drew out the truth, hoping to mitigate damages and paint Reilly as the villain for attacking her. Freda Schwartz poured out her embarrassing story. One of seven children raised on a farm, she only had an eighth-grade education. She left the farm to get work in Chicago as a domestic servant when she was eighteen and met Belosky, a bookmaker, who offered to marry her. He took her to the home of a friend, who performed a marriage service. She soon became pregnant, and just before the baby was born, she and Belosky moved to Hollywood, California. When they later returned to Chicago, she learned that Belosky had duped her; the man who married them was not a real judge. Consequently, she left him, later working in the cabaret as a hat check girl to provide for her daughter, Joy. She had only maintained the last name Bell, to legitimize her daughter.

Reilly did not let up, drawing out that even on her marriage license to Schwartz, she had lied, indicating she had formerly been married to Morris Belosky, even after she knew that was not so.

Whether the members of the jury felt sympathy for her embarrassing situation or anger that she had lied would never be known.

ONCE THE PLAINTIFFS rested their case, John Reilly called a number of witnesses to testify in defense of Northwest Airlines. First up was Edwin Gunnerson, a pilot for Northwest who had successfully flown across the lake that night. He explained how he had flown on Airway Green 2, from Muskegon, Michigan, to Milwaukee, Wisconsin, landing at 11:20 p.m. He had seen lightning north of his flight path and experienced minor turbulence, but had made it across the lake. That proved little, however, because his crossing occurred about an hour before Flight 2501 was last heard from.

Next, Reilly called Captain Renn, the Capital Airlines pilot who departed Milwaukee at 11:45 p.m. and crossed the lake on Red 57, just a short time before Flight 2501 reached the lakeshore. Reilly used his testimony to show that despite crossing the lake through heavy turbulence, Renn made it.

On cross-examination, Kolbrener brought out that Renn was delivering cargo, not passengers. Cargo flights did not operate under the same directives as passenger flights, which had to avoid turbulence.

Reilly next called Northwest radio operator Holland Krotz, who had communicated with Flight 2501 several times that night. Krotz explained that he had given Flight 2501 weather reports for the cities of Minneapolis, Madison, and Milwaukee, when the pilot asked for them.

On cross-examination, Kolbrener discovered that Krotz had a busy evening that night with over 100 separate communications with other Northwest flights. Although his teletype machine delivered all the sequence reports from the eighteen regional airports, he did not offer Flight 2501 any weather information other than what the pilot had specifically requested.

Captain W. F. Dean, the Northwest pilot who flew the same DC-4 used for Flight 2501 into New York earlier that evening, testified on behalf of Northwest. He established that the aircraft was in fine working order during his flight.

Kolbrener was able to use him for a completely different line of questioning: to elicit testimony about how altimeters can be unreliable in the area of thunderstorms. Dean probably did not realize he was being drawn into Kolbrener's trap when offhandedly asked, "Can the company transmit weather reports to you in flight?"

"Yes," he answered, "through radio stations along the line of the flight." Then Dean unwittingly added, "The company can transmit the sequence reports as required or as they deem it necessary for us to have."

Kolbrener must have been happy to get that scathing bit of information to help his case, especially from a witness for the opposition.

Reilly's last two witnesses from Northwest Airlines would offer testimony most critical to the company's case. Minneapolis flight superintendent George Benson and New York flight dispatcher Warren Seifert had jointly made the decision *not* to provide Flight 2501 with the 10:30 p.m. forecast of the National Weather Service or the updated forecast of their own meteorologist, Donald Wertz. Reilly had to show this was not an oversight or mistake, but a calculated decision in the best interest of the flight. He began with George Benson. "Why didn't you send it?" he asked, referring to the new forecast.

"Element of time," Benson answered. Realizing that he had made it sound as if he was too busy, he expanded his answer. "For the twelve-hour forecast period, it appeared the front was moving at about twenty-three or twenty-four miles per hour. I felt the front would still be north of Milwaukee when 2501 was crossing the lake based on the speed of its movement."

Then Reilly called Warren Seifert to the stand. "Did you get Badner's 10:30 p.m. forecast?"

"Yes, at about 11:05 or 11:10 p.m."

"And were you aware of your flights in the air?"

"Yes, I was."

"What did you do when you got the forecast?"

"I compared it with the previous and checked it against the sequence reports and the company forecast. It did not seem a good idea to give this to the flight as it forecast a developing squall in the northern part of Michigan's Lower Peninsula, considerably north of Flight 2501's route of travel, and the company had already provided a warning."

On cross examination Kolbrener asked Seifert, "Is a squall line significant to a pilot?"

"It can be of significance," Seifert replied hesitatingly, trying not to stumble into a trap.

"And is a squall line a place where there can be severe turbulence?"

"It is possible."

"Isn't it so significant that it should be put into the hands of a pilot?"

"That is correct," Seifert replied, ready with what he thought would be a solid response. "We did so!"

"Tell that jury what the forecast you gave the pilot was."

"A cold front lying northeast to southwest between Rochester, Minnesota, and Omaha, Nebraska, moving slowly eastward." Then Seifert added. "The squall line was ahead of the front."

"At the time that forecast was written at 4:45 p.m.," Kolbrener asked, slowly and distinctly, "how far was the squall from Milwaukee?"

"250 miles, roughly west."

That statement alone seemed damning, considering how far away it was, but Kolbrener then posed his key question: "Does the 10:30 p.m. forecast not read, 'developing squall line moving southward over southern lower Michigan?'"

"Objected to!" Reilly shouted, realizing that his witness had not only stumbled into, but gotten himself caught, in a trap. "We concede that is what the forecast reads!"

Kolbrener and his co-counsel probably felt pretty satisfied that they had so effortlessly drawn an opposing witness into their trap. Whether the jurors all realized the significance of the difference between the two forecasts would only be known when they delivered the verdict.

ON NOVEMBER 6, 1957, after eighteen days of testimony, the defense rested its case. Judge Dimock announced that their deliberations would be divided into two phases. "First I am going to submit to you a special question of fact: In what state did the plane strike the waters of Lake Michigan?"

He came out from behind the bench, walked up to the map, and pointed out the mid-lake dividing line between Michigan, Indiana, Illinois, and Wisconsin to make sure the jury understood the boundaries. "It is your exclusive function to determine the facts of this case," he began. "It is not what counsel on either side said or what I may say as to what the facts are, but your judgment of the facts that must govern."

Among other things, he later reminded them, "In this case, the plaintiffs have the burden of proof. The defendant has no burden to establish anything."

Once the jury determined the state in which the accident had occurred, the judge could apply that state's statute to the case.

At 4:35 p.m. that afternoon, the judge dismissed the jury to begin its deliberations. Within twenty minutes, the forelady requested a ruler and the map that defined state boundaries. At 5:00 p.m. the jurors returned to the courtroom.

"Have you determined in which state the plane fell?" Judge Dimock asked the jury.

"We have, your honor."

"What have you determined?"

"The plane fell within the state of Michigan."

Kolbrener and his co-counsel must have been thrilled. They had won on the first question, however, the next questions would be much more critical.

The judge thanked the jurors and dismissed them until the next day when motions and closing arguments would be made.

AT 11:40 A.M. ON NOVEMBER 7, 1957, after the plaintiffs' closing argument, John Reilly began his summation of the case. He addressed each plaintiff's case individually and, as he did in his opening comments, reinforced his contention that three of the plaintiffs had no legal claim to financial damages, all the while reminding the jury how this truly had been a tragedy.

Regarding the Schwartz case, Reilly must have considered that bringing out Freda Schwartz's lies was a double-edged sword. Although it served his purpose well—to discredit the entire testimony of that plaintiff—it made him appear heartless in revealing the embarrassing fact that her daughter was illegitimate. He tried to explain his motivations to gain the jury's forgiveness, "I beg of you to hear it is my sacred and solemn duty to find out who is the next-of-kin and who is entitled to bring an action and certainly I had to be satisfied of the death of Mr. Belosky."

Then he explained that he merely stumbled onto the fact that they had never really been married. His sincerity was short-lived. He then turned on Schwartz. "All she said the day before her confession, although she held up her hand and said 'I swear to tell the truth,' was in fact a lie. She wasn't married as she said, and never had been married."

By painting her a liar on that one issue, Reilly hoped the jury would dismiss all her testimony as lies.

Reilly then turned to the primary issue—the question of whether Northwest was negligent: "I say to you based on what you have heard, can you say why or how this accident happened? If you can't, then can you be arrogant or foolhardy enough to say this was a negligent act? Even if there was negligence about it, there must be a proximate relationship with the accident."

He used an effective analogy to explain proximate cause. "If you were negligent because your automobile headlamp was broken and you were in an accident in the daytime, that negligence would *not* be the proximate cause of the accident."

He reminded the jury of the forecast that Northwest meteorologist Beresford gave the pilots before the flight took off, which he stressed provided them full warning of the developing squall. To drive home that point, he reached for his copy of the forecast and began reading it out loud, but added a personal comment that would be a grievous error, although he didn't realize it at the time. His error could and would render the trial worthless: "Badner's forecast called for 'scattered thunderstorms along the eastern edge'—*thank God we have a pilot on the jury who can give you something about thunderstorms*—'Base 3,000 to 4,000, tops 30,000 to 40,000 feet, with moderate to severe turbulence at all levels. Flights below 10,000 feet to proceed with caution through the frontal zone.'"

Kolbrener, Caddy, and McCann must have looked at each other in disbelief at Reilly's huge impropriety and turned to see if the judge had noticed and would object, but Dimock just sat there calmly listening as Reilly continued. Minutes later, Reilly dug his hole even deeper: "The acumen and ability and the experience of a pilot—*and thank God you have got one on the jury who will tell you about it*—when you are sitting up there and you are watching for all those thousands of hours, you know where the weather is and where you can get through. That is how they get through."

If any of the jurors, including the pilot, saw the smiles of incomprehension on the faces of Kolbrener, Caddy, and McCann or noticed them furiously making notes, they probably had no idea why. The attorneys were marveling at their good fortune. If the jury did not find in favor of their clients, they now had grounds for a mistrial. They knew that although the jurors had the right to talk among themselves and use personal experience to make their decisions or sway others, an attorney did not have the legal right to *direct,* or even suggest, that the jury to listen to an expert within their ranks, as Reilly had just done, not only one, but twice.

Unaware of his blunders, Reilly concluded his summation: "Is there anything that says that it wasn't a twister or a hurricane or lightning that blew this plane out of the sky despite all the ingenuity of the pilots, who I say were straining every minute that night? Who better than they to be the judges of the weather before them? I leave this case with you. In my humble opinion, I can't see how it can be other than a verdict for my client, which I ask of you."

At 3:50 p.m., Judge Dimock began his charge to the court. He told the jury he would ask them three questions: "One, was the defendant negligent? Two, if so, was such negligence the proximate cause of the fall of the plane into Lake Michigan? And three, if so, what damages are the plaintiffs due?"

Then he explained the guidelines for determining those answers. "Every common carrier, like Northwest Airlines, is under duty to exercise a high degree of care with respect to the safety of its passengers. Any breach of that duty to exercise a high degree of care is negligence. You are not to infer negligence from the mere happening of the accident. If you should find that Northwest did violate its duty to its passengers, that alone would not be sufficient to render the defendant responsible. In addition, you would have to find their violation of this duty to be the cause of the loss of the airplane. There must be an unbroken chain of events leading to the accident."

Finally, he addressed the issue of damages, saying, "If you find the defendant negligent and that the negligence was a cause of the accident, then, and only then, will you turn to the question of damages."

Dimock outlined the methods and means they could use to calculate the amounts of the damages for each plaintiff, cautioning, "Remember that neither party is entitled to sympathy. You are not to give weight to the fact that the plaintiffs are individuals, while the defense is a corporation."

At 4:25 p.m., Dimock sent the jury to deliberate. The jurors would not be allowed to go home until they returned their verdict. From 6:15 p.m. to 7:30 p.m., the jurors were given a break for dinner, then they continued deliberating. At 11:30 p.m. the forelady asked for a copy of Julius Badner's testimony. When she was told it was 227 pages long, the clerk of the court recommended they adjourn to a hotel for the night. The jurors agreed, and a marshal escorted them there at 12:40 a.m. They returned in the morning to continue their work at 10:35. By 4:15 p.m., after nearly twelve hours of deliberation, the forelady sent a note to the judge indicating the jury had come to a unanimous decision.

Once all parties had reconvened in the courtroom, the clerk asked, "Madame Forelady, have you arrived at a verdict?"

"Yes," she replied.

"Will you state your verdict?"

To the first question, 'was the defendant negligent?' We answer yes."

Kolbrener, Caddy, and McCann were thrilled, realizing they had successfully convinced the jury of Northwest's negligence. They were totally unprepared for the next answer.

"To the second question," the forelady continued, "'was such negligence the proximate cause of the fall of the plane into Lake Michigan?' The answer is no."

Shocked, the three attorneys began whispering, planning their next move. They would not accept the verdict, and they still had an ace up their sleeves: Reilly's blunders.

Dimock concluded by addressing the jury, "I think it is obvious you have worked with your heads rather than your hearts and that is all we can ask of jurors. In the name of the court, thank you for the work that you have done in the administration of justice over this long trial."

"All RISE! THE UNITED STATES District Court in the southern district of New York is in session," the clerk of the court announced four months later on February 19, 1958, at the beginning of the second wrongful death trial over the loss of Northwest Airlines Flight 2501. This time, a new judge, Thomas F. Murphy, a 1930 graduate of Georgetown University and Fordham Law School, a former New York City Police Commissioner, and former federal prosecutor, presided over the trial. He was best known as the prosecutor in the trials of Alger Hiss, a former State Department official accused of perjury for denying that he had passed confidential documents to a courier for the Communist Party.

Soon after losing the first case, attorneys for the plaintiffs had made a motion for a mistrial to Judge Dimock, pointing out the improper direction by Reilly in encouraging eleven jurors to consider the testimony of the twelfth juror, a pilot. As Judge Dimock had done in a previous case where an attorney had pointed out his error, he readily admitted his own mistake in writing, "I was derelict in not counteracting Mr. Reilly's improper directive on my own. My error requires a new trial."

All the attorneys had agreed to let stand the first verdict that placed the accident in the state of Michigan, so that the whole trial was not a waste. In the second trial, the same three attorneys represented the same four plaintiffs, and the same defense attorney represented Northwest. The attorneys called the same witnesses and elicited much the same testimony, in 11 days rather than 18 days, largely because they did not have to argue in which state the accident had occurred, and Patricia Schwartz admitted forthright that she had never been previously married. The only difference in the second trial was that the judge asked only one question of the jury: "Is Northwest liable for this accident?"

On March 5, 1958, after deliberating from 11:05 a.m. to 11:00 p.m., the jury reached a verdict—as with the first jury—after reviewing all of Julius Badner's testimony. When all the parties returned to the courtroom at that late hour, Judge Murphy asked, "Madam Forelady, how do you find the defendant, liable or not liable?"

"We find the defendant not liable."

For a second time John G. Reilly had presented a brilliant case. He belittled the idea of any pecuniary damages, except Freda Schwartz, whom he again compromised by bringing out her prior impropriety of lying on her marriage license. Then he made any negligence on the part of Northwest Airline's employees unimportant by stressing the competence of the pilots and their ability to make independent decisions regarding the weather. From the beginning, the plaintiffs had little chance for a win.

After everyone left the courtroom, Patricia Schwartz happened to get on the elevator with one of the jurors. With tears in her eyes, she rebuked the decision of the jury, "Well, my husband died at the hands of that airline and we get nothing."

"I'm so sorry," was all the juror could say.

Judge Edward J. Dimock presided over the first wrongful death suit, in 1957.

Judge Thomas F. Murphy presided over the second wrongful death suit in 1958.

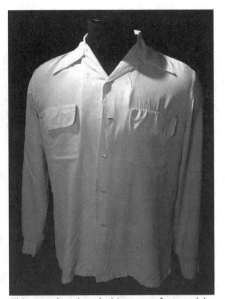

Frederick August Goettel near the time of the crash of Flight 2501. In 1967 a slope on the Dyer Plateau in the Antarctic was named, *The Goettel Escarpment,* in honor of his career accomplishments. *Ancestry. com/Goettel family.*

This peach-colored shirt manufactured by the McGregor Company was in a suitcase, pulled from a commercial fishing net by Captain Julius Allers, one of the first items of flotsam found in the lake after the crash. *Photograph by the author.*

Ensign Lawrence J. Otto as he appeared as a new officer in 1950 (left) and when interviewed by the author in 2007. *Courtesy of Lawrence Otto.*

Identified as belonging to Merle Barton, this suit jacket and hair styling kit were found on the beach days after the accident. The shredded jacket and warped and rusted implements indicate the force of the crash. *Courtesy of Cathy Barton Snyder.*

Captain Julius Allers was fishing from the *Elsie J* when he found a suitcase, a shirt, ties, and human flesh the day after the crash. At the time of this book's publishing, the boat is still operated by the Jensen family in South Haven, Michigan. *Courtesy of Judy Allers Schlaak.*

This photograph appeared in the *News Palladium* of June 27, 1950, with the caption, "Captain Nathaniel Fulford, Coast Guard officer in charge of Lake Michigan search for missing Northwest airliner, phones directions to aides from South Haven Coast Guard station. Looking on is Chief Petty Officer Frank Rydlewics, officer in charge of South Haven station." *Associated Press*.

This photograph appeared in the *News Palladium* of June 27, 1950, with the caption, "These three South Haven Coast Guardsmen were first to find debris and bits of bodies from lost airplane at 6 p.m. Sunday. Left to right, they are Kenneth Richie, seaman, James Bryson, engineman second class, and First Class Boatswain's Mate Joseph Bartunek." *Associated Press*.

These photographs appeared side by side in multiple newspapers. At left, Coast Guardsmen using hooks on poles are pulling a pair of brown, tweed pants from Lake Michigan. At right, Seaman Charles McGuire holds a piece of the aircraft. *Associated Press.*

A seaman carrying clothing wrapped in a Northwest blanket into the boat house at the St. Joseph Coast Guard Station where all the debris was stored. *Universal News Reel.*

Berrien County Coroner Louis Kerlikowske (left) and CAB official George E. Clark examining debris recovered from the lake. *Associated Press.*

A seat cushion and child's undershirt among the recovered debris. *South Haven Tribune.*

This blanket was among the first items recovered from the lake. Its discovery helped lead the larger Coast Guard vessels to the site of the debris. Paul L. Benscoter (left), Chicago Station manager for Northwest Airlines, and Captain Nathaniel Fulford (right), of the Ninth Coast Guard District, identified the debris. *South Haven Tribune.*

Joseph Kimm (left) in 1933 when he was a copilot for Northwest is pictured with, from left to right, Hugh Rueschenberg, Amelia Earhart, and Mal Freeburg after a "proof of the pudding flight" from Minneapolis to Spokane. *Courtesy of Joseph Kimm.*

The Naval Destroyer Escort *Daniel A. Joy,* DE-585, was used primarily for diving operations during the search for Flight 2501 in June 1950. *Author's Collection.*

The Coast Guard Patrol Boat *Frederick Lee,* WSC-139, was the first vessel on the scene at Milwaukee. *Author's Collection.*

The Coast Guard Buoy Tender *Woodbine,* was the first vessel on the scene off South Haven, Michigan. *Author's Collection.*

The Coast Guard Icebreaker *Mackinaw,* WAG-83, was the largest of the vessels used in the search and rescue operation. *Author's Collection.*

The Coast Guard Buoy Tender *Hollyhock,* WAGL/WLM-220. *Author's Collection.*

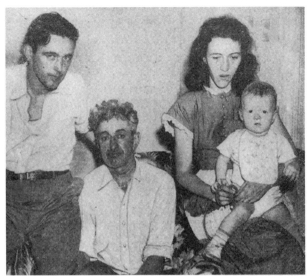

This photograph appeared in the *Seattle Times* on June 25, 1950, with the following caption: "The Hughes family waits at home for news of Mrs. Peter Hughes who was a passenger on the crashed plane. L. to R. Peter Hughes Jr., Peter Hughes, a daughter Mrs. Alice Donovan, and her son Michael, 17 months old."

Seattle Times reporters had little regard for privacy. This photograph was staged to evoke pity according to William Kaufmann. The caption read: "Carefully concealing his own knowledge of the tragedy that has struck at their lives, Winfield Kaufmann reads to his three children, Mary Jean, Richard, and William in Seattle home. Children are unaware mother was passenger on plane."

PART V
THE SEARCH CONCLUDES

"The journey, not the destination, matters."

T. S. Elliot

Chapter 19

A PROMISING TARGET

In April 2010, the National Underwater and Marine Agency returned to South Haven, Michigan, to begin our seventh expedition. Ralph Wilbanks, Steve Howard, and Jim Lesto planned to stay six weeks that year, arriving earlier and leaving later than usual to cover as much ground as possible. That year Clive made the decision to search in the northern segment of the circle within Airway Red 57, which ran from Glenn, Michigan, to Milwaukee, under the theory that Flight 2501 may have actually remained on its scheduled airway. Although, after studying the court transcripts and talking with other pilots, I believed that Robert Lind diverted south to avoid that storm, I could not argue with Clive's logic. We often search on a courseline when looking for shipwrecks.

To fully cover that territory, Ralph would have to scan an area that we had already covered using David Trotter's 50 kHz sonar during a previous unsuccessful search for the *Andaste*. We could not be sure that Dave's low frequency sonar would have "seen" a debris field if that's all that remained of Flight 2501.

About four weeks into the search, Ralph called me. I answered while sitting at the computer in my office, where I worked almost every waking moment. "We found a small boat," he said, "I'm sending you the image now."

Great, I thought sarcastically, *another shipwreck*.

I immediately saw the absurdity of my reaction. Shipwrecks had been almost all I had thought about for the last many years, so a new discovery should be a reason to celebrate. However, I wanted Ralph to find the airplane wreckage so badly that another shipwreck just seemed to get in the way. This would be the eighth shipwreck we had encountered in the course of the search for Flight 2501.

"You missed it." Ralph pointed out. "It's in the area that you already covered."

"How deep?" I asked.

"250 feet. It's pretty small."

The mention of its size told me that Ralph did not blame us for not finding it. He knew that a small target would be hard to see with the 50 kHz fish.

"*Sea Mar III*, maybe?" I asked, realizing I could get excited by that discovery.

"No, it's not *that* small," he said, dashing my momentary hope. "It's about fifty feet long, probably made of wood."

While we were talking, I opened my email to see the target staring me in the face. The database in my head told me that no wooden vessels fifty feet long were known to have gone down in that area, so I knew we had another mystery boat on our hands.

"I'll contact Bob, Todd, and Jeff to see when they can make the dive."

Since Ralph had not yet found the DC-4 on Red 57, I began second-guessing the logic of searching in that airway. I had always given credence to David Schwab's theory that the airplane crashed southwest of where the debris had been found. In addition, I had recently found a newspaper article quoting Northwest Chief Pilot, Joseph Kimm. Although his statement was not completely clear, it suggested that Flight 2501 might have been on Red 28, the southern airway. We knew that the debris had been found north of Red 28. If the airplane crashed on Red 28, then the debris would have drifted northeast just as Schwab concluded.

I brought up my misgivings about searching north. "What about spending some time searching south too this year, down by Airway Red 28?"

"Well, we haven't finished Red 57," Ralph said, "and I don't like to jump around."

I could certainly understand that logic. I could never forgive myself if we moved south and then years later found the wreck north, just a lane or two from where Ralph left off.

"Plus, Ralph added, "I'm not sure we're coming back next year."

That last statement hit me like the seventy pounds of lead he hung on the fish. In about three weeks it would all be over. I hung up feeling physically and emotionally beaten.

A FEW DAYS later on Monday, May 17, 2010, Ralph called again, and seemed to have had a change of heart. "I need you and the team here tomorrow night. We only have ten days left before we call it quits. Clive's going to be here tomorrow night and we want to strategize where to search during our last days here."

"What?" I stammered, my mind racing. *If he didn't want to consider moving the search area a few days ago, why now?*

"Does it have to be tomorrow?" I asked. "I've got another meeting. Can we make it Wednesday night instead?"

"Change your meeting," he ordered like an army sergeant. "Clive wants to meet tomorrow, and he wants everyone's input about where the wreckage might be."

A command performance, it seemed.

"And make sure everyone is here.

"Well, I'm sure everyone will want to see Clive," I acknowledged, "but no one besides Jack and me has been specifically working on the search area. I'm not sure anyone will do much more than throw a dart."

"Darts are fine," he said. "Get them all here at six o'clock." He hung up without waiting for me to say, "Okay."

With the phone still in my hand, I stepped out of my office and hollered over the balcony downstairs to Jack. "Clive's going to be here tomorrow and Ralph wants us down at the house."

"Really?" Jack asked, climbing the stairs. "What's up?"

I recounted our conversation word for word, expressing my frustration at having to cancel my other meeting and my confusion over Ralph wanting to strategize at this late date. Jack hesitated for a few seconds thinking over what I told him, then he said quietly, "They probably found the plane."

Oh, my God. Jack's words slapped me in the face. *Of course, how could I be so stupid?* Ralph was telling me without telling me. I had always wondered how he would share the news if he found the wreck. I thought of how he had announced to Clive that he had found the *Hunley.* Ralph phoned him in the wee hours of the morning and woke him up. "We're done, I'm sending you my bill," he had said, sounding purposely frustrated.

Clive, probably still fighting off grogginess after being so abruptly awakened, began trying to change Ralph's mind. "Why quit now?"

"Because," Ralph said slowly, ready to deliver his punch line, "We found it!"

Apparently we would have to wait until tomorrow night for Ralph to deliver his punch line to us. If Jack was right, I would be attending the meeting with my tail between my legs. I was obviously wrong about the airplane crashing southwest: It probably crashed up north on Red 57, its scheduled airway. Frankly I could care less about being right or wrong; I only cared about providing answers to the victims' families.

I rescheduled my meeting, then started making calls to the team. When that business was taken care of, I phoned Dave Trotter. For years, Dave has been my sounding board. A man of integrity, he has a good grasp on the "shipwreck game," as we call it. Once more, I recounted Ralph's words, then told Dave about Jack's suspicion. I was surprised that he did not agree: "I'd take Ralph on his word and show up prepared to talk strategy."

I immediately wondered if Dave was in on the game. I knew that he and Ralph had become friends, and I knew Dave was good at keeping secrets.

"Dave," I begged, "please tell me if you know something."

"I don't know anything about it, Val," he said very reassuringly.

I didn't doubt him anymore. Dave wouldn't lie.

I spent the next day organizing my files, making notes, and planning how I would present my case for searching southwest, but it seemed a waste. I was sure that Jack was right.

Jack left his office a little early on Tuesday, and we picked up Craig on the way to South Haven. As we got off the highway at the Phoenix Road exit, it hit me. Within the hour, we would learn where the airplane had crashed. I had a hard time keeping calm; my heart beat fast. *How perfect*, I thought. *This coming June would mark the sixty-year anniversary*. This seemed a synergistic finality to the whole project.

When we pulled in the driveway, I left my briefcase in the car; I knew we would not be doing any strategizing.

Everything seemed festive when we walked in the front door. Some of the team had already arrived and had beers in their hands. They were laughing and talking. I greeted Clive, shaking his hand. He looked positively jolly, even more so than two years earlier at our house when he presented us with three new wrecks. We met his wife, Janet, for the first time. She was dressed in corduroy slacks and a plain top; I liked her immediately. She was a regular person just like Clive, down to earth, gracious, and polite.

Ralph greeted me with enthusiasm. He offered me an O'Doul's, my near-beer of choice. Then he walked me over to the pizza and scooped me up a slice. All of us had so much fun, talking and eating and catching up with Clive, that I forgot for a moment why we were there, until Ralph announced, "Everyone in the dining room, please."

Every year since they had first rented the house, Ralph had used the dining room as a command post, shoving the eight-foot table into the corner of the room and filling it with several computers, files, books, and papers stacked high. I saw The Bear God sitting atop one pile, overlooking the scene. In pushing the table up against the wall, he had trapped all of the chairs, except two. They sat in front of the computers on the table, one displaying a Lake Michigan chart zoomed in to the area off South Haven and the other a black screen. Ralph sat down in front of the computer with the chart. "Here, take a seat, Val," he said offering me the chair in front of the other computer.

I looked around for Clive and Janet to offer one of them the seat instead, but saw Clive standing in the opposite corner and Janet leaning up against the kitchen door jamb. Everyone else stood behind the table. I sat down and looked at the black screen. I realized that it was the first slide of a PowerPoint presentation; I wanted to press the enter and see the sonar image of the wreck site, but refrained. Obviously Ralph had a special unveiling planned.

Ralph began clicking the keys on his computer, calling up layer upon layer on the chart. I immediately recognized the familiar colored boxes that marked the areas where we had already searched between Red 57 and Red 28 and a new box where they had been searching that month on Red 57. I saw the dots that represented all the wrecks we had found and the latest discovery up north—the fifty-foot mystery boat. Ralph began his presentation by saying, "Jeff, come on up here and point to the spot where you think the plane is."

By now, everyone knew what was going on, and Jeff Vos played along, sidling up to the table and placing his finger on a spot on the screen. Ralph marked the initials, "JV," at that spot. Then he asked Bob the same question. The ceremony continued with Ross, then Craig, then Todd, then Jack. The chart filled up with initials. Everyone seemed to have fun with the process, throwing their darts south, east, and west. Then it was my turn. "Now you, Valerie," Ralph said, looking me square in the eyes.

"How about I just press here," I said, hovering my finger over the enter key on the computer in front of me, "and let's see what the wreck looks like."

"No, no, no," he said playfully, grabbing my arm. "You have to tell us where you think it is."

I really didn't want to guess, I just wanted to see the target, but I knew I would be a party pooper if I didn't. I quickly weighed two options. I could point randomly to a spot in Airway Red 57 where I knew they had been searching and appear to be "right." Or, I could stay true to myself and point to a spot far south of there in Red 28, knowing I would be proven wrong. I took a few seconds for careful consideration, then pointed to a spot near Red 28. "Somewhere around here," I said.

Ralph typed "VV" at a spot in that general vicinity.

Clive was the only person who had not yet made a guess. As if on cue, Ralph said, with a big smile and an exaggerated southern drawl, "Now, Clive, where do you think it is?"

Clive made his way through the gathered people up to the table. Then he began circling his right hand in the air with his index finger at the ready and finally zeroed into a spot on Red 57 where they had been searching. We all laughed with him at his drama. Ralph marked "CC" at that spot, then reached over to the computer in front of me and hit the enter key, launching the first slide of his PowerPoint presentation. An image I recognized as a magnetometer reading appeared. "Here's the ferrous spike we got," Ralph explained.

The engines of the DC-4, we all knew, were made of steel, a ferrous metal. He tapped enter again, and I saw a side-scan image. If I had to give the Rorschach ink blot a name, I'd call it "Galaxy." It looked like an array of dots and lines forming a loose circle, just what I would have expected to see if an airplane hit the water, exploded, then sank to the bottom in a heap.

Ralph explained his big ceremonial reveal as just having fun, since Clive was coming to town anyway. "This looks the most promising of anything we've found yet all these years, but let's not get too excited," he cautioned. "Y'all are going have to check it out."

I stared at the image and did not hear much of what Ralph was saying. It was as if I had muted the sound around me. I realized how badly the DC-4 had been obliterated when it hit the water. It appeared to be just a jumble of twisted metal, like the Coast Guardsmen I had talked to expected. The target resembled the images I had studied of Swissair Flight 111, a McDonald Douglas MD-11 that crashed off Halifax, Nova Scotia, in 1998, in 180 feet of water. The video of the wreck showed heaps of debris, none of it discernible as an airplane. If Flight 2501 was as badly damaged as Flight 111, I wondered how we would be able to survey the site and learn anything from the mess.

Just then, the volume in the room unmuted and I heard what I can only describe as revelry behind me: Sounds of clinking beer bottles, back patting, and general whooping and hollering. I glanced away from the side-scan and looked at the dot on the map where the "CC" indicated the position of the wreck. I stared at that spot, only then fully realizing the implication of the location. If the airplane crashed in Red 57, that meant that Robert Lind flew right into the heart of the storm, without even trying to divert south. In that instant, I realized how hard it would be for me to have to tell the victims' families that the pilot did not even attempt to avoid the storm—that he flew with complete disregard for the weather. I felt the room starting to spin.

I glanced back at the side-scan, but instead of seeing the dots and lines I saw a grave site of 58 people. I thought of Jean Kaufmann and Kenneth Skoug, and I wondered how their son's Bill and Ken would feel if they saw this image. I looked away from the carnage. Unexpectedly, my eyes met those of Clive's wife, who was still leaning against the kitchen doorway. She looked sad, a mirror of how I felt.

Suddenly, sobs began bubbling up inside me. I pushed the chair back and quickly retreated from the room, stumbling into the living room where I fell down onto the black leather sofa. I looked through blurry eyes to see Steve Howard coming from the bathroom, a wad of toilet paper in his hand. "Here," he said, offering me the crumpled tissues.

Just then, the noise from the dining room hushed. I heard Craig saying, "You don't understand, she knows these people. She knows their families. She's going to have to tell them."

Craig realized what had upset me. Jack did, too. He joined me on the sofa, sitting close and wrapping his arm around me. Steve broke our silence. "We can't know for sure if it's the plane," he said in his soothing southern drawl, "until you get down there."

That was true, of course, but I could not imagine what else it could be. "But there's ferrous metal down there," I said. "That target isn't just clay and rocks."

"Yes, there's definitely ferrous metal down there, but we've been fooled before."

After all these years of waiting and wondering, I so badly wanted to find the wreck, but I didn't want this target to be it. I didn't want to find out that Robert Lind flew right into the storm.

I don't know how long I sat there, but I finally composed myself enough to go back and sit in the chair in the dining room again. Jack accompanied me. Ralph was scrolling though side-scan images of the target. I leaned in, trying to find some excitement in the discovery, but I was still sniffling. Just then, I felt a pair of hands on my shoulders. I looked around to find Clive standing behind me, his touch expressing an unsaid condolence. I stood up and hugged him, thanking him for finally solving the mystery.

"We haven't solved it yet," he said. "That's where you guys come in."

"How deep?" I asked Ralph, trying to morph from emotional female to impassive project manager.

"250."

I could dive this, I thought. *I had been to 230 on the* Hennepin. *I owe a firsthand account to the families.*

I swiveled around, looking for Todd, got up, and walked over to him, ready to ask that he take me along on the dive. I cleared my throat and raised my eyebrows, but before I could form my words, he looked me in the eye and shook his head back and forth. "If you reacted like *that* seeing a picture," he said, "then you can't risk going down there."

I knew he was right, even before he said it. Being alive for my kids is more important than making the dive for someone else's kids. I'd be on the boat when they dived, but not in the water.

We spent the next half hour finishing the pizza and planning the dive for the upcoming weekend. Clive would still be in town, so he could accompany Ralph and crew on *Diversity* to hear the news firsthand.

"BRING ME UP A PIECE OF ALUMINUM," Ralph hollered over the water from his boat to ours, as Todd, holding his video camera, jumped into the water. "I won't believe it until I see some proof."

Jeff followed as soon as Todd swam out of his way.

We had anchored on the target 90 minutes earlier, and kibitzed between the two boats while Bob, Todd, and Jeff suited up. The lake was calm on that Saturday afternoon, the sky overcast, and the temperature cold. While we waited on site for the divers, *Diversity* would motor over to the new, small mystery wreck and Ralph would capture a side-scan image of it for Clive. We had suggested they return in about an hour.

Bundled in my green parka, I bent over and picked up the forty-cubic-foot pony tank filled with Nitrox, lifted it over the transom, and helped Bob Underhill clip it to a D-ring attached to his harness. That tank held his deco gas, the mix he would breathe on his slow ascent from the wreck. Bob did a giant stride into the water. Jack grabbed Bob's still camera, stepped through the opening in the transom, bent down, and handed it to Bob in the water. "Be safe, don't take any chances down there," he said.

Bob secured the camera to yet another D-ring and kicked his way over to join his buddies at the down line. Twenty seconds later, the three heads disappeared beneath the surface. Craig checked his watch: 2:23 p.m. The dive profile called for twenty minutes at 250 feet, then sixty minutes for the ascent, during which time they would be decompressing. By about 3:45 p.m., we would know what the wreckage looked like.

Jack and I retreated to the semi-warmth of the cabin to wait it out, while Craig sat on the back deck. Looking east out the cabin windows, we could not see shore. From our vantage point, we might as well have been in the middle of a vast sea. We had been in the position of waiting for news about a new wreck discovery on many occasions when we had found wrecks deeper than we could safely dive. It was always difficult to wait, wondering what the divers were seeing, knowing that we would have to wait to view the rerun, all the while realizing that one way or another, the discovery could be life-changing.

For non-shipwreck hunters, the tension is hard to understand. I suppose it's like an expectant father who is sitting outside the delivery room while his wife gives birth. He does not know whether his child will be a boy or a girl, healthy or sick, or have all ten fingers and all ten toes, and, sometimes, he has to worry whether his wife will survive the delivery. Whatever happens in the delivery room, the father knows it will forever change his life.

As the boat gently rocked back and forth, I thought of how finding the wreck could change our lives in the near future. I had already printed out the phone numbers of all the family members and would have to start making calls that evening. If the media caught wind of the discovery, we would be inundated with requests for information. New stories would probably bring more family members out of the woodwork, and I would be spending a lot of time talking with them, explaining what we found and what we learned. We would have to contact the NTSB. And if we saw any human remains, the state police would need to know. And we would have to make more dives to try to investigate the wreck. On top of all that, I had not yet figured out how I would juggle all this and my two kids. I looked at my watch; it was 3:15 p.m. In about a half hour we would know.

Just then, I heard bubbles, which meant a diver was up much sooner than we expected. Hoping there was no trouble, Jack and I hurried from the cabin and looked aft. Craig pointed toward the three heads on the surface. "What's up, do you suppose?" I asked Craig.

The divers were still too far away to ask them. "They seem fine," Jack said. "They probably just cut the dive short because it's so cold."

We watched as they kicked their way over to the swim platform. I didn't holler over to them anxiously as I usually did after a first dive on a new wreck. As much as I wanted to know what they saw, deep down I knew it would be upsetting, so I delayed the moment just a bit longer. Todd reached the ladder first while Bob and Jeff hung back, holding the tag line that trailed out behind the boat. Todd took the regulator out of his mouth, wiped his nose of the ever-present, dripping snot that comes forth after a deep dive, looked up, and said something that made no sense: "I didn't know airplanes were made of iron."

"What? Come on, Todd, don't kid around!" I said angrily. I was tired of the flippant teasing, I did not enjoy Ralph's unveiling ceremony, and I didn't appreciate Todd's mocking. "What the hell did the plane look like?"

"It's not a plane," he said more loudly, spit coming out of his mouth, as he handed his camera up to Jack. "It's just a bunch of metal."

Thinking of the Swissair Flight 111 wreckage and how it looked like just a bunch of metal, I said, "You were probably just narked," referring to the drunken-like condition that deep diving can induce. "That's what a demolished plane *would* look like."

Jack set the camera down on a seat as Todd climbed the ladder. Todd slumped down on the deck bench and started unclipping his tank harness. "I wasn't narked, Valerie," he said. "I saw an I-beam. It's a pile of iron covered in zebra mussels. In fact," he said, brushing at an orange streak on his knee patch, "this is rust. Aluminum doesn't rust."

I stared at the streak of rust on his knee. It finally hit me. We were not anchored into the wreckage of Flight 2501. For the better part of a week, I assumed we had found it, and my mind was having a hard time wrapping around anything other than that.

Then I thought of Clive. As difficult as it was for me to accept that this was not Flight 2501, Clive was going to have an even harder time. He might not even believe us. "Did you film it?" I asked Todd.

"It's all there, including the I-beam," he said pointing down at his camera.

While Jack and Craig helped Bob and Jeff out of the water, I grabbed Todd's video camera, struggling to open the clasp on the waterproof housing. "Ralph and Clive are going to have to see this," I said to no one in particular.

I pulled the camera out of the housing and found the rewind button. I waited as the tape scrolled back. Then I hit "play." I held the small screen close to my face and watched the light green color of the water get darker, then I saw the pile of junk. I scrutinized the video, still expecting to see some wiring, a propeller, or anything else that might suggest Todd was wrong, but then I saw a long, I-shaped beam.

In a way I felt relieved, but also disappointed. I didn't want this target to be the wreck, but I did want—finally—to know what happened to Flight 2501. Frankly, my emotions were frazzled. In the last week, I had felt frustration, curiosity, tension, sadness, disbelief, relief, and now I was upset. And if I was upset, I figured Clive would be crushed.

I looked up to see *Diversity* approaching our boat, its crew probably just as tense as I had been five minutes earlier.

"Don't joke with them, please," I implored Todd, Bob, and Jeff. "Just tell them gentle and fast."

Steve idled the engine and came up on our port side. "So what do we have?" Ralph hollered over with a grin on his face, while Jim grabbed the line that Jack threw him and secured the boat.

Clive walked over to the rail and Steve abandoned his post at the helm to come out on deck.

I was livid when I heard Todd deliver the same line. "I didn't know airplanes were made of iron."

Ralph's mouth kept smiling, but his eyes narrowed. I could tell he thought he heard Todd correctly but hoped that he hadn't. "No, really, what's down there?" Ralph asked, his smile now completely gone.

Afraid someone would make another wisecrack, I leaned over said in as soft a voice as I could and still be heard, "It's *not* the plane." I extended the camera over the water toward Ralph. "It's a pile of scrap iron—take a look."

Ralph watched a little of the video, while Bob, Jeff, and Todd, provided some commentary. Clive didn't even look over Ralph's shoulder. He retreated to the cabin. Steve followed.

Five minutes into the video, Ralph handed the camera back over to me. "Cast off, Jim," he said. Steve started the engine, and they motored slowly away from us without so much as a wave. Clearly, they were going off to lick their wounds.

We looked for *Diversity* in South Haven when we reached the harbor, but we didn't see it. I was glad. It would have been too hard.

THE NEXT DAY, I sat down at my computer to search through an on-line source for historic newspapers to see if I could find an article that mentioned the loss of the scrap iron that had caused us so much aggravation. I typically have only minimal success finding articles with this kind of source even when I search for a specific shipwreck incident on a particular day. I did not expect to have any luck finding an article about an unknown boat losing scrap iron on an unknown date. I spent four hours searching through the last 100 years using a combination of keywords like "scrap iron," "I-beam," "sunk," "lost," "South Haven," "Glenn," and a few others, learning, in the process, more than I ever cared to know about scrap iron.

I finally found a promising article in the December 22, 1977, *Herald Palladium,* entitled "Runaway Barge Corralled in Saint Joseph." I clicked to open a larger version. The article explained that a tugboat had left Holland towing two identical 165-foot barges each loaded with 1,200 tons of scrap iron. The trio of vessels encountered forty-knot winds and twelve- to fifteen-foot waves, and "when about five miles northwest of South Haven, the second barge broke loose, capsized, and dumped its load of scrap iron in Lake Michigan."

The article could not have been any more specific, unless the reporter had noted that the barge "dumped its load of scrap iron in Lake Michigan *in a pile that looked like a mangled DC-4.*"

Since I had learned the value of scrap iron as I read through the many articles, I did a quick calculation that made me laugh. Twelve thousand tons of scrap iron, at the current value, was worth well over a quarter million dollars. Ralph had found, in all likelihood, the most valuable thing on the bottom of Lake Michigan, worth, ironically, probably about as much as Clive had already spent on the search effort. Of course, as shipwreck hunter Garry Kozak had realized about the zinc and lead ingots on the *Dean Richmond*, it would cost twice as much as its value to raise it from the bottom.

I called Ralph that evening to tell him about his valuable find. We shared a laugh, but not a big one. Clive had gone home, and Ralph and crew had gone back out searching that day, but no one had their hearts in it any more. He told me they would leave at the end of the week.

This time, he didn't say, "See y'all next year."

ABOUT TWO WEEKS LATER, I received a note from Clive regarding the scrap metal: "I was numb with disappointment, unable to believe the dirty hand that fate dealt us."

Leave it to Clive to express so eloquently what we had all been feeling. Sure, I was disheartened, but Clive felt the disappointment in his heart and in his wallet. He concluded by writing, "As to next year, I'll give it some deep thought."

I hoped that the news I delivered later that summer might remind Clive that although we had not accomplished our primary objective, that year's expedition was not all in vain. The fifty-foot mystery wreck turned out to be a very old, very unusual sloop, making it difficult to identify. Despite extraordinary research efforts, we have only been able to make a guess as to its identity.

Chapter 20

REVELATION

I don't know if the sloop provided incentive or whether Clive just has unbelievable persistence, but in the fall of 2010, I received an email from Ralph informing me that Clive had decided to keep searching. Six months later in mid-April 2011, NUMA descended upon South Haven once again. Same house, same boat, same team. This time they continued searching in the southwest sector of the circle, moving toward Airway Red 28.

About two weeks into the search, Ralph sent me a couple jpeg images. The first was a mosaic created by digitally stitching together a large swath of sonar runs. "The long lines on the image are spaced about 50 feet apart," he wrote, "and are undoubtedly the scars still remaining in the lake bottom from the dragging operations done by the Coast Guard."

I marveled at seeing history before my eyes and what a detailed image Ralph's sonar could produce.

The second target, in 285 feet of water, looked like two small objects. I named it "Double Target" for obvious reasons. Later that summer, Todd, Bob, and Jeff dived on Double Target. It turned out to be two nun buoys, conical-shaped channel markers, probably lost off a Coast Guard buoy tender. It seems that the NUMA/MSRA team had become quite adept at finding and identifying interesting oddities on the bottom of Lake Michigan. But, they found a whole lot of nothing during the last four weeks of the search.

This was particularly discouraging because as our search wrapped up, we heard that the wreck of Air France Flight 447 and its black boxes had just been found after multiple search expeditions in the two years since the airplane crashed. I studied with fascination the side-scan sonar image of the Airbus as it lay on the bottom of the Atlantic in 12,000 feet of water.

PERHAPS THE ANNOUNCEMENT of the discovery of Air France Flight 447 inspired Clive to keep searching. He made a commitment that he would fund yet another expedition—our ninth—in 2012. Unfortunately, we would not have success like the Flight 447 search team had. NUMA spread its efforts over multiple areas covering territory in all directions attempting to completely cover the entire circle of probability established way back in 2007. It was our most barren expedition yet: They did not even find any oddities, just another 35 square miles of flat, featureless sand bottom. Consequently, I was flabbergasted when Ralph left town saying, "See y'all next year."

IN THE BLINK OF AN EYE, the summer of 2012 turned to fall; fall turned to winter; and winter turned to spring. I could hardly believe that I was already a decade older than I was when we began the search.

In anticipation of hopefully having to identify aircraft parts on the lake bottom, our family made a detour to Dayton, Ohio, during our spring vacation that year, to visit the National Museum of the United States Air Force. We had learned that if we queued up at the museum early enough in the morning, we might be among the 60 individuals that day who would be allowed onto the nearby Wright-Patterson Air Force Base to see the display of presidential aircraft in a hanger there. We wanted to see *Sacred Cow*, President Roosevelt's, and later, President Truman's airplane, one of the few remaining DC-4s.

After suffering for an hour in line on a very cold April morning, we received our coveted tickets and boarded a bus. Ten minutes later, the bus driver dropped us off at the hanger and informed us we were to return to the bus in 45 minutes. As Jack and I and our girls passed through the entrance, we immediately saw *Sacred Cow*, the first airplane in the huge hanger. The morning sun pouring radiantly through the wall of windows made the aluminum skin of the DC-4 shimmer. I was struck immediately by how massive and impressive the aircraft was. It seemed a mechanized work of art, beautiful and sophisticated at the same time.

I walked around it to understand its magnitude. The landing gear alone stood taller than me. I realized that it may well be identifiable among the wreckage. Moving back along the starboard side, I reached up to touch the deicer, on the leading edge of the wing. Like a balloon, the long, rubberized surface could be filled with air to crack any ice that might form. I wondered if, like the rubber belt on the wreck of the *Hennepin's* conveyor, the deicers would have deteriorated after so long underwater. As I walked under the tail section, I looked up to see the number painted on the tail, and lamented that the action of the silt in Lake Michigan has probably eradicated number N-95425 from the wreckage. Next, I climbed the stairs leading into the airplane at the port side near the tail. I thought about Flight 2501's passengers boarding at the same place. Like me, they probably marveled at the aircraft's magnificence. It would have seemed indestructible.

When I reached the top of the stairs, I touched the aluminum surrounding the door and felt the rivets holding it in place on the framework, then leaned over to look more closely at the windows. I knew that on the bottom of the lake, we would not see the airplane looking anything like this. It would be a collection of twisted and broken parts.

I entered the airplane and proceeded forward toward the cockpit. I saw how very cramped it was, and realized how Lind's and Wolfe's small statures were of benefit to them as pilots. The six windows that had framed their only view of weather that night were tiny, and I realized how important communication with ground would have been to describe to the pilots all they could not have seen through those small portals.

The 45 minutes passed quickly. As I boarded the bus for the return trip, I hoped that the next time I saw a DC-4, it would be on the lake bottom.

ON APRIL 10, 2013, Ralph Wilbanks and his crew arrived for our tenth expedition. This time he brought a different boat, another twenty-five-foot Parker, but one with a larger cabin and smaller deck space. Clive had commandeered the other Parker for the Cussler Museum in Colorado, in commemoration of all the discoveries that had been made with it. "You know," I said to Ralph at dinner the night after they arrived, "we've been at this longer than we have had our daughter, Taya. I'm ready for this to be over."

"Me too," he laughed.

Their arrival coincided with the worst April weather we had ever seen during our 10-year quest. The team had to wait an entire week before the water calmed enough to begin the search. That year Clive chose to continue venturing farther outside the perimeter of the circle in the northern airway, Red 57. I did not hold my breath waiting for a discovery.

April turned to May, and nothing—not even a stray shipwreck—turned up. By the third week of May, the weather deteriorated, and the search came to an end. We had simply ruled out another forty square miles of lake bottom.

NUMA packed up and bid us goodbye once again. This time, however, Ralph told us he would not return. After ten years and ten expeditions, Clive, reluctantly, thought it best to cut his losses.

"CLIVE MAY BE DONE, but we don't have to be," I said to Jack and Craig after the NUMA crew left and we began discussing our upcoming search effort with David Trotter. "Let's pick up where NUMA left off and find this plane," I proposed.

Craig just laughed. "Didn't you say years ago that it would be impossible for us to find a small plane wreck when we had a hard time finding a big ship?"

"Well, yeah," I backpeddled, "but thanks to Clive, we've ruled out so much territory that we've just about cornered this plane. Maybe it's time we put our money where our mouths are."

I realized that besides our disagreement with NUMA over the hindcasting theories, our single biggest stumbling block in agreeing on a search area had been the lack of detail about Robert Lind's last radio call. The CAB report just summarized his request for descent, noting the plane was "in the vicinity" of Benton Harbor at the time. However, standard protocol suggests that the pilot would have had to provide a more precise location and estimated arrival at the next checkpoint for his request to have been properly evaluated. I found it incredible that the radio operator did not testify at either trial in New York, but recognize that he may have changed jobs in the seven years it took to come to trial. He should have testified at the CAB hearing in Chicago, one month after the accident, but if he did, his words are lost: Relentless attempts to find the transcript have failed. We don't even know what city he was in when he took that radio call, although based on the flight's last known position, it was probably Chicago.

Because so much information exists about this accident and only that one small, but critical detail regarding the last communication is missing, its absence raises the question: Could that information have been purposefully "lost?"

It seems that only four parties would have been able to suppress records of the call: the Civil Aeronautics Board members, Air Traffic Control, the radio operator, or the airline. As government agencies, the CAB and ATC would have had little reason to hide facts that might help determine the accident's cause. However, the radio operator may have feared his actions contributed to the crash. Perhaps he purposely "lost" the little card on which he had typed a transcription of the radio call. Or Northwest Airlines' officials may have confiscated and destroyed that card to hide anything their radio operator said that could be construed as negligence. The airline probably did not want the wreck to be found. Without the wreck, the cause of the accident could not be determined; and without the cause of the accident, it would be hard to prove negligence. But I am not a proponent of conspiracy theories. It seemed more likely that the record of that call has simply been lost due to the passage of time.

I had long ago embraced the last known position of flight in the vicinity of Benton Harbor, despite the vagaries of that notation. On our own now, we could focus on what we had believed for years: that the plane had diverted south toward Benton Harbor and Airway Red 28 in an attempt to fly around the storm.

There was so much information that we had amassed over the years to support that conclusion. Many witnesses had reported seeing an airplane flying south along the lakeshore toward Benton Harbor that night. Benton Harbor lakefront homeowner Commander Helm had reported seeing an explosion offshore sometime after midnight. Additionally, the CAB report concluded that the airplane crashed at approximately 12:25 a.m., soon after it entered the storm front. Based on the testimony of the Weather Bureau's meteorologist Julius Badner, the south-moving squall line would have reached Benton Harbor by 12:25 a.m. And, a number of pilots, including Kevin McGregor, had noted the navigational importance of staying in designated airways, minimizing the chances that Robert Lind would have flown randomly between the airways, particularly at night and in a storm. On top of all that, lake current scientist David Schwab had concluded back in 2006 that the airplane had crashed southwest of where the debris had been found: in other words down by Airway Red 28.

NUMA had already covered some 400 square miles within the circle of probability between the two airways and another 100 square miles north of that and into Airway Red 57. I picked up a pencil and outlined a rectangle within Airway Red 28 that represented about 100 square miles. "This is way more than we can cover in one expedition," I pointed out, "but it seems the most logical place for the plane to have crashed."

David Trotter arrived in early June that year to pick up the search where NUMA had left off. We had rented a house in Benton Harbor to be closer to the new search area, and reserved a slip at the municipal marina. In just a few hours, we had Dave's equipment installed on our boat.

Although we all suspected that the event took place far offshore, we plotted our new search grid to begin where Ralph left off at the edge of the primary search circle, so as to not leave a hole in the coverage. We began the familiar pattern of "mowing the lawn," working west toward deeper water.

Day after day, we searched, hoping we were on the right track now. While Jack or Craig piloted the boat, Dave and a fourth crewman, either me or MSRA members Larry Hatcher or Neel Zoss, sat in the cabin maintaining watch on the plotter. But nothing materialized. After ten days, all we had to show for our effort was 20 square miles in Red 28 that we could rule out.

AFTER WE HELPED DAVE pack up his equipment, I retreated to my office to plot the area we had just covered. The government spent only five days in June 1950 looking for the wreck before it gave up. Between our expeditions with NUMA and our own effort, we had, thus far, spent over 260 days searching during a span of ten years. I agonized, as I calculated how many more expeditions we would have to undertake to fully cover all the likely territory in Airway Red 28.

I suddenly pictured our team as a pack of bloodhounds with noses to the ground sniffing out a trail to the wreck. Every so often the scent had changed direction, and we turned and followed it, never once stopping to take a fresh breath of air and look around. That vision actually forced me to make that stop, take that breath, and look around. When I did, I realized that I had lost sight of the goal. For me, the *goal* had been to solve the mystery of the crash; finding the wreck had only been the *objective* that I thought was critical to achieving the goal.

After 10 years of searching, I came to the conclusion that even if we did find the wreck, that would only provide an X to mark the spot of the accident, not determine its cause. Because black boxes did not exist in 1950, the only way to possibly determine why the airplane crashed would be for investigators to raise the wreckage from the bottom and examine it with the technology available today. Even then, after more than six decades underwater, it is questionable whether that wreckage could offer evidence to solve the mystery.

In all likelihood, our dive team would have to conduct an unofficial examination of the wreckage. We could make broad generalizations: If the wreckage is in a tight area, we might surmise that the airplane hit the surface and sank. If widely scattered, we might conclude that the airplane exploded in mid-air or cartwheeled across the surface. A forward-bent propeller would suggest it crashed with the engines running; a backward bend would indicate that the engines had stopped functioning before impact. However, these conclusions would not prove the cause of the accident and would have little bearing on making aviation safer today.

I finally realized that the answers about what happened to Flight 2501 don't lay on the bottom of Lake Michigan; they lay in our research. Our repeated failures to find the wreck had forced us to keep searching high and low for any small scrap of information that might point us in the right direction. Instead, our research actually uncovered the answers to the questions that have plagued the families of Flight 2501 victims and others interested in this accident.

I thought about what Clive once said to me: "A wreck will only be found when it wants to be found." I don't think Flight 2501 was ready to be found. Instead, I think it wanted us to learn about the airplane, the flight, the crew, the passengers, the search-and-recovery operation, the wrongful death suit, and other similar accidents, all things that we could not possibly learn by studying wreckage on the lake bottom. Only then could we conclude, with a reasonable degree of certainty, the reasons for this tragic accident.

Chapter 21

PROBABLE CAUSE

I n 1950, the Civil Aeronautics Board interviewed dozens of Northwest Airline employees, air traffic controllers, pilots, meteorologists, and witnesses and analyzed wreckage found floating and washed up on the beaches, yet it concluded that there was not sufficient evidence to determine a probable cause for the crash of Northwest Flight 2501. Ever since the CAB began investigating crash sites, it, and subsequently the National Transportation Safety Board (NTSB), which took over in 1967, have worked to determine the causes of accidents and implement changes to reduce their occurrence. The agencies have been quite successful. Between 1921 and the time of this book's publication, there have been more than 16,000 aviation accidents, but only about 175 remain unsolved, more than 100 of those because the wreck was never found.

Flight 2501 falls within the category of unsolved accidents. However, Flight 2501 is *not* listed among the "still missing" airplanes. The CAB apparently found enough wreckage and human remains to consider it "found." Nevertheless, the board could not determine the cause of the accident, noting that perhaps turbulence caused it to break up or the pilot may have lost control of the airplane. Ironically, among those unsolved accidents are two other airplanes that crashed into Lake Michigan. United Flight 389 went down off northern Illinois in August 1965, and a Mack Truck-owned Learjet crashed off Racine, Wisconsin, in January 1969. These have been the only other commercial aviation crashes in the Great Lakes, and, coincidently, they all occurred in the southern third of Lake Michigan.

ONLY ONE OTHER author has ever ventured a speculative cause for this accident. Fred McClement in his book *Anvil of the Gods*, published 14 years after the accident, concluded that weather was principally responsible for the crash. There would seem to be little doubt, after examining all the details surrounding this tragedy, that the violent squall line raging over Lake Michigan played a key role in the DC-4's loss.

Although the Civil Aeronautics Board never officially speculated on what happened, its members undoubtedly had their own opinions. However, in 1950, they little data from prior accidents to provide a comparison. The government only started to maintain detailed accident records of crashes seven years prior to 1950, and in that time span there had been fewer than twenty accidents in the United States in which weather played a major role. Now, after more than seven decades, the CAB, and subsequently the NTSB, have investigated and analyzed over 450 weather-related accidents. Many of those accident reports now provide insight into the possible reasons Flight 2501 crashed.

IN THE WEEK following the loss of Flight 2501, Coast Guard Commander Frederick Goettel and county coroner Jack Fleming, who both analyzed the shards of floating airplane debris and human remains, surmised that the airplane had blown up to cause such damage, although the CAB investigators did not share that assumption. Both insinuated that lightning could have caused the airplane to explode. Only one recorded airline accident had been attributed to lightning prior to 1950. On June 14, 1945, an Army Air Force Curtiss C-46 departed Dallas, Texas, on a passenger flight to Jackson, Mississippi. At an altitude of 3,000 feet, lightning struck the wing, and the crew could not maintain altitude. The airplane crashed into a wooded area; 17 of 18 people on board perished. Even experts at the time did not fully understand this accident. They knew that lightning regularly struck airplanes, but because they are made of aluminum—a good electrical conductor—the electricity typically dissipates into the air causing little or no damage.

The real danger of a lightning strike, what might have happened to Flight 2501, and what probably happened to the C-46 in 1945, was that the bolt of electricity caused a spark to ignite fuel vapor in a fuel tank. Since the 1960s, regulations require that airplanes have built-in systems to ensure that a spark will not ignite fuel vapors. Today, the major concern regarding lightning is the remote possibility that it could damage electrical systems that would affect an aircraft's computer controls. In fact, since 1943, there have been fewer than twenty fatal airplane lightning strikes worldwide.

LIMITED VISIBILITY could have contributed to the crash of Flight 2501. Prior to 1950, three significant accidents in the United States and eleven more in other countries were attributed to low visibility. In the early years when pilots had to rely on land sightings to navigate, any bad weather could minimize visibility and lead to crashes. Most of the early recorded low-visibility incidents involved controlled flight into terrain—and some of these occurred in the daytime. Only after the installation of the radio range station system in the 1940s did pilots have any margin of safety to fly at night or in bad weather.

The radio range signals would have been critical for Lind and Wolfe as they began crossing over the lake. Even if they could have flown below the clouds, they would have had to rely on instruments because they would not have been able to differentiate between the sky and the surface of Lake Michigan at night: Both would have merged into one solid, black mass. Only illumination from an occasional bolt of lightning would have provided minimal visibility. If the altimeter went haywire due to the approaching low-pressure front, then Flight 2501 may have been lower than the 3,500 foot altitude the pilot reported. This may account for all the witnesses who claimed to have seen a low-flying airplane along the lakeshore. Perhaps Flight 2501 simply flew unknowingly into the surface of Lake Michigan. Today's aircraft have radar altimeters and ground proximity warning systems that provide warnings when a airplane is too close to the ground.

The 1965 crash of United Airlines Flight 389 was attributed to low visibility as well as problems with its altimeter; that airplane crashed, coincidentally, into Lake Michigan while flying at night on a course similar to Flight 2501. Utilizing a Boeing 727 jet, Flight 389 departed LaGuardia Airport on August 16 in the early evening headed for O'Hare Airport at Chicago. Soon after 10:00 p.m., when the flight was enveloped in clouds about 40 miles off the coast of Illinois at 35,000 feet, Air Traffic Control cleared the flight to descend to 6,000 feet. Flight 389 exited the clouds at 8,000 feet but was at a point offshore where Lake Michigan would have looked like a solid, black, indistinguishable mass. When the airplane was about twenty miles off Lake Forest, Illinois, Air Traffic Control provided landing instructions. The pilot replied "Roger," and then the control tower lost radio contact with the flight.

Wallace Whigam, a Chicago Park District lifeguard at the North Avenue Beach House, saw an orange flash on the horizon at 9:20 p.m. Three seconds later, he heard a "thundering roar." Similar reports from dozens of witnesses flooded the police and Coast Guard.

Apparently Flight 389 never leveled off at 6,000 feet, but continued down until it crashed into Lake Michigan. All thirty people on board perished. Hours after the crash, members of the Civil Aeronautics Board were on the scene to begin investigating the accident. A salvage firm found and recovered the wreckage, an easier task than trying to find Flight 2501 because by then radar was in use and could pinpoint the site of the crash. Unfortunately, the "black boxes"—the flight data recorders—were damaged. After lengthy analysis, the CAB concluded that the pilots probably misread their altimeter by 10,000 feet and thought they were descending through 16,000 feet, when they were actually descending through only 6,000 feet. It is of significance to note, that like Flight 2501 in which witnesses described seeing a fireball, very little wreckage from Flight 389 showed any signs of burn damage. Therefore it remains possible that the DC-4 exploded in the air or when it hit the water.

TURBULENCE COULD HAVE led to the crash of Flight 2501, one of the possibilities the CAB offered. Before 1950, five fatal accidents in the United States had been attributed to turbulence. In September 1943, an Army Air Force pilot lost control in severe turbulence and his Douglas C-49 crashed on land. A year later, in November 1944, a TWA DC-3 entered a thunderstorm and turbulence caused it to invert. The airplane hit the ground, and all twenty-four people died. Then in 1948 and 1949 Slick Airways lost two airplanes, both Curtis C-46s, one attributed to fuselage breakdown during turbulence and the other to severe icing. In both accidents, everybody died.

The last turbulence-related accident before 1950 occurred just two years prior to the loss of Flight 2501. Northwest Airlines Flight 421, a Martin 202 on a passenger run from Chicago to Minneapolis, entered an area of thunderstorm activity and soon thereafter crashed to the ground. In that case, turbulence contributed to a fatigue crack in a fitting on the left wing, aggravated by the faulty design of that fitting. This conclusion could be drawn only because authorities had the wreckage to examine. There was not enough debris from Flight 2501 to have determined if any structural damage had occurred.

SETTING ASIDE ACCIDENTS in which turbulence causes fuselage breakdown, it is the phenomenon of wind shear, as a part of turbulence, that has caused a number of crashes, and quite possibly caused the loss of Flight 2501. However, in 1950 little about wind shear was understood. Only two pre-1950 accidents were officially attributed to wind shear, and both involved low-flying airplanes in mountainous terrain. In July 1943 American Airlines Flight 63 unexpectedly slammed into rolling hills while flying low near Smith Grove, Kentucky, during a thunderstorm. Just four months before the crash of Flight 2501, a C-47, the military version of the DC-3, hit the side of a mountain in Canada. In both cases CAB analysts determined the force of the wind caused the crashes. These accidents all led to intensive study of the weather's effects on aviation.

Now meteorologists and pilots understand that wind shear refers to the variation of wind over either horizontal or vertical distances, which results in a tearing or shearing action. Although wind shear can occur at any altitude, it is particularly hazardous within 2,000 feet of the ground. A major change in wind velocity can lead to a loss of lift, and if the airplane is at a low altitude, the pilot would have little time to pull out of the problem. Significant shear can occur when temperature changes dramatically and when a front moves in fast, and cold fronts, which often follow squall lines, have more significant horizontal wind shear than warm fronts. Pilots also understand that the velocity of wind offshore can be nearly double the same wind onshore due to differences in friction between water and land masses.

Wind shear associated with thunderstorms can create downdrafts, which are generated when rain-cooled, dense air sinks inside a thunderstorm. These strong winds are carried down by a process called "momentum transfer." As precipitation begins to fall, it drags some of the air with it, initiating the downdraft, which is intensified by evaporative cooling as drier air from the edges of the storm mixes with the moist air within the storm. Downdrafts, which can create hazardous conditions for pilots, are divided into two categories: macrobursts and microbursts. A macroburst is more than two and a half miles in diameter and can produce winds as high as 135 mph. A microburst is a very localized column of sinking air that produces damaging, divergent, and straight-line winds as high as 170 mph, lasting as little as a couple of seconds to several minutes.

Even up to the 1980s, not enough was known about downdrafts and their effects. The 1985 crash of Delta Airlines Flight 191 may provide insight into Flight 2501 even though it involved a newer jet. In fact, the decisions made by the Delta pilot, understood only because the black boxes were later found, may have been quite similar to those made by Robert Lind in June 1950.

On August 2, 1985, Flight 191's Lockheed L-1011, took off from Florida for Dallas-Fort Worth International Airport. As the aircraft flew over Louisiana, a thunderstorm formed directly in its path. Captain Edward Connors immediately changed his heading to avoid the turbulent weather. As he descended toward Dallas, the crew spotted an isolated thunderstorm in the vicinity of the airport, but decided to proceed through it. At about 1,500 feet above ground level, First Officer Rudolph Price mentioned to Captain Connors that he saw lightning in one of the clouds ahead. At about 800 feet above the ground, the aircraft's airspeed increased significantly without crew intervention. Price tried to stabilize the aircraft's speed, but Connors recognized the speed increase as a sign of wind shear and warned Price to watch the speed, yelling, "You're going to lose it all of a sudden . . . there it is."

Suddenly, their airspeed dropped from 173 to 133 knots and Price pushed the throttles forward, giving temporary lift. The airspeed then dropped again, to 119 knots, and Connors cried out, "Hang on to the son of a bitch!"

In addition to the sudden tailwind flowing outward from the microburst, the aircraft also experienced a downdraft of more than 30 feet per second; a side gust, which caused a rapid roll to the right; and an increase in the aircraft's angle toward the ground. Price attempted to regain control by pushing the aircraft's nose down to fly out of the stall, but the severe wind conditions continued to force the airplane toward the ground. There was not enough time to recover, and the aircraft struck the ground, the tail section broke off, and the fuselage bounced back into the air, came down on a highway, hit a car, and killed its occupant. Of the 163 people on board, 134 died. Only those passengers in the tail section survived. Eventually the NTSB blamed the crash of Flight 191 on a microburst, however, the board also duly noted Captain Price's fatal decision to fly into the storm.

Flight 2501 could have crashed due to a microburst, but it is surprising to note that the CAB and the attorneys representing Flight 2501 families never blamed Captain Lind for his decision to continue the flight.

The tragic crash of Flight 191 provided immense information that enabled pilots to learn about and avoid downdrafts. Most of today's airplanes also have wind shear detection systems to further assist the pilots.

AS EVIDENCED IN THE DELTA Flight 191 crash, wind shear can contribute to the stall of an aircraft and remains one last thing to consider in the case of Flight 2501. In 1950, a stall had never been officially blamed for an airplane crash. However, a number of retired pilots who flew propeller airplanes have since conjectured that Flight 2501 may have been the victim of just that. A stall is a condition in aerodynamics wherein the angle of the airplane increases beyond a certain point such that the wing's lift begins to decrease. The angle at which this occurs is called the "critical angle of attack," which is dependent upon the profile of the wing and other factors, but is typically in the range of 8 to 20 degrees relative to the incoming wind. An instantaneous loss of headwind or a tailwind can reduce airspeed. That low airspeed can cause an airplane's wings to stall, thus, the aircraft descends.

One symptom of an approaching stall is slow and sloppy controls. As the speed of the aircraft decreases, there is less air moving over the wing, and, therefore, less air will be deflected by the ailerons, elevators, and rudder. Any yawing of the aircraft as it begins to stall can result in a spin because air no longer flows smoothly over the wings. Today airplanes are equipped with stick shakers, intended to provide aural and tactile awareness of a low-speed condition, giving pilots an even earlier chance to react properly.

An examination of two recent, high-profile accidents may offer some insight into what could have happened to Flight 2501. Both crashes occurred as a result of a stall and both involved secondary blame as well, blame that cannot be overlooked in Flight 2501.

On February 12, 2009, a Colgan Air Bombardier DHC-8-400, operating as Flight 3407 from Newark, New Jersey, to Buffalo, New York, crashed into a house eight miles from the Buffalo runway. Like Flight 2501, the flight crew made no radio calls to inform air traffic control what they were experiencing. This accident can only be fully understood because the cockpit voice recorder was recovered from the wreckage.

The flight had been normal in every respect until the landing approach. At the approach, the pilots extended the aircraft's flaps and landing gear, and the airspeed decayed to 145 knots. The captain responded by lowering the flaps to the fifteen-degree position. As the flaps transitioned past the 10-degree mark, the airspeed further slowed to 135 knots. Six seconds later, the aircraft's stick shaker activated, warning the crew of the impending stall. The automated system disengaged the autopilot, and the pilot took manual control, but by then the speed had reduced to a dangerously slow 131 knots. Instead of following the established stall recovery procedure of adding full power and lowering the nose, the captain added only about three-quarter power and angled the nose up. Although the pilot probably understood the aerodynamics of flying out of a stall, it may have seemed completely counterintuitive to angle his airplane toward the ground at full power. Because of this error, the aircraft came even closer to stalling. The captain disregarded the stick shaker and continued forcing the nose up. The airplane pitched up at a steep angle, then pitched down even steeper, then rolled to the left, and snapped back to the right. Occupants aboard experienced forces estimated at nearly twice that of gravity. The airplane descended for about twenty-five seconds, then crashed into a house about five miles from the end of the runway. All four crew, forty-five passengers, and one person in the house were killed.

Although the stall technically caused the crash, the pilot was blamed for his inappropriate response to the stall. Unlike the case of Flight 2501, examiners looked into the career record of the Colgan pilot and found that he had several unsatisfactory grades and on four occasions was disapproved for advanced licenses, including an airline transport pilot license, a single-engine license, a multi-engine license, and his instrument rating. Following each failure, he took the exam a second time and passed.

It is interesting to note that Robert Lind's testing record, which was similar to the Colgan pilot's record, was never questioned by the CAB.

Less than four months later, another accident occurred that involved a stall and resulted in blame leveled squarely on the shoulders of the pilots for their inappropriate response to the situation. On June 1, 2009, Air France Flight 447 crashed into the Atlantic Ocean in circumstances that were eerily similar to Flight 2501. Unlike Flight 2501, Flight 477 carried black boxes, and accident investigators did not stop trying to locate them on the bottom of the Atlantic, hoping they would explain the unfathomable accident. It would take nearly two years and millions of dollars until a side-scan sonar team led by the Woods Hole Oceanographic Institution discovered a large portion of debris from Flight 447. One hundred fifty bodies, still trapped in the partly intact remains of the aircraft's fuselage, were located in depths exceeding 12,000 feet. In May 2011, the Bureau d'Enquetes et d'Analyses (BEA), the French equivalent of the NTSB, released details from the flight data recorder and voice recorder which explained the accident.

Flight 447's Airbus A330-200 took off from Rio de Janeiro at 7:30 p.m. on a flight across the Atlantic to Paris. The last radio contact took place when the flight was approximately one-third of the way across the ocean. At that time, Captain Marc Dubois, a veteran with more than 11,000 hours of flight time, reported his altitude at 35,000 feet and indicated that he would be entering Senegalese-controlled airspace in fifty minutes. He did not mention bad weather or any other problems.

In fact, the airplane was heading right for an area of severe tropical thunderstorms with one of the two copilots, Pierre-Cédric Bonin, an inexperienced 32-year-old, in control. At approximately 2 a.m., the other copilot, thirty-seven-year old David Robert, returned to the cockpit after a rest break. Captain Dubois gave Robert his seat and retreated for a nap. Despite having more seniority and twice Bonin's experience, Robert left Bonin in charge.

Suddenly at 2:08 a.m., a strange aroma flooded the cockpit, and the temperature suddenly increased. At first Bonin thought that something was wrong with the air-conditioning system, but Robert assured him that the effect was from the severe weather. Bonin announced that he was going to reduce the speed. Just then an alarm sounded, indicating that the autopilot was disconnecting because the pitot tubes, externally mounted sensors that determine airspeed, had iced over. The pilots now had to fly manually. Neither Bonin nor Roberts had ever received training in how to deal with an unreliable airspeed indicator or in flying manually under such conditions.

Bonin pulled back on the side stick to put the airplane into a steep climb. Seconds later, the stall warning sounded. Pilots are trained to push the controls forward when they're at risk of a stall so the airplane will dive and gain speed. However, Bonin was inexperienced, and because the Airbus controls are on the outside of each pilot's seat and act independently of each other, Robert, did not know that Bonin was pulling back on the stick.

The stall alarm would have been impossible to ignore. Yet neither of the pilots mentioned it or acknowledged the possibility that the airplane had indeed stalled. Although the airplane continued to climb at 7,000 feet per minute, it kept losing speed, until it was flying at only ninety-three knots, a speed more typical of a small aircraft. Robert noticed the speed and tried to correct him at 2:10, "Pay attention to your speed. Pay attention to your speed."

They conversed in short sentences to try to adjust the speed and orientation. Thirty seconds later, Bonin said, "Here we go, we're descending."

Bonin eased pressure on the stick, and the airplane gained speed. The stall warning fell silent. Recognizing they were not out of the woods yet, Robert pushed a button to summon the captain. For reasons unknown, Bonin once again increased his back pressure on the stick to raise the nose. Again the stall alarm began to sound. Still the pilots continued to ignore it, perhaps believing that an Airbus was incapable of stalling.

By this time both pitot tubes and the cockpit's avionics all began to function normally, yet the pilots did not revert to computerized flying.

At 02:11, Bonin said, "I'm in TOGA, huh?" referring to the acronym for "Take Off, Go Around." When an airplane takes off, a pilot must increase engine speed and raise the nose to gain speed and altitude quickly at ground level. However, doing that at 37,500 feet, where the engines generate less thrust and the wings generate less lift, causes an airplane to instead descend. While Bonin's behavior was irrational, intense psychological stress could have been responsible for his action. The airplane soon reached its maximum altitude and then began to sink toward the ocean. The stall warning continued to sound.

At 02:11:32, Bonin exclaimed, "Damn it, I don't have control of the plane, I don't have control of the plane at all!"

"Left seat taking control!" Robert hollered.

Unfortunately, Robert seemed unaware that the airplane had again stalled, and he pulled back on the stick. Finally Captain Dubois returned to the cockpit at 02:11:43 and realized the airplane was descending rapidly, "What the hell are you doing?"

"We've totally lost control of the plane. We don't understand at all.... We've tried everything."

Inexplicably, Dubois did not take control. The three men argued back and forth until Bonin finally said something that alerted the other two pilots to the problem: "But I've had the stick back the whole time!"

"No, no, no.... Don't climb.... No, no," Dubois immediately screamed.

"Descend, then," Robert blared, "Give me the controls.... Give me the controls!"

Bonin yielded the controls, Robert quickly forced the nose down, and the airplane began to regain speed, but by that point, the airplane was only 2,000 feet above the ocean. There was not enough time to fly down and out of the stall. Without warning his colleagues, Bonin took back the controls and forced the side stick all the way back. At 2:14:23 a.m., Robert screamed "Damn it, we're going to crash.... This can't be happening!" Apparently up to the moment of his death, Bonin had no idea that his response to the problem had made it worse. Three seconds before impact, he screamed, "But what's happening?"

IF ROBERT LIND AND VERNE WOLFE found themselves inside a lightning storm or experienced a stall, a downdraft, or extreme turbulence, they may have had a similar horrific realization moments before their lives ended. More than fifty-six years after the crash of Flight 2501, ninety-eight-year-old retired Northwest Airlines Captain Joseph E. Kimm, among Northwest's earliest pioneering airline pilots and the chief pilot at the time the crash, provided his opinion of what happened that night.

Not hampered by any bureaucracy that may have inhibited him from drawing a conclusion right after the crash, Kimm—who flew thousands of hours in propeller airplanes, had experience in thunderstorms, and who personally examined the debris from Flight 2501—concluded that Flight 2501 experienced severe turbulence. This, he noted, "could have caused an 'upset,' meaning thrown up and over on its back. That could have induced a high-speed stall, which caused the airplane to angle down."

His conclusion matched that drawn in 1950 by the Douglas Aircraft Company's investigator who indicated that the DC-4s tended to invert in high winds. Kimm also explained that once a DC-4 departed controlled flight—in other words a stall—it was difficult to get it back under complete control in a timely manner. If the airplane was as low as the witnesses reported, then he felt, "there would be little distance to try to pull out of the stall."

Based on his analysis of the debris, Kimm was convinced the airplane hit the water angled down and to the left at about 400 miles per hour. The force of an impact at that speed could have caused fuel tanks in the wings to explode, creating a fireball, and shredding the aircraft and passengers.

Tragically for the passengers of Flight 2501, Kimm's scenario, suggests that their last moments would have been horrifying.

IN THE WEE HOURS OF JUNE 24, 1950, Robert Lind and Verne Wolfe were likely too consumed in dealing with their emergency to have radioed their situation to air traffic control or even informed the passengers of what was happening. Lind's eyes probably hurt from staring into the blackness punctuated by flashes of lightning, trying to see something, anything, to tell him what his actual altitude was. A quick glance at the altimeter might have shown he was at 3,500 feet, but he would have known the low-pressure front could have affected that. During his prior radio communication, he had not asked for, or received, a local barometric reading to calibrate his altimeter. The lake, he knew, was at 600 feet altitude, so at best he had 2,900 feet of clearance above the water, but maybe less. He might have pulled up to try to gain altitude, with little care at that point to inform ATC of his actions.

He probably fought back a sick feeling in his stomach, as much from the gyrations as the thought that perhaps he should not have attempted to cross the lake. He might have swallowed hard, only to find his mouth dry. The aircraft might have felt on even keel, but the compass could have been turning slowly. In response, he might have pushed a little rudder and added a little pressure on the controls to stop the turn, but that probably felt unnatural, and he might have returned the controls to their original position. His mind must have been swirling as he thought back to other occasions when he had taken decisive action to fly out of bad weather, but the pressure of this situation and the realization that this was worse than anything he had ever been in might have paralyzed him.

Perhaps stewardess Bonnie Ann Feldman would have had the wherewithal to warn the passengers to secure their seat belts as the turbulence increased, and would have, herself, taken a seat and belted in. As the airplane banked in one direction as a result of Lind's actions, anything not secured, like briefcases, blankets, purses, or carry-on satchels stowed on the open shelves above the passengers' heads, could have been hurled around the cabin, perhaps severely injuring or even killing someone. Many of the passengers would likely have screamed uncontrollably. Others may have vomited as a natural reaction to the force. The stench of the sick may have contributed to the illness of others. Some may have fainted, mercifully. In the last minute—and it could hardly have been more than that—those who maintained any semblance of composure would have had fleeting visions of their lives, goals not accomplished, and perhaps sadness for those they would leave behind.

If he was in any condition or frame of mind to have acted, Father Augustine Walsh may have said a prayer, mumbled to himself or perhaps loudly for the benefit of those around him, perhaps from I John: "He that believeth on the Son hath everlasting life." He may have asked for wisdom for the pilots or perhaps salvation for himself and his fellow passengers.

Prayers of all kinds were probably being said in those last moments. Miriam Frankel and Joseph Sirbu may have whispered the Sh'ma, a familiar Hebrew prayer.

Christian Scientist, Louise Spohn, might have recited in her mind the scientific statement of being from the writing of Mary Baker Eddy: "Spirit is immortal Truth; matter is mortal error. Spirit is the real and eternal; matter is the unreal and temporal. Spirit is God, and man is His image and likeness. Therefore man is not material; he is spiritual."

Even those who were not religious may have recalled the first few words of Psalm 23, "The Lord is my Shepherd, I shall not want."

Little three-year-old Dana Malby probably cried inconsolably, clutching his mother: She would have held him tight in her arms. John Schafer would have, likewise, held onto his mother and may have screamed for his stepfather even though he was not with them. Youngsters Tommy and Janice Hokanson may have grabbed for their parents, having no idea what was going wrong. Although they would not have given it a thought at the time in their fear and misery, the Hokansons were perhaps the most fortunate people on the flight. They would die arm and arm with the most important people in their lives beside them and would not have to suffer the traumatic loss of a spouse, parent, or child, like the families of their fellow victims would have to do.

The Ajemians, Frengs, Heustons, and Schlachters had their spouses for comfort, sitting side by side holding hands, perhaps managing a kiss or stammering a last "I love you." The Ajemians had been through much tragedy in their lives and, consequently, they may well have handled this better than anyone. They had their faith, they had each other for 40 years, and they had the comfort that their two daughters were grown, married, and successful musicians.

The married people traveling alone would have had a rough time thinking of their spouses, and in some cases children, feeling alone in their final moments. Any thoughts that Jean Kaufmann, who had been in Europe for two months, may have had about leaving her husband probably left her mind. Instead, she may have realized that she would have already been home with her three children had she gotten to the airport earlier the previous evening.

Kenneth Skoug probably regretted his last angry conversation with his son over the car repair bill.

Rosalie Gorski would have clutched the unborn child in her belly. She may have been overwhelmed with grief that she would never give birth to the baby that her husband did not yet know was growing inside her.

The two doctors, Cardle and Anderson, may have found strength. Their pride and professionalism would have kept them calm, at least on the outside. Leo Wohler, William Kelty, and Jo Longfield, all buyers with department stores in Billings, may have sat near each other. One of the two men may have offered his hand to Longfield, for father-like comfort.

The single people traveling by themselves—and there were many— would have felt terribly alone. They would not have had the comfort of a loved one's touch and presence, but may have reached out to the man or woman seated beside them in those last few moments of their lives, an indefinable bond that would forever link them.

Only Marie Rorabaugh, already elderly and widowed, probably did not scream or become sick. She would have held on to an arm rest with one hand and the chamois bag containing all her jewelry in the other, enjoying the ups and downs much like she loved riding roller coasters. At least that's how her daughter, Helen Rorabaugh Seymour, chose to picture her mother's last moments for the 55 years she outlived her. Any other thoughts about what her mother may have endured were too gruesome and painful to imagine.

In the last few seconds in the cockpit, Lind would have been sweating and shaking, trying to stay on course and hoping he would pass through the storm and keep flying With the wind tearing at the aircraft and lightning flashing all around him, he may have had a vision of his wife and baby daughter in his head.

When the end came, Robert Lind, Verne Wolfe, Bonnie Ann Feldman, and passengers would have died painlessly in an instant. Those fifty-eight men, women, and children, with faith in their respective gods, and their loved ones beside them or in their thoughts, were simply gone.

MORE THAN SIX DECADES after the loss of Flight 2501, it is clear that the storm was the primary reason that Flight 2501 crashed. Even in 1951, the Civil Aeronautics Board accident investigation report acknowledged that the airplane entered an area of severe turbulence and crashed shortly thereafter. With dozens of similar accidents offering hindsight now, we have a much better idea of exactly what might have taken place in that storm. However, as the previous review of a number of similar accidents indicates, there is rarely just one reason that an airplane crashes, and the human factor must also be considered, something that investigators in 1950 would not have addressed.

In fact, until the book *The Human Factor in Aircraft Accidents* by David Beaty was published in 1969, the term "human factor" was not even recognized. As Beaty pointed out, even after his book came out, airlines, aircraft manufacturers, and even pilots resisted its acceptance. But the Tenerife disaster in 1977, when two 747s collided and 583 people perished, prompted the aviation industry to begin to make moves toward understanding the problem. Since then the study of human factors in aviation has blossomed into an industry.

Even scuba divers understand a chain of events and the human factor. One problem is usually compounded by another. Then poor decisions in response to those problems become the last link in the chain that can make an accident fatal. These accidents often happen to even the most practiced people, who, by virtue of their experience, sometimes let down their guard.

There was—most certainly—a chain of events that led to the crash of Flight 2501. It was definitely unfortunate that the FAWS report by Captain Mitchell in the Lockheed Lodestar, indicating turbulence on Red 57, never reached Lind. That might have prompted him to turn back. It was also tragic that the ATC denied Lind's request to descend due to traffic still on the ground as far away as Milwaukee. If Lind had been given that permission, perhaps the accident could have been avoided. However, these are minor in comparison to the fact that Northwest Airlines did not tell the pilots about the changing squall line.

It will be recalled that during preflight planning, Northwest Airlines' meteorologist Beresford provided the pilots with his 4:45 p.m. forecast that predicted an *east*-moving squall over the Great Lakes. Then, at 10:30 p.m., Julius Badner of the National Weather Bureau issued, via teletype, a new forecast that called for widespread thunderstorm activity and a squall line extending from southern Wisconsin eastward into Lower Michigan moving decidedly *southeastward*. In addition, he put sequence reports on the teletype at 11:30 p.m. indicating that the squall line stretched across the lake just a mile or two north of Glenn; it had been moving southeast like a snow plow, churning up winds along its leading edge.

Except for receiving current weather reports for Milwaukee, Madison, and Minneapolis about thirty minutes before he began the lake crossing, Lind was not told that a squall line had in fact formed. It will also be recalled that Northwest personnel responsible for the flight at that time—Warren Seifert, and George Benson—together made the decision not to advise Flight 2501 of the new forecast because they believed the thunderstorms were still north of the flight and did not want to lessen the pilots' attentiveness to the conditions.

Obviously, both men completely missed the significance of the updated weather reports that indicated the north-south orientation of the squall line had clocked around 45 degrees and now extended east-west across Lake Michigan, moving south at a very rapid pace. They should have realized that if Flight 2501 crossed the lake anywhere south of the squall line, the leading edge of the south-moving storm would soon catch up to it. Even the national weather maps, printed in every newspaper in the country on Saturday June 24, 1950, made this fact exceedingly clear—a thick, black kidney-shaped mass ran east-west cutting though Lake Michigan with arrows indicating it was moving south. It would not have taken a meteorologist to understand the potential peril of this, but the pilots were deprived of this information.

Given the only information Robert Lind had about the storm—that thunderstorms were moving east and would likely form a squall line—it is possible that after Flight 2501's last radio sign off at 12:15 a.m., Lind presumed that he had already flown south of the east-moving squall line. He probably continued across the lake, assuming he was flying around the southern end of the storm. Joseph Kimm, system chief pilot for Northwest, supported this when he told reporters right after the accident, "Robert Lind would not deliberately fly into a storm."

Tragically, since the squall line was moving straight south at 12:13 a.m. when Flight 2501 reported being near Benton Harbor, any path west across the lake would have exposed it to the leading edge of the *south-moving* squall line where lightning, wind shear, and downdrafts could be deadly. Within minutes, the squall line would have enveloped the airplane.

The Civil Aeronautics Board did not consider human factors in its 1951 accident report, as the NTSB would later do after the April 1977 crash of Southern Airway Flight 242. The DC-9 jet crashed, killing 72 people, after penetrating a storm and losing the function of the engines from water intake. In that case, the airline informed the crew of a storm, but did not tell them that the storm had intensified and formed a squall line. The conclusion, as determined by the NTSB after that accident, should have been the same conclusion arrived at by the CAB regarding Flight 2501: "If the company's dispatcher system had provided the flight crew with timely weather information pertaining to the aircraft's intended route of flight, it is possible that the severe weather would not have been penetrated."

Although the plaintiffs' attorney Martin Kolbrener clearly understood Northwest Airlines' negligence in not passing the squall's changing velocity and direction to its pilots, he did not have any such evidence from the official report as reference. Whether the members of the CAB truly did not draw that conclusion, or chose not to put that conclusion in writing, the absence of such a conclusion led directly to the airline being exonerated for negligence.

Likewise, the CAB report omitted any reference to Captain Robert Lind's poor training record. Consequently his career did not undergo scrutiny in the trial. However, in finding cause for this accident, human factors in regard to Lind must be considered. Now, more than six decades after Lind's death, there are no living next-of-kin who can attest to his character or skills as a pilot. His parents and his wife have long since passed away. His brother, a fellow Northwest pilot, died tragically in a car crash in 1967. His nieces and nephews were too young to have known him well. His coworkers at Northwest only recalled that he was a "good man and competent pilot, not a hot-dogger."

Only Lind's FAA records provide a glimpse of his skills and personality. Those records show that Lind had difficulty passing his flight examinations. He might not have worked well under pressure, a trait unfortunate in a storm, at night, over a lake. However, in the nine years he had been flying for Northwest, he would have had the time to hone his skills. The real issue with Robert Lind was what Joseph Kimm pointed out at the CAB hearing weeks after the accident: He chose to continue his flight across the lake in a storm when other pilots in a similar position that night decided to turn back.

THIS BEGS THE BIGGEST QUESTION—the mother of all questions regarding this accident: What prompted Robert Lind to risk crossing Lake Michigan in a storm? To answer that question is to solve the mystery of this accident by placing the last link at the end of the chain of events behind the faulty FAWS system, ATC's descent denial, the shifting direction of the squall, Northwest Airline's failure to inform the pilot of that shift, and Robert Lind's skills. That last link in the chain—the fatal link—is Robert Lind's motivation, and that link could never be found among the wreckage of Flight 2501 on the bottom of Lake Michigan.

Certainly Lind was persistent, a trait apparent by his refusal not to give up until he passed his flight exams. Unquestionably Lind had experience flying across Lake Michigan—he had done so hundreds of times. However, there was one factor that may have motivated Lind that no one on the Civil Aeronautics Board knew about. The only people alive at the time of this book's writing who understood Lind's personal situation were his nieces and nephews and the copliot's wife. They knew that Lind had a needy wife at home who had little tolerance for her husband's long trips away from her. More significantly, they knew that the couple had a new baby, who Lind had seen little of during her first weeks of life. And at the time of his last radio transmission at 12:15 a.m., Lind was little more than two hours from Minneapolis: a tempting proximity. It seems reasonable that Robert Lind's motivation to make it home to his wife and his daughter—the loves of his life—would have been his ultimate reason for continuing across Lake Michigan that night.

In the wee hours of Saturday, June 24, 1950, Robert Lind was probably struck by a malady that many pilots, even today, struggle to overcome. "Get-home-itis," as flyers call the condition, may have been the overriding—and most tragic—human factor in the worst American aviation accident of its time when 58 men, women, and children lost their lives in that fatal crossing.

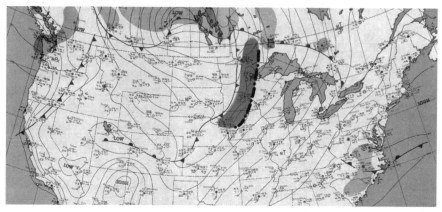

The daily weather charts for June 23, 1950 (top) and June 24, 1950, created at 12:30 a.m. each day, were printed in newspapers the following morning. The kidney bean-shape indicated the position of the squall line and how it drastically changed direction just as Flight 2501 reached the Michigan lakeshore near midnight. However, Robert Lind was not advised of that change. His last radio call, when near Benton Harbor, suggested that he tried to fly south around what he believed to be a still-east-moving squall. In fact, that move would have put the airplane on a collision course with the storm, where turbulence or downdrafts likely caused it to crash. *NOAA Central Library Data Imaging Project.*

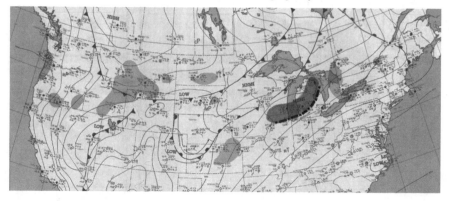

EPILOGUE

On June 24, 2015, the 65th anniversary of the loss of Flight 2501, I stood quietly in the sun with my teenaged daughters, Cella and Taya, on a small rise of land in Lakeview Cemetery in South Haven. I gazed at the newly placed memorial stone—an actual boulder—inscribed, "Northwest Airlines Flight 2501 June 24, 1950." The grass was still damp from a storm just two nights before, reminding me of the terrible storm that took the lives of 58 good people in 1950. I pondered how my life had, over the last dozen years, become intertwined with the lives of people I did not know personally. They were lost in an accident that took place before I was born, yet somehow they had compelled me to make sure their lives, their loss, and the ones they left behind would never be forgotten.

Just three weeks earlier, I had received a brief, surprising email from a stranger Beverly Smith. "Are you aware the South Haven Lakeview Cemetery has body parts from NWA flight 2501? They were buried one year after the accident. The plot is not marked."

I had thought it was all over. In the previous two years, although I spent time on the lecture circuit speaking about Flight 2501, I had moved on. I was busy with my museum exhibit design firm. I began working on another book. Cella and Taya had become certified scuba divers. Jack and I had explored shallow-water shipwrecks with our girls. Our team had just located a new shipwreck—the *John V. Moran*—a steamer holed by ice in 1899. I no longer pondered, on a daily basis, where Flight 2501 had crashed. I was satisfied that we had done all that we could to solve the mystery of this airline accident.

Then it all came rushing back with Beverly's email. I immediately wrote back to her, and later that day we spoke. I learned that her daughter, Mary Ann Frazer, the sexton for the city-owned cemetery, and Beverly often place flags at the graves of soldiers. She had been in Mary Ann's office looking in the "N" register for a veteran whose last name was Norman. Just below his name, she spotted an unusual listing: "Northwest Airlines crash victims, June 1950." The burial had taken place in May 1951. Beverly called the listing to her daughter's attention and immediately went to the library to look up the accident. There, she found an early edition of this book and learned, surprisingly, that her great uncle, Joseph Bartunek, was among the Coast Guard crew who found the first debris offshore. Then, she sent me the email.

After some local inquiries, we came to realize that the remains recovered from the beaches of South Haven—those collected by county health inspector Jack Fleming and others—had been buried at this plot almost a year after the accident. Apparently county jurisdictions required that the remains recovered in South Haven be buried in Van Buren County and the remains recovered offshore and brought to St. Joseph be buried in Berrien County.

We had spent considerable time back in 2008 arranging for a memorial stone at the plot in the Riverview Cemetery, planning a service, and inviting the Flight 2501 families. With the 65th anniversary of the accident just weeks away, I envisioned another marker stone and memorial service on that day.

Arrangements happened quickly, thanks in large part to Mary Ann and her mother. They contacted the St. Joe Monument Works in Benton Harbor, which not only offered to donate a stone, but also promised to have it installed in record time. The two women also made arrangements for flowers and a bugler to play Taps. South Haven's mayor, Robert Burr, and my teammate, Craig Rich, offered to read the victims' names. Together, we reached out to Jeff Filbrandt at the Filbrandt Family Funeral Home in South Haven again, and he offered to organize the service. I contacted Pastor Robert Linstrom, who had officiated at the 2008 service. He agreed to lead this new service as well.

I emailed all the Flight 2501 families to tell them about this new discovery. In the seven years since the last service, some relatives had died, others were too elderly to travel, and there was too little time for anyone else to arrange flights. However, they all expressed gratitude for the efforts on their behalf. We also informed the local media of the grave discovery and memorial service in hopes that some members of the public would help us honor and remember the victims.

As my daughters and I stood graveside just before noon on June 24, 2015, I noticed a nearby stone engraved with the name Charles H. Tate. I thought how ironic that Mayor Tate, who had closed the beaches in June 1950 to prevent the public from stumbling upon the remains of the airplane, was buried so near them. As I contemplated that, the latest in a long string of inexplicable coincidences, Mary Ann, Beverly, Jeff Filbrandt, Pastor Linstrom, Mayor Burr, and Craig Rich joined us. *Would anyone else come*, I wondered.

Just then I heard a car door shut and moments later saw a small group of people approach over the rise. Then another car drove up and parked nearby. And another. And another. From all directions in the large cemetery people came, walking carefully between the other stones, whispering quietly among themselves. Some carried flowers and placed them at the base of the stone. Everyone approached the stone and spent a few moments looking at the photographs of the victims displayed on an easel nearby. My eyes welled with tears of joy that so many people chose to spend their lunch hour that day showing their respect for individuals lost somewhere off our shores.

At noon, Pastor Linstrom began the service:

"A couple of nights ago as the pounding rain and tornadic winds pummeled our shores, many of those who might have been sleeping soundly were awakened by the storm. Sixty-five years ago it was on a night much like that night that South Haven neighbors were awakened by the storm and heard a low-flying plane…We are gathered today in memory of the 55 passengers and three crew, the 58 people who died that night 65 years ago. We gather here with all of you who are witnesses and keepers of the legacy of those who died. We gather to give thanks this day for the proper accommodation of them. We give thanks for the privilege of marking this place as hallowed ground. We give thanks for this moment in time made sacred by our gathering in this hallowed place."

After leading the group in prayer, Pastor Linstrom introduced me to speak about those lost:

"I did not lose a loved one on Northwest Airlines Flight 2501, nor did I personally know any of the people lost in Flight 2501 somewhere on Lake Michigan 65 years ago today. However, in the last dozen years, I have gotten to know each of them quite personally, through the recollections of their children, grandchildren, and siblings who suffered such a terrible loss so long ago:

"I feel honored to have gotten to know these individuals—victims whose lives will forever be commingled when their plane hit the surface of Lake Michigan somewhere off our shores—an event that touched this community so long ago. A dozen years ago, our team set out to locate the wreck and solve the mystery of why this plane crashed. Year after year, we combed the bottom of the lake hoping to find a trace of the lost airliner. Year after year we were unsuccessful. And, year after year, we continued our research to try to find some remnant of information that might pinpoint the sight of the crash. Instead of finding the plane, however, we found people: witnesses who remembered the stormy night, airline employees working that night, Coast Guardsmen who recovered debris and human remains, and the Van Buren county health inspector, Jack Fleming, who was responsible for everything that washed ashore on the beaches of South Haven—the remains that are interred here."

Then Craig Rich and Mayor Burr read, one by one, the names of the victims, punctuated by the ringing of a bell. I heard audible sighs and saw people wiping their eyes when Craig noted the children and pregnant women. More emotions swept through those gathered when a bugler, standing beyond the stone in a small grove of trees, played a slow, mournful Taps.

I choked up when delivering my final words, words that I have tried to live by each day, words that I read seven years earlier at the other service to honor Flight 2501 victims buried in Riverview Cemetery, words written by Mary Ann Fenimore who lost her grandmother, grandfather, and aunt on Flight 2501:

"Despite the decades that have passed since this accident, its message remains clear: we must appreciate each day for what it is, love the ones we love more deeply today than we did yesterday, and remember those who have passed because although they are gone, our memory keeps them close."

Since the publication of this book, the Michigan Shipwreck Research Association has independently resumed its search for the wreck site.

In February 2020 the author appeared in a two-hour special episode of the Discovery Channel television show *Expedition Unknown* entitled "America's Vanished Airliner" (Season 8, episode 2) sharing the story of NWA Flight 2501 and inviting the host, Josh Gates, along on MSRA's expedition. MSRA team members Jack Van Heest, Jeff Vos, Todd White, and David Schwab, as well as three descendants of passenger Ken Skoug also appear in the program. That episode can be seen on line or through a television provider.

If the wreckage is discovered in the future, the author will post the discovery story at:

www.NorthwestAirlinesFlight2501.com

Jack and Valerie van Heest with *Expedition Unknown* host Josh Gates at right.

The Flight 2501 stone monument marks the grave of Flight 2501 victims in the Lakeview Cemetery in South Haven, Michigan. It was donated by the St. Joe Monument Works in Benton Harbor, Michigan. *Photograph by Tom Renner.*

APPENDIX

T he families and friends of the 58 victims of the crash of Flight 2501 all grieved in their own ways and most found the strength and resilience to go on. Even the professionals involved in the aftermath of the accident had difficulties in the wake of the tragedy. The following are the stories of a handful of people who were affected by this accident.

NEXT-OF-KIN

The Cardle Family: Since Mary Cardle had no idea that her husband Archibald had taken Flight 2501 on Friday night, rather than the Saturday night flight that he held a ticket on, she went to the Minneapolis airport on June 25 and was told her husband was not on that flight. She learned that he had taken the earlier flight only after hearing his name listed as a victim in a radio news broadcast. Days later, Northwest Airlines contacted her asking that she come to the airport to claim her husband's luggage, which had arrived on the later flight.

The family held a memorial service at the Westminister Presbyterian Church, but had difficulty coping emotionally, especially without a body to bury.

A year after the accident, Mary Cardle married R. Dean Todd, who had also recently lost his wife. The Todds and Cardles had been friends before Todd lost his wife and Mary lost her husband.

Cardle's daughter, Mary, married her boyfriend at about the same time as her mother married Dean Todd. They eventually had four children. Mary Jr. refused to fly anywhere on the same airplane with her husband, acknowledging that as hard as it was to lose her father, she had the comfort of her mother. She did not want to risk her children losing both parents.

Just as he had planned, John Cardle eventually became a successful doctor, like his father. As he and his sister got older, they lost touch with each other in the course of their busy lives. When the two siblings learned of the NUMA/MSRA search for their father's airplane wreck, they found reason to reconnect.

A Feldman Family Friend: Bonnie Ann Feldman, the stewardess on the flight, was very close friends and roommates with Joan Marie Somerville Mann. Bonnie served as maid of honor when Joan married. Seven years after the accident, Joan had a baby daughter and named her Bonnie after Bonnie Ann Feldman. Bonnie Mann grew up hearing wonderful stories about Feldman from her mother.

When she was twelve, Bonnie Mann found an old postcard in a box in her attic that Feldman had sent to her mother from Bermuda. Bonnie noticed the distinct style of Feldman's signature on the postcard, copied it, and adopted it as her own. Now in her fifty's, Bonnie Mann Goldstein still signs her name the same way that Bonnie Ann Feldman usually did, keeping her memory alive in that way.

The Freng Family: Mary Ann Freng White, the only surviving member of the Freng family, gave birth to her first child in September 1950, three months after the accident. She named her daughter Barbara after her sister. The following year, she and the baby traveled cross-country to visit a relative in California, taking a train because she did not want to fly. The long trip was grueling, so she decided to make the return trip by airplane. Just days before leaving California, she got cold feet about flying and canceled her ticket. She later learned that the aircraft—believed to have been United Airlines Flight 610—had crashed, killing everyone on board.

The Whites had four more children in the next five years. They named their fourth child William Freng White after Mary's father. Three years after having their last child, the couple divorced and Mary later married Swagar Sherley, Jr., the son of Congressman Sherley from Louisville, Kentucky. She gave birth to yet another child and named her Mary Beth, for herself. Her closest friend believed that Mary chose to have a large number of children to replicate the family that she had lost so that she would never be alone.

The Gorski Family: Rosalie Gorski's husband, Bill, never knew that his wife was pregnant when she died. She had only shared that news with her sister and planned to surprise her husband at the airport. Bill Gorski had a difficult time after his wife's death, particularly because he had no time to grieve; he was called into active duty weeks after the accident to serve in

Korea after hostilities broke out. About five years after Rosalie's death, when the Basilica of the National Shrine of the Immaculate Conception was being built in Washington, D.C., Gorski made a donation and had a granite plaque engraved in the Memorial Hall in the lower level. It reads, "In memory of Rosalie Gorski, nee Kurinka."

The Kaufmann Family: Life was very difficult for the Kaufmann family in the wake of Dorothy Jean Kaufmann's death. Her husband, Winfield, exhibited worsening emotional problems and had a difficult time raising his three young children as a single parent. He never remarried.

The children suffered without their mother. One day when young Bill Kaufmann was given the rare opportunity to play at a friend's house, his friend's mother offered him a piece of cake, fresh from her oven. Bill broke down in tears, thinking of his mother who used to do the same for him.

Mary Jean, who later changed her name to Brandi, sought grief counseling through the organization Motherless Daughters. She later married and had two daughters, but had no example to model her mothering after and had difficulties at first. Then, she made the decision to give them all the emotional support and love that she had always wished for. Now Brandi is a loving grandmother too.

The third child, Richard, took his own life when in his early twenties.

For years, William and Brandi each had desires to meet other members of the victims' families to learn how they coped in the wake of that accident. They finally had that opportunity when they attended the memorial service in Michigan in 2008.

Margaret Lind, wife of Captain Robert Lind: Some time after losing her husband in the crash and losing her beloved adopted baby daughter in the aftermath, Margaret Lind remarried. Her new husband had children from a prior marriage, so Margaret had the opportunity to experience parenthood. However, she never really recovered from her double tragedy.

The Malby Family: Wesley Malby, the 30-year-old husband of Yvette and father of three-year-old Dana Richard Malby, married shortly after the death of his family. In December 1952, his new wife, Helen, gave birth to Kathleen and less than a year later, in November 1953, Helen gave birth to a boy, her first son and Wesley's second son. The couple named the boy Dana Malby, after Wesley's lost son, changing only the middle name from Richard to Robert.

The Schwartz Family: Although Warren Johnson and Joy Bell married under the most difficult of circumstances on the same day that Joy's stepfather, Frank Schwartz, died on Flight 2501, their marriage has been long and happy. In 2000 they celebrated their fiftieth anniversary. They live on an island in Minnesota in the summer and spend winters in South America.

The Reid Family: Before he boarded the flight, William Reid sent his niece, Ann, a beautiful bride doll in a white satin dress, with a card saying he would be home soon. The doll sat on top of Ann's jewelry box for many years, and now, more than six decades after the accident, she still cherishes both the doll and the card.

The Schlachter Family: Shortly before the accident, Carl and Louise Schlachter gave their young niece, Daisy, a book called "Gigi: The Story of a Merry-Go-Round Horse." To inscribe the book, Carl drew a sun, its rays, and a smiley face in the middle, forming the sun's circle with the words, "To Daisy from *Carlou*," his way of referring to himself and his wife, as if they were one. When the author contacted Daisy for the first time fifty-eight years after the accident, she happened to have the book sitting right next to her telephone. It remains among her most prized possessions.

The Sirbu Family: A few days after the crash, Joseph Sirbu's wife, Alma, received a blue-gray mink stole in the mail that her husband had sent to her during his buying trip in New York. The stole must have been too painful a reminder of her great loss because she never wore it. In memory of her husband, Alma and her sons established a foundation to provide financial aid to independent manufacturers' representatives who fell on hard times. Flush with funds after a number of years, the Foundation endowed a building at the City of Hope Hospital, just outside Los Angeles, California, known as the Joseph Sirbu Building.

Alma never remarried, remaining a widower for forty-one years—longer than she had been married. On the few occasions when a man tried to court her, she sent her son Jerry to dissuade him.

The Skoug Family: The Skougs honored their patriarch, Kenneth, by naming every subsequent son Kenneth. To this day the Minnesota State division of the American Legion baseball program annually honors the state's winning team with the Ken Skoug Championship Trophy, which has been given since 1951 in honor the department's former baseball director. Baseball has been a favorite pastime for all the Skoug boys. Ken II had difficulty playing baseball due to his eyesight, but he has always enjoyed watching the games. He attended various Washington Senators' games over the years and then took his son to many games at Memorial Stadium in Baltimore, although his favorite team has been the Minnesota Twins since their origination in 1961. He continues to be a fan and has attended several games near where he lives.

Ken III is a fan, a player, and a coach. He has attended numerous Major League Baseball games throughout the country. He played seven years of baseball, reaching a summer league All Star game once and playing every position except catcher. He spent two years as an assistant coach on his son Ken IV's (Kenny's) team.

Kenny played his fourth year of baseball in 2013. He enjoys going to Comerica Park to see the Detroit Tigers play and watches the postseason games on television.

In 2020 Ken Skoug II, Ken Skoug III, and Ken Skoug IV appeared in the Discovery Channel show Expedition Unknown, sharing the story of the man after whom they were named with the host, Josh Gates.

The Wohler Family: Leo Wohler's wife, Gladys, never married after her husband died on Flight 2501. She did not participate in a lawsuit and received only a few hundred dollars for each child as a death settlement. Despite that, she was proud to be able to put all her children through college while taking up a new career. In 1969, she was voted Mother of the Year in Montana.

Soon before her death at the age of ninety-three in 1991, she asked that her ashes be spread near her husband. Her son David contacted a Coast Guard officer who was able to give him the coordinates where the oil slick was found off South Haven, Michigan. The family hired a fisherman in South Haven to take them out to the site, where they conducted a memorial service and spread their mother's ashes. Then, in 2008, all seven children participated in the memorial service at the Riverview Cemetery in St. Joseph, Michigan.

The Wolfe Family: Kristine Wolfe, who was just a baby when her father died, grew to be a lovely little girl. Her mother, Ruth, saw to it that although she never had a chance to know her father, she would be surrounded by family. She had dozens of aunts, uncles, and cousins, and two loving grandparents who cared greatly for her. Her grandparents had a big home and welcomed their daughter and granddaughter into it. Ruth used some of the $10,000 settlement from her husband's life insurance policy to remodel the upstairs into an apartment. "I invested most of the insurance money for our future, but it was not enough. I sold our big Cadillac and bought a little Ford. And I knew I would have to go back to work," Ruth said in 2007.

She had worked in offices before she was married, and took up a career again after her husband's death. Years later, her coworkers encouraged her to run for Clerk of Circuit Court in Vilas County, Wisconsin. "I recall some people who supported my campaign referring to me as 'the poor widow.'" She later explained. "I did not like the election process, but certainly did not want to be elected out of pity." She was elected and that position would change her life.

George Ellis, a Wisconsin state accountant, with whom she often consulted, began flirting with her. She had never dated after her husband's death, focusing instead on raising her daughter. However, with Kristy then in college, she decided the time was right. When Ellis said, "I think selective services owes you a dinner for all your help," Ruth found her flirtatious abilities resurfacing and responded, "Yes, I think YOU owe me a dinner." A new romance began.

George Ellis later recounted a surprising coincidence. "I told my sister's husband, Leonard "Doc" Alexander, about Ruth and mentioned that she had been married to Verne Wolfe, a pilot, who had died in an airplane crash."

Alexander was amazed. He pulled up his sleeve and showed Ellis the shrapnel scar he had received while flying over Kiska, Alaska, during the war. "Verne was flying the plane when I was hit!" he said.

That was just one more connection that sealed the new couple's relationship. On May 4, 1968, they snuck off to be married by the county commissioner in Stillwater, Minnesota. They had a long and wonderful life together.

OTHERS TOUCHED BY THE ACCIDENT

Julius Allers, fisherman who found the first airplane debris: Julius Allers wore the ties he had recovered from among the wreckage of Flight 2501 to church regularly. He continued fishing for Jensen Fisheries until the late 1960s when he purchased his own fishing boat, but the downturn in fish populations and increased regulations caused him to give up the business. He then worked at a local factory and died in 1986.

His wife, Paula, kept the shirt that her husband had recovered from the wreckage neatly folded in a box with a note explaining how her husband acquired it. Her daughter, Judy Schlaak, the registrar at the Michigan Maritime Museum in South Haven, came to have the shirt after her mother's passing in 1997. In 2007, Schlaak gave the shirt to the author of this book and shared the story of the discovery, hoping it might help point the team to the wreck.

Jackie Eldred, Ear Witness: Eldred always felt guilty that she had not told the police about hearing what she believed to be an airplane crashing that night so long ago. She and her husband were concerned at the time about not being believed. When the Eldreds learned about the renewed search effort, the couple did all they could to recount the memories of that night in an effort to help find the wreck.

Richard H. Miller, Northwest Airlines flight superintendent: Miller was tied up for years with bureaucratic paperwork, interviews, and testifying about his role in the crash of Flight 2501. Although he never thought that his decision *not* to provide new weather information to Robert Lind had any bearing on the accident, he admitted in private to Bob Gibson, the dispatcher with whom he had traded shifts, that he was plagued "wondering what he could have done differently" to have changed the outcome. He told Gibson, "I will never again trade shifts with anyone," blaming fate for putting him in charge that night.

Lawrence J. Otto, ensign on the *Woodbine*: A few months after the 2501 search in 1950, Larry met a woman, Betty, on a group outing. They dated for about nine months and were getting serious, so Otto took her on a car trip to meet his parents in Milwaukee. Although he had no intention of proposing until after his parents gave their approval, just when they were crossing the bridge between Benton Harbor and St. Joseph, Otto blurted out, "Would you like to be the mother of my children?"

Perhaps the site of the St. Joseph Coast Guard Station reminded him of the gruesome work there and the fragility of life, causing a desire to secure his future. The couple married on June 23, 1951, coincidentally, one year to the day after Flight 2501 took off on that fateful journey. They eventually had nine children. In time, Otto was promoted to commander and served many years on the famous Coast Guard Icebreaker *Mackinaw*, also used in the search for Flight 2501.

Otto was thrilled to help the NUMA/MSRA team and surprised to see his handwriting and signature in the log book records obtained to aid in the search. He and his wife paid their respects to family members during the graveside memorial in 2008, and Otto had the chance to express how very sad he was that a rescue was not possible.

Otto faithfully attended Coast Guard reunions after his retirement and lived to celebrate his 61st anniversary before dying in 2012. One of his daughters said, "His passing was peaceful, he could speak very little but kept reaching up and gazing skyward."

"Dad, do you see God?" she asked.

"Yes."

"What do you see?"

"Light.... Beautiful.... Funny."

Then he smiled and closed his eyes and was gone.

Arlene Savit, passenger who gave up ticket on Flight 2501: "I've been waiting for this call for fifty-six years," Savit said when contacted by the author in 2006. She felt like her life had been spared when she gave up her ticket on Flight 2501, instead deciding to drive home to Minneapolis. *Newsday* interviewed her after the accident and published a photograph of her with her suitcase. "That was my opportunity for a re-birth," she recalled.

Savit married in 1951, less than a year after the accident. She believes her close call prompted her boyfriend, Richard, to propose. The Savits had four children. "I knew there was a reason I was spared," Savit said. "and it took me a while to figure out what it was."

She believes that she was saved because of her children and her music. Three of her children became chiropractors and between the ages of sixty-two and sixty-six she wrote and performed 227 songs. She feels that both endeavors provide comfort and happiness for others, which she sees as an important mission in life.

Frederic Stripe, Capital Airlines pilot flying just behind Flight 2501: Once Captain Stripe landed at Milwaukee on June 24, 1950, after waiting at Detroit for the storm to pass, he was swarmed with questions about possibly seeing Flight 2501 the previous night. Although he had not seen the DC-4, he followed the investigation as it unfolded and became interested in the modern-day search effort when he learned about it. He offered the author his insight into conditions that night and in early aviation.

He lived a long life and was a most highly respected pilot and friend to many. Just a few days before his 100th birthday, his son read to him the chapter of this book in which he appeared. "His eyes lit up," Frederic Jr. said. "It was one of his few cognizant moments in his last weeks."

He died just four days after his centennial birthday celebration.

NORTHWEST AIRLINES

Soon after the accident, Northwest Airlines received the Stratocruisers it had ordered and began to phase out its use of the DC-4s. In 1959, the company began flying jets when its first turboprop jet aircraft, the Lockheed L-188 Electra, arrived, and later jets like the Douglas DC-8, which were able to offer the shortest flight times on routes to Asia. In October 1960, Northwest retired the last Boeing 377 Stratocruiser. The airline took delivery of the Boeing 720B in 1961, and the new Boeing 707 in 1963. Upon the retirement of the last propeller aircraft soon thereafter, Northwest became the first U.S. airline with an all-turbofan jet fleet, hence the slogan "Northwest Orient: The Fan-Jet Airline." Northwest began operating the Boeing 727 in 1964. (Although Northwest Airlines is sometimes referred to as Northwest Orient Airlines, that name was only used to advertise its overseas flights, never as a legal name of the company.)

Over the duration of Northwest Airline's operation, from 1926 to 2008, when it began merging with Delta Airlines, the company experienced 28 fatal accidents killing a total of 692 people, including the 58 lost on Flight 2501. Flight 2501 holds rank as Northwest Airlines' third worst accident. Two Northwest accidents exceeded Flight 2501 in fatalities. On June 3, 1963, Flight 293, a DC-7 used for a military air transport flight, crashed in the Pacific Ocean off Annette Island in Alaska, killing all 101 people on board. Then on August 16, 1987, Flight 255, a DC-9, crashed on takeoff at Detroit, killing 154 people on the flight and two on the ground. Only a four-year-old girl survived.

STATISTICS

Of the 1242 DC-4s built, 120 were destroyed in accidents. Flight 2501 is the tenth worst accident involving DC-4s. Flight 2501, along with a United, an Eastern, and an American Airlines crash—all that resulted in fifty-eight deaths—share rank as the United States' 44th worst commercial carrier airline disasters.

Not considering the terrorist-induced crashes on September 11, 2001, American Airlines Flight 191, which crashed at Chicago's O'Hare Airport on May 25, 1979, because of a mechanical failure, currently holds rank as the worst airline disaster in the United States with the loss of 273 people, including two on the ground.

NOTES & ACKNOWLEDGEMENTS

I did not set out to write a book about the loss of Northwest Airlines Flight 2501. Rather, I intended to research the accident in search of information that might lead our team to the wreckage. Solving historical mysteries is how I prefer to spend my free time. This pastime often feeds my professional pursuits, which include writing, video production, and museum exhibit design. I find it most satisfying when passion and profession merge.

I share an interest in finding long-lost shipwrecks with a handful of other eccentric people who, for many of the same reasons as me, have made such quests a significant part of their lives. One of the world's most recognizable shipwreck hunters, author Clive Cussler, has such great love for saving history that he invests his book royalties into searches for the cultural benefit of mankind. He, too, has found a way to merge passion and profession, providing an inspiration for me and others like me.

When we joined forces to search for the wreck of Flight 2501, and I began to find relatives of the victims, I realized that what began as a challenge to solve a long-standing mystery would be infinitely more significant to those people. And I also realized that this project fell within a little sliver of time when I could find people associated with the crash, thanks to the internet, and before those same people would be gone. By talking to them, I was able to flush out most of the details regarding the accident.

I knew that after stirring the pot, I had an obligation to write this book, but thought it necessary to find the wreck before I could do that. Then, in 2012, I learned that a Coast Guard officer I had interviewed had died. That's when I realized I had to write this book before anyone else I had interviewed, particularly the victims' family members, might die. Unfortunately, I could not write fast enough. Even before the first edition of this book was published, many of the people quoted here had passed away.

I felt that this book would be a way to honor the memory of the victims, considering how little Northwest Airlines or the government had done for their families after the accident. After a fatal crash today, the authorities go to great lengths to offer condolences to the families, erect memorials, find all the bodies for proper burial, and return any personal possessions to the families. In the case of airplanes that crash in deep water, the Federal Aviation Administration and National Transportation Safety Board expend tremendous effort to search for the wreckage so that they can determine the cause and either correct mechanical defects or set forth new policies to avoid similar accidents. Those efforts often provide some solace for family members, but the families of Flight 2501's victims were never even told that the remains of their loved ones had been interred, complicating their process of mourning. I hope that in some small way this book can serve as a requiem and a memorial.

I also hope that through the input of witnesses, meteorological experts, retired pilots, and modern-day pilots ,who have assisted me in analyzing the crash, this book provides a plausible explanation for the accident, and in so doing teaches a valuable lesson. Consequently, perhaps the families of these 58 good people will realize their loved ones did not die in vain.

Fatal Crossing is a work of nonfiction. It depicts the lives of the crew and passengers, the last hours of the flight, the effect of the crash on surviving family members, and the efforts to find the wreckage and explain the tragedy. As the author and a participant in the search, I have two voices: one in the "third-person" as the chronicler of the events that took place in the twentieth century, and the other in the "first-person" to depict the search effort in which I was involved. The dialogue that is quoted has been done to the best recollection of those who participated in the conversations, although I have had to put words in the mouths of some participants when after more than five decades they could recall only the general gist of what took place. Anything written as fact comes from an individual with a pertinent connection to the people or events surrounding the loss of Flight 2501 or from primary documents such as newspapers, official records, or court transcripts, which amounted to over 5,000 pages. Collectively, the interviews and documents form the content.

Even though this is nonfiction, it does include conjecture. I have elected to put forth some speculation and judgments, but have done so with great care after discussions with experts or people who knew the victims. That conjecture, however, is clearly stated in the text. While writing this book, I was constantly reminded that it is all true by a peach-colored shirt pulled from the floating debris and given to me to be its caretaker.

After this book was first published in 2013 and updated with later printings, including this edition, the search for Flight 2501 has continued.

Only time will tell if a discovery will be made and if the wreckage will provide any new evidence. Until then, this book must suffice as insight into the accident.

THERE ARE NUMEROUS PEOPLE I wish to thank for making the project and book possible. I am grateful to Clive Cussler for investing more than a decade in the search for Flight 2501. Without him, there would have been no search, and without the search there would not have been a reason to conduct research. He encouraged my to write this book, allowed me to write about him, and endorsed two of my books.

Ralph Wilbanks, an archaeologist and side-scan operator, spent considerable time out on the lake. Though paid for his services, the work was stressful, dangerous, and exhausting. Ralph's boat pilot and childhood friend, Steve Howard, was with him every step of the way. Harry Pecorelli, Cameron Fletcher, Jim Lesto, and Matt Thompson have all served as crewmen during one or more expeditions, Jim steadily during many years. Each of them contributed to the effort that led to the discovery of many shipwrecks that otherwise may not have been found.

Technical divers Bob Underhill, Jeff Vos, and Todd White, volunteered their time and talents to make dozens of deep, dangerous dives during this project. Not only did they help rule out numerous targets as Flight 2501, but their documentation dives helped to solve other mysteries and contributed to the historical record.

I am also indebted to David Trotter, the Great Lakes' most renowned side-scan operator, who has over the years been my mentor, providing his expertise, counsel, and wisdom and is our great friend.

The work of Craig Rich, a volunteer member of both the search team and the research team, was invaluable: His article captured the attention of Clive Cussler and lit a fire under me that simmered for a while until it started boiling. I appreciate that he encouraged and assisted me in continuing what he had began.

Two other researchers I met during the course of this project provided invaluable assistance as project volunteers: pilot Kevin McGregor and forensic genealogist Chriss Lyon. Kevin served as my connection to the FAA, NTSB, and all things aviation, and was available at a moment's notice to talk about the project. He even flew me in his airplane on the last leg of the route that Flight 2501 so I could better write about the event based on experience. He also located invaluable court transcripts and accompanied me to New York to pore over them. Chriss helped me to find a great many family members and was instrumental in locating the St. Joseph, Michigan, gravesite as well as several important documents. Through this project, Kevin, Chriss, and I became good friends, sharing a deep understanding that coincidences, like our meeting, are anything but random. Tragically, Kevin died in 2015. He, like the victims of Flight 2501, left us too soon and is greatly missed.

Jeff Filbrandt, Pastor Robert Linstrom, Beverly Smith, and Mary Ann Frazier, who orchestrated the memorial services, deserve praise and recognition for helping bring a measure of closure to this tragic accident.

Those whom I interviewed—and there were many—all deserve my gratitude. They include the many dozens of witnesses, Northwest Airlines employees, and other officials quoted in the book, as well as experts not specifically quoted, including pilots Tim Choke, David Field, Bill Yocious, John Wegg, Mark Werkema, Mathew Rodina, John Olivia, and Steve Wolff; retired Northwest president Donald Nyrop; Northwest retirees Jerry Nielson, Pete Paske, Felix Perry, and Bob Gibson; author Mike Fornes; Kalamazoo Air Zoo staff Robert Ellis, William Cleary, and Bill Painter; Coast Guardsman Mike Moran; aviation photographer Leo Kohn; historian Dale Ridder; and Yankee Air Force Museum Director Gaye Roberts. I wish to extend a special thanks to retired Northwest radio operator Rick Cochran for helping me write about aviation communication in 1950; aviation expert Chuck Bois, who helped find several key witnesses and offered important critique of the book; Captain Freddie Stripe for sharing information about early aviation and his experience that night; Joe Kimm for his personal recollections of Flight 2501; aviation weather specialist Martin Hendren, who tracked down all kinds of information and photographs about the building of the C-54 that would eventually be used for Flight 2501; Judy Allers Schlaak, who entrusted me with the shirt her father recovered from the Flight 2501 floating debris; and Cathy Barton Snyder, who for a museum exhibit, loaned items belonging to her father that had been pulled from Lake Michigan.

I am particularly thankful to the relatives of the victims who shared memories of their loved ones, their travel details, and the raw emotions they experienced after the accident, all of which give substance to this book. I wish to especially recognize Bill Kaufmann and Ken Skoug, Jr. and Sr., the first relatives with whom I connected. They encouraged my pursuit of other families, who collectively helped me bear witness to what the crew and passengers might have seen and thought and felt. I apologize to them for the graphic details which were included so that other readers could understand the immensity of this tragedy. I am especially sad that many of the people whom I interviewed did not live to see the book in print.

I must also recognize Elizabeth Trembly, an English professor and author, who first identified the potential for a book about this project and shepherded me through the early writing. She served as a guide, advisor, critic, and friend through the multi-year effort. Ann Weller provided her keen abilities at editing and proofreading that eliminated my many stumbles and blunders. Many individuals, including authors Craig Rich, Kevin McGregor, and J. Ryan Fenzel read early drafts and offered critical input.

Last, but not least, my husband and fellow MSRA founding board member, Jack van Heest, deserves significant recognition. He has been at my side every step of the way. He brought me to Michigan and opened up a whole new world for me. He has maintained gainful employment as an engineer, which has allowed me to pursue ventures that often have little financial reward. He encouraged my first writing endeavor, has been an invaluable member of the Flight 2501 search team, is a partner in all my professional ventures, and offered research, insight, and editing for this book. He even saved my life once on a deep shipwreck.

Many times in the course of interviewing family members of the victims, I relived the aftermath of the crash and found myself grieving alongside them. As horrible as the death of the passengers and crew was, being left behind seemed to me the more sorrowful position. When I think of my own losses, my mother, my "nieces," and my friend Kevin McGregor, who all died prematurely like the people on Flight 2501, I turn to Jack, and our daughters, Cella and Taya, to give me comfort. Knowing that we are a family gives me peace to go on and do the other things that matter significantly less than they do. And most importantly, I realized that if I hold precious the memories of those who are lost, they are never really gone.

If you enjoyed *Fatal Crossing*, please consider reading
Flight of Gold by the late Kevin A. McGregor.
In-DepthEditions.com

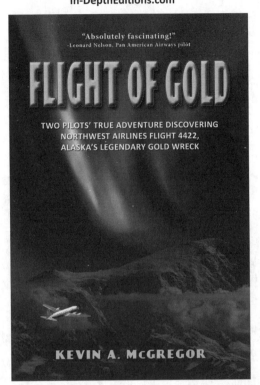

On March 12, 1948, Northwest Airlines Flight 4422, a DC-4 with a crew of six, carrying twenty-four Merchant Marines from Shanghai to New York, crashed high up on Alaska's Mt. Sanford. Air reconnaissance flights spotted the charred remains of the plane, but the site was too remote for recovery teams. Rumors that the plane had been transporting gold and diamonds immediately erupted and enticed treasure hunters to the mountain, but life-threatening conditions kept them from reaching what became known as "Alaska's Legendary Gold Wreck."

Flight of Gold is the first-person account of commercial airline pilot and mountain climber Kevin McGregor, who with commercial and bush pilot Marc Millican, an experienced mountain climber as well, attempted to accomplish what dozens of other expeditions failed to do: discover the remains of the plane and solve the mystery of the reputed treasure. Working in secret, these two daring and adventurous explorers journeyed into the vast Wrangell-Saint Elias National Park. Facing horrific winds, avalanches, and threats of wild animals, the courageous and determined men returned year after year in search of the truth.

After four years of near-obsessive efforts, they made a monumental discovery: After half a century, wives, siblings, and children of the victims were still alive and seeking answers. Continuing their efforts for the sake of the families, McGregor and Millican made two more startling discoveries: one led them into leading-edge forensics and the other gave substance to the treasure rumor.

"The Final Moments of Flight 2501." *A painting by Bryan David Snuffer.*

BIBLIOGRAPHY

BOOKS

Beaty, David. *The Naked Pilot: The Human Factor in Aircraft Accidents*. United Kingdom: Airlife Publishing LTD, 1995.

Bilstein, Roger E. *Flight in America, From the Wrights to the Astronauts*. Revised Edition. Baltimore: Johns Hopkins University Press, 1994.

Breslau, Alan Jeffry. *The Time of My Death*. E. P. Dutton & Co., Inc, 1977.

Burkhardt, Robert. *The Federal Aviation Administration*. New York: Frederick A. Praeger, 1967.

Cussler, Clive, and Craig Dirgo. *The Sea Hunters*. New York: Simon & Schuster, 1996.

Cussler, Clive, and Craig Dirgo. *The Sea Hunters II*. New York: Penguin Putnam, 2002.

Fornens, Mike. *USCGC Mackinaw: An Illustrated History of a Great Lakes Queen*. Michigan: Cheboygan Tribune Printing Co, 2005.

Gann, Ernest K. *Fate Is The Hunter*. New York: Simon & Schuster, 1961.

Gero, David. *Aviation Disasters: The World's Major Civil Airliner Crashes Since 1950*. United Kingdom: The History Press, 2010.

Gordon, Alastair. *Naked Airport: A Cultural History of the World's Most Revolutionary Structure*. New York: Metropolitan Books, Henry Holt and Company, 2004

Gourley, Jay. *The Great Lakes Triangle*. United States of America: Fawcett Publications, 1977.

Harvey, Lola. *Derevina's Daughters: Saga of an Alaskan Village*. Kansas: Sunflower University Press, 1991.

Hicks, Brian, and Schuyler Kropf. *Raising the* Hunley: *The Remarkable History and Recovery of the Lost Confederate Submarine*. United States of America: Ballantine Publishing Group, 2002.

Jacobs, Lou. *Highways in The Sky: The Story of Air Traffic Control*. United States of America: Bobbs-Merrill Company, 1975.

Jones, Geoff. *Northwest Airlines The First Eighty Years*. Illinois: Arcadia, 2005.

Knight, Clayton and K. S. *Plane Crash! The Mysteries of Major Air Disasters and How They Were Solved*. New York: Greenberg Publisher, 1958.

Komons, Nick A. *Bonfires to Beacons: Federal Civil Aviation Policy Under the Air Commerce Act, 1926-1938.* Washington, DOT/FAA, 1980.

McClement, Fred. *Anvil of the Gods: The airline pilot and his aircraft vs. natural violence--ice, hail, squalls, wind-shear and giant thunderstorms.* New York: J. B. Lippincott Company, 1964.

Michigan Maritime Museum: Maritime South Haven 1900-1950. Illinois: Arcadia Publishing, 2004.

Ruble, Kenneth D. *Flight To The Top.* United States of America: Viking Press, 1986.

Saroyan, William. *Obituaries.* California: Creative Arts Book Company, 1979.

Truman, Margaret (ed). *Where the Buck Stops: The Personal and Private Writings of Harry S. Truman.* New York: Warner Books, 1989.

Veronico, Nicholas A. (et al.). *Wreckchasing 2: Commercial Aircraft Crashes & Crash Sites.* United States of America: World Transport Press, 1996.

Volgenau, Gerald. *Shipwreck Hunter: Deep, Dark and Deadly in the Great Lakes.* Michigan: Ann Arbor Media Group, 2007.

WEBSITES

http://en.wikipedia.org/wiki/Northwest_Airlines_Flight_255
http://en.wikipedia.org/wiki/Northwest_Orient_Airlines_Flight_293
http://aviation-safety.net/index.php
http://www.faa.gov/about/media/b-chron.pdf
http://en.wikipedia.org/wiki/Aeropostal_Alas_de_Venezuela
http://libraryonline.erau.edu/online-full-text/ntsb/aircraft-accident-reports/AAR67-AA.pdf
http://propspistonsandoldairliners.blogspot.com/2009/12/how-to-fly-airways-1950-style.html
http://www.pilotfriend.com/training/flight_training/nav/rad_nav_overview.htm
http://www.hlswilliwaw.com/aleutians/Shemya/html/northwest_airlines_on_shemya.htm
http://www.nwahistory.org/index.htm
http://ir.lawnet.fordham.edu/cgi/viewcontent.cgi?article=1931&context=flr
http://www.law.du.edu/documents/transportation-law-journal/past-issues/v02/air-traffic-technology.pdf

OFFICIAL DOCUMENTS

Civil Aeronautics Board Report, January 18, 1951.
Log of the US Coast Guard Cutter *Woodbine.* June 24, 1950 to June 28, 1950.
Log of the US Coast Guard Cutter *Mackinaw.* June 24, 1950 to June 28, 1950.
Log of the US Coast Guard Cutter *Hollyhock.* June 24, 1950 to June 28, 1950.
Log of the US Coast Guard Cutter *Frederick Lee.* June 24, 1950 to June 28, 1950.
Log of the US Navy Destroyer *Daniel A. Joy.* June 24, 1950 to June 28, 1950.

National Transportation Safety Board. Loss of Control on Approach Colgan Air, Inc. Operating as Continental Connection Flight 3407 Bombardier DHC-8-400, N200WQ Clarence Center, New York, February 12, 2009.

United States Department of Commerce Weather Bureau. Daily weather reports. Muskegon, Michigan, June 1950.

United States Department of Commerce Weather Bureau. Daily weather reports. Milwaukee, Wisconsin, June 1950.

United States Department of Commerce Weather Bureau. Daily weather reports. Chicago, Illinois, June 1950.

United States Department of Commerce Weather Bureau. Daily weather reports. St. Joseph, Michigan, June 1950.

United States District Court Southern District of New York. John. V. Rorabaugh, Freda Larson Schwartz, William and May Ramsey, Oscar S. Schafer vs. Northwest Airlines. October 11, 1957. 2000+ pages of court transcripts.

United States District Court Southern District of New York. John. V. Rorabaugh, Freda Larson Schwartz, William and May Ramsey, Oscar S. Schafer vs. Northwest Airlines. February 19, 1958. 1000+ pages of court transcripts.

NEWSPAPERS June 23 – July 18, 1950

Chicago Daily Tribune.

Chicago Sun Times.

Grand Rapids (Michigan) *Press.*

Herald Palladium. Benton Harbor, MI.

Holland (Michigan) *Sentinel.*

Los Angeles Times.

Miami Daily News.

New York Times.

San Francisco Examiner.

The Billings (Montana) *Gazette.*

The Boston Herald.

The Bridgeport (Connecticut) *Post.*

The Daily Courier. Connellsville, PA.

The Daily Plainsman. Huron, SD.

The Dallas Morning News.

The Denver Post.

The Herald-Press. St. Joseph, Michigan.

The Independent Record. Helma, Montana.

The Kalamazoo (Michigan) *Gazette.*

The Minneapolis Star.

The Milwaukee Journal.

The Oregonian. Portland, Oregon

The Seattle Times.

The Sheboygan (Wisconsin) *Press.*

The St. Paul (Minnesota) *Pioneer Press.*

The Tacoma (Washington) *News Tribune.*

The Yakima (Washington) *News Tribune.*

Philadelphia Inquirer.

South Haven (Michigan) *Tribune.*

Spokane Daily Chronicle.

Walla Walla (Washington) *Union Bulletin.*

Washington (DC) *Democrat.*

Washington (DC) *Post.*

INTERVIEWS

Victims' Relatives
Ajemian Family
Anderson Family
Barton Family
Cardle Family
Eastman Family
Feldman Family
Freng Family
George Family
Goldsbury Family
Gorski Family
Heenan Family
Heuston Family
Hill Family
Hokanson Family
Jackson Family
Kaufmann Family
Keating Family
Kelty Family Lind Family
Longfield Family
Malby Family
McNickle Family
Meyer Family
Neilsen Family
Olsen Family
Reid Family
Rorabaugh Family
Ross Family
Shafer Family
Schlachter Family
Schwartz Family
Sirbu Family
Skoug Family
Spohn Family
Walsh Family
Wohler Family
Wolfe Family

Former Northwest Officials
Rick Cochran
Bob Gibson
Joseph Kimm

Jerry Nielson
Donald Nyrop
Pete Paske
Felix Perry

Pilots
Chuck Bois
Tim Choke
David Field
John Olivia
Mathew Rodina
Frederic Stripe
John Wegg
Mark Werkema
Steve Wolff
Bill Yocious

Coast Guard Officials
Carl Gilbow
Larry Otto
Wayne Tovey

Witnesses
David Allers
George Bartholomew
Oscar Bergstrom
Donald Bassi
Verley Bunyea
Doyle Cleveland
Jackie Eldrid
John Fleming
Web and Romona Geezer
Marilynn Kelly
Jenine Kucera
Evelyn Kulczy
Doug McCain
Mary Meyer
Jim Mitchel
Stella Nowlan
Jeanette Stieve
Dave Schlaak
Judy Schlaak
Diane Savage
Norma Quinn

Dale Wickham

Others
Clive Cussler
Steve Howard
Robert Ketelhut
Kevin McGregor
Dale Ridder
Arlene Savit
Jack Schlosser
David Trotter
Ralph Wilbanks

INDEX

PRAISE FOR FATAL CROSSING

"This book wonderfully balances the details, which have been exhaustively researched: The carnage with the strings of the heart; the searches in the water and in the archives; in the lives of those ended that day; and in those loved ones who lived on, scarred by lack of closure. This book provides that closure. My search has ended. It put me softly by Ben and Slava's graveside. It quieted my questions and brought light to still the dark thoughts of my loved one's mysterious passings. This book, and the untiring efforts to find answers to this fatal crossing, honor my grandparents, my family, and me."

— George Heuston, Grandson of Benjamin and Slava Heuston, victims of Flight 2501.

"Fascinating and very well written. Van Heest's a better reporter/investigator than most people who do it for a living."

— David Moore, news reporter WGVU Public Media.

"Brava to V. O. van Heest who has done an incredible job of researching and writing this story. I loved the way she began the book and how I was pulled in with the NWA history and that of the crew and families. I was completely absorbed in the pages of this book. I could not leave it alone. In fact, I usually don't take books on trips with me, but I did because I had to know what happened next."

— Ann Kerr, former Northwest Airlines flight attendant.

"This is a very engrossing tale. Van Heest has done deep research into this tragic event and leads the reader through the attempts at finding the wreckage of the plane and a step-by-step process as her crew of investigators find other ships that disappeared over the years. Van Heest takes great care when profiling the crew of the aircraft and its passengers, leaving a touching human quality to the mystery of the crash and its aftermath. The night of the flight is brought back to life as we learn of the experienced flight crew, the seemingly routine flight path, and the severe weather encountered on the way to Minneapolis. Every element of this tragic tale is well written, thoroughly documented, and emotionally felt. High points and frustrations abound as the difficulty in finding this plane and its occupants is deftly expressed by the author. FATAL CROSSING is a both a window to the past and a relevant look at where exploration is today. Excellent!"

— Steven S. Airheart, Reader.

PRAISE FOR FATAL CROSSING

"Riveting and compassionate, FATAL CROSSING honours the mystery of Flight 2501 with the comprehensive investigation it so richly deserves. Van Heest's meticulous research vividly recounts the events of the doomed flight as well as the grim scope of the dramatic aftermath. Interspersed with the history, Van Heest's personal odyssey to locate the elusive wreckage reads like a marine detective tale, where she and her team separate promising leads from maddening red herrings, and parse vague scraps of data in their effort to find a 94-foot long needle in a 1,000 square-mile haystack. FATAL CROSSING is one captivating read."
> - J. Ryan Fenzel, author of ALLIED IN IRONS, an adventure novel based on the loss of Flight 2501.

"A true artist with words, V. O. van Heest provided depth and detail, which adds so much to the experience of reading this book. The thoroughness of the research and study resulted in a fascinating story. I loved it! "
> - Charles Boie, retired pilot, aviation artist, and historian.

"The aviation and underwater worlds of past and present collide in the depths of one of Lake Michigan's greatest true mysteries. Van Heest's incredible research and tenacity come full circle in this passionate tale of amazing determination. This wonderful story redefines the term, Never Give Up!"
> - Kevin A. McGregor, Commercial Airline Pilot, and author of FLIGHT OF GOLD.

"Though I lived through all the ups and downs of the past decade of researching and searching with MSRA and our friends at NUMA, van Heest still managed to bring tears to my eyes as the events leading to the loss of Flight 2501 played out. This true tale of tragedy is highlighted by van Heest's own compulsion to solve the mystery, her dogged determination to discover the few participants still alive after almost six decades, and her compassion and empathy for the families of those lost on that June night in 1950. Nearly forgotten for half a century, the fateful story of the loss of Flight 2501 and its 58 victims told in FATAL CROSSING will now take its rightful place among the roll call of great American tragedies."
> - Craig Rich, Director, MSRA, and author of FOR THOSE IN PERIL and THROUGH SURF AND STORM.